Legal Foundations of Environmental Planning

Legal Foundations of Environmental Planning:

Cases and Materials on Environmental Law

Jerome G. Rose

CENTER FOR URBAN POLICY RESEARCH
Rutgers University—The State University of New Jersey
New Brunswick, New Jersey

CENTRAL MISSOURI
STATE UNIVERSITY
Warrensburg,
Missouri

THE CUPR SURVEY SERIES

Series Editors George Sternlieb and Virginia Paulus

Copyright © 1974 by Jerome G. Rose
Published by Center for Urban Policy Research
Rutgers University, The State University
New Brunswick, New Jersey

Acknowledgments

I am particularly indebted to Nathan Edelstein, a student in the J.D.–MCRP joint program at Rutgers University, for his assistance in collecting and editing the material and to Hilary Levine, Librarian, at the Center for Urban Policy Research, who assisted in preparing that material for press.

CONTENTS

TABLE OF CASES

Legal Foundations of Environmental Planning

I. LEGAL THEORIES AND PROCEDURES

A. Legal Theories On Which Suites May Be Based

1. <u>Nuisance</u>

<u>HULBERT v. CALIFORNIA PORTLAND CEMENT CO.</u>, 161 Cal. 239, 118 p. 928 (1911).

MELVIN, J. Petitioner has made an original application to this court to suspend the operation of a certain injunction until the decision of the appeals in two cases, in each of which the California Portland Cement Company, a corporation, is the defendant, on the ground that the property of the corporation would be so greatly damaged by the operation of the injunction pending the appeals that a judgment in defendant's favor would be almost fruitless; while it is contended the damage to plaintiffs is easily susceptible of satisfaction by a payment of money. Petitioner offers to furnish any bond this court may require, if the order which is prayed for shall be granted. As this was the first case in America, so far as this court knew, in which the operation of a cement plant had been enjoined because of the dust produced in the processes of manufacture, and as the showing which was made indicated that petitioner's loss would be very great if the injunction were enforced at once, an order was entered, temporarily staying its operation until both sides to the controversy could be heard. The court was moved somewhat to such action also because the trial court had made an order staying the operation of the injunction for 60 days, so that this court might have the opportunity of passing upon this application. Two principal questions are presented: (1) Has the Supreme Court the authority in aid of its appellate jurisdiction, under section 4 of article 6 of the Constitution, to suspend the operation of an injunction pending appeal? (2) If it have such power, is this a proper case for the exercise thereof? Owing to the conclusion which we have reached, it is unnecessary to answer the first question authoritatively, because, assuming a reply to it in the affirmative, we cannot say that the facts of this case warrant any other response to the second inquiry than a negative one.

The salient facts shown by the petitioner are that the California Portland Cement Company is engaged in the manufacture of cement on property situated nearly two miles from the center of the city of Colton, in the county of San Bernardino, but not within the limits of said city; that said manufactory is located at Slover mountain, where the substances necessary to the production of Portland cement are quarried; that long before the surrounding country had been generally devoted to the production of citrus fruits Slover mountain had been known as a place where limestone was produced; that quarries of marble and limestone had been established there; that lime kilns had been operated upon said mountain for many years; that in 1891 the petitioner obtained title to said premises, and commenced thereon the manufacture of Portland cement; that the said corporation has expended upon said property more than $800,000; that at the time when petitioner began the erection of the cement plant the land surrounding the plant was vacant and unimproved, except some land lying to the north, which had been planted to young citrus trees; that these trees were first planted about a year before the erection of the cement plant was commenced (but long after the lime kilns and the marble quarries had been operated) that subsequently other orange groves have been planted in the neighborhood; that the petitioner's plant on Slover mountain has a capacity of 3,000 barrels of cement per day; but that by the judgment of the superior court in two certain actions against petitioner, entitled Lillie A. Hulbert, Administratrix, etc., v. California Portland Cement Company, a Corporation, and Spencer E. Gilbert, plaintiff, v. Same Defendant, the corporation aforesaid was enjoined from operating its plant in such manner as to produce an excess of 88,706 barrels of finished cement per annum; that the regular pay roll of the company includes the names of about 500 men, who are paid about $35,000 a month; that the fixed, constant monthly expenses for supplies and materials amount to $35,000; that the California Portland Cement Company employs the best, most modern methods in its processes of manufacture, but that nevertheless there is an unavoidable escape into the air of certain dust and smoke; that petitioner has no other location for the conduct of its business at a profit; that the land of the Hulbert estate is located from 1,500 to 2,500 feet from petitioner's cement works, and that Spencer E. Gilbert's

HULBERT v. CALIFORNIA PORTLAND CEMENT

land is all within 1,000 feet therefrom; that petitioner has diligently sought some means of preventing the escape of dust from its factories; that it has consulted the best experts and sought the best information obtainable, and that it is now and has been for a long time conducting experiments along the lines suggested by the most eminent engineering authorities upon this subject, and that, as soon as any process can be evolved for preventing the escape of the dust, the petitioner will adopt such process in its works, and it is believed that a process now constructing with all diligence by petitioner will effectually prevent the escape of dust. Petitioner also alleges that it is easily possible to estimate the damages of the plaintiffs in money, while it is utterly impracticable to estimate the damage in money which will be caused to the petitioner by the closing of the plant, and that stopping the plant pending the appeals will cause financial ruin to the chief stockholders of the petitioner, and that the elements of loss averred are irreparable on account of the disorganization of petitioner's working force, loss of market, and deterioration of machinery.

The learned judge of the superior court, in deciding the cases in which petitioner here was defendant, described the method of manufacturing cement and the injury to the trees. He said, in part: "The output from these two mills at the present time is about 2,500 barrels of cement every 24 hours, and to produce this there is fed into the various kilns of the defendant, during the time mentioned, about 1,500,000 pounds of raw mix, composed of limestone and clay, ground as fine as flour and thoroughly mixed. This raw mix is fed into the tops of kilns, wherein the temperature varies from 1,800 to 3,000 degrees Fahrenheit, and through which kilns the heated air and combustion gases pass at the rate of many thousands of feet per minute. The result of this almost inconceivable draft is to carry out, in addition to the usual products of combustion, particles of the raw mix, to the extent of probably 20 tons per day or more, the greater part of which, without question, is carried up into the air by the rising gases, and thereafter, through the action of the winds and force of gravity, distributed over the surrounding territory." Speaking of the premises of the plaintiffs, he said that, because of prevailing westerly winds and on account of the proximity of the mills, said lands were almost continually subject to the deposit of dust. In this regard he said: "It is the fact incontrovertibly established by both the testimony of witnesses and personal inspections made by the court that a well-nigh continuous shower of cement dust, emanating from defendant's cement mills and caused by their operation, is, and for some years past has been, falling upon the properties of the plaintiffs, covering and coating the ground, filtering through their homes, into all parts thereof, forming an opaque semi-cemented incrustation upon the upper sides of all exposed flowers and foliage, particularly leaves of citrus trees, and leaving ineradicable, yet withal plainly discernable, marks and evidence of dust, dusty deposits, and grayish colorings resulting therefrom, upon the citrus fruits. The incrustations above mentioned, unlike the deposits occasionally occurring on leaves because of the presence of undue amounts of road dust or field dust, are not dissipated by the strongest winds, nor washed off through the action of the most protracted rains. Their presence, from repeated observations, seems to be as continuous as their hold upon the leaves seems tenacious." The court further found that the deposit of dust on the fruit decreased its value; that the constant presence of dust on the limbs and leaves of the trees rendered the cultivation of the ground and the harvesting of the crop more costly than it would have been under ordinary conditions; and that said dust added to the usual and ordinary discomforts of life by its presence in the homes of the plaintiffs. The court also found that the operation of the old mill of the defendant corporation had occurred with the acquiescence of the plaintiffs, and that the defendant had acquired a prescriptive right to manufacture the maximum quantity of cement produced annually by that factory.

In view of such facts solemnly found by the court after trial, we cannot say that there is reason for a suspension by this court of the injunction, even conceding that we have power under proper circumstances thus to prevent a disturbance of existing conditions, pending an appeal. We are not insensible to the fact that petitioner's business is a very important enterprise; that its location is peculiarly adapted for the manufacture of cement; and that great loss may result to the corporation by the enforcement of the injunction. Even if the officers of the corporation are willing to furnish a bond in a sum equal to the value of the properties of Gilbert and of the Hulbert estate here involved, we cannot, under plain principles of equity, compel these plaintiffs to have recourse to their action at law only, and take from them the benefit of the injunctive relief accorded them by the chancellor below. To permit the cement company to continue its operations, even to the extent of destroying the property of the two

HULBERT v. CALIFORNIA PORTLAND CEMENT

plaintiffs and requiring payment of the full value thereof, would be, in effect, allowing the seizure of private property for a use other than a public one—something unheard of and totally unauthorized in the law. Hennessy v. Carmony, 50 N. J. Eq. 616, 25 Atl. 374; Sullivan v. Jones & Laughlin Steel Co., 208 Pa. 540, 57 Atl. 1065, 66 L. R. A. 712. Nor may we say, as petitioner urges us to declare, that cement dust is not a nuisance, and therefore that the restraint imposed is illegal, even though this is one of the first cases, if not the very first, of its kind, in which the emission of cement dust from a factory has been enjoined, for we are bound by the findings of the court in this proceeding, and may not consider their sufficiency or lack of it until we take up the appeals on their merits. The court has found that the plaintiffs in the actions tried were specially damaged by a nuisance maintained by the cement company. This entitles the plaintiffs, not only to damages, but to such relief as the facts warrant, and the chancellor has determined that limiting the production in the manner selected is a proper form of protection to their rights. It is well settled in California that a nuisance which consists in pouring soot or the like upon the property of a neighbor in such manner as to interfere with the comfortable enjoyment of the premises is a private nuisance, which may be enjoined or abated, and for which, likewise, the persons specially injured may recover pecuniary damages. Code Civ. Proc. § 731; Fisher v. Zumwalt, 128 Cal. 493, 61 Pac. 82; Melvin v. E. B. & A. L. Stone Co., 7 Cal. App. 328, 94 Pac. 390; Judson v. Los Angeles Sub. Gas Co., 157 Cal. 172, 106 Pac. 583, 26 L. R. A. (N. S.) 183. The last-named case was one in which the operation of a gas factory had been enjoined, and the following language was used: "A gas factory does not constitute a nuisance per se. The manufacture in or near a great city of gas for illuminating and heating is not only legitimate, but is very necessary to the comfort of the people. But in this, as in any other sort of lawful business, the person conducting it is subject to the rule, "Sic utere tuo ut alienum non lœdas," even when operating under municipal permission, or under public obligation to furnish a commodity. Terre Haute Gas Co. v. Teel, 20 Ind. 131; Attorney General v. Gaslight & Coke Co., L. R. 7 Chan. Div. 217; Sullivan v. Royer, 72 Cal. 248 [13 Pac. 655]. Nor will the adoption of the most approved appliances and methods of production justify the continuance of that which, in spite of them, remains a nuisance. Evans v. Fertilizing Co., 160 Pa. 223 [28 Atl. 702]; Susquehanna Fer. Co. v. Malone, 73 Md. 276 [20 Atl. 900, 9 L. R. A. 737, 25 Am. St. Rep. 595]; Susquehanna Fer. Co. v. Spangler, 86 Md. 562 [39 Atl. 270, 63 Am. St. Rep. 533]."

Petitioner contends for the rule that the resulting injuries must be balanced by the court, and that, where the hardship inflicted upon one party by the granting of an injunction would be very much greater than that which would be suffered by the other party if the nuisance were permitted to continue, injunctive relief should be denied. This doctrine of "the balance of hardship" and the associated rule that "an injunction is not of right but of grace" are the bases of petitioner's argument, and many authorities in support of them have been called to our attention. In petitioner's behalf are cited such cases as Richards' Appeal, 57 Pa. 105, 98 Am. Dec. 202, where an injunction which had been sought to restrain defendant from using large quantities of bituminous coal to plaintiff's damage was refused, and the plaintiff was remitted to his action at law; the court saying, among other things: "Whatever of injury may have or shall result to his (the plaintiff's) property from the defendant's works, by reason of a nuisance complained of, is only such as is incident to a lawful business conducted in the ordinary way, and by no unusual means. Still, there may be injury to the plaintiff, but this of itself may not entitle him to the remedy he seeks. It may not, if ever so clearly established, be a cause in which equity ought to enjoin the defendant in the use of a material necessary to the successful production of an article of such prime necessity as good iron, especially if it be very certain that a greater injury would ensue by enjoining than would result by refusal to enjoin." The same rule was announced in Dilworth's Appeal, 91 Pa. 248, a case involving the building of a powder house near plaintiff, and in Huckenstine's Appeal, 70 Pa. 102, 10 Am. Rep. 669. Petitioner admits that in the later case of Sullivan v. Jones & Laughlin Steel Co., supra, the Supreme Court of Pennsylvania reached a different conclusion, but contends that the opinion in that case merely defines the word "grace" as used in Huckenstine's Appeal; the real meaning of the expression "an injunction is a matter of grace" being that a high degree of discretion is exercised by a chancellor in awarding or denying an injunction. An examination of the case, however, shows that the court went very much further than a mere definition of the phrase "of grace." In that case the defendant had erected a large factory for the manufacture of steel on land purchased from one of the plaintiffs, but after many years defendant had commenced the use of "Mesaba" ore, which caused the emission of great quantities of fine dust upon the property of plaintiffs. The Supreme Court of Pennsylvania, in reversing the decree of the lower court, dismissing the bill, went into the matter of "balancing injuries" and "injunctions of

HULBERT v. CALIFORNIA PORTLAND CEMENT

grace" very thoroughly, and we may with propriety, I think, quote and adopt some of its language upon these subjects as follows:

"It is urged that, as an injunction is a matter of grace, and not of right, and more injury would result in awarding than refusing it, it ought not to go out in this case. A chancellor does act as of grace, but that grace sometimes becomes a matter of right to the suitor in its court, and, when it is clear that the law cannot give protection and relief—to which the complainant in equity is admittedly entitled—the chancellor can no more withhold his grace than the law can deny protection and relief, if able to give them. This is too often overlooked when it is said that in equity a decree is of grace, and not of right, as a judgment at law. In Walters v. McElroy et al. [151 Pa. 549] 25 Atl. 125, the defendants gave as one of the reasons why the plaintiff's bill should be dismissed that his land was worth but little, while they were engaged in a great mining industry, which would be paralyzed if they should be enjoined from a continuance of the acts complained of; and the principle was invoked that, as a decree in equity is of grace, a chancellor will never enjoin an act where, by so doing, greater injury will result than from a refusal to enjoin. To this we said: 'The phrase "of grace," predicated of a decree in equity, had its origin in an age when kings dispensed their royal favors by the hands of their chancellors; but, although it continues to be repeated occasionally, it has no rightful place in the jurisprudence of a free commonwealth, and ought to be relegated to the age in which it was appropriate. It has been somewhere said that equity has its laws, as law has its equity. This is but another form of saying that equitable remedies are administered in accordance with rules as certain as human wisdom can devise, leaving their application only in doubtful cases to the discretion, not the unmerited favor or grace, of the chancellor. Certainly no chancellor in any English-speaking country will at this day admit that he dispenses favors or refuses rightful demands, or deny that, when a suitor has brought his cause clearly within the rules of equity jurisprudence the relief he asks is demandable ex-debito justitiæ, and needs not to be implored ex gratia. And as to the principle invoked, that a chancellor will refuse to enjoin when greater injury will result from granting than from refusing an injunction, it is enough to observe that it has no application where the act complained of is in itself, as well as in its incidents, tortious. In such case it cannot be said that injury would result from an injunction, for no man can complain that he is injured by being prevented from doing to the hurt of another that which he has no right to do. Nor can it make the slightest difference that the plaintiff's prop-

erty is of insignificant value to him, as compared with the advantages that would accrue to the defendants from its occupation.' There can be no balancing of conveniences when such balancing involves the preservation of an established right, though possessed by a peasant only to a cottage as his home, and which will be extinguished if relief is not granted against one who would destroy it in artificially using his own land. Though it is said a chancellor will consider whether he would not do a greater injury by enjoining than would result from refusal, and leaving the party to his redress at the hands of a court and jury, and if, in conscience, the former should appear, he will refuse to enjoin (Richards' Appeal, supra), that 'it often becomes a grave question whether so great an injury would not be done to the community by enjoining the business that the complaining party should be left to his remedy at law' (Dilworth's Appeal, supra), and similar expressions are to be found in other cases, 'none of them, nor all of them, can be authority for the proposition that equity, a case for its cognizance being otherwise made out, will refuse to protect a man in the possession and enjoyment of his property, because that right is less valuable to him than the power to destroy it may be to his neighbor or to the public' (Evans v. Reading Chem. Fer. Co., 160 Pa. 209 [28 Atl. 702]). The right of a man to use and enjoy his property is as supreme as his neighbor's, and no artificial use of it by either can be permitted to destroy that of the other." * * *

Let the temporary order staying the operation of the injunction be dismissed, and the petition be denied.

ROSE, THE LEGAL ADVISER ON HOME OWNERSHIP 223 to 231 (1964).

1. NUISANCES CREATED BY YOUR NEIGHBOR

A. Definition of a Nuisance

The ownership of your house gives you the legal right to enjoy its use without unreasonable interference by your neighbor. Your neighbor is entitled to these same rights and privileges. Conflict can arise if your neighbor uses his property in a manner causing annoyance, inconvenience, discomfort, or damage to you. It is possible for him to inflict this harm without ever crossing his boundary line and without ever coming into personal contact with you. If your neighbor creates noises or smells, or carries on any activity which is offensive or dangerous, and thus deprives you of reasonable enjoyment of your property, then the law calls this activity a "nuisance" and gives you legal remedies.

In determining whether a particular activity constitutes a nuisance, it is difficult to define just how much annoyance or inconvenience is necessary to make it objectionable. It is always a question of degree, depending upon the circumstances. In every case the right of one landowner to use his property freely must be balanced against the right of the other landowner·to enjoy his own property without unreasonable interference and annoyance by his neighbor. Each case is also a question of balancing the usefulness and social need of the activity against the amount of harm which it inflicts. The concept of "nuisance" will become clearer as you examine various examples.

B. Illustrations of Nuisances

(1) NOISES. There are some noises so annoying that they appreciably diminish the enjoyment of your house. Some noises are so disturbing that they can affect the peace and health of your family. If your neighbor habitually makes noises which are so loud and unusual in the neighborhood that you cannot sleep, read, concentrate, or converse normally until it stops, this noise is an unreasonable invasion of your rights and is a nuisance. Of course, if your house is in the center of a city, you cannot insist upon the quiet that you expect in the country. Also, to be a nuisance the noise must be of such a nature as to disturb a person of normal sensitivity. If you or a member of your family is sick or otherwise especially sensitive to sound, you cannot impose your need for unusual quiet and stillness on your neighbors.

The question of whether any particular noise or sound constitutes a nuisance depends again upon the particular circumstances. In one case a court held that the ringing of church bells caused a substantial annoyance to the residents of the adjoining houses and that it was a nuisance. Another court ruled that the ringing of church bells in a heavily populated area was not a nuisance even though it did disturb a particular sick and sensitive person. In other cases courts have held that the noise of music lessons is not a nuisance and that practising a musical instrument is not a nuisance. However, if your neighbor makes noises and sounds maliciously and for the sole purpose of disturbing you, that does constitute a nuisance.

(2) SMELLS, SMOKE, AND FUMES. Every homeowner is entitled to have in and around his property reasonably pure and wholesome air, consistent with the locality in which he lives. If someone carries on any activity or business which creates smells, smoke, or fumes which are offensive and make living in your house uncomfortable, then such activity or business may constitute a nuisance.

Whether any particular smell or amount of smoke constitutes a nuisance depends upon the circumstances. The locality and surroundings must be considered. A smell may be objectionable in a residential area but common in a manufacturing area. Furthermore, the smell or smoke must cause an appreciable amount of annoyance or discomfort. It is not enough to claim that you are an unusually delicate or fastidious individual. One court held that the smell and smoke of burning leaves did not constitute a nuisance, but excessive smoke from burning rags and other offensive materials is a nuisance. Other courts have held that offensive cesspools and defective septic tanks constitute a nuisance. In various cases courts have held a fertilizer factory, a slaughter house, and a garbage plant to be nuisances because of the offensive odors which they produced.

(3) PETS AND OTHER ANIMALS. If your neighbor keeps a dog, or other pet, which is vicious, he must keep the animal so confined that it cannot inflict injury. A pet can also become a nuisance by howling, screeching, crying, barking, or making such noise as to deprive the neighbors of the peace and quiet of their homes. In an early New York case a court held that a person had a right to kill a neighbor's dog because the dog came onto his property constantly and caused disturbance by howling and barking during the night, after the person had notified the owner and the owner failed to restrain the dog. Some states have statutes which give a person the right to kill a trespassing dog under certain circumstances. There is another old case which held that it is a nuisance to use animals in such a manner as to offend the sense of decency of the neighbors. In this case the defendant kept stallions for breeding, which was conducted in full view of neighbors on the adjoining property.

(4) OFFENSIVE PERSONAL CONDUCT.

(a) Cohabitation. There is an old Kentucky case holding that it is a public nuisance for a man and woman known to the community to be unmarried to live together as man and wife. This ruling is unusual because at common law it is not a crime for an unmarried couple to live together as man and wife.

(b) Indecency, Lewdness, and Profanity. Most states have statutes which prohibit conduct that is grossly vulgar, unfit to be seen or heard, lustful, offensive to morality, indecent, or nasty. Under certain circumstances, such conduct may constitute a private nuisance. The morality of the community will determine whether particular conduct is indecent or lewd. The standards of morality may vary greatly from a sophisticated suburban community to a provincial rural community. **For** example, in one case a court held that the question, "Will you go to bed with me?" when spoken to a woman without provocation, was vulgar and obscene.

Complaints of indecent exposure sometimes arise in areas where houses are placed so close to each other that each owner must be ·constantly vigilant to screen his personal activities from view from the outside. Most states have statutes which make it a misdemeanor to "wilfully and lewdly expose his person, or the private parts thereof . . . in any place where others are present . . ." These statutes are directed at exhibitionists and nudists, but in one case a court held that if a person bathes without a screen, shade, or other obstruction and can be seen distinctly from a nearby house, he is guilty of indecent exposure.

Under some circumstances, abusive language and profanity may be considered to be a nuisance, or even a breach of the peace.

(c) Eavesdroppers and Peeping Toms. Eavesdropping is a common law offense. It was originally directed against those who listened under windows or eaves of a house to overhear conversation for the purpose of creating slanderous or troublemaking stories. Peeping Toms do not commit a crime at common law, but most states make their action an offense by statute, either directly or indirectly. One decision was that peeking into a window of a house, by someone who has no business there, at a time of the night when the residents are likely to be preparing for bed, is disorderly conduct within the meaning of a criminal statute. Both activities would deprive a homeowner of the peaceful enjoyment of his home and would probably constitute a nuisance.

(5) DANGEROUS OR OFFENSIVE CONDITIONS.

(a) Garbage. Your neighbor creates a nuisance if he deposits his garbage on his own property in such place and manner as to cause offensive odors or to invite vermin and rodents. However, in one case a court held that it is not a nuisance for a person to use his vacant lot to dump refuse when the only objection was that it is unsightly.

(b) Insects. In one case a court held that it is a nuisance to permit to exist conditions which lead to the breeding of mosquitos, flies, or other disease-carrying insects.

(c) Cesspools and Septic Tanks. Cesspools and septic tanks which do not function properly, or are so constructed or maintained as to threaten or impair health, are nuisances.

(d) Overgrown or Noxious Weeds. Many states and local communities have laws which require the owner of property to cut all noxious weeds or any weed which grows over a given height. Some of these statutes declare overgrown weeds to be a nuisance and also provide penalties for failure of the owner to remove the condition. In Washington, D. C., Congress has seen fit to impose a fine on property owners who, after notice fail to remove weeds over four inches in height.

(e) Dilapidated Condition of House. Most homeowners take pride in their houses, try to keep them in repair, and are usually disturbed by a neighbor's house which is allowed to become dilapidated. But the mere fact that a house is unsightly, old, and in need of paint and repair does not make it a nuisance unless it creates an unmistakable and imminent danger.

(f) Malicious Acts. If your neighbor commits an act or creates a condition for no purpose other than to annoy you or to destroy the peace and quiet of your home, then what he does is a nuisance.

(g) Funeral Homes. In a well-governed community, zoning laws will protect you against the possibility of having a funeral home established next to your house. In the absence of zoning laws, you still may be protected by the courts, which have recognized that the constant reminder of death has a depressing effect which impairs a homeowner's enjoyment of his property. However, the courts also recognize the necessity of permitting funeral homes somewhere in the community. The question of whether a funeral and embalming business will be permitted in any particular location will depend upon the particular circumstances and use of the surrounding property. In one case a court refused to permit a funeral home to be established 400 feet from a plaintiff's house.

C. Legal Remedies against Nuisance

If your neighbor does create a condition which constitutes a nuisance, it is usually wise to exhaust every method of persuasion and social influence to induce him to remove the nuisance before resorting to legal remedies. The existence of the nuisance may impair the enjoyment of your house, but open hostility with a neighbor can seriously and permanently impair peaceful enjoyment of your home. If all attempts at persuasion, compromise, and reconciliation fail, the following legal remedies are available to abate a nuisance.

(1) INJUNCTION. Under some circumstances, a court will issue an injunction ordering the offending neighbor to cease the activity or remove the conditions creating the nuisance. The remedy of injunction is usually available where irreparable injury may result and where the nuisance is continuous or recurrent. In any case, the remedy is a matter of discretion of the court.

(2) DAMAGES. You may sue to recover damages caused by the nuisance, no matter how slight or difficult to assess in monetary terms. If your monetary damages are insignificant, you are entitled to nominal damages. If the nuisance is willful or malicious, you may be entitled to punitive damages.

(3) CRIMINAL ACTION. Your neighbor may be subject to criminal penalties for creating a public nuisance. A public nuisance is an offense against the state. A condition which creates a hazard or annoyance to the public at large is a public nuisance.

(4) SELF-HELP. If you suffer from the injury of a private nuisance, you may resort to self-help to abate the nuisance, but you must do it without a breach of the peace. In every instance when you take the law into your own hands, you do so at the risk of liability if you exceed your rights. Before resorting to self-help, you must give notice to the offending neighbor so that he will have an opportunity to remove the nuisance himself. You may enter onto your neighbor's premises for the

purpose of abating a nuisance only if you can do so in a peaceable manner. You must go no further than is reasonably necessary to abate the nuisance, and you must use care to prevent unnecessary damage. At all times you act at your peril and will be liable for damages if it is later determined that the condition is not a nuisance. If you provoke a breach of the peace, you will be subject to criminal penalties. In spite of all of these dangers, there are circumstances where the need for quick action may justify the risk. However, you would be wise to discuss the problem with your lawyer before proceeding.

D. Objectionable Community Activities

Closely related to the problem of private nuisance caused by a neighbor is the troublesome question of governmental activities which may interfere with and disturb the quiet enjoyment of your home. In this situation, the activity itself is socially desirable or even necessary, but it creates noise, lights, crowds, or other disturbance to homeowners in the immediate vicinity. Examples of this type of activity are airports, firehouses, schools, and churches.

(1) AIRPORTS. A homeowner whose house is located in the immediate vicinity of an airport may be deprived of the peaceful enjoyment of his home by the noise, vibration, dust, and lights. Most homeowners whose houses are so situated do not have a legal remedy because the courts have held that the existence of an airport, in and of itself, is not a nuisance. In order to obtain help from the courts, a complaining homeowner must be able to prove that the airport is operated in an unreasonable manner that creates a nuisance. Some of the complaints which the courts have been asked to pass upon are excessive dust, low-flying planes, and noise.

(a) Dust. In one case a court held that the operation of a municipal airport was a nuisance because it created excessive amounts of dust which filtered into nearby houses and caused inconvenience, injury, and illness to the residents. In spite of this case, the general rule seems to be that a certain amount of dust and noise are incidental to the operation of an airport and they will not constitute a nuisance even though they cause discomfort and injury to residents nearby.

(b) Low-Flying Planes. Low-flying planes raise another interesting legal issue. Historically, the ownership of land has always included the right to all the land downward, indefinitely, and the right to all the airspace upward, indefinitely. With the development of the airplane, the right to the airspace above has been limited to only the amount that the owner reasonably needs. It is clear that an airplane which flies at a high altitude does not commit a trespass on the land below. However, if an airplane flies low enough, it will commit a trespass on the land below by flying through airspace which is the private property of the owner of the land. This legal issue has been raised in lawsuits against airports by owners of houses in the airport's

THE LEGAL ADVISER ON HOME OWNERSHIP

immediate periphery, where planes pass close to their rooftops when taking off and landing.

(c) Noise. The noise problem exists all year long, but becomes acute in warm weather when the windows of the house are open wide and the average homeowner spends more time on his patio or in his backyard. During this time of year, a homeowner who lives in or around a major city must expect the quiet and tranquility of his home to be jarred by the recurrent deafening roar of transcontinental jets. The demand for faster transportation has led to ever bigger and more powerful aircraft engines that only aggravate the noise problem. This technological development has raised legal questions which still have not been resolved.

The problem of aircraft noise is another interesting illustration of two social forces which create a legal conflict for which there is no easy solution. One social force consists of the local homeowners, who have demanded that aircraft use mufflers and other sound inhibitors to lessen the noise, that they be limited to flight patterns which avoid populated areas, and that in taking off they be required to gain altitude at a steep angle, rather than at a gradual angle causing disturbance for a greater distance around the airport. The other social force is represented by the various governmental agencies responsible for the safety of aircraft; they oppose any suggestion tending to increase the hazard to aircraft, pilots, or passengers.

This problem can be acute in the suburban areas around major cities. The homeowner in Nassau County, New York, is near both Kennedy International Airport and LaGuardia Airport, which service much of the domestic and all of the international air traffic into New York. To meet this problem, the Nassau County government has engaged experts to make acoustical studies to determine the amount of noise produced under varying circumstances. With these studies as ammunition, the county has started legal proceedings to limit the noise nuisance. In time, the courts and legislature will probably provide new laws to clarify and define the rights of homeowners whose enjoyment of their homes is impaired by a nearby airport.

(2) SCHOOLS, FIREHOUSES, HOSPITALS, AND PLAYGROUNDS. No one can reasonably deny the need for and desirability of schools, firehouses, hospitals, and similar community facilities. However, most homeowners would also prefer to have these functions performed next to someone else's house rather than their own.

Zoning laws give some protection from the establishment of one of these community projects. But this protection is limited. The existing zoning law may prohibit anything but a particular type of dwelling in your residential zone. But it has been held that zoning regulations are not contracts with the local government, and the government may amend these laws at a later date and at that time authorize the building of a firehouse, school, etc. Furthermore, the Federal government is not bound by local zoning laws because Federal law is the supreme law of the land. The possibility of a community project being built next to your house is one of the reasons why it has already been suggested that a vacant lot next to a house should be regarded by a home buyer as a potential threat. Of course, even if there are no vacant lots, a community project can still be built by the government by using the power of condemnation, but this is less likely.

(3) CHURCHES. A church or other place of worship may be objectionable to the adjoining homeowner even if he is a member of that same congregation. The crowds, traffic, parked cars, and activity associated with church services and functions do impair the quiet enjoyment of a house. Zoning laws usually determine the areas in which churches may be built. Restrictive covenants may also prevent the building of a church. In a famous case in New York, the court held that where a restrictive covenant limited the use of the land to "dwellings," a church could not be built where the adjoining homeowner (who was a member of the same church) would not consent to it.

BOOMER v. ATLANTIC CEMENT CO., 26 N.Y. 2d 219,
309 N.Y. Supp. 2d 312 (1970).

BERGAN, Judge.

Defendant operates a large cement plant near Albany. These are actions for injunction and damages by neighboring land owners alleging injury to property from dirt, smoke and vibration emanating from the plant. A nuisance has been found after trial, temporary damages have been allowed; but an injunction has been denied.

The public concern with air pollution arising from many sources in industry and in transportation is currently accorded ever wider recognition accompanied by a growing sense of responsibility in State and Federal Governments to control it. Cement plants are obvious sources of air pollution in the neighborhoods where they operate.

But there is now before the court private litigation in which individual property owners have sought specific relief from a single plant operation. The threshold question raised by the division of view on this appeal is whether the court should resolve the litigation between the parties now before it as equitably as seems possible; or whether, seeking promotion of the general public welfare, it should channel private litigation into broad public objectives. ● ● ●

It is a rare exercise of judicial power to use a decision in private litigation as a purposeful mechanism to achieve direct public objectives greatly beyond the rights and interests before the court.

Effective control of air pollution is a problem presently far from solution even with the full public and financial powers of government. In large measure adequate technical procedures are yet to be developed and some that appear possible may be economically impracticable.

It seems apparent that the amelioration of air pollution will depend on technical research in great depth; on a carefully balanced consideration of the economic impact of close regulation; and of the actual effect on public health. It is likely to require massive public expenditure and to demand more than any local community can accomplish and to depend on regional and interstate controls.

[1] A court should not try to do this on its own as a by-product of private litigation and it seems manifest that the judicial establishment is neither equipped in the limited nature of any judgment it can pronounce nor prepared to lay down and implement an effective policy for the elimination of air pollution. This is an area beyond the circumference of one private lawsuit. It is a direct responsibility for government and

BOOMER v. ATLANTIC CEMENT COMPANY

should not thus be undertaken as an incident to solving a dispute between property owners and a single cement plant—one of many—in the Hudson River valley.

The cement making operations of defendant have been found by the court at Special Term to have damaged the nearby properties of plaintiffs in these two actions. That court, as it has been noted, accordingly found defendant maintained a nuisance and this has been affirmed at the Appellate Division. ● ● ●

The rule in New York has been that such a nuisance will be enjoined although marked disparity be shown in economic consequence between the effect of the injunction and the effect of the nuisance. ● ● ●

Thus the unconditional injunction granted at Special Term was reinstated. The rule laid down in that case, then, is that whenever the damage resulting from a nuisance is found not "unsubstantial", viz., $100 a year, injunction would follow. ● ● ●

Although the court at Special Term and the Appellate Division held that injunction should be denied, it was found that plaintiffs had been damaged in various specific amounts up to the time of the trial and damages to the respective plaintiffs were awarded for those amounts. ● ● ●

This result at Special Term and at the Appellate Division is a departture from a rule that has become settled; but to follow the rule literally in these cases would be to close down the plant at once. This court is fully agreed to avoid that immediately drastic remedy; the difference in view is how best to avoid it.*

One alternative is to grant the injunction but postpone its effect to a specified future date to give opportunity for technical advances to permit defendant to eliminate the nuisance; another is to grant the injunction conditioned on the payment of permanent damages to plaintiffs which would compensate them for the total economic loss to their property present and future caused by defendant's operations. For reasons which will be developed the court chooses the latter alternative.

If the injunction were to be granted unless within a short period—e. g., 18 months—the nuisance be abated by improved methods, there would be no assurance that any significant technical improvement would occur.

---

* Respondent's investment in the plant is in excess of $45,000,000. There are over 300 people employed there.

BOOMER v. ATLANTIC CEMENT COMPANY

The parties could settle this private litigation at any time if defendant paid enough money and the imminent threat of closing the plant would build up the pressure on defendant. If there were no improved techniques found, there would inevitably be applications to the court at Special Term for extensions of time to perform on showing of good faith efforts to find such techniques.

Moreover, techniques to eliminate dust and other annoying by-products of cement making are unlikely to be developed by any research the defendant can undertake within any short period, but will depend on the total resources of the cement industry nationwide and throughout the world. The problem is universal wherever cement is made.

For obvious reasons the rate of the research is beyond control of defendant. If at the end of 18 months the whole industry has not found a technical solution a court would be hard put to close down this one cement plant if due regard be given to equitable principles.

On the other hand, to grant the injunction unless defendant pays plaintiffs such permanent damages as may be fixed by the court seems to do justice between the contending parties. All of the attributions of economic loss to the properties on which plaintiffs' complaints are based will have been redressed.

The nuisance complained of by these plaintiffs may have other public or private consequences, but these particular parties are the only ones who have sought remedies and the judgment proposed will fully redress them. The limitation of relief granted is a limitation only within the four corners of these actions and does not foreclose public health or other public agencies from seeking proper relief in a proper court.

It seems reasonable to think that the risk of being required to pay permanent damages to injured property owners by cement plant owners would itself be a reasonable effective spur to research for improved techniques to minimize nuisance. ● ● ●

The present cases and the remedy here proposed are in a number of other respects rather similar to Northern Indiana Public Service Co. v. W. J. & M. S. Vesey, 210 Ind. 338, 200 N.E. 620 decided by the Supreme Court of Indiana. The gases, odors, ammonia and smoke from the Northern Indiana company's gas plant damaged the nearby Vesey greenhouse operation. An injunction and damages were sought, but an injunction was denied and the relief granted was limited to permanent damages "present, past, and future" (p. 371, 200 N.E. 620).

Denial of injunction was grounded on a public interest in the operation of the gas plant and on the court's conclusion "that less injury would be occasioned by requiring the appellant [Public Service] to pay the appellee [Vesey] all damages suffered by it * * * than by enjoining the operation of the gas plant; and that the maintenance and operation of the gas plant should not be enjoined" (p. 349, 200 N.E. p. 625). ● ● ●

BOOMER v. ATLANTIC CEMENT COMPANY

Thus it seems fair to both sides to grant permanent damages to plaintiffs which will terminate this private litigation. The theory of damage is the "servitude on land" of plaintiffs imposed by defendant's nuisance. (See United States v. Causby, 328 U.S. 256, 261, 262, 267, 66 S.Ct. 1062, 90 L.Ed. 1206, where the term "servitude" addressed to the land was used by Justice Douglas relating to the effect of airplane noise on property near an airport.)   ●   ●   ●

The orders should be reversed, without costs, and the cases remitted to Supreme Court, Albany County to grant an injunction which shall be vacated upon payment by defendant of such amounts of permanent damage to the respective plaintiffs as shall for this purpose be determined by the court.

JASEN Judge (dissenting).

It has long been the rule in this State, as the majority acknowledges, that a nuisance which results in substantial continuing damage to neighbors must be enjoined. (Whalen v. Union Bag & Paper Co., 208 N.Y. 1, 101 N.E. 805; Campbell v. Seaman, 63 N.Y. 568; see, also, Kennedy v. Moog Servocontrols, 21 N.Y.2d 966, 290 N.Y.S.2d 193, 237 N. E.2d 356.) To now change the rule to permit the cement company to continue polluting the air indefinitely upon the payment of permanent damages is, in my opinion, compounding the magnitude of a very serious problem in our State and Nation today.

In recognition of this problem, the Legislature of this State has enacted the Air Pollution Control Act (Public Health Law, Consol.Laws, c. 45, §§ 1264 to 1299-m) declaring that it is the State policy to require the use of all available and reasonable methods to prevent and control air pollution (Public Health Law § 1265 [1]).

The harmful nature and widespread occurrence of air pollution have been extensively documented. Congressional hearings have revealed that air pollution causes substantial property damage, as well as being a contributing factor to a rising incidence of lung cancer, emphysema bronchitis and asthma.[2]

The specific problem faced here is known as particulate contamination because of the fine dust particles emanating from defendant's cement plant. The particular type of nuisance is not new, having appeared in many cases for at least the past 60 years. (See Hulbert v. California Portland Cement Co., 161 Cal. 239, 118 P. 928 [1911].) It is interesting to note that cement production has recently been identified as a significant source of particulate contamination in the Hudson Valley.[3] This type of pollution, wherein very small particles escape and stay in the atmosphere, has been denominated as the type of air pollution which produces the greatest hazard to human health.[4] We have thus a nuisance which not only is damaging to the plaintiffs,[5] but also is decidedly harmful to the general public.

I see grave dangers in overruling our long-established rule of granting an injunction where a nuisance results in substantial continuing damage. In permitting the injunction to become inoperative upon the payment of permanent damages, the majority is, in effect, licensing a continuing wrong. It is the same as saying to the cement company, you may continue to do harm to your neighbors so long as you pay a fee for it. Furthermore, once such permanent damages are assessed and paid, the incentive to alleviate the wrong would be eliminated, thereby continuing air pollution of an area without abatement.

It is true that some courts have sanctioned the remedy here proposed by the majority in a number of cases,[6] but none of the authorities relied upon by the majority are analogous to the situation before us. In those cases, the courts, in denying an injunction and awarding money damages, grounded their decision on a showing that the use to which the property was intended to be put was primarily for the public benefit. Here, on the other hand, it is clearly established that the cement company is creating a continuing air pollution nuisance primarily for its own private interest with no public benefit.

This kind of inverse condemnation (Ferguson v. Village of Hamburg, 272 N.Y. 234, 5 N.E.2d 801) may not be invoked by a private person or corporation for private gain or advantage. Inverse condemnation should only be permitted when the public is primarily served in the taking or impairment of property. (Matter of New York City Housing Auth. v. Muller, 270 N.Y. 333, 343, 1 N.E.2d 153, 156; Pocantico Water Works Co. v. Bird, 130 N.Y. 249, 258, 29 N.E. 246, 248.) The promotion of the interests of the polluting cement company has, in my opinion, no public use or benefit. ● ● ●

I would enjoin the defendant cement company from continuing the discharge of dust particles upon its neighbors' properties unless, within 18 months, the cement company abated this nuisance.[7]

It is not my intention to cause the removal of the cement plant from the Albany area, but to recognize the urgency of the problem stemming from this stationary source of air pollution, and to allow the company a specified period of time to develop a means to alleviate this nuisance.

● ● ●

In a day when there is a growing concern for clean air, highly developed industry should not expect acquiescence by the courts, but should, instead, plan its operations to eliminate contamination of our air and damage to its neighbors.

2. Negligence

KELLEY v. NATIONAL LEAD COMPANY, 210 S.W. 2d 728, (Mo. 1948).

BENNICK, Commissioner.

This is an action to recover compensation for personal injuries and property damage allegedly sustained by plaintiffs, Harry Kelley and Florence L. Kelley, his wife, as a consequence of the negligence of defendant, National Lead Company, in causing and permitting gases, fumes, and chemical particles to be emitted from its chemical plant and discharged over the neighborhood where plaintiffs resided.

The action was brought pursuant to the authority of the new code, which permits all persons to join in one action as plaintiffs if they assert any right to relief jointly or severally in respect to or arising out of the same transaction or occurrence, and if any question of law or fact common to all of them will arise in the action. Laws Mo. 1943, p. 360, sec. 16, Mo.R.S.A. § 847.16.

● ● ●

Upon a trial to a jury, a verdict was returned awarding plaintiff Harry Kelley the sum of $500 for personal injuries, and awarding both plaintiffs the sum of $500 for damage to their property, but denying plaintiff Florence L. Kelley a recovery on her claim for personal injuries.

Judgment was entered in accordance with the verdict; and following an unavailing motion for a new trial, defendant gave notice of appeal, and by subsequent steps has caused the case to be transferred to this court for our review.

Defendant's plant is located in St. Louis County just south of the city limits of the City of St. Louis at the point where the River Des Peres flows into the Mississippi River. The surrounding territory is utilized for both industrial and residential purposes.

The plant was originally operated by the Titanium Pigment Company, but was taken over as a division of defendant company around 1935. The plant was constructed for the manufacture of titanium pigments, which are chiefly consumed in the making of paints.

An essential ingredient in the process of making pigments out of titanium ore is sulphuric acid, which, prior to 1934, had been purchased on the open market. However in that year the original company decided to begin the manufacture of its own sulphuric acid; and in the period from 1934 to 1941 four separate units were designed and constructed under contracts with reputable, established firms with experience throughout the country in that particular undertaking. As a matter of fact, there is no suggestion in the record of any defect or insufficiency in the construction or installation of the plant.

The four units were designed to manufacture 93% sulphuric acid, and in the course of the process of operating the units certain fumes and mists escaped through stacks and were discharged into the surrounding atmosphere. There was some dispute regarding the density of such fumes and mists during the time before the war that defendant was merely engaged in the manufacture of 93% sulphuric acid. Defendant admitted that a few complaints were received during that period, but offered the explanation that the situation in those instances was usually found to be due to some particular set of circumstances occurring in connection with atmospheric conditions that would bring the fumes to the ground in the surrounding residential area. Indeed, defendant's evidence showed that prior to the outbreak of war, it was not unusual to delay operations, sometimes for several days, until the atmospheric conditions and wind direction would be such that if any undue amount of

KELLEY v. NATIONAL LEAD CO.

fumes and gases should be emitted from the stacks, they would not be carried into a residential area. On the other hand, plaintiffs' evidence disclosed that between 1939 and 1941, the Smoke Commissioner of the City of St. Louis, because of complaints received in his office, was prompted to conduct an investigation in the neighborhood, and not only detected the presence of sulphur fumes in the air as well as a white mist or vapor which reduced visibility to a matter of feet, but also traced such fumes and mist to their point of origin, which he found to be defendant's plant.

But whatever may have been the difficulty encountered during the period before the war when defendant was merely engaged in the manufacture of 93% sulphuric acid in connection with its regular peacetime activities, the situation was in any event greatly aggravated and intensified in the latter part of 1941 when one of the units was converted to the manufacture of 40% oleum at the direction of the Ordnance Department of the United States Army.

● ● ●

The direction for the conversion of defendant's plant was made under the authority of an act for the conscription of industry, which was enacted by the Congress in 1940. 50 U.S.C.A.Appendix, § 309.

Suffice it to say that by the provisions of such act, the President was empowered, through the War and Navy Departments, to place an order with any manufacturer for such product or material as might be required, and which was of the nature and kind usually produced or capable of being produced by such manufacturer. Compliance with all such orders for products or material was made obligatory upon the manufacturer, and the orders were required to be given precedence over all other orders and contracts theretofore placed with the manufacturer. In the event of the refusal of any manufacturer to comply with any such order, the President, through the War and Navy Departments, was authorized to take over the operation of the plant for the Government; and it was further provided that any corporation or its responsible officers who should fail to comply with the provisions of the act should be deemed guilty of a felony, and upon conviction should be punished by imprisonment for not more than three years and a fine not exceeding $50,000.

Oleum, which is sometimes referred to as fuming sulphuric acid, is made by dissolving sulphur trioxide in concentrated sulphuric acid. ● ● ●

Before the war emergency it had only been manufactured in very limited quantities; and in undertaking to carry out the direction of the Ordnance Department, not only had defendant never made oleum at any time, but it had no experience to guide it derived from any prior instance where a plant constructed for the manufacture of sulphuric acid was converted into a plant for the manufacture of oleum. As might have been expected, serious difficulties were encountered from the very outset. Moreover there was no opportunity for shutting down the plant while awaiting favorable atmospheric conditions and wind direction as in the case of the manufacture of sulphuric acid during peacetime. The amount of oleum furnished the Weldon Springs Ordnance Works determined how much T.N.T. could be made available for the progress of the war, and all during the duration of the war defendant was under constant pressure from the Ordnance Department to increase its output. The result of all this was that the discharge of fumes was greatly intensified over what had been the situation before the manufacture of oleum was begun. ● ● ●

The gist of plaintiffs' cause of action was embodied in paragraph 4 of their petition, in which they charged that defendant then and for some years past had "negligently and carelessly" caused large quantities of poisonous and deleterious gases, fumes, and chemical particles, including concentrated sulphuric acid and oleum, to be discharged from a number of very tall stacks at its plant, and that whenever the wind blew from the direction of the stacks towards plaintiffs' home, it caused such gases, fumes, and chemical particles to be deposited in plaintiffs' neighborhood, resulting in injury to their persons and damage to their property.

they lived. Throughout the trial counsel emphasized on repeated occasions that the issue was one of negligence; and in the submission of the case both sides requested and received instructions upon such theory. There can be no doubt that the parties themselves, as well as the lower court, construed the pleadings as putting negligence in issue, and they will therefore be given the same construction in disposing of the case on this appeal.

By the time of the submission of the case, this issue had been reduced to the question of whether defendant could have remedied or prevented the escape of fumes and gases from its plant, but negligently failed to do so.

The question involved the use of a device or principle known as the Cottrell Precipitator ● ● ●

It seems to be unquestioned that owing to the higher strength of the materials employed as well as the difference in temperature at which the process is required to be carried on, the manufacture of oleum results in the giving off of far larger amounts of fumes and gases than in the case of the manufacture of sulphuric acid. Not only is the production of fumes and gases inherent in the very nature of the process, but there is no known way of preventing it.

When defendant converted its plant to the manufacture of oleum, it did not know what to expect in the way of fumes and gases, but the result was beyond its worst foreboding. Immediate efforts were made by defendant's own officials to study the problem and find its reason and solution, ● ● ● and while their recommendations may have helped the condition to some extent, they did not succeed in eliminating the fumes.

Early in 1942 the question of the application of the Cottrell process was taken up with the Research Corporation of America. It was known that Cottrell Precipitators had been used successfully in other classes of sulphuric acid plants for various purposes, and it was thought that the process was worthy of a trial, though the same had never before been employed in a plant converted to the manufacture of oleum. ● ● ●

On the contrary, all the evidence, including that for plaintiffs, disclosed that the application of the Cottrell principle to any particular situation requires testing and experimentation, and that in each and every instance it has to be what some of the witnesses referred to as a tailor-made job.

In the summer of 1943 a test plant was constructed upon defendant's premises according to specifications furnished by the Research Corporation of America. The evidence showed that the test plant was required because of the fact that the Research Corporation of America had had no previous experience in designing equipment for a plant of the type and nature of defendant's plant. ● ● ●

On January 14, 1944, defendant was instructed by the Ordnance Department to discontinue the manufacture of oleum, and negotiations with the Research Corporation of America for the installation of a Cottrell Precipitator were thereupon abandoned. However in October, 1944, defendant was directed to resume the manufacture of oleum, and negotiations for the installation of a Cottrell Precipitator were once again begun. On V-J Day, which was August 15, 1945, the manufacture of oleum was finally terminated. Some time later a Cottrell Precipitator was completed and installed; and while defendant's assistant superintendent testified in his direct examination that it had accomplished the desired purpose of eliminating the fumes in the manufacture of sulphuric acid, it was brought out in his cross-examination that there was still a certain amount of gas and mist coming out of the stacks at the time of the trial in May, 1946. ● ● ●

Plaintiffs' petition charged mere general negligence, that is, that defendant carelessly and negligently caused gases, fumes, and chemical particles to be emitted from its plant and deposited in plaintiffs' neighborhood. ● ● ●

But while referring to the case as one of res ipsa loquitur, what plaintiffs doubtless mean to urge is that it comes within the principle of Fletcher v. Rylands, L.R. 1 Exch. 265, L.R. 3 H.L. 330, which is that one, who for his own purposes collects and keeps anything upon his land which is likely to do mischief if it escapes, must keep it at his peril, and if he does not do so is prima facie actionable for all the damage which is the natural consequence of its escape. In any event, the petition was drawn upon this theory. It is enough to say, however, that such principle has been seriously questioned in practically all jurisdictions, and at any rate is not the law in our own jurisdiction, where it is held that liability cannot be imposed upon the owner or occupant for damage caused by the escape of substances from his premises except upon proof of some fault or negligence on his part. Murphy v. Gillum, 73 Mo.App. 487; Greene v. Spinning, Mo.App., 48 S.W.2d

● ● ●

It is interesting to note that while plaintiffs drew their petition upon the principle announced in Fletcher v. Rylands, and while they presented their evidence upon that theory, when they came to the submission of the case they abandoned their reliance upon the mere fact of the escape of the fumes and gases, and included the element of whether defendant had permitted such fumes and gases to escape, when, in the exercise of ordinary care, it could have remedied or prevented said condition, but failed to do so. Such specific element of liability was undoubtedly suggested by the evidence regarding the eventual designing and installation of a Cottrell Precipitator; and the obvious purpose of the instruction was to submit the question of whether defendant had been guilty of negligence in failing to prevent the escape of fumes and gases by at all times making use of such a device.

Having due regard for the fundamental concepts of the law of negligence, we cannot escape the conclusion that plaintiffs failed to make a case for the jury upon this issue.   ● ● ●

There is a distinction to be drawn between negligence and actionable negligence. Hight v. American Bakery Co., 168 Mo.App. 431, 151 S.W. 776. Even though a given act or omission might be thought to indicate a lack of care and thus to constitute negligence from the viewpoint of the ordinary layman, it does not follow that a cause of action will inevitably arise therefrom. On the contrary, in order to impose liability there must not only be a lack of care, but such lack of care must involve a breach of some duty owed to another under the particular circumstances existing at the time of the act or omission complained of, which act or omission must have proximately resulted in such other person's injury.   ● ● ●

It may be that defendant was in one sense negligent in so long delaying its experimentation with the Cottrell principle, but such negligence, if any, lacked the essential elements to make it actionable in this character of proceeding. If a Cottrell Precipitator had been readily procurable on the market, defendant would no doubt have owed plaintiffs the duty of promptly installing one, but since such a device was not available on the market, defendant was not guilty of any breach of duty so as to have afforded plaintiffs a remedy by an action for negligence.

[10] The whole trouble is that while plaintiffs may have a cause of action, they have mistaken the remedy to be pursued for its enforcement. If they are to obtain redress for whatever injury and damage they have sustained, it seems clear that it must be upon the theory of nuisance. It is well recognized that for one to permit fumes and gases to escape from his premises and be deposited on the premises of another to his injury and damage may constitute an actionable wrong in the maintenance of a nuisance.   ● ● ●

KELLEY v. NATIONAL LEAD CO.

What is of course meant is that such a condition may constitute a nuisance in fact, depending on the circumstances of the particular case, such as the location and character of the neighborhood; the nature of the use to which the property is put; the extent and frequency of the injury; and the effect upon the enjoyment of life, health, property, and the like. ● ● ●

The doctrine is not limited to any particular character of industry, and it has been expressly held that the emission of fumes and gases from a sulphuric acid plant may constitute a nuisance, although the business itself is not unlawful, nor is the plant a nuisance per se. ● ● ●

But notwithstanding the relevancy of any of the evidence to the questions that would arise in the case of nuisance, plaintiffs appreciate that a petition based on the theory of negligence will not sustain a recovery on the theory of nuisance. ● ● ●

It has been repeatedly held that where it appears from the record that the plaintiff has rights growing out of an occurrence but has misconceived his remedy, it is within the province of an appellate court to remand the case to permit the petition to be amended, if the plaintiff is so advised, and the case retried upon the cause of action disclosed. ● ● ●

It follows from what has been said that the judgment of the circuit court should be reversed and the cause remanded for a new trial.

2. Negligence (Continued)

REYNOLDS METALS COMP. v. YTURBIDE, 258 F. 2d 321 (9th Cir.) cert. den. 358 U.S. 840 (1958).

POPE, Circuit Judge.

In July, 1946, Reynolds Metals Company, a Delaware corporation, acquired through lease, an aluminum plant belonging to the Government and located at Troutdale, Oregon. It commenced operation of its first potline for the production of aluminum in September of that year. In the operation of the plant chemical compounds containing aluminum were collected in the reduction cells of the so-called "pots" and were reduced or separated by the process of electrolysis or passage of current through the cell. In the process, temperatures up to 1775° F. were developed. As the compounds with which the cells were charged, (cryolite or sodium fluoride or calcium fluoride and aluminum fluoride) contain large percentages of fluorine ranging around 50 percent, a considerable portion of fluoride material was volatilized in the process and reached the atmosphere.[1]

Shortly after the operation of the plan began, and in December, 1946, the appellees in these three appeals, Paul Martin, his wife, Verla Martin, and his daughter, Paula Martin (now Mrs. Yturbide), moved to their cattle farm or ranch near Troutdale located about a mile to a mile and one-half from the aluminum plant, and they resided there until November, 1950. The law suits out of which these appeals grew were based upon claims that during the period of their residence on the farm they were poisoned by fluorides which originated at the appellant's plant and were borne on the air to the farm where they breathed these fluoride effluents claimed to be highly toxic and also ate vegetables growing in their garden which also had been absorbing the same toxic elements.[2]

The principal question presented here is whether the evidence adduced at the trial below, (the three cases were tried together and upon the same evidence) was sufficient to permit the case to go to the jury. Upon the part of the appellant it is contended, (1) that there was insufficient proof to demonstrate that the damage to the persons of the plaintiffs,

of which they complain, was caused by the fluorides escaping from defendant's plant; and (2), that there was no evidence of any negligence, or any other breach of duty, on the part of the defendant.

[1] With respect to the question of causation:—whether the escaping fluorides did in fact cause plaintiffs' injuries, —the evidence was sufficient to warrant the jury's conclusion that the escaping fluorides were the cause of the injuries.

● ● ●

A horticulturist from the Oregon State College, in the years 1948, 1949 and 1950 made test samples of plants grown on selected plots in the vicinity of the Martin property, for the purpose of determining the fluorine content of such plants. ● ● ●

The plants tested on plots which were farther away from the plant showed a subtantially decreasing fluorine content, thus indicating that relatively speaking the nearer the aluminum plant the greater the concentration of the gases, fumes and particulates, (i. e. fine solids). ● ● ●

REYNOLDS METALS COMPANY v. YTURBIDE

In general there was an absence of proof as to just what quantities of fluorides contained in these gases, fumes, and particulates, passed over the Martin land or were inhaled by them or ingested from the garden vegetables eaten by them. There was, however, proof that these fluorides were toxic. • • •

That very large quantities of these gases, fumes, and particulates, did leave the plant and were diffused into the air, was unquestioned. Appellant's own exhibits disclose that with the equipment which was used to control the escape of gases during the period that the Martins lived on their farm, hundreds of pounds of these effluents escaped each day. Thus in the year 1947, the amount of fluorine alone escaping per day from the plant averaged 2845 pounds. Comparable amounts escaped in the years 1948–1949 and throughout the first half of 1950, after which time the appellant began the installation of a new control system which was much more efficient in arresting the escape and fall-out.

There is no showing as to where these large quantities of effluents finally settled. The experiments mentioned above would indicate that the greater portion settled on those areas nearest the plant, and those areas included the Martin farm. That the effluents did have some degree of toxic or harmful effect was indicated by proof that cattle upon the Martin place showed damage from fluorosis. Generally with respect to cattle it does not appear to have been controverted that cattle damage from an aluminum plant is a fairly common phenomenon.[3]

[2] Of course it does not follow from mere proof of some damage to cattle on the Martin place that the plaintiffs' physical injuries were due to excessive amounts of fluorides from the plant.

• • •

A significant bit of testimony adduced was proof that glass in the Martin home became etched by acid, probably hydrofluoric acid which was one of the effluents from the aluminum plant. One of the expert witnesses, the British doctor who had some prior experience with similar etching of glass located near industrial plants abroad, testified that the glass from the Martin window which he was shown during the testimony was an indication of excessive quantities of fluoride contamination in the atmosphere.

Although the cases of the Martins are unique in that they were unable to produce either from medical literature or expert witnesses histories of persons situated as they were, namely, persons not working in the plant but simply living outside and near the plant, who developed symptoms similar to theirs in consequence of the fall-out of emanations from an aluminum plant, (see footnote 5a infra) nevertheless they did produce substantial medical testimony which did connect their disabilities and physical injuries with the fluorides escaping from the plant. Of course there was also testimony to the contrary, but the evidence adduced on their behalf, principally from the British medical expert referred to in footnote 3, supra, and from a Dr. Capps, a Chicago specialist on diseases of the liver, was substantial, and in our view, fully worthy of credit. • • •

The medical witnesses expressed confidence in their conclusions because of the fact that they found substantially the same symptoms in the three individuals, thus lessening the possibility that the symptoms were attributable to individual idiosyncracies. Neither one was able to testify as to the degree of concentration,—how many parts per million of fluorides,—would be required to bring about the injuries found, but both attached some significance to the fact that the window in the house was etched by acid. As stated by Dr. Capps, "I think that if there is enough fluorine to etch a window, it should be able to etch a lung." Dr. Hunter related his own experience in finding in England a family with the same symptoms as the Martins who lived in a house near an industrial plant [7] whose windows were similarly etched and said that the etching he observed in the glass taken from the Martin home was an indication of excessive quantities of fluorine in the atmosphere. He referred to studies made in 1946 warning the industrial world "against throwing into the atmosphere an effluent which would etch glass."

A further circumstance which the medical witnesses emphasized was that in the case of the Martins their abnormal symptoms were reduced and lessened after they had moved away from the vicinity of the plant. We are thus led to the conclusion that the jury was warranted in finding, as they did, that physical injuries to the Martins were caused by the fluoride emanations from the plant

which found their way to the Martin place.

On behalf of the defendant evidence was adduced to show that only a very small concentration of fluorides could have reached the Martin home. We think the jury were warranted in accepting plaintiffs' testimony, and the inferences therefrom, that excessive amounts of fluorides reached them, for they actually suffered fluoride poisoning. There was no proof on the part of plaintiffs as to what particular percentage or concentration of fluorides was necessary to produce such results. Plaintiffs were obliged to accept in that respect the concession made by the defendant to the effect that such fluorides are "poisonous in excessive amounts." The only possible conclusion is that because the damage was actually caused by the fluorides, they somehow managed to

The important question is whether there was proof of any negligence or other breach of duty on the part of the defendant which brought about these injuries as its proximate result. ● ● ●

Appellant argues that there is a complete absence of proof of any want of care on its part in the operation of the aluminum plant. In this respect its contention is that before the plant was put in operation it equipped it with facilities for minimizing the amount of effluents that escaped from the plant. ● ● ●

The result of this spray system was that it removed some 60 percent of the fluorides from the air coming through the roof so that only 40 percent of these compounds actually escaped from the plant.

Defendant's Assistant Vice-President testified that during this period from 1946 to 1950, when the spray system of fluorides elimination was in use, the company was carrying on experiments to devise and find better ways of making a more efficient capture of the effluents.

● ● ●

The result of the use of this improved system was to eliminate 90 percent of the fluoride compounds from the air which escaped from the plant. ● ● ●

In short, by this improved method, the portion of the emanating fluorides which reached the air was 10 percent of the total as against 40 percent under the earlier system.

In determining the duty of care the law imposed upon the defendant, it is to be borne in mind that the ordinary care which the law requires of such a defendant is measured in part by the defendant's knowledge of potential dangers. ● ● ●

get there in excessive quantities. We think we must accept this as a permissible finding of the jury.

As stated in the Restatement of Torts, § 289, in determining the standard of reasonable conduct, "the actor should recognize that his conduct involves a risk of causing an invasion of another's interest, if a person, possessing * * * such superior perception as the actor himself has * * * would infer that the act creates an appreciable chance of causing such invasion." Comment (n) under this section headed "Superior knowledge" recites: "If the actor has a wider knowledge, whether gained from personal experience or otherwise, the propriety of his judgment as to the risk involved in his conduct is determined by what a reasonable man having such knowledge would regard as probable."

● ● ●

Not only that, but it was the duty of one in the position of the defendant to know of the dangers incident to the aluminum reduction process. As the last named authors point out in § 16.5, "The manufacturer must learn of dangers that lurk in his processes and his products."

The record here amply demonstrates that the defendant was fully aware of the potential dangers in the escape of fluorides. It is not questioned that numerous claims of injury to cattle from the operation of such plants had been presented to this and other manufacturers. The defendant's senior chemist at the Troutdale laboratory testified that he was familiar with the literature upon the toxic qualities of these fluorides; that he knew that in quantities they were toxic; that some of these were heavier than air and would reach the earth after being air-borne; that quantities of them would drift in the direction of the Martin land and that there were publications which dealt with dangers to human beings from fluorides.

The question is whether in view of the knowledge which the company was reasonably required to have as a manufacturer in this field, and the knowledge which it actually did have of the potential dangers of these escaping fluorides there was evidence of a failure to use reasonable care for the protection of persons in the situation of the Martins.

On behalf of the defendant it was testified that at all these times defendant was utilizing and had installed the latest and best known means of protecting against the escape of the fluorides; that the company, continually studying the problem, installed an experimental pilot plant to develop a new process and then changed over to the improved process as soon as its feasibility was developed.

On behalf of plaintiffs it was urged that the evidence warranted a conclusion that the company did not exercise the care in this direction which it might have done in that it allowed the plant to be operated with the less efficient elimination system from 1946 until 1950 whereas proper care required an earlier use of the better devices. ● ● ● we are of the opinion that the trial court properly submitted to the jury the question of negligence on the part of the defendant on the theory that this was a case correctly permitting the application of the doctrine of res ipsa loquitur.

The court instructed the jury as follows: "Under the law and the facts of these actions, the defendant was the sole operator and in exclusive possession and direct control of the aluminum plant involved during the time involved, namely, between on or about September 23, 1946, and November 30, 1950. Further, that under the ordinary course of events, it is unexpected that persons being in the vicinity of such a plant would be injured or harmed by fluorine compounds emanating therefrom, and that such a mishap would not occur." The statement in the first of these two sentences is unquestionable; the second sentence is in conformity with defendant's theory and much of the evidence adduced by it at the trial. The instruction was consistent with the testimony that the plant as equipped and operated, would not cause fluorosis to persons who had not been employed in the plant itself. The

REYNOLDS METALS COMPANY v. YTURBIDE

court noted that there was no evidence as to the amount or concentration of fluorides that would bring about fluorosis in the case of such persons. While during the critical period here 40 percent of the gases, fumes and particulates got by the sprinkler system and escaped into the air, the fluorine contents aggregating hundreds of pounds all told, the tests made at various localities near the plant and on every side thereof, according to defendant's witnesses, produced no significant concentration of fluorides at the time the tests were made. Hence, the court, accepting this proof, told the jury that, "under the ordinary course of events, it is unexpected that persons being in the vicinity of such a plant would be injured or harmed by fluorine compounds emanating therefrom."

In so ruling the court in effect determined that the accident was of a kind which ordinarily does not occur in the absence of someone's negligence. That is a prime condition for the application of the so-called rule of res ipsa loquitur. Said the court (135 F.Supp. at page 381): "Here was an instrumentality that was in the exclusive possession and control of the defendant. Something that ordinarily we would not expect to happen did happen and damage resulted. This is the pure and simple test as the Court sees it, of res ipsa loquitur."9 ● ● ●

Viewing plaintiffs' case in the most favorable light, as we are required to do, we have the following: (1), Damage to persons in the position of the Martins was possible from "excessive amounts" of fluorides; (2), the Martins were poisoned and from this plant and by these fluorides; (3), from this it is permissible to infer that "excessive amounts" reached them,—that there were such excessive amounts; (4), the emission of exces-

sive amounts from the plant was circumstantial evidence of negligence. Res ipsa loquitur.

Appellant says that the res ipsa rule was misapplied here. ● ● ● "Defendant in a res ipsa case may show by evidence how the accident happened, but ordinarily this does not entitle him to a directed verdict. The jury may still reject the evidence or find that the explanation does not preclude the likelihood of negligence. * * * In most res ipsa loquitur cases defendant cannot definitely explain the accident. His usual defense consists of proof of the precautions he did take in constructing, maintaining, and operating the injuring instrumentality. Once in a great while such proof may conclusively show that the accident did not in fact happen, or that it was not caused by defendant. But this is seldom the outcome. And where it is not, defendant is in this dilemma: the less effective his precautions to prevent the occurrence the more apt they are to appear negligent; the more effective the precautions testified to, the less likely they are to have [been] taken in this case since the accident *did happen.*"10 ● ● ●

When res ipsa loquitur is applied the facts of the occurrence warrant the inference of negligence. They furnish substantial evidence of negligence where the direct evidence of it may be lacking, but they make a case to be decided by the jury.12 In finding itself in the dilemma mentioned by Harper & James in the language quoted above, appellant is in no different situation than any other defendant who finds itself in a res ipsa case and before a jury. It is not, as appellant asserts, the victim of the application of a rule of absolute liability. ● ● ●

The judgments are affirmed.

3. Trespass

REYNOLDS METALS COMPANY v. MARTIN, 337 F. 2d 780 (9th Cir. 1964).

The action was commenced on December 18, 1961, in the Circuit Court of the State of Oregon for the County of Multnomah. The plaintiffs, Paul Martin and Verla Martin, his wife, were citizens and residents of Oregon,[1] and defendant, Reynolds Metals Company, is a Delaware corporation.[2]

The original purpose of the action was to recover actual damages in the sum of three hundred thousand dollars and punitive damages in the sum of one hundred thousand dollars, by reason of the alleged contamination of plaintiff's fifteen-hundred acre cattle ranch. Such contamination, it was asserted, was caused by the emanation of fluoride fumes and particulates from defendant's nearby aluminum reduction plant at Troutdale, Oregon, during the years 1956 to 1961.[3]

● ● ●

After pretrial proceedings had been in progress for some time the plaintiffs, on October 28, 1963, filed their second amended complaint. By that time plaintiffs were seeking actual damages in the sum of $1,428,342 and punitive damages in the sum of one million dollars. Injunctive relief against continued operation of the Troutdale plant was also sought, unless adequate controls were installed to eliminate the emanation of fluorides.

Defendants thereupon moved to dismiss the action for lack of jurisdiction over the subject matter and for failure to state a claim upon which relief can be granted. Both grounds for the motion were premised on the assertion that primary administrative jurisdiction rests with the Sanitary Authority of the State of Oregon, which has certain functions and duties with respect to air pollution pursuant to ORS 449.760 to 449.830. Because of the primary jurisdiction of that agency, defendant contended, the exercise of jurisdiction by the district court must be suspended pending administrative determination of the matters involved in the suit.

The district court denied the motion and this appeal followed.

The doctrine of primary administrative jurisdiction, unlike the rule requiring exhaustion of administrative remedies, applies where a claim is originally cognizable in the courts. It comes into play, as the Supreme Court said in United States v. Western Pac. R. Co., 352 U. S. 59, 64, 77 S.Ct. 161, 165, 1 L.Ed.2d 126:

"* * * whenever enforcement of the claim requires the resolution of issues which, under a regulatory scheme, have been placed within the special competence of an administrative body; in such a case the judicial process is suspended pending referral of such issues to the administrative body for its views."

Appellant concedes that since this is a diversity action the law of Oregon governs in determining whether the doctrine of primary administrative jurisdiction should be applied in this case. It urges that the courts of Oregon will apply the doctrine in a proper case, and that this is such a case.

While the doctrine may not have been mentioned by name in the decisions of the Supreme Court of Oregon, it appears to have been applied in at least one case. See Valley & Siletz R. R. Co. v. Flagg, 195 Or. 683, 247 P.2d 639, 654, which involved the railroad rate-making function of the Oregon Public Utilities Commissioner. We can therefore assume, and appellee does not argue to the contrary, that cases can arise in which the courts of Oregon, applying the doctrine of primary administrative jurisdiction, would suspend judicial proceedings pending referral of the issues to a state administrative body for its views.

REYNOLDS METALS COMPANY v. MARTIN

The precise question presented, therefore, is whether the courts of Oregon would hold that effectuation of the purpose of the legislature in enacting ORS 449.760 to 449.830, requires that the Sanitary Authority should first pass on some or all of the matters in dispute.[4]

One section of the statutes in question, namely ORS 449.820, gives the Sanitary Authority power to institute suits for injunction to compel compliance with the agency's rules, regulations and orders pertaining to air pollution. The last sentence of subsection (1) of ORS 449.-820 reads:

"The provisions of this section shall not prevent the maintenance of actions or suits relating to private or public nuisances brought by any other person, or by the state on relation of any person without prior order of the Sanitary Authority."

The question of whether this statutory language evidenced a legislative purpose that the doctrine of primary administrative purpose should not apply with regard to the air pollution statutes, ORS 449.760 to 449.830, was before the Supreme Court of Oregon in the recent case of Diercks v. Hodgdon, Or., 390 P.2d 935. On review in that case was a decree enjoining the operator of a shingle mill from permitting smoke, cinders and ashes to invade the plaintiff's residential property, and awarding damages in the sum of three hundred dollars.

On the basis of the quoted provision of ORS 449.820(1), the court rejected the argument that the plaintiff should have instituted administrative proceedings under ORS 449.760 to 449.830, before resorting to a suit in equity. The court said (at page 936):

"ORS 449.820 specifically provides that resort to administrative abatement proceedings is not a condition precedent to relief in law or equity from public or private nuisance."

The company argues, however, that the Diercks decision is not controlling here because that case sounded in nuisance, and the provision of ORS 449.820(1) on which the court relied in Diercks refers to the maintenance of actions or suits relating to "private or public nuisances." Our case, it is contended, does not sound in nuisance, but in trespass.

The complaint in Diercks made no mention of either nuisance or trespass, but the decree which was entered referred to the grievance as a "nuisance." Likewise the Oregon Supreme Court regarded the condition caused by the invasion of the plaintiff's property by smoke, cinders and ashes emanating from the defendant's shingle mill as a "nuisance." In our case, on the other hand, the complaint refers to the contamination of the plaintiff's ranch by reason of fluorides emanating from the Troutdale plant as a "trespass" upon the lands of the plaintiff, the term "nuisance" not being used.

The distinction between trespass and nuisance in the law of Oregon is dealt with at length in Martin v. Reynolds Metals Co., 221 Or. 86, 342 P.2d 790, involving these same parties and the identical kind of grievance, but for an earlier period of time. In that suit, as here, the complaint made reference to "trespass" and not to "nuisance," but the company contended that, in actuality, only a cause of action in nuisance was stated. In taking this position the company sought to apply the two-year statute of limitations applicable to nuisance ac-

---

4. That this is the applicable test for determining whether the doctrine of primary administrative jurisdiction is to be applied in a particular case, see United States v. Western Pac. R. Co., 352 U.S. 59, 65, 77 S.Ct. 161.

tions (ORS 12.110), instead of the six-year statute applicable to actions sounding in trespass. ORS 12.080.

Upholding a trial court determination that the suit sounded in trespass, the Supreme Court (342 P.2d at page 794) defined trespass as:

"* * * any intrusion which invades the possessor's protected interest in exclusive possession, whether that intrusion is by visible or invisible pieces of matter or by energy which can be measured only by the mathematical language of the physicist."

Measured by this definition, and especially in view of the fact that this case involves precisely the same kind of grievance between the same parties, the conduct complained of in the case before us constituted a trespass, as alleged in the complaint.

In the course of its opinion in the Oregon Martin case, however, the court defined trespass and nuisance in a way which indicates that they overlap. Citing 4 Restatement, Torts 224, Intro. Note Chapter 40, the court defined a trespass as "* * * an actionable invasion of a possessor's interest in the exclusive possession of land * * *" and a nuisance as "* * * an actionable invasion of a possessor's interest in the use and enjoyment of his land. * * *." 342 P.2d at 792. The Supreme Court of Oregon itself recognized this overlap, saying:

"The same conduct on the part of a defendant may and often does result in the actionable invasion of both of these interests, in which case the choice between the two remedies is, in most cases, a matter of little consequence. * * *" Ibid.

At least where a trespass, consisting of an interference with the possessor's interest in the exclusive possession of land, is of a continuing nature, it would seem also to interfere with that possessor's interest in the use and enjoyment of his land, and thus be a nuisance. Such is the kind of interference complained of in our case, for it has assertedly continued over a long period of time.

[1] We are therefore of the opinion that, under Oregon law, the conduct complained of is both a trespass and a nuisance but that the trespass aspect of the case will govern in determining which statute of limitations is to be applied.

We see no reason why the trespass aspect of the case should govern in determining whether the quoted provision of ORS 449.820(1) stands in the way of applying the doctrine of primary administrative jurisdiction. That provision speaks of actions or suits "relating" to private or public nuisances. For the reasons indicated above we think this suit relates to a private nuisance even though it sounds in trespass for purposes of the statute of limitations.

Under the company's interpretation of this statutory provision, the doctrine of primary administrative jurisdiction will or will not apply, depending upon whether the plaintiff calls the same conduct, warranting the same relief, a trespass or a nuisance. Such a demarcation between cases in which the doctrine would or would not apply borders on the capricious and could serve no perceivable purpose relevant to the air pollution statutes of Oregon. We do not believe that in ORS 449.820(1), the legislature used the term "nuisance" in a restricted sense that would produce such an arbitrary result.

In our opinion the quoted provision in ORS 449.820 renders inapplicable, under the circumstances of this case, the doctrine of primary administrative jurisdiction. It is unnecessary to consider the other reasons advanced by appellee why the doctrine is inapplicable.

Affirmed.

4. Ultrahazardous Activities

LUTHRINGER v. MOORE, 31 Cal. 2d 489, 190 P. 2d 1
(1948).

CARTER, Justice.

Plaintiff recovered a judgment on a verdict for damages for personal injuries against defendant, R. L. Moore. Plaintiff stated his action in two counts, the first predicated upon an absolute liability or liability without fault, and the second, alleged negligence of defendants. The defendants are Bedell, the tenant of the restaurant building hereafter mentioned and the operator of the restaurant therein, Sacramento Medico-Dental Building Company, a corporation, the owner of the office and restaurant buildings, and Moore, an individual engaged in the pest eradication business. A nonsuit was granted as to all defendants as to the second count in the complaint. Bedell and Medico-Dental Building Company were exonerated. Plaintiff appeals from the unfavorable result as to those defendants but advises this court that he urges that appeal only in the event the judgment is reversed as to Moore who is the only appealing defendant. In view of the result (affirmance of the judgment) reached herein we will treat plaintiff's position as an abandonment of his appeal, and accordingly, it is dismissed.

From the foregoing it is apparent that we have presented, the question of whether Moore was absolutely liable for the injury —was liable without fault—whether the doctrine of strict liability is applicable.

The locale of the accident giving rise to the action is commercial buildings in the business district of the City of Sacramento. Defendant, Sacramento Medico-Dental Building Company, is the owner of two contiguous buildings, one a ten story concrete office building and the other a restaurant building. Tenants of that defendant occupy the buildings. Beneath the first floor of both buildings are basement rooms. They are connected by passageways. A room on the street level floor of the office building was occupied by a tenant Flynn in which he conducted a pharmacy. There was also a dress shop on that floor. A restaurant occupied the restaurant building. Flynn's store was adjacent to the main entrance lobby of the office building.

Defendant Moore was engaged to exterminate cockroaches and other vermin in the basement under the restaurant and that part under the dress shop. He made his preparations and released hydrocyanic acid gas in those rooms about midnight on November 16, 1943. Plaintiff, an employee of Flynn in the latter's pharmacy, in the course of his employment, arrived at the pharmacy about 8:45 a.m. on November 17, 1943, with the purpose of opening the store. Although there is a conflict in the evidence, there is testimony that none of the three entrances to the drug store bore any signs or notices warning of the presence or danger of the above mentioned gas. The evidence is clear that there was none on the door used by plaintiff. He entered by a door from the office building lobby. He was suffering from a cold. After entering the store he proceeded to a small mezzanine floor to put on his working clothes. Feeling ill he returned to the main floor and lost consciousness. He was discovered in that condition by Flynn's bookkeeper who arrived at the pharmacy between 9:15 and 9:30 a.m. Plaintiff was removed from the store, treated by the firemen of the city with a resuscitator and taken to the hospital where he received medical attention. He was found suffering from hydrocyanic acid gas poisoning and his injuries are from that source.

Counsel for defendant Moore contends that the evidence is insufficient to justify the verdict in favor of plaintiff. He asserts that there is no evidence of the escape of hydrocyanic acid gas from the basement to the pharmacy or the presence of such gas when plaintiff was there; that there is no evidence that plaintiff suffered from such gas poisoning on the morning in question or that his condition since was due to such poisoning.

It is beyond dispute that Moore released the gas in the basement of the building the night preceding the morning of plaintiff's injury. It is unlikely that such lethal gas was present and released at any other place in the vicinity. The evidence shows the gas is lighter than air, readily diffuses in air, is very penetrating and in the language of witness Bell: "It will penetrate behind baseboards, cracks and crevises that we couldn't get at with any type of liquid insecticide. It will go through mattresses, chesterfields, furniture, some types of porous walls.

"Q. It does a good job of fumigating? A. That's right.

"Q. Because it can get into small cracks and apertures? A. That's right."

● ● ●

The foregoing evidence points unerringly to the conclusion that there was cyanide gas in the pharmacy; that it came from the fumigation operation in the basement; and that plaintiff was poisoned by such gas. Moore's arguments with reference to the care used to confine the gas, the failure of some persons to detect any gas odor, the possibility that the presence of gas in the lobby of the office building and elsewhere was due to the gas being blown from the restaurant by Moore and the like, pose nothing more than conflicts in the evidence.

Moore alleges error in the giving of the instruction reading: "I instruct you that any person engaging in an ultra-hazardous activity, who knew, or in the exercise of reasonable care, should have known its ultra-hazardous character, and thereby proximately causes injury to another by a miscarriage of such activity, is liable to the person harmed, unless the latter knew or in the exercise of reasonable care should have known its ultra-hazardous nature and failed to exercise reasonable care for his own safety, or unless he knowingly and voluntarily invited the injury, and brought it upon himself.

"Likewise, any person, firm or corporation who brings, or permits to be brought upon its premises that which is of an ultra-hazardous nature, and who knew, or in the exercise of reasonable care should have known its ultra-hazardous nature, is liable for any injury proximately caused another, by its miscarriage, unless the person so harmed knew, or in the exercise of reasonable care should have known of its ultra-hazardous nature and failed to exercise reasonable care for his own safety or unless he knowingly and voluntarily invited the injury, and brought it upon himself.

"This principal of law does not require a finding of negligence upon those so engaging in such activity, or upon those bringing or permitting it to be brought upon the premises.

"I instruct you as a matter of law that under all the facts and circumstances of this case, the use and release of hydrocyanic acid gas by the defendant Moore, in the premises of defendants Bedell and Sacramento Medico-Dental Building, a corporation, all as appears in the evidence, constituted an ultra-hazardous activity." He asserts that it advised the jury on questions of fact, such as that gas did escape from the basement to the pharmacy which was present when plaintiff entered the pharmacy, and such condition was unknown to plaintiff; that plaintiff came in contact with the gas and became ill therefrom, and that plaintiff was acting in the course of his employment when he entered the pharmacy. Suffice it to say, a mere reading of the instruction refutes Moore's argument. In any event, the jury were fully instructed on proximate cause and fully informed with relation to ultra-hazardous activities (later discussed) as follows: "You are instructed that defendant R. L. Moore, doing business as 'Orchard Supply Company,' was engaged under all the facts and circumstances of this case in what the law considers to be an ultra-hazardous activity when he used hydrocyanic acid gas to fumigate the connected basement rooms which have been referred

LUTHRINGER v. MOORE

to as Bedell's storeroom and the Superintendent's office, ~~the latter being located in the basement of the Medico Dental Office Building.~~ A person who carries on an ultra-hazardous activity is liable to another whom the actor should recognize as likely to be harmed by the ~~unpreventable~~ miscarriage of the activity for harm resulting to said person from that which makes the activity ultra-hazardous, although the utmost care is exercised to prevent the harm, unless the person injured knew or in the exercise of reasonable care should have known its ultra-hazardous nature and fails to exercise reasonable care to avoid the harm threatened thereby ~~after acquiring knowledge that the ultra hazardous activity is being carried on~~ and after it has miscarried or is about to miscarry. In the present case, if you find from a preponderance of the evidence that defendant R. L. Moore, doing business as 'Orchard Supply Company,' should have recognized that persons in nearby parts of the Medico-Dental Office Building were likely to be harmed if hydrocyanic acid gas escaped from the rooms being fumigated and that hydrocyanic acid gas did in fact escape and find its way to the Medico-Dental Pharmacy premises thereby coming in contact with and causing harm to the plaintiff Albert L. Luthringer, unless you also find from a preponderance of the evidence that plaintiff Albert L. Luthringer knew or in the exercise of reasonable care should have known that fumigation with hydrocyanic acid gas was being carried on and that the gas had escaped or was about to escape to the pharmacy premises and then failed to exercise reasonable care to avoid the harm threatened, or unless he knowingly and voluntarily invited the injury and brought it upon himself, your verdict must be for the plaintiff Albert L. Luthringer and against defendant R. L. Moore, doing business as 'Orchard Supply Company.' "

[1] In connection with the foregoing it is urged that the instructions declare as a matter of law that the release of such gas on the premises constitutes an ultrahazardous activity. It appears to be settled that the question of whether the case is a proper one for imposing absolute or strict liability is one of law for the court. See, Green v. General Petroleum Corp., 205 Cal. 328, 270 P. 952, 60 A.L.R. 475; Munro v. Pacific Coast Dredging, etc., Co., 84 Cal. 515, 24 P. 303, 18 Am.St.Rep. 248; Rest.,Torts, sec. 520, Com.h.

Turning to the question of whether absolute or strict liability is appropriate in the instant case, we find that according to witness Bell (a man engaged in the pest control business), there are only three operators licensed to use lethal gas in pest control in Sacramento. And in regard to the nature of hydrocyanic acid gas he testified: ● ● ●

A. The operator going into a building isn't too familiar with the construction of the building. There might be a hidden flue and cracks some place you might miss. If you did miss that, the people above the area would be fumigated. That gas might leak up there. They would be subject to being gassed that way. The safest way is to vacate the building, no matter how careful you are to always be careful of every piece of construction of the building." Hydrocyanic acid gas is defined as a "dangerous or lethal chemical" in the statutes dealing with licensing of those engaged in the pest control business (Business & Professions Code, sec. 8513.) Bell testified on cross examination that the gas was generally used in the community, and that it is used for fumigating railroad cars, homes, apartments, and fruit trees, but as seen there are only three licensed operators in Sacramento.

Defendant Moore introduced a written notice which he claims was attached to the door of the pharmacy directing that he be contacted before entering the building because of possible gas leakage, indicating that he believed a leakage possible although he testified that he took every precaution to seal the basement before he released the gas. This evidence, as above discussed, clearly points to the conclusion

LUTHRINGER v. MOORE

that the gas escaped from the basement into the pharmacy although great care to prevent it was exercised by Moore. As before seen, the activity in releasing the gas was carried on in the basement of commercial buildings where there are a great many tenants. Under these circumstances we have a case which calls for liability without fault—a case falling within the category of what has been defined as the miscarriage of an ultra-hazardous activity. It has been said: "One who carries on an ultra-hazardous activity is liable to another whose person, land or chattels the actor should recognize as likely to be harmed by the unpreventable miscarriage of the activity for harm resulting thereto from that which makes the activity ultra-hazardous, although the utmost care is exercised to prevent the harm. * * * An activity is ultra-hazardous if it (a) necessarily involves a risk of serious harm to the person, land or chattels of others which cannot be eliminated by the exercise of the utmost care, and (b) is not a matter of common usage. * * * An activity is a matter of common usage if it is customarily carried on by the great mass of mankind or by many people in the community. It does not cease to be so because it is carried on for a purpose peculiar to the individual who carries it on. Certain activities may be so generally carried on as to be regarded as customary. Thus, automobiles have come into such general use that their operation is a matter of common usage. This, together with the fact that the risk involved in the careful operation of a carefully maintained automobile is slight, is sufficient to prevent their operation from being an ultrahazardous activity. However, the use of an automotive vehicle of such size and weight as to be incapable of safe control and to be likely to crush water and gas mains under the surface of the highway is not as yet a usual means of transportation and, therefore, the use of such an automobile is ultrahazardous. ● ●●
* * The rule stated * * * does not apply if the activity is carried on in pursuance of a public duty imposed upon the actor as a public officer or employee or as a common carrier. * * * The rule stated * * * does not apply where the person harmed by the unpreventable miscarriage of an ultrahazardous activity has reason to know of the risk which makes the activity ultrahazardous and (a) takes part in it, or (b) brings himself within the area which will be endangered by its miscarriage, (i) without a privilege, or (ii) in the exercise of a privilege derived from the consent of the person carrying on the activity, or (iii) as a member of the public entitled to the services of a public utility carrying on the activity. * * * (1) A plaintiff is not barred from recovery for harm done by the miscarriage of an ultrahazardous activity caused by his failure to exercise reasonable care to observe the fact that the activity is being carried on or by intentionally coming into the area which would be endangered by its miscarriage. (2) A plaintiff is barred from recovery for harm caused by the miscarriage of an ultrahazardous activity if, but only if, (a) he intentionally or negligently causes the activity to miscarry, or (b) after knowledge that it has miscarried or is about to miscarry, he fails to exercise reasonable care to avoid harm threatened thereby." Rest., Torts, secs. 519, 520, 521, 523. In the case of Green v. General Petroleum Corporation, supra, an oil well had "blown out" due to natural gas pressure while in the process of being drilled, and plaintiff's property was damaged by debris being cast thereon. The court declared the driller of the well to be liable although he had used all care possible to avoid the accident, and announced the rule that: "Where one, in the conduct and maintenance of an enterprise lawful and proper in itself, deliberately does an act under known conditions, and, with knowledge that injury may result to another, proceeds, and injury is done to the other as the direct and proximate consequence of the act, however carefully done, the one who does the act and causes the injury should, in all fairness, be required to compensate the other for the damage done." Page 333 of 205 Cal., page 955 of 270. P. ● ● ●

LUTHRINGER v. MOORE

Whatever the situation may be in that regard, there can be no doubt that the case of Green v. General Petroleum Corporation, supra, enunciated a principle of absolute liability which is applicable to the instant case. It is not significant that a property damage, as distinguished from a personal injury, was there involved. The important factor is that certain activities under certain conditions may be so hazardous to the public generally, and of such relative infrequent occurrence, that it may well call for strict liability as the best public policy.

The above quoted evidence shows that the use of gas under the circumstances presented is a hazardous activity; that it is perilous and likely to cause injury even though the utmost care is used; that defendant Moore knew or should have known that injury might result; and that the use of it under these circumstances is not a matter of "common usage" within the meaning of the term. In regard to the last feature it may be used commonly by fumigators, but they are relatively few in number and are engaged in a specialized activity. It is not carried on generally by the public, especially under circumstances where many people are present, thus enchancing the hazard, nor is its use a common everyday practice. It is not a common usage within the definition: "An activity may be ultra-hazardous because of the instrumentality which is used in carrying it on, the nature of the subject matter with which it deals or the condition which it creates." Rest., Torts, sec. 520(b), com. Cl. (b). And in this connection the instruction advising the jury that the usage was not common, was proper.

Moore claims error in respect to the refusing of instructions offered by him dealing with inevitable accident, negligence on his part and refuting the rule of strict liability. Manifestly such instructions are not appropriate in a case of strict liability.

Moore complains that the modification of an instruction offered by him was error. The instruction was: "The court instructs the jury that it was plaintiff's duty to exercise his faculties of sight and smell to apprise himself of danger and to use ordinary care at all times in exercising such senses. (To look in a careless manner, or to exercise his sense of smell in a careless manner, is not to look or smell at all.)" The court did not give the portion in parenthesis. Assuming the instruction was applicable, it is clear the part given was sufficient.

Complaint is made of the refusal to give an instruction reading: "The court instructs you that no man is responsible for that which no man can control." Such an instruction would only lead to confusion in the type of case under consideration and is based on cases where there was common usage in the sense used in the Restatement.

Error is urged in the refusal to give Moore's instructions on contributory negligence of plaintiff phrased in the language used in an ordinary negligence case. Such an instruction was improper as seen from the foregoing discussion of what conduct on part of plaintiff bars his recovery, and was correctly covered by plaintiff's instruction No. 10 heretofore quoted.

● ● ●

The judgment against defendant Moore is affirmed. Plaintiff's appeal is dismissed.

CHAPMAN CHEMICAL CO. v. TAYLOR, 215 Ark. 630, 222 S.W. 2d 820 (1949).

FRANK G. SMITH, Justice.

Mrs. Virginia C. Wilson owns a farm in Jefferson County, which she rented in the year 1947 to G. E. Taylor for an agreed share of the crops grown on the land, the principal crop being cotton. She and her tenant filed this suit against Elms Planting Co., a corporation, to recover damages to their crop occasioned by the use of a chemical dust by the Elms Co. called 2-4-D, in spraying a rice crop on land owned by the Elms Co. which was three-fourths of a mile from plaintiffs' crop.

The testimony shows that within very recent years there has been developed a powerful chemical referred to as 2-4-D, which is very damaging to any broad leaved plant with which it has contact, but which does no harm to grasses and plants which are not broad leaved. The Elms Co. used this chemical in spraying its rice crop and particles thereof drifted and settled on plaintiffs' cotton crop, greatly reducing the yield thereof and this suit was brought to recover compensation for this damage.

The Elms Co. filed an answer in which liability was denied. In addition it filed a cross-complaint against Chapman Chemical Co. and others who have passed out of the case. ● ● ●

These contentions of the Elms Co. and of the Chemical Co. bring us to a consideration of the case on its merits, and we shall treat the two contentions together, as they are inseparately connected. ●●●

It is undisputed that 2-4-D powder will answer the purpose for which it was designed, that is of killing plants with large leaves which appear in fields of rice. The most noxious of those weeds is the coffee bean plant which matures about the same time the rice does, and, if allowed to mature its seed will mix with the rice when threshed and will destroy or greatly lessen the marketability of the rice, unless separated from the rice at great expense and trouble, usually by hand.

The chief objection to the use of the powder is that it is very dangerous to such plants as cotton, potatoes, vegetables, etc., when it comes in contact with them. This characteristic of the powder was well known, in fact the literature which the Chemical Co. published and circulated gave warning of that fact. The plaintiffs; or cross-appellants, insist therefore that both the Chemical Co. and the Elms Co. are liable to them for the damage to their cotton crop caused by the use of this powder. It is undisputed that the use of the powder caused the damage for which plaintiff sued.

It was shown by testimony, which is undisputed, that the practice of dusting agricultural crops, as well as truck farms, etc., has prevailed for a number of years and is becoming a common practice. Some of these chemicals are dangerous to live stock and others to plants of certain kinds and they are used for various purposes. Extensive and experienced planters who have used chemical dust for a number of years for different purposes, testified that when the areas to be treated are sufficiently large, aeroplanes are used in scattering the dust or chemical, and that if properly applied even by planes, the dust does not float or extend more than fifty or one hundred fifty feet beyond the area intended to be treated, and that no damage results beyond that distance to plants which would be damaged if touched by the dust

The testimony developed the fact of which the Elms Co. was unaware and it was not shown that the Chemical Co. was aware, and that is that the 2-4-D dust possessed the quality of floating for great distances when cast in the air, even for miles. None of the experienced farmers who dusted their crops for various purposes had ever known any other dust, when properly applied, to float for a greater distance than from fifty to one hundred fifty feet. As has been said, cross

CHAPMAN CHEMICAL CO. v. TAYLOR

appellants cotton crop was three-fourths of a mile from the Elms Co. rice field at the nearest point.

The testimony shows that the Elms Co. used the dust on a morning when no wind was blowing and that it was distributed over the rice field by an aviator whose regular business it was to dust crops with the use of his plane, and who testified that but little of the dust was cast upon any land except the rice crop as he was careful to shut off the distribution of the dust when making the necessary turns of his plane.

The operator supervising the dusting process testified that he had been engaged in the crop dusting business for 22 years, operating from California to Florida and from Mexico to Canada and that when properly distributed the dust did not extend more than 40 to 50 feet beyond the area treated, but this testimony did not relate to 2–4–D

The question of foreseeability of probable injury from the use of 2–4–D was submitted to the jury in instructions given at the request of cross appellants over the objections of both Elms Co. and the Chemical Co.

The jury might well have found, and evidently did find, that there was no previous experience in the use of agricultural chemicals which gave any indication of the danger of using 2–4–D to a crop three-fourths of a mile away, or that its use was "a cause from which a person of ordinary experience and sagacity could foresee that the result might probably ensue". Alaska Lumber Co. v. Spurlin, 183 Ark. 576, 37 S.W.2d 82, 83.

[2] The testimony shows that before buying or applying the 2–4–D chemical the manager of the Elms Co. consulted one L. C. Carter of Ark. Rice Growers Assn. regarding the use of 2–4–D. Carter had been and was a manager of the Rice Experimental Station near Stuttgart, 7 or 8 years, and was at that time manager of the Rice Growers Coop. Assn. and the Elms Co. manager was informed by Carter that he, Carter thought its use would

be all right. In other words, there is no evidence upon which to predicate liability against the Elms Co. except the fact alone that the Elms Co. did use a dangerous chemical, and we conclude that the verdict of the jury in favor of the Elms Co. was not unsupported by the testimony and should be affirmed.

As to the Chemical Co. a different test as to liability must be applied. The three chemical companies operated under a single officer, Chapman being the president of all three and the owner of practically all of the stock of all the corporations. The Illinois company did not manufacture the 2–4–D chemical dust, but its Memphis affiliate did. Appellant Chemical Co. was the distributor and sole agent for the Tennessee company in this State, and the testimony shows that it was selling an extremely hazardous product and was selling it as its own product. Indeed the testimony shows that the Tennessee Co. was in effect and in fact the agent of the Chemical Co. in manufacturing the dust, as all sales thereof here involved were made by the appellant Chemical Co. The testimony shows that the Chemical Co. was selling the dust as its own product. It controlled and distributed all advertising material which recommended its use and gave directions therefor. At Sec. 400 of the Chapter on Torts, Restatement of the Law, it is said that one who puts out as his own product a chattel manufactured by another is subject to the same liability as though he were its manufacturer.

It is said there was no privity of contract between the Chemical Co. and cross appellants. This showing was at one time, and for some time considered necessary to occasion liability, the line of decisions to that effect going back to the early English case of Winterbottom v. Wright, 10 Mees. & W. 109, 152 Eng. Reprint 402, decided in 1842. But the courts have been getting away from that doctrine and many have entirely repudiated it and discarded it. The opinion of Justice Cardozo, then a member of the Court of Appeals of New York, and later an Associate Justice of the United States Supreme Court in the case of Mac-

CHAPMAN CHEMICAL CO. v. TAYLOR

Pherson v. Buick Motor Co., 217 N.Y. 382, 111 N.E. 1050, L.R.A.1916F, 696, Ann.Cas. 1916C, 446, is credited with the inception of the modern doctrine of manufacturer's liability based upon foreseeability rather than privity of contract. ● ● ●

"The question in each case was whether the danger was sufficient to require the manufacturer to guard against it." In other words, that foreseeability and not privity was the proper test. See also Sec. 824, Chapter on Sales, Sec. 824, 46 Am. Jur. page 946.

Now this 2–4–D powder is highly efficient for its intended purposes, that is to kill broad leaved plants, but its very efficiency for that purpose makes its use extremely hazardous to other plant life.

An article appeared in the Ark. State Plant Board News in July, 1948, which began, "Effective June 24th the U. S. Civil Aeronautics Administration prohibits the use of 2–4–D dust by aeroplanes. This action was taken at the request of the U. S. Dept. of Agriculture following many complaints that drifting dust had injured cotton and other broad leaved crops."

This was subsequent to the spraying of the Elms rice crop which damaged appellants cotton crop and in the law of negligence it is generally true that foresight and not retrospect is the standard of negligence. But here we are dealing with an extra hazardous chemical known to be highly dangerous.

The essence of this case is contained in instruction number 10–A given over the objection of the Chemical Co., which reads as follows: "It was the duty of the defendant Chapman Chemical Company before putting an inherently dangerous product on the market to make tests to determine whether or not it would damage crops of others; if you believe from a preponderance of the evidence in this case that the lants. We think this testimony presents the question whether absolute or strict liability should apply.

2–4–D dust applied on July 1, 1947, by the Elms Planting Company was an inherently dangerous product liable to damage the property of others, and that such tests were not made, then you are told that the defendant Chapman Chemical Company is negligent."

If this instruction is correct, the judgment against the Chemical Co. should be affirmed, if it is not it should be reversed. Now a test was made but its purpose was to ascertain whether or not 2–4–D could be distributed by aeroplane as other dusts could be. It was found that it could be, but no test was made as to the floating quality of the dust, and it is this characteristic or quality of 2–4–D which makes its use extra hazardous. In other words, was the Chemical Co. under the duty of testing and knowing that 2–4–D dust, unlike other chemical dusts, would float for great distances. The undisputed testimony is that this 2–4–D, unlike other dusts, does not immediately or soon settle, but on the contrary floats in the air for long periods of time and for great distances, as much as 10, 15 or 20 miles, and one witness placed the distance at 35 miles.

That peril attended the use of the dust is undisputed. Indeed the literature circulated by the Chemical Co. contained this caution, "Chapman 2–4–D weed killer should be applied in such a manner as to avoid contacting crop plants such as cotton, sweet potatoes, vegetables, ornamental trees, etc." With this knowledge the Chemical Co. sold the dust, knowing that it would in its ordinary use be distributed from an aeroplane and it did this without making any test to determine what the effect thereof would be. Its literature referred to the dust as a proved weed killer and recommended the application of it by means of an aeroplane.

The undisputed testimony is that the Elms Co. bought the dust from the Chemical Co. and applied it in the manner directed for the known purpose for which it was sold and that this use thereof resulted in serious damage to cross appel-

In the case of Luthringer v. Moore, 31 Cal.2d 489, 190 P.2d 1, 5, it was said by the Supreme Court of California that, "It appears to be settled that the question of whether the case is a proper one for imposing absolute or strict liability is one of law for the court." Among other authorities cited to support this statement is the restatement of the Law of Torts, Section 520, Com. H.

If one casts into the air a substance which he knows may do damage to others, and in some circumstances will certainly do so, principles of elementary justice, as well as the best public policy require that he know how far the substance will carry or be conveyed through the air and what damage it will do in the path of its journey, and if he releases such a substance either from ignorance of, or in indifference to the damage that may be done, the rule of strict liability should be applied.

● ● ●

We do not think the Chemical Company excused itself from liability by the mere showing that it was unaware of the peculiar carrying quality of the dust it was selling. Ordinary care required that it should know in view of the dangerous nature of the product it was selling, and it was charged with the knowledge which tests would have revealed. The case is therefore one in which the rule of strict liability should be applied. ● ● ●

Justices Holt and McFaddin are of the opinion that the judgment for the Elms Co. should be reversed. Other members of the court are of the opinion that the judgment in favor of that Company should be affirmed. Justice George Rose Smith is of the opinion that Instruction No. 10–A above copied, which we said was of the essence of the case was erroneous and that the judgment against the Chemical Co. should be reversed for that reason. The result of these views is that the judgment for the Elms Co. should be affirmed and that the judgment against the Chemical Co. should also be affirmed. It is therefore so ordered.

GEORGE ROSE SMITH, Justice (dissenting in part).

I agree that the standard of ordinary care is applicable in the case of the Elms Company, but I am unable to concur in the rule of absolute liability on the part of the Chemical Company. Instruction 10–A in effect told the jury that the latter company was negligent if it failed to discover by tests any possible harm that might result from the use of 2–4–D. Similarly, the majority hold that the manufacturer who puts a dangerous commodity on the market is responsible for the consequences of its use, no matter how unexpected or unforeseeable they may be.

I think the manufacturer's duty should be that of making such tests as are reasonably necessary in the circumstances—it being understood, of course, that the duty to take precautions increases proportionately with the degree of danger inherent in the commodity. It is shown that 2–4–D is harmless to narrow-leaved plants, but suppose for argument's sake that there is in the world one narrow-leaved plant that the dust will injure. Upon the majority's reasoning the Chemical Company would be liable for failing to test the dust on that particular plant, even though it may have made experiments with ten thousand other species. So as to the drifting quality of the chemical. The proof shows that many agricultural dusts have been widely used during a quarter of a century, yet none has ever before been known to drift more than a few rods. I think the jury should have had the opportunity to decide whether the Chemical Company acted with ordinary prudence in assuming that 2–4–D would float in the same way as other dusts. ● ● ●

I find no reason for bringing into our law the principle of absolute liability. Experience elsewhere has shown that this doctrine is hard to confine, once its existence has been recognized. We shall be asked to extend the scope of this case in the future, and I can hardly see the point at which its application may logically be said to end.

NEW JERSEY SPORTS EXPOSITION AUTHORITY v. McCRANE, 119 N.J. Super. 457, 292 A. 2d 580 (1971).

VI   The Public Trust

(A)   *Tidelands*

Section 6 of the act authorizes the Authority to "effectuate a project to be located in the Hackensack meadowlands upon a site not to exceed 750 acres * * *." The Authority has stipulated that the projected site will include substantial acreage designated by the State to be tideland. Cheval and the Audubon Society contend that this property is vested in the public trust and cannot be conveyed, leased or utilized in any way by the State for any purpose not related to the public trust. Specifically, Cheval and Audubon make a two-pronged attack. First, they urge that the proposed racetrack usage is in violation of the public trust. Secondly, they argue that section 17 of the act permits the granting, leasing or conveying of "meadowlands, riparian lands or lands under water and similar lands" without compensation.

The New Jersey Const. (1947), Art. VIII, § IV, par. 1, concerns itself with the perpetual fund for the support of free public schools.[3] By statute, N.J.S.A. 18A:56-5 provides:

All lands belonging to this state now or formerly lying under water are dedicated to the support of public schools. All moneys hereafter received from the sales of such lands shall be paid to the board of trustees, and shall constitute a part of the permanent school fund of the state.

N.J.S.A. 18A:56-6 provides similarly for income arising from leases of such lands.

● ● ●

The following statutory authorities are relevant to the contemplated conveyance. N.J.S.A. 13:1B-13.7(b) provides that an "instrumentality of the State * * *

may apply to the [Natural Resource Council] for a conveyance * * * of the State's interest in the meadowlands * * *." N.J.S.A. 13:1B-13.8(c) states that the Hackensack Meadowland Negotiation Board shall fix the consideration for the conveyance. Pursuant to N.J.S.A. 13:-1B-13.9, the Natural Resource Council "shall approve an application for conveyance, if * * * it is satisfied that the conveyance will be in the public interest." N.J.S.A. 12:3-7 declares that riparian lands may be conveyed for a reasonable compensation, which shall be fixed by the Natural Resource Council, the Governor and the Attorney General.

N.J.S.A. 13:1B-13.13 is addressed to the aforementioned constitutional provision:

The net proceeds from the sale, lease or transfer of the State's interest in the meadowlands shall be paid to the Fund for the Support of Free Public Schools established by the Constitution, Article VIII, Section IV, after deducting from the net proceeds any expenditures of the Hackensack Meadowlands Development Commission for reclaiming land within the district. The amount of said deduction for reclamation shall be paid to the Hackensack Meadowland Development Commission.

Clearly, the statutes cited provide for compensation to be paid to the Fund for the Support of Free Public Schools. This is in exact accord with the New Jersey Constitution. The deduction of costs of reclamation from the proceeds is no argument for ambiguity. There is no confusion as to the meaning of this portion of the legislative enactment. ● ● ●

The argument raised in regard to the tidelands, however, goes much deeper than the just compensation claim. It goes to the very core of the act, for Cheval and Audubon vigorously submit that no conveyance can be permitted in view of the proposed use by the Authority. They opt for a re-examination of the means utilized for protection of the tidelands and seek to revisit the proposition that the tidelands belong to the sovereign in trust for the people, i. e., a public trust. As they view it, the trust will be violated *per se* by a conveyance of the type proposed and will be further breached by the destruction of the ecological balance of the area. More broadly, East Rutherford and public counsel strongly urge that the proposed complex will have a deleterious effect, not solely on the tidelands but on the surrounding area as well. It can be seen, then, that while counsel focus on different areas, the thrust is essentially the same, to wit, the abrogation by the Legislature of its duties as trustee of the tidelands and as overseer of the people's right to a clean and healthy environment. This latter position will be included in the discussion under (B) of this section, captioned "Environment and Ecology."

As stated previously, the parties have stipulated that "the projected site includes substantial acreage designated by the State to be state-owned tideland." In O'Neill v. State Highway Dept., 50 N.J. 307, 235 A.2d 1 (1967), Chief Justice Weintraub defined these lands as follows:

The State owns in fee simple all lands that are flowed up to the high-water line or mark. The high-water line or mark is the line formed by the intersection of the tidal plane of mean high tide with the shore. The mean (sometimes called "ordinary") high tide is defined as the medium between the spring and the neap tides. [at 323] 235 A.2d at 9.

The genesis of the public trust doctrine can be gleaned from the opinion by Chief Justice Kirkpatrick in Arnold v. Mundy, 6 N.J.L. 1, 69–78 (Sup.Ct.1821). There are two types of public property, one "reserved for the necessities of the state, and * * * used for the public benefit" (at 71), the other "common to all the citizens, who take of them and use them,

each according to his necessities, and according to the laws which regulate their use, and are called common property." *Id.* This common property consisted of navigable rivers,[4] ports, bays, sea coasts, including the land under the water which could be utilized for "navigation, fishing, fowling, sustenance, and all the other uses of the water and its products (a few things excepted * * *)." *Id.* at 77. Since by its nature common property did not permit title to vest in the people, the common law "placed it in the hands of the sovereign power, to be held, protected, and regulated for the common use and benefit." *Id.* at 71. Subsequent to the American Revolution, the sovereign's power vested in the people of each State, to be exercised through their representatives, the Legislature. *Id.* at 78.

Arnold was cited favorably in the landmark decision of the United States Supreme Court in Illinois Central Railroad Co. v. Illinois, 146 U.S. 387, 13 S.Ct. 110, 36 L.Ed. 1018 (1892). In discussing the duties incumbent upon the State in carrying out its fiduciary duty, the court declared that there could be no abdication of the trust. However, this statement was not without qualification.

The control of the State for the purposes of the trust can never be lost, *except as to such parcels as are used in promoting the interests of the public therein, or can be disposed of without any substantial impairment of the public interest in the lands and waters remaining.* [13 S.Ct. at 118; emphasis added]:

It can be seen, then, that subject to the aforementioned qualifications, there is nothing that prevents the alienability of the trust lands. The New Jersey Legislature has recognized this in its enactment of N.J.S.A. 18A:56–5 and N.J.S.A. 13:1B–13.13.

NEW JERSEY SPORTS & EXPOSITION AUTH. v. McCRANE

The conveyance of land envisioned in the act clearly meets the trust qualifications. As previously indicated, just compensation has been safeguarded and the proceeds will be applied to the support of free public schools. Most importantly, the conveyance will promote a purpose which has been deemed beneficial to the public. The inclusion of a racetrack in no way detracts from the public purpose character of the project. Accordingly, the conveyance of the tidelands will not violate the public trust.

I will now consider the argument raised in regard to the tidelands in its broadest and perhaps most serious impact, that is, the ecological or environmental controversy.

(B) *Environment and Ecology*

In fashioning their arguments, Cheval, Audobon, East Rutherford and public counsel all concede, as they must, that they are required to exhibit a right to relief. Two approaches are taken, one via the Ninth Amendment, to the United States Constitution, the other via the Fourteenth.

The Ninth Amendment states:

The enumeration in the Constitution, of certain rights, shall not be construed to deny or disparage others retained by the people.

In Griswold v. Connecticut, 381 U.S. 479, 85 S.Ct. 1678, 14 L.Ed.2d 510 (1965), the majority and concurring opinions concerned themselves with this amendment and both spoke of "penumbral rights" as rights guaranteed in addition to those specifically enumerated in the first eight amendments. One commentator has constructed the following theory:

The rule of construction embodied in the Ninth Amendment could be the foundation for a declaration by the Supreme Court of a constitutional right to an uncontaminated environment. Perhaps no principle is as fundamental as the preciousness of every human life. The Fifth and Fourteenth Amendments offer no less protection to "life" than to "liberty." Surely liberty and the various rights specifically enumerated in the Constitution are meaningless abstractions if life itself is ended through pollution's often invisible but unrelenting and imminently cataclismic environmental assault on the human body. [Esposito, "Air and water pollution: What to do while waiting for Washington," 5 Harv.Civ.Lib.—Civ.Rights L.Rev. 32, 47–48 (1970)].

Another commentator would combine the "public trust concept with the constitutional basis given by the Ninth Amendment" as a weapon in the battle against the defiling of our environment. Cohen, "The Constitution, The Public Trust Doctrine and The Environment," 1970 Utah L.Rev. 388, 399 (1970).

The theory based upon the Fourteenth Amendment is that certain civil rights, i. e., environmental rights, are being abridged by state action, in contravention of 42 U.S.C.A. § 1983. ● ● ●

The challengers come armed with more than theory. They point to case law which they believe supports their environmental and ecological claims. ● ● ●

In the landmark case of Scenic Hudson Preservation Conference v. FPC, 354 F.2d 608 (2 Cir. 1965), cert. den. 384 U.S. 941, 86 S.Ct. 1462, 16 L.Ed.2d 540 (1966), various conservation groups were successful in setting aside action taken by the Federal Power Commission (FPC). This case involved the controversial "Storm King Project" wherein Consolidated Edison sought to construct a pumped storage hydroelectric project adjacent to the Hudson River. The Second Circuit, in remanding, held that the FPC failed to follow its statutory mandate, which required it to consider the conservation aspects of the project. It was noted that the FPC had refused to receive certain testimony, including some pertaining to fish protection devices. ● ● ●

In Citizens Committee for Hudson Valley v. Volpe, 425 F.2d 97 (2 Cir. 1970), plaintiffs challenged the issuance of a permit to allow dredging and filling for the construction of the Hudson River Expressway. In answer to defendant's claim that one of the plaintiffs lacked standing, the court noted (at 105) that unless that plaintiff had standing at that stage of the project, it would be in a very difficult position "at some later date to overbalance the equities in favor of the State such a large commitment of public funds would engender and its legitimate concern could be irretrievably subverted even though the permit was issued unlawfully."

These decisions hold that the courts will intervene to prevent agency action in contravention of a statutory mandate to consider a project's environmental and ecological ramifications.

The Authority, for the purposes of this motion, has stipulated an assumption that a "factual issue exists with respect to the impact of a major project such as the sports complex upon the environment of the meadowlands district." However the Authority claims that the issue is premature in view of the fact that no decisions have been made and no action has been taken which will affect the environment or ecology. Cheval, Audubon, East Rutherford and public counsel submit that the issue should be considered now, since a considerable investment is contemplated. The challengers rely upon the foregoing federal court decisions in support of their argument that irreparable damage will result if they are foreclosed from a hearing at this time.

I fail to discern the parallel in the case at hand. The foregoing cases and other authorities are clearly based upon statutory mandates which require the particular agency or commission to consider the conservation aspects of the project. These federal mandates support the legal holding that the applicable agency explore all issues relevant to the "public interest" before any action is taken. Each agency is required to make factual findings concerning the environmental and ecological ramifications. But, I repeat, this is the result of a statutory directive—not a constitutional mandate. All parties agree that the United States Supreme Court has not spoken on the constitutional right to a clean environment to the exclusion of various other rights. This does not mean that any one is opposed to wholesome ecology.

This court is most alert to the changing attitudes of society. I understand fully the prevailing reform in the manner we look at our problems and even in the fashion that we make decisions. I am unequivocally sensitive to the fact that we should view the law in the light of what it good for the people. There must be an awareness of the necessity for environmental balance.

The tempo of the times is such that the Ninth Amendment may carry such a constitutional interpretation. And even if this comes to pass, in the absence of statute, there is no bar to a declaration of constitutionality of this act and then the necessity for the administrative hearings as to the environmental balance. If the act is unconstitutional, there is no need for environmental hearings. Such determinations are to be made only by virtue of a constitutional act. The cases cited by counsel in support of a statement that it may be too late to wait do not involve the determination of the constitutionality of a statute.

NEW JERSEY SPORTS & EXPOSITION AUTH. v. McCRANE

No case has been cited to demonstrate that the time is ripe at this stage of the proceedings to consider the environmental impact of the act. Public counsel points to the alleged legislative failure during the one-day hearing to consider any of the environmental repercussions. But an examination of the hearing shows this to be inaccurate. • • •

The act itself addresses the issue. The Legislature specifically provided in section 23 that the Authority

* * * shall consult with the Meadowlands Commission and the Department of Environmental Protection with respect to the ecological factors constituting the environment of the Hackensack meadowlands to the end that the delicate environmental balance of the Hackensack meadowlands may be maintained and preserved. • • •

Thus, the Legislature was aware of N.J.S.A. 13:17–1 et seq., wherein it declared that the meadowlands area

* * * is a land resource of incalculable opportunity for new jobs, homes and recreational sites, which may be lost to the State through piecemeal reclamation and unplanned development; that much of this acreage may be subject to redevelopment under section 3, Article VIII, of the State Constitution; that the orderly, comprehensive development of these areas due to their strategic location in the heart of a vast metropolitan area with urgent needs for more space for industrial, commercial, residential, and *public recreational* and other uses, can no longer be deferred. * * * [N.J.S.A. 13:17–1; emphasis added]

This section goes on to state that the area needs "special protection from air and water pollution" and that "the necessity to consider the ecological factors constituting the environment of the meadowlands and the need to preserve the delicate balance of nature must be recognized to avoid any artificially imposed development that would adversely affect not only the area but the entire State. * * *" *Id.*

It is from this vantage point that the act in its entirety, and section 23 in particular, must be viewed. It cannot be assumed that the Legislature, on the one hand, carefully drafted an act for the development of the area and then, on the other hand, in callous and utter disregard thereof, passed a further enactment which would frustrate the former's purpose. To opt for this result is to read the enactments in a vacuum, in utter disregard of the historical background and policy considerations. • • •

A further observation is proper. The executive and legislative branches of the State Government have clearly made known their awareness to environmental problems by the passage of such acts as the Clean Ocean Act, Pesticide Control Act, Greenacres Act, Air Pollution Control Act, etc. And it must be emphasized that N.J.S.A. 13:1D established the Department of Environmental Protection in 1970. This Department, referred to in section 23 of the act, was established and is empowered to initiate complaints, to hold hearings and institute legal proceedings, etc. N.J.S.A. 13:1D–9. Thus, the executive and legislative branches have brought the problem of environment and pollution to the door of every citizen and industry. If these are the facts, it cannot be argued that section 23 is not meaningful and not responsive to the need. • • •

I am satisfied that the Legislature has given much consideration to the environmental and ecological issues. In any case, the issue is not relevant at this time. The day may come when a decision or act by the Authority will affect the environment. At that time judicial and/or administrative relief, if necessary, will undoubtedly be available. For example, if after consultation

NEW JERSEY SPORTS & EXPOSITION AUTH. v. McCRANE

with the Authority, the Department of Environmental Protection claims the project will have ill effects, it has the machinery necessary to pursue the matter further. The court must presume that the Department will serve vigorously. And when building is undertaken one day, all legal requirements outlined in anti-pollution legislation, in upgrading waste treatment facilities and in maintaining an ecological balance will be enforced. I cannot agree with public counsel that the State will stand committed in the absence of an immediate environmental hearing.

I fully agree that the public should be and is entitled to a further opportunity to be heard on the environmental and ecological overtones of the legislation. Although the court may not have the facilities or power to be able to police the ecological factors, it may perhaps oversee the actions of the administrative agencies in this vital area. It is before these agencies that experts may appear if the Authority is violating any provision of environmental law. But to determine that this is not the juncture for such a hearing is not to deny the right. Every piece of legislation carries its advantages and disadvantages. The mere passage of the act is not enough to bring about judicial intervention. And this is as it should be, because in the final analysis government by judges is inferior to government by legislators.

The environmental issue is ripe for summary judgment under existing law. The judgment of the court declares that the arguments as to the trusteeship of the tidelands and the legal objections surrounding the environmental and ecological factors do not affect the constitutionality of this act.

. . . .

For additional information about the public trust doctrine see:

1. Sax, "The Public Trust Doctrine in Natural Resource Law: Effective Judicial Intervention," 86 Mich. L. Rev. 471 (1970).

2. Cohen, "The Constituion, Public Trust Doctrine, and the Environment," 1970 Utah L. Rev. 388.

3. Note, "The Public Trust in Tidal Areas: A Sometime Submerged Traditional Doctrine," 79 Yale L. J. 762 (1970).

6. The Ninth Amendment

GRISWOLD v. CONNECTICUT, 381 U.S. 479 (1965).

● ● ●

The foregoing cases suggest that specific guarantees in the Bill of Rights have penumbras, formed by emanations from those guarantees that help give them life and substance. See *Poe* v. *Ullman*, 367 U. S. 497, 516–522 (dissenting opinion). Various guarantees create zones of privacy. The right of association contained in the penumbra of the First Amendment is one, as we have seen. The Third Amendment in its prohibition against the quartering of soldiers "in any house" in time of peace without the consent of the owner is another facet of that privacy. The Fourth Amendment explicitly affirms the "right of the people to be secure in their persons, houses, papers, and effects, against unreasonable searches and seizures." The Fifth Amendment in its Self-Incrimination Clause enables the citizen to create a zone of privacy which government may not force him to surrender to his detriment. The Ninth Amendment provides: "The enumeration in the Constitution, of certain rights, shall not be construed to deny or disparage others retained by the people." ● ● ●

Reversed.

MR. JUSTICE GOLDBERG, whom THE CHIEF JUSTICE and MR. JUSTICE BRENNAN join, concurring.

I agree with the Court that Connecticut's birth-control law unconstitutionally intrudes upon the right of marital privacy, and I join in its opinion and judgment. ● ● ●
I do agree that the concept of liberty protects those personal rights that are fundamental, and is not confined to the specific terms of the Bill of Rights. My conclusion that the concept of liberty is not so restricted and that it embraces the right of marital privacy though that right is not mentioned explicitly in the Constitution [1] is supported both by numerous decisions of this Court, referred to in the Court's opinion, and by the language and history of the Ninth Amendment. In reaching the conclusion that the right of marital privacy is protected, as being within the pro-

tected penumbra of specific guarantees of the Bill of Rights, the Court refers to the Ninth Amendment, *ante,* at 484. I add these words to emphasize the relevance of that Amendment to the Court's holding.

The Court stated many years ago that the Due Process Clause protects those liberties that are "so rooted in the traditions and conscience of our people as to be ranked as fundamental." *Snyder* v. *Massachusetts,* 291 U. S. 97, 105. ● ● ●

This Court, in a series of decisions, has held that the Fourteenth Amendment absorbs and applies to the States those specifics of the first eight amendments which express fundamental personal rights.[2] The language and history of the Ninth Amendment reveal that the Framers of the Constitution believed that there are additional fundamental rights, protected from governmental infringement, which exist alongside those fundamental rights specifically mentioned in the first eight constitutional amendments.

The Ninth Amendment reads, "The enumeration in the Constitution, of certain rights, shall not be construed to deny or disparage others retained by the people." The Amendment is almost entirely the work of James Madison. It was introduced in Congress by him and passed the House and Senate with little or no debate and virtually no change in language. It was proffered to quiet expressed fears that a bill of specifically enumerated rights[3] could not be sufficiently broad to cover all essential rights and that the specific mention of certain rights would be interpreted as a denial that others were protected. ● ● ●
the Framers did not intend that the first eight amendments be construed to exhaust the basic and fundamental rights which the Constitution guaranteed to the people.[5]
● ● ● this Court has had little occasion to interpret the Ninth Amendment ● ● ●

The Ninth Amendment to the Constitution may be regarded by some as a recent discovery and may be forgotten by others, but since 1791 it has been a basic part of the Constitution which we are sworn to uphold. To hold that a right so basic and fundamental and so deep-rooted in our society as the right of privacy in marriage may be infringed because that right is not guaranteed in so many words by the first eight amendments to the Constitution is to ignore the Ninth Amendment and to give it no effect whatsoever. Moreover, a judicial construction that this fundamental right is not protected by the Constitution because it is not mentioned in explicit terms by one of the first eight amendments or elsewhere in the Constitution would violate the Ninth Amendment, which specifically states that "[t]he enumeration in the Constitution, of certain rights, shall not be *construed* to deny or disparage others retained by the people." (Emphasis added.)

A dissenting opinion suggests that my interpretation of the Ninth Amendment somehow "broaden[s] the powers of this Court." *Post,* at 520. With all due respect, I believe that it misses the import of what I am saying. I do not take the position of my Brother BLACK in his dissent in *Adamson* v. *California,* 332 U. S. 46, 68, that the entire Bill of Rights is incorporated in the Fourteenth Amendment, and I do not mean to imply that the Ninth Amendment is applied against the States by the Fourteenth. Nor do I mean to state that the Ninth Amendment constitutes an independent source of rights protected from infringement by either the States or the Federal Government. Rather, the Ninth Amendment shows a belief of the Constitution's authors that fundamental rights exist that are not expressly enumerated in the first eight amendments and an intent that the list of rights included there not be deemed exhaustive. ● ●●

The Ninth Amendment simply shows the intent of the Constitution's authors that other fundamental personal rights should not be denied such protection or disparaged in any other way simply because they are not specifically listed in the first eight constitutional amendments. I do not see how this broadens the authority of the Court; rather it serves to support what this Court has been doing in protecting fundamental rights. ● ● ●

I agree fully with the Court that ● ● ● the right of privacy is a fundamental personal right, emanating "from the totality of the constitutional scheme under which we live." ● ● ●

The entire fabric of the Constitution and the purposes that clearly underlie its specific guarantees demonstrate that the rights to marital privacy and to marry and raise a family are of similar order and magnitude as the fundamental rights specifically protected.

Although the Constitution does not speak in so many words of the right of privacy in marriage, I cannot believe that it offers these fundamental rights no protection. The fact that no particular provision of the Constitution explicitly forbids the State from disrupting the traditional relation of the family—a relation as old and as fundamental as our entire civilization—surely does not show that the Government was meant to have the power to do so. Rather, as the Ninth Amendment expressly recognizes, there are fundamental personal rights such as this one, which are protected from abridgment by the Government though not specifically mentioned in the Constitution. ● ● ●

In sum, I believe that the right of privacy in the marital relation is fundamental and basic—a personal right "retained by the people" within the meaning of the Ninth Amendment. Connecticut cannot constitutionally abridge this fundamental right, which is protected by the Fourteenth Amendment from infringement by the States. I agree with the Court that petitioners' convictions must therefore be reversed.

7. Inverse Condemnation

UNITED STATES v. CAUSBY, 328 U.S. 256 (1946).

Mr. Justice Douglas delivered the opinion of the Court.

This is a case of first impression. The problem presented is whether respondents' property was taken, within the meaning of the Fifth Amendment, by frequent and regular flights of army and navy aircraft over respondents' land at low altitudes. The Court of Claims held that there was a taking and entered judgment for respondents, one judge dissenting. 104 Ct. Cls. 342, 60 F. Supp. 751. The case is here on a petition for a writ of certiorari which we granted because of the importance of the question presented.

Respondents own 2.8 acres near an airport outside of Greensboro, North Carolina. It has on it a dwelling house, and also various outbuildings which were mainly used for raising chickens. The end of the airport's northwest-southeast runway is 2,220 feet from respondents' barn and 2,275 feet from their house. The path of glide to this runway passes directly over the property—which is 100 feet wide and 1,200 feet long. The 30 to 1 safe glide angle [1] approved by the Civil Aeronautics Authority [2] passes over this property at 83 feet, which is 67 feet above the house, 63 feet above the barn and 18 feet above the highest tree. [3] The use by the United States of this airport is pursuant to a lease executed in May, 1942, for a term commencing June 1, 1942 and ending June 30, 1942, with a provision for renewals until June 30, 1967, or six months after the end of the national emergency, whichever is the earlier.

Various aircraft of the United States use this airport— bombers, transports and fighters. The direction of the prevailing wind determines when a particular runway is used. The northwest-southeast runway in question is used about four per cent of the time in taking off and about seven per cent of the time in landing. Since the United States began operations in May, 1942, its four-motored heavy bombers, other planes of the heavier type, and its fighter planes have frequently passed over respondents' land and buildings in considerable numbers and rather close together. They come close enough at times to appear barely to miss the tops of the trees and at times so

close to the tops of the trees as to blow the old leaves off.
The noise is startling. And at night the glare from the
planes brightly lights up the place. As a result of the
noise, respondents had to give up their chicken business.
As many as six to ten of their chickens were killed in one
day by flying into the walls from fright. The total
chickens lost in that manner was about 150. Production
also fell off. The result was the destruction of the use of
the property as a commercial chicken farm. Respondents
are frequently deprived of their sleep and the family has
become nervous and frightened. Although there have
been no airplane accidents on respondents' property, there
have been several accidents near the airport and close to
respondents' place. These are the essential facts found
by the Court of Claims. On the basis of these facts, it
found that respondents' property had depreciated in
value. It held that the United States had taken an easement over the property on June 1, 1942, and that the value
of the property destroyed and the easement taken was
$2,000.

I. The United States relies on the Air Commerce Act
of 1926, 44 Stat. 568, 49 U. S. C. § 171, as amended by the
Civil Aeronautics Act of 1938, 52 Stat. 973, 49 U. S. C.
§ 401. Under those statutes the United States has "complete and exclusive national sovereignty in the air space"
over this country. 49 U. S. C. § 176 (a). They grant
any citizen of the United States "a public right of freedom
of transit in air commerce⁴ through the navigable air
space of the United States." 49 U. S. C. § 403. And
"navigable air space" is defined as "airspace above the
minimum safe altitudes of flight prescribed by the Civil
Aeronautics Authority." 49 U. S. C. § 180. And it is
provided that "such navigable airspace shall be subject
to a public right of freedom of interstate and foreign air
navigation." Id. It is, therefore, argued that since these
flights were within the minimum safe altitudes of flight
which had been prescribed, they were an exercise of the
declared right of travel through the airspace. The United
States concludes that when flights are made within the
navigable airspace without any physical invasion of the
property of the landowners, there has been no taking of
property. It says that at most there was merely incidental damage occurring as a consequence of authorized
air navigation. It also argues that the landowner does
not own superadjacent airspace which he has not subjected
to possession by the erection of structures or other occu-

pancy. Moreover, it is argued that even if the United States took airspace owned by respondents, no compensable damage was shown. Any damages are said to be merely consequential for which no compensation may be obtained under the Fifth Amendment.

It is ancient doctrine that at common law ownership of the land extended to the periphery of the universe—*Cujus est solum ejus est usque ad coelum.*[5] But that doctrine has no place in the modern world. The air is a public highway, as Congress has declared. Were that not true, every transcontinental flight would subject the operator to countless trespass suits. Common sense revolts at the idea. To recognize such private claims to the airspace would clog these highways, seriously interfere with their control and development in the public interest, and transfer into private ownership that to which only the public has a just claim.

But that general principle does not control the present case. For the United States conceded on oral argument that if the flights over respondents' property rendered it uninhabitable, there would be a taking compensable under the Fifth Amendment. It is the owner's loss, not the taker's gain, which is the measure of the value of the property taken. *United States v. Miller*, 317 U. S. 369. Market value fairly determined is the normal measure of the recovery. *Id.* And that value may reflect the use to which the land could readily be converted, as well as the existing use. *United States v. Powelson*, 319 U. S. 266, 275, and cases cited. If, by reason of the frequency and altitude of the flights, respondents could not use this land for any purpose, their loss would be complete.[6] It would be as complete as if the United States had entered upon the surface of the land and taken exclusive possession of it.

We agree that in those circumstances there would be a taking. Though it would be only an easement of flight which was taken, that easement, if permanent and not merely temporary, normally would be the equivalent of a fee interest. ● ● ●

We have said that the airspace is a public highway. Yet it is obvious that if the landowner is to have full enjoyment of the land, he must have exclusive control of the immediate reaches of the enveloping atmosphere. Otherwise buildings could not be erected, trees could not be planted, and even fences could not be run. ● ● ● The landowner owns at least as much of the space above the ground as he can occupy or use in connection with the land. See *Hinman* v. *Pacific Air Transport*, 84 F. 2d 755. The fact that he does not occupy it in a physical sense— by the erection of buildings and the like—is not material. As we have said, the flight of airplanes, which skim the surface but do not touch it, is as much an appropriation of the use of the land as a more conventional entry upon it. ● ● ●   The reason is that there would be an intrusion so immediate and direct as to subtract from the owner's full enjoyment of the property and to limit his exploitation of it. While the owner does not in any physical manner occupy that stratum of airspace or make use of it in the conventional sense, he does use it in somewhat the same sense that space left between buildings for the purpose of light and air is used. The superadjacent airspace at this low altitude is so close to the land that continuous invasions of it affect the use of the surface of the land itself. We think that the landowner, as an incident to his ownership, has a claim to it and that invasions of it are in the same category as invasions of the surface.[11]

● ● ●

    For the findings of the Court of Claims plainly establish that there was a diminution in value of the property and that the frequent, low-level flights were the direct and immediate cause. We agree with the Court of Claims that a servitude has been imposed upon the land. ● ● ●

Since on this record it is not clear whether the easement taken is a permanent or a temporary one, it would be premature for us to consider whether the amount of the award made by the Court of Claims was proper.

The judgment is reversed and the cause is remanded to the Court of Claims so that it may make the necessary findings in conformity with this opinion.

Reversed.

MR. JUSTICE BLACK, dissenting.

CITY OF WALLA WALLA v. CONKEY, 6 Wash. App. 300, 492 P. 2d 589 (1971).

PEARSON, Judge.

The respondent, City of Walla Walla, commenced a declaratory judgment action, naming as defendants the numerous appellants and others [1] who own property near Mill Creek, some 3 miles west of Walla Walla, and whose property is in close proximity to respondent's sewage treatment plants. Many of the appellants use the waters from Mill Creek and an irrigation ditch known as "Gose Ditch" for farm irrigation purposes. The city has for years been depositing sewage from its treatment plants into Mill Creek and Gose Ditch.

The properties of appellants were benefited by a 1927 decree of the Superior Court for Walla Walla County, which required the city to:

[D]ischarge, deliver, and return into the bed of the natural channel of Mill Creek . . . all of the sewage water and other waters accumulating from time to time in the sewer system of the . . . City of Walla Walla, and when the said City of Walla Walla shall treat, purify or otherwise sterilize the sewage of the City of Walla Walla, to then return the purified or sterilized product to said point . . . to the end that each of the plaintiffs . . . may use the same for irrigation purposes . . .

The decree also provided that the appellants whose property was served for irrigation by Gose Ditch were entitled to a prior right to 1.77 cubic feet of water per second of time at all seasons of the year.

The city alleged in its complaint that because of increased population and industrial expansion it was now using 6 wells in addition to the Mill Creek water and that it was now treating sewage waters from various institutions which had not existed in 1927 and which institutions had their own water supply systems. Accordingly, the city claimed that sewage and industrial waste was being created far in excess of the amounts the city could treat and purify, despite the addition of an industrial sewage treatment facility.

The city sought to have the 1927 decree modified, so as to obligate the city to supply the appellants

only an amount of treated sewage waste that bears the same proportion to the total sewage effluent as plaintiff's [the city's] water right of 22 cubic feet per second of water from Mill Creek bears to the total water supplies available to plaintiff which contribute to the production of sewage waters.

The appellants filed counterclaims, alleging that their property rights had been unconstitutionally taken through the operation of the city's sewer plants because of noxious odors emanating from the discharge of polluted water into Gose Ditch and Mill Creek. There was testimony at trial that the pollution also caused the appellants' sprinkling systems to become plugged, and covered the creek and ditch beds with a slimy material.

The declaratory judgment action was tried separately to the court and the disposition of that action is not before us. [2] The counterclaims were tried to a jury. At the conclusion of appellants' case, the court granted respondent's motion challenging the sufficiency of the evidence and entered judgments of dismissal from which this appeal is taken.

The dismissal of the counterclaims was granted on two grounds. First, the trial court believed that appellants had not established when the unconstitutional "taking" had occurred. Accordingly, there was insufficient evidence to allow the jury to apply the proper measure of damages, namely, the value of the property immediately before and after the taking. Secondly, the trial court believed that appellants' claims were barred because of more than 10 years of adverse use of or interference with appellants' property rights by the city.

The questions raised on appeal are these. (1) Have respondent's actions in dumping raw and partially treated waste matter into Mill Creek and Gose Ditch, causing noxious odors, clogging irrigation sprinklers, and so forth, constituted a constitutional taking of appellants' property, requiring constitutional compensation? (2) Was it necessary for appellants to prove the exact time of "taking" so as to permit a factual determination of damages, and if so, was the offered evidence sufficient to make a prima facie case? (3) Does the statute of limitations applicable to adverse prescription apply to the type of constitutional taking or damaging which occurred in this case?

There is no question that pollution of a stream by a municipality in carrying out its sewage disposal functions constitutes a constitutional taking, where the disposal results in pollution of the stream on such a scale as to create a public nuisance. Snavely v. Goldendale, 10 Wash.2d 453, 117 P.2d 221 (1941).

2 J. Sackman, Nichols on Eminent Domain § 5.795(2) (3d ed. 1970) states at page 5–383:

> When a city or town gathers the sewage of its inhabitants and pours it into a private watercourse there is a serious impairment of the enjoyment of riparian rights and the injury resulting therefrom undoubtedly constitutes a "damage", but whether such injury is of such a character as to constitute a "taking" is not entirely clear. In a few states it is held that a lower riparian owner upon a private watercourse is not entitled to compensation for the pollution of the water by a municipal sewer system. But the weight of authority favors the principle that the court cannot balance the public convenience and inconvenience; that the pollution of a stream by sewage or for any other public purpose is a taking of property in the constitutional sense and that it cannot be effected without compensation.

(Footnotes omitted.)

We thus conclude that there was clearly established a prima facie case of an inverse condemnation in the nature of a taking, which occurred as a result of the city's sewage disposal activities. ● ● ●

We now turn to the question of whether appellants established a prima facie case of damages which are not barred by the applicable statute of limitations. ● ● ●

Respondent city also argues persuasively and the trial court ruled that the evidence showed a long history of pollution dating back to the 1920's, with gradual aggravations in the 1930's and 1940's when vegetable processing plant residue was added to the city sewage disposal system. Respondent urges that the prescriptive use period had long since established the city's rights to interfere with the use and enjoyment of appellants' property. This argument would persuade us were it not for the undisputed fact that it was not until the 1960's that the city started accepting large quantities of industrial waste which its plants could not properly treat, to the end that sewage and industrial waste were deposited into Mill Creek and Gose Ditch with no treatment at all. ● ● ●

The unique problems presented in the inverse condemnation situation are exemplified by the two rulings made by the learned trial judge in dismissing the cross-complaints. They are these. When did the interference with the use and enjoyment of appellants' property reach the proportions where the law recognizes that a "taking" in the constitutional sense has occurred? It is necessary to answer that question because when an inverse condemnation has occurred, the right to claim compensation must be asserted within 10 years of the "taking." In Ackerman v. Port of Seattle, 55 Wash.2d 400, 405, 348 P.2d 664, 667 (1960), the rule was aptly stated:

> We have held that an action for constitutional taking is not barred by any statute of limitations and may be brought at any time before title to the property taken is acquired by prescription. The prescriptive period in this state has been held to be ten years. [Citing cases.]

It is also necessary to ascertain the time the taking has occurred because the measure of compensation is usually determined at that time. Again, in Ackerman v. Port of Seattle, *supra,* at page 413, 348 P.2d at page 371, the rule was announced that damages for an inverse condemnation would be "the difference between the value of their property before the airport was *extensively used* and the value thereafter, plus interest from that date." ● ● ●

We view the policies and problems of the interference with the use and enjoyment of property by noxious odors and water pollution caused by the municipality's sewage disposal system, strikingly similar to the airport cases. Remedies of trespass or nuisance are largely inappropriate. Martin v. Port of Seattle, *supra.* There is no less reason to allow the property owners in this case the decline in market value of their property than in the airport noise cases. The harm is only different in kind. However, there is one marked distinction in the two types of cases and we must determine whether that distinction is sufficient to call for a different application of the rules cited above. That difference has to do with the permanence of the damages caused by the acts of the municipality.

In the airport cases, there is little likelihood that the airplane noise will ever be abated, unless, of course, the genius of American technology develops the noiseless aircraft. However, when it comes to sewage pollution of air and water, there is a compelling and urgent necessity for municipal governments to solve that problem; and in fact, the City of Walla Walla has been required by court order to deliver effluent from its treatment facilities, meeting purity standards set by either the state or federal government. In the event such order is complied with, appellants' market value decline may be minimized. Therefore, to assess damages, as is done in the airport case, at the time *extensive* use has been established, would be unfair to the public who in all likelihood will also bear the cost, as it ultimately must, of treatment facilities sufficient to reduce or eliminate the air and water pollution. Such a result could also be grossly unfair to the property owner in cases where the pollution is allowed to worsen as the city grows and develops industrially.

We also point out that where inverse condemnation by air and water pollution has taken place, the degree of harm, as demonstrated by the facts of this case, is seasonable and subject to wide variations from month to month or from year to year. The variations are affected by (1) the weather, (2) the amount of industrial wastes or sewage discharged, and (3) the effectiveness of the treatment facilities. Accordingly, a determination of damages at some unpredictable time in the past will neither accurately measure the loss to a particular property owner, nor will it enable him to guess with any degree of accuracy *when* the jury will determine that his property rights have been taken.[3] This will make it necessary for him to place before the jury numerous obsolete evaluations of the decline in market value, to the confusion of the jury, when the interests of justice would best be served by a determination of the current effect the pollution has on the market value of the land involved.

Accordingly, it is our view that in this unique type of inverse condemnation, damages should be measured as the decline in market value at the time of trial. ● ● ●

In Wilshire v. Seattle, 154 Wash. 1, 6, 280 P. 65, 67 (1929) the court stated:

This court has held that in case possession of land is taken prior to the initiation of condemnation proceedings the compensation to the owner, based upon the market value of the land, is to be determined as of the date of trial, and not as of the date possession was taken.

We are of the opinion that such rule is workable and fair when applied to inverse condemnation by air and water pollution. Since appellants' evidence showed the decline in market value as of the time of trial, we conclude that a prima facie case was made on the issue of damages.

However, because of the city's claim of adverse prescription, we do think it was necessary for appellants to establish a prima facie case that substantial or extensive pollution occurred within 10 years prior to the commencement of the actions, which was different in kind or substantially greater in degree than that which existed before that period commenced. Cheskov v. Port of Seattle, *supra*.

We think there was sufficient evidence from appellants' witnesses and from respondent's plant supervisor to create an issue of fact for the jury. The pollution worsened in the early 1960's and became severe in the mid-1960's when sewage without treatment was deposited in Mill Creek in great quantities.

Consequently, the jury should have been allowed to make that factual determination under instructions to the effect that, to recover, appellants must establish by a preponderance of the evidence that the damage to their property had, within 10 years prior to the commencement of the action,

differed substantially in kind or was substantially greater in degree than it had been prior to the commencement of that period. *See* Ackerman v. Port of Seattle, *supra;* Cheskov v. Port of Seattle, *supra;* Anderson v. Port of Seattle, 66 Wash.2d 457, 403 P.2d 368 (1965).

We think the trial court should also submit to the jury the question of which of the appellants, if any, acquired his property *after* the time of "taking." No damages should be allowed any appellant found to have acquired his property for a price commensurate with its diminished value. Such parties should not be entitled to recover damages which they did not, in fact, sustain, even though the current market value of their land may be less than it would be without the pollution.

Reversed and remanded.

. . . .

For additional information on inverse condemnation, see:

1. Mandelker, "Inverse Condemnation: The Constitutional Limits of Public Responsibility," 1966 Wisc. L. Rev. 3.

2. Russell, "Recent Developments in Inverse Condemnation of Airspace," 39 J. of Air L. and Comm. 81 (1973).

3. Note, "Inverse Condemnation - Stream Pollution as Taking of Property for Public Use," 40 Tenn. L. Rev. 514 (1973).

4. Van Alstyne, "Modernizing Inverse Condemnation: A Legislative Prospectus," 8 Santa Clara L. R. 1 (1967).

8. Statutory Basis of Action

a.) MICHIGAN ENVIRONMENTAL PROTECTION ACT (1970) Mich Stats Ann 14.528(201)-14.528(207).

14.528(202) Action in circuit court; granting of relief.) Sec. 2 (1) The attorney general, any political subdivision of the state, any instrumentality or agency of the state or of a political subdivision thereof, any person, partnership, corporation, association, organization or other legal entity may maintain an action in the circuit court having jurisdiction where the alleged violation occurred or is likely to occur for declaratory and equitable relief against the state, any political subdivision thereof, any instrumentality or agency of the state or of a political subdivision thereof, any person, partnership, corporation, association, organization or other legal entity for the protection of the air, water and other natural resources and the public trust therein from pollution, impairment or destruction.

(2) In granting relief provided by subsection (1) where there is involved a standard for pollution or for an antipollution device or procedure, fixed by rule or otherwise, by an instrumentality or agency of the state or a political subdivision thereof, the court may:

(a) Determine the validity, applicability and reasonableness of the standard.

(b) When a court finds a standard to be deficient, direct the adoption of a standard approved and specified by the court.

(CL'48, 691.1202.;

14.528(202a) Posting of bond or cash.) Sec. 2a. If the court has reasonable ground to doubt the solvency of the plaintiff or the plaintiff's ability to pay any cost or judgment which might be rendered against him in an action brought under this act the court may order the plaintiff to post a surety bond or cash not to exceed $500.00.

14.528(203) Evidentiary showing; principles applicable; master or referee; costs.) Sec. 3. (1) When the plaintiff in the action has made a prima facie showing that the conduct of the defendant has, or is likely to pollute, impair or destroy the air, water or other natural resources or the public trust therein, the defendant may rebut the prima facie showing by

the submission of evidence to the contrary. The defendant may also show, by way of an affirmative defense, that there is no feasible and prudent alternative to defendant's conduct and that such conduct is consistent with the promotion of the public health, safety and welfare in light of the state's paramount concern for the protection of its natural resources from pollution, impairment or destruction. Except as to the affirmative defense, the principles of burden of proof and weight of the evidence generally applicable in civil actions in the circuit courts shall apply to actions brought under this act.

(2) The court may appoint a master or referee, who shall be a disinterested person and technically qualified, to take testimony and make a record and a report of his findings to the court in the action.

(3) Costs may be apportioned to the parties if the interests of justice require.

(CL'48, 691.1203.)

58

b.) NATIONAL ENVIRONMENTAL POLICY ACT
(1970) 42 U.S.C. 4332.

i. TITLE 42. -- THE PUBLIC HEALTH AND WELFARE

§ 4332. Cooperation of agencies; reports; availability of information; recommendations; international and national coordination of efforts.

The Congress authorizes and directs that, to the fullest extent possible: (1) the policies, regulations, and public laws of the United States shall be interpreted and administered in accordance with the policies set forth in this chapter, and (2) all agencies of the Federal Government shall—

(A) utilize a systematic, interdisciplinary approach which will insure the integrated use of the natural and social sciences and the environmental design arts in planning and in decisionmaking which may have an impact on man's environment;

(B) identify and develop methods and procedures, in consultation with the Council on Environmental Quality established by subchapter II of this chapter, which will insure that presently unquantified environmental amenities and values may be given appropriate consideration in decisionmaking along with economic and technical considerations;

(C) include in every recommendation or report on proposals for legislation and other major Federal actions significantly affecting the quality of the human environment, a detailed statement by the responsible official on—

(i) the environmental impact of the proposed action,

(ii) any adverse environmental effects which cannot be avoided should the proposal be implemented,

(iii) alternatives to the proposed action,

(iv) the relationship between local short-term uses of man's environment and the maintenance and enhancement of long-term productivity, and

(v) any irreversible and irretrievable commitments of resources which would be involved in the proposed action should it be implemented.

Prior to making any detailed statement, the responsible Federal official shall consult with and obtain the comments of any Federal agency which has jurisdiction by law or special expertise with respect to any environmental impact involved. Copies of such statement and the comments and views of the appropriate Federal, State, and local agencies, which are authorized to develop and enforce environmental standards, shall be made available to the President, the Council on Environmental Quality and to the public as provided by section 552 of Title 5, and shall accompany the proposal through the existing agency review processes;

(D) study, develop, and describe appropriate alternatives to recommended courses of action in any proposal which involves unresolved conflicts concerning alternative uses of available resources;

(E) recognize the worldwide and long-range character of environmental problems and, where consistent with the foreign policy of the United States, lend appropriate support to initiatives, resolutions, and programs designed to maximize international cooperation in anticipating and preventing a decline in the quality of mankind's world environment;

(F) make available to States, counties, municipalities, institutions, and individuals, advice and

information useful in restoring, maintaining, and enhancing the quality of the environment;

(G) initiate and utilize ecological information in the planning and development of resource-oriented projects; and

(H) assist the Council on Environmental Quality established by subchapter II of this chapter. (Pub. L. 91–190, title I, § 102, Jan. 1, 1970, 83 Stat. 853.)

. . . .

For information on the preparation of an environmental impact statement see:

Burchell & Hagevik, THE ENVIRONMENTAL IMPACT HANDBOOK (Center for Urban Policy Research) 1974.

ii. WHAT CONSTITUTES A "MAJOR FEDERAL ACTION SIGNI-FICANTLY AFFECTING THE ENVIRONMENT"?

SAN FRANCISCO TOMORROW v. ROMNEY, 472 F. 2d 1021 (9th Cir. 1973)

McGOVERN, District Judge:

By Complaint filed January 13, 1972, plaintiff individuals, community and environmental organizations alleged that the United States, through Housing and Urban Development Secretary George Romney, had illegally approved and financed the Yerba Buena Center Redevelopment Project in San Francisco and the West Berkeley Industrial Park Redevelopment Project in Berkeley, California. Plaintiffs' claims were premised upon the theory that the Secretary of Housing and Urban Development (hereafter HUD) had failed to file for each project an Environmental Impact Statement as required by Section 102(2)(C) of the National Environmental Policy Act (NEPA), 83 Stat. 853, 42 U.S.C. § 4332, which provides:

"The Congress authorizes and directs that, to the fullest extent possible: . . . (2) all agencies of the Federal Government shall * * *

(C) include in every recommendation or report on proposals for legislation and other major Federal actions significantly affecting the quality of the human environment, a detailed statement by the responsible official on—

(i) the environmental impact of the proposed action,

(ii) any adverse environmental effects which cannot be avoided should the proposal be implemented,

(iii) alternatives to the proposed action,

(iv) the relationship between local short-term uses of man's environment and the maintenance and enhancement of long-term productivity, and

(v) any irreversible and irretrievable commitments of resources which would be involved in the proposed action should it be implemented.

Prior to making any detailed statement, the responsible Federal official shall consult with and obtain the comments of any Federal agency which has jurisdiction by law or special expertise with respect to any environmental impact involved. Copies of such statement and the comments and views of the appropriate Federal, State, and local agencies, which are authorized to develop and enforce environmental standards, shall be made available to the President, the Council on Environmental Quality and to the public as provided by section 552 of Title 5, and shall accompany the proposal through the existing agency review processes." ● ● ●

The West Berkeley Project consists of a 20-block area in West Berkeley along the eastern edge of the Eastshore Freeway. When renewed as planned, the area will enclose primarily commercial buildings and other facilities intended for industrial purposes. The project was contemplated originally to be part of a federal urban renewal program, but subsequently was converted to a Neighborhood Development Program.

● ● ●

San Francisco Yerba Buena Project consists of 87 acres in the City and County of San Francisco ● ● ●

As currently planned, the presently blighted area will have new commercial buildings, parking facilities for 4,000 automobiles, a convention center, a large hotel and other facilities. ● ● ●

These projects represent two types of HUD urban renewal projects which may qualify for federal financial assistance under the slum clearance and urban renewal provision of the Housing Act of 1949, 68 Stat. 622, as amended, 42 U.S. C. § 1450 et seq. The conventional Yerba Buena Center project is planned and funded as one unit, the other, the Neighborhood Development, or West Berkeley Industrial Park, project is funded in annual increments, and the Government may terminate the project at the end of any year.

The trial court concluded that the plaintiffs had no standing to challenge the projects because the plaintiffs' property or other legal interests in the project were neither greater nor lesser than those of other organizations or persons.

While it might properly be said that the Articles of Incorporation of the Sierra Club clearly indicate that its corporate purposes do not include suits, or activities, of the specific type here involved, yet it appears that the principal plaintiff, San Francisco Tomorrow, is not so corporately restricted. The Complaint alleges sufficiently that San Francisco Tomorrow has been adversely affected, at least in non-economic ways, by agency inaction under NEPA. That should be, and is, sufficient under case law to give San Francisco Tomorrow sufficient standing to sue. Sierra Club v. Hickel, 433 F.2d 24 (Ninth Circuit, 1970).

As for the Berkeley project, an individual plaintiff, William Walker, resides within the project area and has alleged sufficient environmental injury to be entitled to his day in Court.

We also note that the federal appellees here have changed their position on the question of standing, and now state in their brief on appeal: "Since it appears from the record that at least some of the plaintiffs have satisfied recent Supreme Court requirements for standing, the Government is not challenging standing before this Court."

The controversy before us should be decided by an examination of the facts, as is necessarily required in every NEPA case.

The National Environmental Policy Act became effective on January 1, 1970 and its terms are applicable to all agencies of the Federal Government which thereafter engage in further "major federal actions significantly affecting the quality of the human environment

The Act does not by direct language or by implication call for retrospective application. In fact, the Council on Environmental Quality, the agency created by NEPA to enforce the Act, states in its interim guidelines of April 23, 1971 that existing federal projects and programs are affected only by further major action, as follows:

"11. Application of section 102(2) (C) procedure to existing projects and programs. To the maximum extent practicable the section 102(2)(C) procedure should be applied to further major Federal actions having a significant effect on the environment even though they arise from projects or programs initiated prior to enactment of the Act on January 1, 1970. Where it is not practicable to reassess the basic course of action, it is still important that further incremental major actions be shaped so as to minimize adverse environmental consequences. It is also important in further action that account be taken of environmental consequences not fully evaluated at the outset of the project or program. ● ● ●

The controlling question before us is whether or not subsequent to January 1, 1970, some further major action which would significantly affect the quality of the human environment, was required of the Federal Government in the development of either the Yerba Buena Center or the West Berkeley Industrial Park projects. ● ● ●

Urban renewal funds were committed to the project for limited purposes only. The Redevelopment Agency may use the funds to purchase the land within the renewal area, relocate the displaced residents, demolish buildings in the area, and provide for site grading streets and utilities. The funds may not be used for building construction and the Federal Government does not acquire or redevelop the properties.

When the National Environmental Policy act became effective on January 1, 1970, the federal involvement in the Yerba Buena Center project was virtually complete. In fact, for purposes of NEPA, major *federal* action had terminated on December 2, 1966 when HUD became contractually obligated to the San Francisco Redevelopment Agency for the loan and grants. The record before us shows no further major federal involvement subsequent to that time.

Appellants argue that the June 26, 1970 and April 28, 1972 amendatory grants to the San Francisco Redevelopment Agency and Hud's contractual right to monitor the project as it develops to assure compliance with statutory and contractual requirements constituted major federal actions subsequent to the passage of NEPA. We hold otherwise.

Amendatory contracts which increase the federal funding only to provide for the rising costs of land acquisition and relocation of displaced residents do not constitute "further major federal action" within the meaning of the Act. Instead, such amendments represent but

confirmation of the Federal Government's earlier decision that the project proposal conformed to HUD requirements and was therefore eligible for a grant and loan. The major federal action was the execution of the initial grant and loan contract which occurred over four years before the effective date of NEPA. Monitoring the project only assures HUD that the undertakings of SFRA under its contract of December 2, 1966 will be fulfilled and involves no further major federal action. ● ● ●

It is otherwise, however, as to the West Berkeley Project. HUD's agreement of February 10, 1970 with the Berkeley Redevelopment Agency significantly changed an industrial park project to a neighborhood development program. This constituted major federal action. Since that date is subsequent to the effective date of NEPA, the project may go forward only upon compliance with the terms of the Act.

● ● ●

The order of the trial court is affirmed as to the Yerba Buena Center Redevelopment Project in San Francisco and reversed as to the West Berkeley Industrial Park Redevelopment Project.

SAVE OUR TEN ACRES v. KREGER, 472 F. 2d 463 (5th Cir. 1973).

CLARK, Circuit Judge:

What is the proper standard for judicial review of an agency's threshold determination *not to file* an environmental impact statement under the National Environmental Policy Act of 1969 (NEPA)?[1]

This is an action to enjoin the construction of a federal office building on a downtown site in Mobile, Alabama, brought by an organization known as Save Our Ten Acres (alphabetically shorthanded: "SOTA"). SOTA is a voluntary unincorporated association comprised of approximately 572 employees of the Corps of Engineers, formed to resist the selection of the urban site. The Corps of Engineers is to occupy the greater part of the new building on completion. The site selection decision was made by the General Services Administration (GSA). The basis of SOTA's attack on that decision in the court below and in the instant appeal is limited to an alleged failure of the GSA to comply with the NEPA requirement that all federal agencies file a detailed statement of the environmental impact of all major federal actions which may significantly affect the quality of the human environment.[2]

It is undisputed that the defendants have proceeded with this site selection and construction without preparing an NEPA statement. However, they argue that no such environmental impact statement was required in this case because the building, even if it be a major federal action within the meaning of the statute,[3] will not significantly affect the quality of the human environment. The court below refused any relief, reasoning that the foregate determination by GSA that this project did not significantly affect the quality of the human environment could not be disturbed unless the court found it to be arbitrary, capricious or an abuse of discretion. To best effectuate the Act this decision should have been court-measured under a more relaxed rule of reasonableness, rather than by the narrower standard of arbitrariness or capriciousness. We therefore vacate and remand.

The question presented in this case has not yet been addressed by this circuit, though the question has arisen in a number of reported cases.[4] In support of its argument that the arbitrary or capricious standard should govern, the agency relies on the well-settled proposition that, in the absence of fraud, administrative findings of fact are conclusive if supported by any substantial record evidence. However, this usual fact determination review rule ought not be applied to test the basic jurisdiction-type conclusion involved here. NEPA was intended not only to insure that the appropriate responsible official considered the environmental effects of the project, but also to provide Congress (and others receiving such recommendation or proposal) with a sound basis for evaluating the environmental aspects of the particular project or program. The spirit of the Act would die aborning if a facile, ex parte decision that the project was minor or did not significantly affect the environment were too well shielded from impartial review. Every such decision pretermits all consideration of that which Congress has directed be considered "to the fullest extent possible." The primary decision to give or bypass the consideration required by the Act must be subject to inspection under a more searching standard. ● ● ●

Under the review standard we hold is required, the court must determine whether the plaintiff has alleged facts which, if true, show that the recommended project would materially degrade any aspect of environmental quality. In this case SOTA charges, *inter alia,* that the construction of the building will create severe urban parking and traffic congestion problems, will aggravate an already substantial air pollution problem, and is to be improperly located on the floodplain of the Mobile River. Though we express no opinion on the merits of SOTA's claim, we note that SOTA's allegations on their face may well satisfy the criteria of GSA's own statement of policy for implementation of the NEPA.[6]

Since SOTA has raised substantial environmental issues concerning the proposed recommended project here, the court should proceed to examine and weigh the evidence of both the plaintiff and the agency to determine whether the agency reasonably concluded that the particular project would have no effects which would significantly degrade our environmental quality. ● ● ● If the court concludes that no environmental factor would be significantly degraded by the project, GSA's determination not to file the impact statement should be upheld. On the other hand, if the court finds that the project may cause a significant degradation of some human environmental factor (even though other environmental factors are affected beneficially or not at all),[7] the court should require the filing of an impact statement or grant SOTA such other equitable relief as it deems appropriate.

Not only do we iterate that this decision has not the slightest intent of indicating what ruling should eventuate from the retest we require, but we also would emphasize that it is not the province of the courts to review any actual decision on the merits (if one be required) as to the desirability *vel non* of the project. We merely hold that it is the courts' function to insure that the mandate of the statute has been carried out and that all relevant environmental effects of the project be given appropriate consideration by the responsible official whenever it is unreasonable to conclude that the project is without the purview of the Act.

● ● ●

The judgment of the court below is Affirmed, in part, vacated, in part, and remanded with directions.

B. Who May Sue

I. Standing To Sue

SIERRA CLUB v. MORTON, 405 U.S. 727 (1972).

MR. JUSTICE STEWART delivered the opinion of the Court.

The Mineral King Valley is an area of great natural beauty nestled in the Sierra Nevada Mountains in Tulare County, California, adjacent to Sequoia National Park. It has been part of the Sequoia National Forest since 1926, and is designated as a national game refuge by special Act of Congress.[1] Though once the site of extensive mining activity, Mineral King is now used almost exclusively for recreational purposes. Its relative inaccessibility and lack of development have limited the number of visitors each year, and at the same time have preserved the valley's quality as a quasi-wilderness area largely uncluttered by the products of civilization.

The United States Forest Service, which is entrusted with the maintenance and administration of national forests, began in the late 1940's to give consideration to Mineral King as a potential site for recreational development. Prodded by a rapidly increasing demand for skiing facilities, the Forest Service published a prospectus in 1965, inviting bids from private developers for the construction and operation of a ski resort that would also serve as a summer recreation area.

• • •

The final Disney plan, approved by the Forest Service in January 1969, outlines a $35 million complex of motels, restaurants, swimming pools, parking lots, and other structures designed to accommodate 14,000 visitors daily. This complex is to be constructed on 80 acres of the valley floor under a 30-year use permit from the Forest Service. • • •

SIERRA CLUB v. MORTON

To provide access to the resort, the State of California proposes to construct a highway 20 miles in length. A section of this road would traverse Sequoia National Park, as would a proposed high-voltage power line needed to provide electricity for the resort. Both the highway and the power line require the approval of the Department of the Interior, which is entrusted with the preservation and maintenance of the national parks.

Representatives of the Sierra Club, who favor maintaining Mineral King largely in its present state, followed the progress of recreational planning for the valley with close attention and increasing dismay. ● ● ●

In June 1969 the Club filed the present suit in the United States District Court for the Northern District of California, ● ● ●

The petitioner Sierra Club sued as a membership corporation with "a special interest in the conservation and the sound maintenance of the national parks, game refuges and forests of the country," and invoked the judicial-review provisions of the Administrative Procedure Act, 5 U. S. C. § 701 *et seq.*

After two days of hearings, the District Court ● ● ● rejected the respondents' challenge to the Sierra Club's standing to sue, ● ● ●

The respondents appealed, and the Court of Appeals for the Ninth Circuit reversed. 433 F. 2d 24. With respect to the petitioner's standing, the court noted that there was "no allegation in the complaint that members of the Sierra Club would be affected by the actions of [the respondents] other than the fact that the actions are personally displeasing or distasteful to them," *id.*. at 33, and concluded:

"We do not believe such club concern without a showing of more direct interest can constitute standing in the legal sense sufficient to challenge the exercise of responsibilities on behalf of all the citizens by two cabinet level officials of the government acting under Congressional and Constitutional authority."

Alternatively, the Court of Appeals held that the Sierra Club had not made an adequate showing of irreparable injury and likelihood of success on the merits to justify issuance of a preliminary injunction. The court thus vacated the injunction. The Sierra Club filed a petition for a writ of certiorari which we granted, 401 U. S. 907, to review the questions of federal law presented.

The first question presented is whether the Sierra Club has alleged facts that entitle it to obtain judicial review of the challenged action. Whether a party has a sufficient stake in an otherwise justiciable controversy to obtain judicial resolution of that controversy is what has traditionally been referred to as the question of standing to sue. Where the party does not rely on any specific statute authorizing invocation of the judicial process, the question of standing depends upon whether the party has alleged such a "personal stake in the outcome of the controversy," *Baker* v. *Carr*, 369 U. S. 186, 204, as to ensure that "the dispute sought to be adjudicated will be presented in an adversary context and in a form historically viewed as capable of judicial resolution." *Flast* v. *Cohen*, 392 U. S. 83, 101. Where, however, Congress has authorized public officials to perform certain functions according to law, and has provided by statute for judicial review of those actions under certain circumstances, the inquiry as to standing must begin with a determination of whether the statute in question authorizes review at the behest of the plaintiff.[3]

The Sierra Club relies upon § 10 of the Administrative Procedure Act (APA), 5 U. S. C. § 702, which provides:

> "A person suffering legal wrong because of agency action, or adversely affected or aggrieved by agency action within the meaning of a relevant statute, is entitled to judicial review thereof."

Early decisions under this statute interpreted the language as adopting the various formulations of "legal interest" and "legal wrong" then prevailing as constitutional requirements of standing.[4] But, in *Data Processing Service* v. *Camp*, 397 U. S. 150, and *Barlow* v. *Collins*, 397 U. S. 159, decided the same day, we held more broadly that persons had standing to obtain judicial review of federal agency action under § 10 of the APA where they had alleged that the challenged action had caused them "injury in fact," and where the alleged injury was to an interest "arguably within the zone of interests to be protected or regulated" by the statutes that the agencies were claimed to have violated.[5]

In *Data Processing*, the injury claimed by the petitioners consisted of harm to their competitive position in the computer-servicing market ● ● ●

In *Barlow*, the petitioners were tenant farmers who claimed that certain regulations of the Secretary of Agriculture adversely affected their economic position *vis-à-vis* their landlords. ● ● ●

Thus, neither *Data Processing* nor *Barlow* addressed itself to the question, which has arisen with increasing frequency in federal courts in recent years, as to what must be alleged by persons who claim injury of a noneconomic nature to interests that are widely shared.[7] That question is presented in this case.

The injury alleged by the Sierra Club will be incurred entirely by reason of the change in the uses to which Mineral King will be put, and the attendant change in the aesthetics and ecology of the area. Thus, in referring to the road to be built through Sequoia National Park, the complaint alleged that the development "would destroy or otherwise adversely affect the scenery, natural and historic objects and wildlife of the park and would impair the enjoyment of the park for future generations." We do not question that this type of harm may amount to an "injury in fact" sufficient to lay the basis for standing under § 10 of the APA. Aesthetic and environmental well-being, like economic well-being, are important ingredients of the quality of life in our society, and the fact that particular environmental interests are shared by the many rather than the few does not make them less deserving of legal protection through the judicial process. But the "injury in fact" test requires more than an injury to a cognizable interest. It requires that the party seeking review be himself among the injured.

The impact of the proposed changes in the environment of Mineral King will not fall indiscriminately upon every citizen. The alleged injury will be felt directly only by those who use Mineral King and Sequoia National Park, and for whom the aesthetic and recreational values of the area will be lessened by the highway and ski resort. The Sierra Club failed to allege that it or its members would be affected in any of their activities or pastimes by the Disney development. Nowhere in the pleadings or affidavits did the Club state that its members use Mineral King for any purpose, much less that they use it in any way that would be significantly affected by the proposed actions of the respondents.[8]

The Club apparently regarded any allegations of individualized injury as superfluous, on the theory that this was a "public" action involving questions as to the use of natural resources, and that the Club's longstanding concern with and expertise in such matters were sufficient to give it standing as a "representative of the public." [9] This theory reflects a misunderstanding of our cases involving so-called "public actions" in the area of administrative law.

The origin of the theory advanced by the Sierra Club may be traced to a dictum in *Scripps-Howard Radio v. FCC*, 316 U. S. 4. ● ● ●

Taken together, *Sanders* and *Scripps-Howard* thus established a dual proposition: the fact of economic injury is what gives a person standing to seek judicial review under the statute, but once review is properly invoked, that person may argue the public interest in support of his claim that the agency has failed to comply with its statutory mandate.[12] It was in the latter sense that the "standing" of the appellant in *Scripps-Howard* existed only as a "representative of the public interest." It is in a similar sense that we have used the phrase "private attorney general" to describe the function performed by persons upon whom Congress has conferred the right to seek judicial review of agency action. ● ● ●

The trend of cases arising under the APA and other statutes authorizing judicial review of federal agency action has been toward recognizing that injuries other than economic harm are sufficient to bring a person within the meaning of the statutory language, and toward discarding the notion that an injury that is widely shared is *ipso facto* not an injury sufficient to provide the basis for judicial review.[13] We noted this development with approval in *Data Processing*, 397 U. S., at 154, in saying that the interest alleged to have been injured "may reflect 'aesthetic, conservational, and recreational' as well as economic values." But broadening the categories of injury that may be alleged in support of standing is a different matter from abandoning the requirement that the party seeking review must himself have suffered an injury.

Some courts have indicated a willingness to take this latter step by conferring standing upon organizations that have demonstrated "an organizational interest in the problem" of environmental or consumer protection. *Environmental Defense Fund* v. *Hardin*, 138 U. S. App. D. C. 391, 395, 428 F. 2d 1093, 1097.[14] It is clear that an organization whose members are injured may represent those members in a proceeding for judicial review. See, e. g., *NAACP* v. *Button*, 371 U. S. 415, 428. But a mere "interest in a problem," no matter how longstanding the interest and no matter how qualified the organization is in evaluating the problem, is not sufficient by itself to render the organization "adversely affected" or "aggrieved" within the meaning of the APA. The Sierra Club is a large and long-established organization, with a historic commitment to the cause of protecting our Nation's natural heritage from man's depredations. But if a "special interest" in this subject were enough to entitle the Sierra Club to commence this litigation, there would appear to be no objective basis upon which to disallow a suit by any other bona fide "special interest" organization, however small or short-lived. And if any group with a bona fide "special interest" could initiate such litigation, it is difficult to perceive why any individual citizen with the same bona fide special interest would not also be entitled to do so.

The requirement that a party seeking review must allege facts showing that he is himself adversely affected does not insulate executive action from judicial review, nor does it prevent any public interests from being protected through the judicial process.[15] It does serve as at least a rough attempt to put the decision as to whether review will be sought in the hands of those who have a direct stake in the outcome. That goal would be undermined were we to construe the APA to authorize judicial review at the behest of organizations or individuals who seek to do no more than vindicate their own value preferences through the judicial process.[16] The principle that the Sierra Club would have us establish in this case would do just that.

As we conclude that the Court of Appeals was correct in its holding that the Sierra Club lacked standing to maintain this action, we do not reach any other questions presented in the petition, and we intimate no view on the merits of the complaint. The judgment is

Affirmed.

MR. JUSTICE DOUGLAS, dissenting.

I share the views of my Brother BLACKMUN and would reverse the judgment below.

The critical question of "standing"[1] would be simplified and also put neatly in focus if we fashioned a federal rule that allowed environmental issues to be litigated before federal agencies or federal courts in the name of the inanimate object about to be despoiled, defaced, or invaded by roads and bulldozers and where injury is the subject of public outrage. Contemporary public concern for protecting nature's ecological equilibrium should lead to the conferral of standing upon environmental objects to sue for their own preservation. ● ● ● This suit would therefore be more properly labeled as *Mineral King* v. *Morton.*

Inanimate objects are sometimes parties in litigation. A ship has a legal personality, a fiction found useful for maritime purposes.[2] The corporation sole—a creature of ecclesiastical law—is an acceptable adversary and large fortunes ride on its cases.[3] The ordinary corporation is a "person" for purposes of the adjudicatory processes, whether it represents proprietary, spiritual, aesthetic, or charitable causes.[4]

So it should be as respects valleys, alpine meadows, rivers, lakes, estuaries, beaches, ridges, groves of trees, swampland, or even air that feels the destructive pressures of modern technology and modern life. The river, for example, is the living symbol of all the life it sustains or nourishes—fish, aquatic insects, water ouzels, otter, fisher, deer, elk, bear, and all other animals, including man, who are dependent on it or who enjoy it for its sight, its sound, or its life. The river as plaintiff speaks for the ecological unit of life that is part of it. Those people who have a meaningful relation to that body of water—whether it be a fisherman, a canoeist, a zoologist, or a logger—must be able to speak for the values which the river represents and which are threatened with destruction. ● ● ●

Perhaps the bulldozers of "progress" will plow under all the aesthetic wonders of this beautiful land. That is not the present question. The sole question is, who has standing to be heard?

Those who hike the Appalachian Trail into Sunfish Pond, New Jersey, and camp or sleep there, or run the Allagash in Maine, or climb the Guadalupes in West Texas, or who canoe and portage the Quetico Superior in Minnesota, certainly should have standing to defend those natural wonders before courts or agencies, though they live 3,000 miles away. Those who merely are caught up in environmental news or propaganda and flock to defend these waters or areas may be treated differently. That is why these environmental issues should be tendered by the inanimate object itself. Then there will be assurances that all of the forms of life [9] which it represents will stand before the court—the pileated woodpecker as well as the coyote and bear, the lemmings as well as the trout in the streams. Those inarticulate members of the ecological group cannot speak. But those people who have so frequented the place as to know its values and wonders will be able to speak for the entire ecological community.

Ecology reflects the land ethic; and Aldo Leopold wrote in A Sand County Almanac 204 (1949), "The land ethic simply enlarges the boundaries of the community to include soils, waters, plants, and animals, or collectively: the land."

That, as I see it, is the issue of "standing" in the present case and controversy.

MR. JUSTICE BRENNAN, dissenting.

I agree that the Sierra Club has standing for the reasons stated by my Brother BLACKMUN in Alternative No. 2 of his dissent. I therefore would reach the merits. Since the Court does not do so, however, I simply note agreement with my Brother BLACKMUN that the merits are substantial.

MR. JUSTICE BLACKMUN, dissenting.

The Court's opinion is a practical one espousing and adhering to traditional notions of standing as somewhat modernized by *Data Processing Service* v. *Camp*, 397 U. S. 150 (1970); *Barlow* v. *Collins*, 397 U. S. 159 (1970); and *Flast* v. *Cohen*, 392 U. S. 83 (1968). If this were an ordinary case, I would join the opinion and the Court's judgment and be quite content.

But this is not ordinary, run-of-the-mill litigation. The case poses—if only we choose to acknowledge and reach them—significant aspects of a wide, growing, and disturbing problem, that is, the Nation's and the world's deteriorating environment with its resulting ecological disturbances. Must our law be so rigid and our procedural concepts so inflexible that we render ourselves helpless when the existing methods and the traditional concepts do not quite fit and do not prove to be entirely adequate for new issues? ● ● ●

Rather than pursue the course the Court has chosen to take by its affirmance of the judgment of the Court of Appeals, I would adopt one of two alternatives:

1. I would reverse that judgment and, instead, approve the judgment of the District Court which recognized standing in the Sierra Club and granted preliminary relief. I would be willing to do this on condition that the Sierra Club forthwith amend its complaint to meet the specifications the Court prescribes for standing. If Sierra Club fails or refuses to take that step, so be it: the case will then collapse. ● ● ●

2. Alternatively, I would permit an imaginative expansion of our traditional concepts of standing in order to enable an organization such as the Sierra Club, possessed, as it is, of pertinent, bona fide, and well-recognized attributes and purposes in the area of environment, to litigate 'environmental issues. ● ● ●

2. Class Actions

RULE 23, FEDERAL RULES OF CIVIL PROCEDURE

Rule 23. Class Actions

(a) Prerequisites to a Class Action. One or more members of a class may sue or be sued as representative parties on behalf of all only if (1) the class is so numerous that joinder of all members is impracticable, (2) there are questions of law or fact common to the class, (3) the claims or defenses of the representative parties are typical of the claims or defenses of the class, and (4) the representative parties will fairly and adequately protect the interests of the class.

(b) Class Actions Maintainable. An action may be maintained as a class action if the prerequisites of subdivision (a) are satisfied, and in addition:

(1) the prosecution of separate actions by or against individual members of the class would create a risk of

(A) inconsistent or varying adjudications with respect to individual members of the class which would establish incompatible standards of conduct for the party opposing the class, or

(B) adjudications with respect to individual members of the class which would as a practice matter be dispositive of the interests of the other members not parties to the adjudications or substantially impair or impede their ability to protect their interests; or

(2) the party opposing the class has acted or refused to act on grounds generally applicable to the class, thereby making appropriate final injunctive relief or corresponding declaratory relief with respect to the class as a whole; or

· (3) the court finds that the questions of law or fact common to the members of the class predominate over any questions affecting only individual members, and that a class action is superior to other available methods for the fair and efficient adjudication of the controversy. The matters pertinent to the findings include: (A) the interest of members of the class in individually controlling the prosecution or defense of separate actions; (B) the extent and nature of any litigation concerning the controversy already commenced by or against members of the class; (C) the desirability or undesirability of concentrating the litigation of the claims in the particular forum; (D) the difficulties likely to be encountered in the management of a class action.

BIECHELE v. NORFOLK & WESTERN RAILWAY CO., 309 F. Supp. 354 (1969, D.C. Ohio).

DON J. YOUNG, District Judge.

This action was originally commenced in the Court of Common Pleas of Erie County, Ohio, and was removed to this Court by defendant on the ground of diversity of citizenship. The action was intended as a class action, and seeks damages and an injunction because of an alleged nuisance created by defendant in the operation of its coal storage and shipping facilities in Sandusky.

After some preliminary skirmishing the Court concluded that this was properly maintainable as a class action and that a representative class was present. Federal Rules of Civil Procedure 23(a). Actually, there are two separate and distinct class actions involved. The first and principal action is that for injunctive relief. The action is founded upon Rule 23(b) (1) and (2) of the Federal Rules of Civil Procedure. Jurisdiction for this action is based upon diversity, 28 U.S.C. § 1332, the amount in controversy being the value of the right involved. Hulsenbusch v. Davidson Rubber Co., 344 F.2d 730 (8th Cir. 1965); Pennsylvania R. R. Co. v. City of Girard, 210 F.2d 437 (6th Cir. 1954); John B. Kelly, Inc. v. Lehigh Nav. Coal Co., 151 F.2d 743 (3rd Cir. 1945); Wisconsin Electric Co. v. Dumore Co., 35 F.2d 555 (6th Cir. 1929). It appears to the Court that the right of each member of the class to live in an environment free from excessive coal dust and conversely, the right of defendant to operate its coal loading facility are both in excess of $10,000.00.

The second action is one for damages resulting from the action of defendant. This action has predominating factual questions in common with the injunctive action and requiring the same evidence as presented in that action. The damage action is properly maintainable as a class action under Rule 23(b) (3) of the Federal Rules of Civil Procedure, common questions of fact predominating. Although diversity of citizenship exists between the parties, the Court does not believe that any of the claims exceed $10,000.00. These claims cannot be aggregated to achieve the jurisdictional amount. Snyder v. Harris, 394 U.S. 332, 89 S.Ct. 1053, 22 L.Ed.2d 319 (March 25, 1969).

Jurisdiction properly lies in this Court under 28 U.S.C. § 1441(c). The claims are sufficiently separate to allow removal of the injunctive action alone. Therefore this Court, in the interest of judicial efficiency, will assume jurisdiction over the entire controversy. Climax Chemical Co. v. C. F. Braun & Co., 370 F.2d 616 (10th Cir. 1966); Moosbrugger v. McGraw-Edison Co., 215 F. Supp. 486 (D.Minn.1963).

Delineation of the class in the damage action through the establishment of geographical boundries was undertaken. Evidence taken at a hearing for a temporary restraining order before Senior District Judge Kloeb as to the extent and locations of the complaints together with a knowledge of the prevailing winds was employed in ascertaining the geographical boundries to be employed. Without such geographical delineation any person who felt that he had been aggrieved by defendant's operation of its coal dock, regardless of the geographical remoteness of his claim, would have had the right to gain redress in this Court. Through this limitation the Court is able to give attention to the vast body of claims for which a reasonably plausible geographical basis can be determined, avoid placing great strain on its docket with numerous actions with only nuisance value, and preserve to the truly aggrieved individual whose claim is geographically remote his right of action (since he, not being a member of the class, is not bound by the judgment).

BIECHELE v. NORFOLK & WESTERN RAILWAY CO.

In furtherance of the policy of the 1966 amendment to Rule 23 to prevent one way intervention and to prevent as much as possible the solicitation of claims as well as to provide the court and the parties with some idea of the real magnitude of the controversy, the Court entered an order requiring all those desiring to present damage claims to enter an appearance in the case on or before November 8, 1968. ● ● ●

No list of the potential members of the class in the damage suit was available nor could one have been compiled. Therefore the Court determined that the best possible service would be by publication of its orders delineating the class and requiring the presentation of claims together with the notice required by Rule 23(c) (2) of the Federal Rules of Civil Procedure. It was, however, determined that the publication in the Sandusky Register would not be a standard legal notice, but would be prominently placed so that the class members would better have the attention drawn to it. See, Booth v. General Dynamics Corp., 264 F.Supp. 465 (N.D.Ill.1965). As a result of this notice, seven hundred thirty-one (731) persons joined the damage action as plaintiffs, five hundred thirty-two (532) filed declinations to participate and several thousand others took no action.

Promptly thereafter, by agreement of the parties, the case was submitted to the Court upon evidence and written argument for a determination of the question of whether or not there was an actionable nuisance, and, if there was, whether plaintiffs were entitled to an injunction, to damages, or to both. The agreement provides that if the Court finds there is an actionable nuisance entitling plaintiffs to damages, a special master will be appointed to hear the evidence as to the amount of damages suffered by each of the seven hundred thirty-one individual parties plaintiff.

Several days were required to present the evidence, and very extensive briefs were filed by the parties, as a result of which the Court has come to the findings of fact and conclusions of law that are expressed in this opinion. ● ● ●

Defendant determined to modernize the facilities to use them for the loading and storage of industrial coals, which are much smaller in size than heating coals, and include large quantities of "fines", which are actually coal dust.

● ● ●

These operations commenced in earnest about in September of 1967. As the time passed, and the amount of coal in storage on the defendant's pier increased, the citizens of Sandusky, particularly those near the pier, began to be troubled by black dust accumulating on their houses and furniture. By March of 1968, the situation was causing a great deal of difficulty, which continued through the summer into the early fall. It was obvious to the casual observer that coal dust was blowing off defendant's storage piles, and the black dust observed by the irate citizenry was assumed to be coal dust. The evidence in the case leaves no doubt whatever of the correctness of this assumption. ● ● ●

At the trial of the case, the overwhelming weight of the evidence showed that persons who lived in various parts of Sandusky, and had had no more problem with dust and dirt than is common in cities, started to have serious problems when the defendant began to stockpile coal. Black, greasy, dirt, which was difficult to wash or clean off, accumulated on their sidewalks, porches, outdoor furniture, and automobiles. ● ● ●

The factual conclusion is inescapable that the plaintiffs were injured in various respects, and to various extents, in their real estate, their personal property and effects, and in their persons by large quantities of coal dust blown from the shipping and storage facilities of the defendant.

As is frequently the case when the factual situation is clear and simple, the legal issues are of some complexity, and the defendant has used great technical skill in taking advantage of the tendency of the courts to use loose, ambiguous, and confusing language in discussing legal problems in this area. The problems arise because there is no sharp line of demarcation between the fields of negli-

BIECHELE v. NORFOLK & WESTERN RAILWAY CO.

gence and nuisance, and in cases in the borderline area, the courts will use expressions relating to both fields interchangeably and imprecisely.

It is not this Court's intention to write a learned treatise on the law of nuisance. The facts of the present case bring it squarely within the following statement of the law of nuisance:

"Strict or absolute liability is always applied where one does anything, or permits anything under his control or direction, to be done, without just cause or excuse, the necessary consequence of which interferes with or annoys another in the enjoyment of his legal rights. In such case the actor commits an intentional act involving a culpable wrong. Where the harm and resulting damage are the necessary consequences of just what the defendant is doing, or is incident to the activity itself or the manner in which it is conducted, the law of negligence has no application and the rule of absolute liability applies." Taylor v. Cincinnati, 143 Ohio St. 426, 432, 433, 55 N.E. 2d 724, 727, 155 A.L.R. 44 (1944).

The *Taylor* case, of course, bears not the remotest resemblance to the present case upon its facts, but it contains an elaborate treatise upon the law of nuisance generally which, while it might arguably be dictum, is generally followed as summarizing and expressing the law of Ohio upon the subject, and hence is binding upon this Court in this case.

The defendant makes much point in argument that it is and has been doing everything possible to prevent the difficulty, and was not negligent in its operation of coal storage and loading, and hence is not liable to the plaintiffs. Assuming this to be true, which plaintiffs strenuously deny, this argument may be answered by reference to an old case, citation unknown, dealing with the action of a man whose house was being shaken to pieces by blasting in a neighbor's quarry. The court held that it was no comfort to the plaintiff to know that his house was being demolished by the defendant in the most careful manner possible.

We are, happily, departing from the era in which it was considered proper for any commercial enterprise, in the name of those profits which are not a dirty word in Ohio, to pollute the atmosphere, earth, and water beyond the endurance of the general public. The defendant may or may not have succeeded to some of Commodore Vanderbilt's enterprises, but his attitude is an impermissible anachronism, and ill becomes defendant.

It is possible that this Court has the burden of deciding whether the plaintiffs must continue to suffer in defendant's filth, or become citizens of a ghost town on an abandoned railway line and a silted-up harbor. If so, the latter seems the lesser of two evils, especially in view of the maxim "Sufficient unto the day is the evil thereof." The present difficulty is certain, but the future disasters are uncertain. It may well be that the citizens of Sandusky can jump out of the frying pan and still avoid falling into the fire.

Plaintiffs are entitled to judgment in this case, but the form that the judgment should take presents serious questions. Certainly each of the individual plaintiffs is entitled to a judgment for the damages that he can show he has suffered as a result of defendant's activities. Necessarily, this means that if the amounts of damages to each of the seven hundred thirty-one plaintiffs cannot be stipulated, the evidence will have to be heard in order to establish them.

The only practical means of working out the damage matters appears to be to refer the matter to a special master, who should be a resident of the Sandusky area. The special master should fix a deadline to file a written statement of claim, either personally or by counsel, before the deadline. All counsel should consult with the special master to work out the forms and procedures for filing and processing the damage claims, with the objective of reducing to a minimum the number of claims which will have to be heard upon the evidence. With respect to claims which cannot be stipulated as to amount, those claimants whose recovery does not exceed the sum of one hundred dollars shall have to pay the fees of the special master for conducting the hearing upon their claims, together with the other costs of the hearing.

*   *   *

The question of whether the award of damages up to the time of commencement of the action, with the right to bring successive actions if the nuisance continues, affords an adequate remedy at law, is not a simple one. The weight of authority appears to be that since the nuisance is a continuing one, actions at law for damages are not an adequate remedy since a multiplicity of damage suits for each individual plaintiff would result. Hence equitable relief by way of injunction is permissible. However, just as the defendant has no right to destroy the property of the plaintiffs by its operations, it is questionable whether plaintiffs have a right to relief which would destroy the legitimate activities of defendant.

Under the principles of equity, the Court has broad powers to fashion effective relief, even though it may have to retain a continuing jurisdiction to modify or change orders granted.

A mandatory order of injunction must issue, requiring defendant to continue the various methods of dust control it has been employing on the coal docks, until further order of the Court.

*   *   *

From the evidence, it appears to the Court that it should be possible to work out economically feasible methods of controlling the emission of coal dust without inhibiting the operations of defendant's facilities, and even permitting defendant to expand the operations should it desire to do so.

Counsel should, within ten days, endeavor to agree upon an order, or should submit to the Court their separate forms of order, if they cannot agree, which will embody the foregoing conclusions, and vest in this Court a continuing jurisdiction until the coal dust problems are resolved.

. . . .

For additional information on class actions see:

1. Note, "Rule 23 Class Action Enforcement of the Clean Air Act of 1970," 7 U. Rich. L. R. 549 (1973).

2. Lamm & Davison, "Environmental Class Actions for Damages," 16 Rocky M. Min. Law. Inst. 59 (1971).

LEGAL   LEGAL   LEGAL   LEGAL

LEGAL NOTICE

TO ALL PERSONS CLAIMING TO BE AFFECTED BY COAL DUST FROM THE LOWER LAKE DOCKS OF THE NORFOLK & WESTERN RAILWAY COMPANY

IN THE UNITED STATES DISTRICT COURT FOR THE NORTHERN DISTRICT OF OHIO WESTERN DIVISION

Dallas Biechele, et al.,
Plaintiffs,

vs.

Norfolk & Western Railway Company,
Defendant.

No. C 68-139

TO ALL PERSONS LIVING OR OWNING REAL ESTATE WITHIN THE AREA OUTLINED ON THE MAP BELOW, AND THE BOUNDARIES SET FORTH IN THE BODY OF THIS NOTICE:

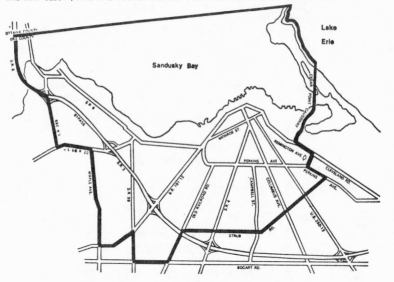

You are hereby notified that the District Court of the United States for the Northern District of Ohio, Western Division, has ordered that this action proceed as a class action, wherein all persons living or owning property within the following described boundaries are members of the class:

Commencing on the shore of Lake Erie at the northernmost point of Cedar Point; thence southeasterly along the shore of Lake Erie to the beginning of the Cedar Point Causeway; thence southerly along the center of the Cedar Point Causeway and Causeway Drive to the center of Cleveland Road; thence easterly along the center of Cleveland Road to Remington Avenue; thence southerly along the center of Remington Avenue to Perkins Avenue; thence easterly along the center of Perkins Avenue to Strub Road; thence southwesterly and westerly along the center of Strub Road to Old Railroad Road; thence southwesterly along the center of Old Railroad Road to Bogart Road; thence westerly along the center of Bogart road to State Route 99; thence northerly along the center of State Route 99 to State Routes 12 and 101; thence westerly along the center of State Routes 12 and 101 to Maple Avenue; thence northerly along the center of

BIECHELE v. NORFOLK & WESTERN RAILWAY CO.

Maple Avenue to U.S. Route 6 and State Route 22; thence westerly along the center of U.S. Route 6 and State Route 22 to State Route 269; thence northerly along the center of State Route 269 to State Route 2; thence northerly along the center line of State Route 2 to its point of intersection with the Erie-Ottawa County Line; thence easterly across Sandusky Bay to the place of beginning.

IF YOU LIVE OR OWN REAL ESTATE WITHIN THOSE BOUNDARIES, you are a member of the class, and unless you make a written request to be excluded. YOU WILL BE INCLUDED IN AND BOUND BY THE JUDGMENT RENDERED BY THE COURT, whether it is favorable or unfavorable to you.

IF YOU WANT TO BE EXCLUDED from membership in the class, you must complete and sign the form headed REQUEST FOR EXCLUSION at the bottom of this notice or write a letter requesting exclusion, and mail it to the Clerk of the United States District Court, 1716 Spielbusch Avenue, Toledo, Ohio, 43624, or have your lawyer do this for you.

IF YOU DO NOT WANT TO BE EXCLUDED, but want to have your own lawyer represent you, you should instruct him to enter your appearance.

This action involves two matters, a claim for an order of injunction restraining the defendant Norfolk & Western Railway Company from continuing the activities alleged to cause coal dust to be blown about, and claims for damages to person and property alleged to have been caused by coal dust.

As to the claim for injunction, all persons living or owning real estate within the boundaries described above will be bound by the judgment in this action whether it is favorable or unfavorable, unless they request exclusion. They need take no action of any kind to be assured of the protection of an order of injunction if one is ultimately issued.

As to claims for damages to person or property, regardless of the outcome of this lawsuit, all such claims will be barred unless the person asserting such claim enters his appearance in this action on or before November 8, 1968.

IF YOU WANT TO MAKE A CLAIM FOR DAMAGES, you may preserve your right to do so by completing the form headed ENTRY OF APPEARANCE at the bottom of this notice, or by writing a letter saying that you enter your appearance in this lawsuit, and mailing the notice or letter to the Clerk of the United States District Court, 1716 Spielbusch Avenue, Toledo, Ohio, 43624, or by having your lawyer do this for you.

ALL REQUESTS FOR EXCLUSION OR ENTRIES OF APPEARANCE MUST BE FILED WITH THE CLERK OR POSTMARKED NO LATER THAN MIDNIGHT ON FRIDAY, NOVEMBER 8, 1968, OR THEY WILL BE INEFFECTUAL.

This action is presently at issue, and may be called for hearing by the Court at any time after November 8, 1968.

THE COURT'S ORDER THAT THIS ACTION SHALL PROCEED AS A CLASS ACTION IS NOT A DETERMINATION OF THE MERITS OF THE CLAIMS ASSERTED, AND IS ONLY A PRELIMINARY PROCEDURAL DETERMINATION AS TO THE POTENTIAL PARTIES INVOLVED. THE DECISION AS TO WHETHER ANY INJUNCTIVE RELIEF WILL BE GRANTED OR ANY DAMAGES AWARDED WILL FOLLOW A TRIAL ON THE MERITS OF THE ACTION.

DON J. YOUNG
United States District Judge

REQUEST FOR EXCLUSION

Dallas Biechele, et al.,
    Plaintiffs,

    v.

Norfolk & Western Railway Company,
    Defendant.

No. C 68-139

The undersigned requests to be excluded from the class of parties plaintiff to the above captioned action.

Name ....

Address ....

....

ENTRY OF APPEARANCE

Dallas Biechele, et al.,
    Plaintiffs,

    v.

Norfolk & Western Railway Company,
    Defendant.

No. C 68-139

I hereby enter my appearance as a member of the class of parties plaintiff to the above action.

Name ....

Address ....

....

3. Intervention

RULE 24, FEDERAL RULES OF CIVIL PROCEDURE

Rule 24. Intervention

(a) Intervention of Right. Upon timely application anyone shall be permitted to intervene in an action: (1) when a statute of the United States confers an unconditional right to intervene; or (2) when the applicant claims an interest relating to the property or transaction which is the subject of the action and he is so situated that the disposition of the action may as a practical matter impair or impede his ability to protect that interest, unless the applicant's interest is adequately represented by existing parties.

(b) Permissive Intervention. Upon timely application anyone may be permitted to intervene in an action: (1) when a statute of the United States confers a conditional right to intervene; or (2) when an applicant's claim or defense and the main action have a question of law or fact in common. When a party to an action relies for ground of claim or defense upon any statute or executive order administered by a federal or state governmental officer or agency or upon any regulation, order, requirement, or agreement issued or made pursuant to the statute or executive order, the officer or agency upon timely application may be permitted to intervene in the action. In exercising its discretion the court shall consider whether the intervention will unduly delay or prejudice the adjudication of the rights of the original parties.

(c) Procedure. A person desiring to intervene shall serve a motion to intervene upon the parties as provided in Rule 5. The motion shall state the grounds therefor and shall be accompanied by a pleading setting forth the claim or defense for which intervention is sought. The same procedure shall be followed when a statute of the United States gives a right to intervene. When the constitutionality of an act of Congress affecting the public interest is drawn in question in any action to which the United States or an officer, agency, or employee thereof is not a party, the court shall notify the Attorney General of the United States as provided in Title 28, U.S.C., § 2403.

LADUE v. GOODHEAD, 44 N.Y.S. 2d 783, 181 Misc. 807
(Erie County Ct., 1943).

WARD, Judge

The law of this forum for the intervention of a third person into a pending action as a party is set forth in Section 193 of the Civil Practice Act, which provides, in part:

"1. The court may determine the controversy as between the parties before it where it can do so without prejudice to the rights of others or by saving their rights; but where a complete determination of the controversy cannot be had without the presence of other parties the court must direct them to be brought in."

"3. Where a person not a party to the action has an interest in the subject thereof, * * * and makes application to the court to be made a party, it must direct him to be brought in by the proper amendment."

Generally, it is the duty of the court to direct that necessary parties be brought in, and to refuse the determination of the controversy affecting their rights, until they are all made parties to the action. Mahr v. Nowich Union Fire Ins. Soc., 127 N.Y. 452, 459, 28 N.E. 391. The purpose of Section 193, Civil Practice Act, is to avoid circuity and multiplicity of suits and to encourage and authorize the determination of damage and liability in one suit, in the sound, judicial discretion of the court. Mirsky v. Seaich Realty Co., 256 App.Div. 658. 11 N.Y.S.2d 191, 194; Lepel High Frequency Laboratories, Inc., v. Capita, 168 Misc. 583, 6 N.Y.S.2d 171, 172, affirmed 256 App.Div. 804, 9 N.Y.S.2d 896. The words "the interest in the subject" of the action mean a direct interest in the cause of action pleaded, which would allow the intervener to litigate a material fact in the complaint. Bulova v. E. L. Barnett, Inc., 194 App.Div. 418, 185 N.Y.S. 424, 426. "This interest must be individual and not public, direct and not indirect, present and not remote. Interest in the result or outcome of the action will not suffice." Town of Irondequoit v. Monroe County, 171 Misc. 125, 11 N.Y.S.2d 933, 939, and see cited cases. Where the plaintiff seeks a money judgment merely, he cannot be compelled under this Section 193 to bring a third person into the action as a party upon the stranger's application. Brooklyn Cooperage Co. v. A. Sherman Lumber Co., 220 N.Y. 642, 643, 115 N.E. 715. In order to bring in a new party, the application must be based upon a moving affidavit or affidavits containing sufficient probative facts. George A. Moore & Co. v. Heymann, 207 App.Div. 416, 202 N.Y.S. 99, 101. ● ● ●

"An intervener is a person who voluntarily interposes in an action or other proceeding with the leave of the court." (Black's Dictionary) Intervention in practice may be defined as: "A proceeding in a suit or action by which a third person is permitted by the court to make himself a party, either joining the plaintiff in claiming what is sought by the complaint, or uniting with the defendant in resisting the claims of the plaintiff, or demanding something adversely to both of them." Black's Dictionary. ● ● ●

4. The Government As Plaintiff

(a) Action by Federal Government

U.S. v. BISHOP PROCESSING COMPANY, 287 F. Supp. 624 (D. Md. 1968).

THOMSEN, Chief Judge.

This action has been brought by the United States under the Clean Air Act (the Act), 42 U.S.C. § 1857 et seq., particularly section 108(g) (1) of the Act, as amended November 21, 1967, 81 Stat. 496, 507, now codified as 42 U.S.C. § 1857d(g) (1).[1] The government seeks to enjoin Bishop Processing Company (the defendant), the operator of a rendering and animal reduction plant near Bishop, Worcester County, Maryland, from discharging malodorous air pollutants, which it is alleged, move across the state line and pollute the air in and around Selbyville, Delaware. Defendant has filed a motion to dismiss the complaint on four grounds, namely: ● ●●
(III) that the requisite administrative steps have not been adequately defined or properly concluded as required by law; and (IV) that remedial action concerning defendant's alleged pollution was and is currently pending in a state court in Maryland, and that this Court cannot take jurisdiction under the Act while such an action is pending.

● ● ●

The administrative proceeding which led to this suit was initiated by a request from the Delaware State Air Pollution Authority under section 1857d(d) (1) (A).[3] In response to that request the Secretary called a conference, which was held in Selbyville, Delaware, on November 9 and 10, 1965. The statute [4] specified the parties who should be invited to participate in such a conference, namely, representatives of the air pollution control agencies of the states and municipalities concerned, and provided that the agencies called to attend such conference might bring such persons as they desired

to the conference. Bishop was not invited to the conference and did not request an opportunity to participate.

Pursuant to section 1857d(e) [5] the Secretary forwarded to the participants a summary of the conference discussions and recommendations for remedial action. Those recommendations called upon the Maryland authorities to require Bishop to complete certain remedial action on or before September 1, 1966. The recommended remedial action was not taken.

Under section 1857d(f) (1)[6] the Secretary is authorized to call a public hearing if "at the conclusion of the period so allowed, such remedial action or other action which in the judgment of the Secretary is reasonably calculated to secure abatement of such pollution has not been taken".

Appropriate findings to that effect were included in a Notice of Public Hearing Concerning Interstate Air Pollution in the Selbyville, Delaware-Bishop, Maryland area, which the Secretary issued on April 21, 1967. ● ● ●

The composition of the Board and the hearing procedures were in accordance with Part 81 of Title 42, C.F.R., set out in the Notice of Proposed Rule Making, dated March 28, 1967, published in the Federal Register on April 3, 1967.

The Hearing Board met on May 17 and May 18, 1967, heard testimony and received other evidence. Bishop was represented by counsel, who made and raised 38 objections to evidence and other points, challenging inter alia the authority and composition of the Hearing Board.

The Hearing Board made findings and recommendations and forwarded them to the Secretary, as required by section 1857d(f) (2).[7] Such a Board is not authorized to issue any order, but its recommendations are not subject to review or modification by the Secretary, who is required by law to forward the findings and recommendations of the Board to the polluter, together with a notice specifying a reasonable time (not less than six months) to secure abatement of the pollution. See section 1857d(f) (3).[8] Accordingly, on May 25, 1967, the Secretary sent the following notice to Bishop:

"THE SECRETARY OF HEALTH, EDUCATION, AND WELFARE WASHINGTON

In the Matter of

INTERSTATE AIR POLLUTION IN SELBYVILLE, DELAWARE-BISHOP, MARYLAND, AREA

NOTICE

"There are attached hereto, and made a part hereof, the Findings, Conclusions, and Recommendations, dated May 19, 1967, of the Hearing Board convened pursuant to the provisions of section 105(e) (1) of the Clean Air Act [42 U.S.C. 1857d(e) (1)] which held a public hearing in the matter of the interstate air pollution in the Selbyville, Delaware-Bishop, Maryland area.

"In accordance with section 105(e) (3) of the Clean Air Act [42 U.S.C. 1857d(e) (3)] the Bishop Processing Company, Bishop, Maryland is hereby notified and directed to cease and desist from discharging malodorous air pollutants and to abate such air pollution not later than December 1, 1967, by the installation, completion and placing into operation adequate and effective control systems and devices, as recommended by the Hearing Board.

"Dated: May 25, 1967.

(S) John W. Gardner
Secretary"

The Secretary is not authorized to impose any sanctions for failure to comply with such a "notice" and what is "directed" therein. What the Secretary may do is set out in section 1857d(g) (1),[9] which provides in pertinent part:

"If action reasonably calculated to secure abatement of the pollution within the time specified in the notice following the public hearing is not taken, the Secretary—

"(1) in the case of pollution of air which is endangering the health or welfare of persons (A) in a State other than that in which the discharge or discharges (causing or contributing to such pollution) originate, * * * may request the Attorney General to bring a suit on behalf of the United States in the appropriate United States district court to secure abatement of the pollution."

Section 1857d(h) [10] provides:

"The court shall receive in evidence in any suit brought in a United States court under subsection (g) of this section a transcript of the proceedings before the board and a copy of the board's recommendations and shall receive such further evidence as the court in its discretion deems proper. The court, giving due consideration to the practicability of complying with such standards as may be applicable and to the physical and economic feasibility of securing abatement of any pollution proved, shall have jurisdiction to enter such judgment, and orders enforcing such judgment, as the public interest and the equities of the case may require." ● ● ●

To support its contention that the requisite administrative steps have not been adequately defined nor properly concluded as required by law, defendant argues several points, which will be considered below. Preliminarily, however, the nature of the administrative proceedings and of the present suit should be reviewed. The history of those proceedings has been outlined above.

UNITED STATES v. BISHOP PROCESSING COMPANY

The *conference*, which was held in 1965, was a conference between representatives of public agencies to consider the problem. Due process did not require that the alleged polluter be invited to that conference, which was neither a rule-making nor an adjudicative hearing. The 1967 amendments do require that in the future, thirty days notice of such a conference be given by publication, and that "interested parties" be given an opportunity to present their views. Section 1857d(d) (2). The Report of the House Committee [13] indicates that the purpose of this amendment was to provide the conferees with the broadest review of the pollution problems in a given area. The amendment was not required by due process or by any provisions of the APA.

The *hearing* in May 1967, some eighteen months after the conference, was held in strict accordance with the provisions of the Act. Section 1857d(f) provides, with minor amendments made in November 1967:

"(1) If, at the conclusion of the period so allowed, such remedial action or other action which in the judgment of the Secretary is reasonably calculated to secure abatement of such pollution has not been taken, the Secretary shall call a public hearing, to be held in or near one or more of the places where the discharge or discharges causing or contributing to such pollution originated, before a hearing board of five or more persons appointed by the Secretary. Each State in which any discharge causing or contributing to such pollution originates and each State claiming to be adversely affected by such pollution shall be given an opportunity to select one member of such hearing board and each Federal department, agency, or instrumentality having a substantial interest in the subject matter as determined by the Secretary shall be given an opportunity to select one member of such hearing board, and one member shall be a representative of the appropriate interstate air pollution agency if one exists, and not less than a majority of such hearing board shall

be persons other than officers or employees of the Department of Health, Education, and Welfare. At least three weeks' prior notice of such hearing shall be given to the State, interstate, and municipal air pollution control agencies called to attend such hearing and to the alleged polluter or polluters. All interested parties shall be given a reasonable opportunity to present evidence to such hearing board.

"(2) On the basis of evidence presented at such hearing, the hearing board shall make findings as to whether pollution referred to in subsection (a) of this section is occurring and whether effective progress toward abatement thereof is being made. If the hearing board finds such pollution is occurring and effective progress toward abatement thereof is not being made it shall make recommendations to the Secretary concerning the measures, if any, which it finds to be reasonable and suitable to secure abatement of such pollution.

"(3) The Secretary shall send such findings and recommendations to the person or persons discharging any matter causing or contributing to such pollution; to air pollution control agencies of the State or States and of the municipality or municipalities where such discharge or discharges originate; and to any interstate air pollution control agency whose jurisdictional area includes any such municipality, together with a notice specifying a reasonable time (not less than six months) to secure abatement of such pollution."

The Secretary was not authorized before the 1967 amendments and is not now authorized to impose any sanctions for failure to comply with such a "notice" and what is "directed" therein. What the Secretary *may* do is set out in section 1857d(g), quoted in the first part of this opinion, namely, ask the Attorney General to bring such an action as the present suit.

UNITED STATES v. BISHOP PROCESSING COMPANY

The *hearing*, therefore, is not an adjudicative hearing. It is not subject to the provisions of the APA dealing with adjudicative hearings, 5 U.S.C.A. § 555. The conference and the hearing were merely the statutory prerequisites to the bringing of the lawsuit. ● ● ●

(a) Defendant complains because no procedural rules for hearings called for by section 1857d(f) (1)[15] were adopted by the Secretary before the hearing in defendant's case.[16] Defendant's case was the first case which had ever proceeded to hearing under the Act, and this suit is the first suit ever filed by the government under the Act. ● ● ●

Since that was the first hearing to be held under the Act, and since the procedures established for that hearing were appropriate therefor, the Court finds no violation of due process by reason of the fact that similar procedures for future hearings had not been adopted. The equal protection argument made by defendant is not supported by the present record, since it does not appear that any other hearings have ever been held, or that any different hearing procedures have ever been adopted.

(b) Defendant argues that the issuance of air quality criteria and control and emission standards are a prerequisite to an administrative hearing under section 1857d(f) (1)[17] and such an action as this under section 1857d(g).[18] There is no merit in this contention. Courts of equity have always had the power to abate nuisances. Section 1857d gives the district courts jurisdiction to abate "pollution of the air in any State or States which endangers the health and welfare of any persons", subject to other provisions in the Act which limit the

● ● ●

jurisdiction of the federal courts under section 1857d(g) (1) to cases which properly come within the commerce power.

● ● ● Under section 1857d(c) (4), the Secretary may now, when an air quality standard is violated, request that suit be instituted without invoking the conference-hearing procedure. Separate provisions are made in that subsection for judicial action in such a case.

● ● ●

Defendant's final challenge to the complaint is that this Court cannot take jurisdiction under the Act because of a suit pending in the Circuit Court for Worcester County, Maryland, filed against defendant on February 2, 1967, by the State of Maryland on the relation of the Maryland State Board of Health and Mental Hygiene, the Maryland State Department of Health, and the Maryland Department of Water Resources, raising similar issues, inter alia. It is true that the philosophy of the Act is not to displace but to encourage state, local and interstate action to abate air pollution. But a pending suit in a state court does not oust the jurisdiction of a district court over such a suit as this. The action in this Court arises out of proceedings instituted under the federal Act a year and a half before the filing of the state court suit, which has not proceeded to judgment. Moreover, it appears that the state court suit is addressed primarily to defendant's water pollution. Comity does not require this Court to abstain from proceeding with the present action instituted by the United States.

Defendant's motion to dismiss must be and it is hereby denied.

(b) Action by Municipal Government

HURON CEMENT COMPANY v. DETROIT, 362 U.S. 440 (1960).

Mr. Justice Stewart delivered the opinion of the Court.

This appeal from a judgment of the Supreme Court of Michigan draws in question the constitutional validity of certain provisions of Detroit's Smoke Abatement Code as applied to ships owned by the appellant and operated in interstate commerce.

The appellant is a Michigan corporation, engaged in the manufacture and sale of cement. It maintains a fleet of five vessels which it uses to transport cement from its mill in Alpena, Michigan, to distributing plants located in various states bordering the Great Lakes. Two of the ships, the S. S. *Crapo* and the S. S. *Boardman,* are equipped with hand-fired Scotch marine boilers. While these vessels are docked for loading and unloading it is necessary, in order to operate deck machinery, to keep the boilers fired and to clean the fires periodically. When the fires are cleaned, the ship's boiler stacks emit smoke which in density and duration exceeds the maximum standards allowable under the Detroit Smoke Abatement Code. Structural alterations would be required in order to insure compliance with the Code.

Criminal proceedings were instituted in the Detroit Recorder's Court against the appellant and its agents for violations of the city law during periods when the vessels were docked at the Port of Detroit. The appellant brought an action in the State Circuit Court to enjoin the city from further prosecuting the pending litigation in the Recorder's Court, and from otherwise enforcing the smoke ordinance against its vessels, "except where the emission of smoke is caused by the improper firing or the improper use of the equipment upon said vessels." The Circuit Court refused to grant relief, and the Supreme Court of Michigan affirmed, 355 Mich. 227, 93 N. W. 2d 888. An appeal was lodged here, and we noted probable jurisdiction, 361 U. S. 806.

In support of the claim that the ordinance cannot constitutionally be applied to appellant's ships, two basic arguments are advanced. First, it is asserted that since

the vessels and their equipment, including their boilers, **have** been inspected, approved and licensed to operate in **interstate** commerce in accordance with a comprehensive **system** of regulation enacted by Congress, the City of Detroit may not legislate in such a way as, in effect, to impose additional or inconsistent standards. Secondly, the argument is made that even if Congress has not expressly pre-empted the field, the municipal ordinance "materially affects interstate commerce in matters where uniformity is necessary." We have concluded that neither of these contentions can prevail, and that the Federal Constitution does not prohibit application to the appellant's vessels of the criminal provisions of the Detroit ordinance.[1]

The ordinance was enacted for the manifest purpose of promoting the health and welfare of the city's inhabitants. Legislation designed to free from pollution the very air that people breathe clearly falls within the exercise of even the most traditional concept of what is compendiously known as the police power. In the exercise of that power, the states and their instrumentalities may act, in many areas of interstate commerce and maritime activities, concurrently with the federal government.

● ● ●

The basic limitations upon local legislative power in this area are clear enough. The controlling principles have been reiterated over the years in a host of this Court's decisions. Evenhanded local regulation to effectuate a legitimate local public interest is valid unless preempted by federal action, *Erie R. Co.* v. *New York*, 233 U. S. 671; *Oregon-Washington Co.* v. *Washington*, 270 U. S. 87; *Napier* v. *Atlantic Coast Line*, 272 U. S. 605; *Missouri Pacific Co.* v. *Porter*, 273 U. S. 341; *Service Transfer Co.* v. *Virginia*, 359 U. S. 171, or unduly burdensome on maritime activities or interstate commerce. *Minnesota* v. *Barber*, 136 U. S. 313; *Morgan* v. *Virginia*, 328 U. S. 373; *Bibb* v. *Navajo Freight Lines*, 359 U. S. 520.

In determining whether state regulation has been pre-empted by federal action, "the intent to supersede the exercise by the State of its police power as to matters not covered by the Federal legislation is not to be inferred from the mere fact that Congress has seen fit to circumscribe its regulation and to occupy a limited field. In other words, such intent is not to be implied unless the act of Congress fairly interpreted is in actual conflict with the law of the State." ● ● ●

HURON CEMENT CO. v. DETROIT

In determining whether the state has imposed an undue burden on interstate commerce, it must be borne in mind that the Constitution when "conferring upon Congress the regulation of commerce, . . . never intended to cut the States off from legislating on all subjects relating to the health, life, and safety of their citizens. though the legislation might indirectly affect the commerce of the country. Legislation, in a great variety of ways, may affect commerce and persons engaged in it without constituting a regulation of it, within the meaning of the Constitution." *Sherlock* v. *Alling*, 93 U. S. 99, 103; *Austin* v. *Tennessee*, 179 U. S. 343; *Louisville & Nashville R. Co.* v. *Kentucky*, 183 U. S. 503; *The Minnesota Rate Cases*, 230 U. S. 352; *Boston & Maine R. Co.* v. *Armburg*, 285 U. S. 234; *Collins* v. *American Buslines, Inc.*, 350 U. S. 528. But a state may not impose a burden which materially affects interstate commerce in an area where uniformity of regulation is necessary. ● ● ●

As is apparent on the face of the legislation, however, the purpose of the federal inspection statutes is to insure the seagoing safety of vessels subject to inspection. Thus 46 U. S. C. § 392 (c) makes clear that inspection of boilers and related equipment is for the purpose of seeing to it that the equipment "may be safely employed in the service proposed." The safety of passengers. 46 U. S. C. § 391 (a), and of the crew, 46 U. S. C. § 391 (b), is the criterion. The thrust of the federal inspection laws is clearly limited to affording protection from the perils of maritime navigation. Cf. *Ace Waterways* v. *Fleming*, 98 F. Supp. 666. See also *Steamship Co.* v. *Joliffe*, 2 Wall. 450.

By contrast, the sole aim of the Detroit ordinance is the elimination of air pollution to protect the health and enhance the cleanliness of the local community. Congress recently recognized the importance and legitimacy of such a purpose, when in 1955 it provided:

> "[I]n recognition of the dangers to the public health and welfare, injury to agricultural crops and livestock, damage to and deterioration of property, and hazards to air and ground transportation. from air pollution, it is hereby declared to be the policy of Congress to preserve and protect the primary responsibilities and rights of the States and local governments in controlling air pollution, ● ● ●

Congressional recognition that the problem of air pollution is peculiarly a matter of state and local concern is manifest in this legislation. Such recognition is underlined in the Senate Committee Report:

> "The committee recognizes that it is the primary responsibility of State and local governments to prevent air pollution. The bill does not propose any exercise of police power by the Federal Government and no provision in it invades the sovereignty of States, counties or cities." S. Rep. No. 389, 84th Cong., 1st Sess. 3.

We conclude that there is no overlap between the scope of the federal ship inspection laws and that of the municipal ordinance here involved.[2] For this reason we cannot find that the federal inspection legislation has pre-empted local action. To hold otherwise would be to ignore the teaching of this Court's decisions which enjoin seeking out conflicts between state and federal regulation where none clearly exists. *Savage* v. *Jones,* 225 U. S. 501; *Welch Co.* v. *New Hampshire,* 306 U. S. 79; *Maurer* v. *Hamilton,* 309 U. S. 598.

An additional argument is advanced, however, based not upon the mere existence of the federal inspection standards, but upon the fact that the appellant's vessels were actually licensed, 46 U. S. C. § 263, and enrolled, 46 U. S. C. §§ 259–260, by the national government. It is asserted that the vessels have thus been given a dominant federal right to the use of the navigable waters of the United States, free from the local impediment that would be imposed by the Detroit ordinance.

The scope of the privilege granted by the federal licensing scheme has been well delineated. A state may not exclude from its waters a ship operating under a federal license. *Gibbons* v. *Ogden,* 9 Wheat. 1. A state may not require a local occupation license, in addition to that federally granted, as a condition precedent to the use of its waters. ● ●●

The mere possession of a federal license, however, does not immunize a ship from the operation of the normal incidents of local police power, not constituting a direct regulation of commerce. Thus, a federally licensed vessel is not, as such, exempt from local pilotage laws, ●●●

HURON CEMENT CO. v. DETROIT

Indeed this Court has gone so far as to hold that a state, in the exercise of its police power, may actually seize and pronounce the forfeiture of a vessel "licensed for the coasting trade, under the laws of the United States, while engaged in that trade." *Smith* v. *Maryland,* 18 How. 71, 74. The present case obviously does not even approach such an extreme, for the Detroit ordinance requires no more than compliance with an orderly and reasonable scheme of community regulation. The ordinance does not exclude a licensed vessel from the Port of Detroit, nor does it destroy the right of free passage. We cannot hold that the local regulation so burdens the federal license as to be constitutionally invalid. ● ● ●

The claim that the Detroit ordinance, quite apart from the effect of federal legislation, imposes as to the appellant's ships an undue burden on interstate commerce needs no extended discussion. State regulation, based on the police power, which does not discriminate against interstate commerce or operate to disrupt its required uniformity, may constitutionally stand. ● ● ●

It is a regulation of general application, designed to better the health and welfare of the community. And while the appellant argues that other local governments might impose differing requirements as to air pollution, it has pointed to none. The record contains nothing to suggest the existence of any such competing or conflicting local regulations. Cf. *Bibb* v. *Navajo Freight Lines,* 359 U. S. 520. We conclude that no impermissible burden on commerce has been shown.

The judgment is affirmed.

MR. JUSTICE DOUGLAS, with whom MR. JUSTICE FRANK-FURTER concurs, dissenting.

The Court treats this controversy as if it were merely an inspection case with the City of Detroit supplementing a federal inspection system as the State of Washington did in *Kelly* v. *Washington,* 302 U. S. 1. There a state inspection system touched matters "which the federal laws and regulations" left "untouched." *Id.,* at 13. This is not that type of case. Nor is this the rare case where state law adopts the standards and requirements of federal law and is allowed to exact a permit in addition to the one demanded by federal law. *California* v. *Zook*, 336 U. S. 725, 735. Here we have a criminal prosecution against a shipowner and officers of two of its vessels for using the very equipment on these vessels which the Federal Goverment says may be used. At stake are a possible fine of $100 on the owner and both a fine and a 30-day jail sentence on the officers. ● ●●

Appellant, operating the vessel in waters at the Detroit dock, is about to be fined criminally for using the precise equipment covered by the federal certificate because, it is said, the use of that equipment will violate a smoke ordinance of the City of Detroit. ● ● ●

The requirements of the Detroit smoke ordinance are squarely in conflict with the federal statute. ●●●

The fact that the Federal Government in certifying equipment applies standards of safety for seagoing vessels, while Detroit applies standards of air pollution seems immaterial. Federal pre-emption occurs when the boilers and fuel to be used in the vessels are specified in the certificate. No state authority can, in my view, change those specifications. Yet that is in effect what is allowed here. ● ● ●

by what authority can a local government fine people or send them to jail for using in interstate commerce the precise equipment which the federal regulatory agency has certified and approved?
● ●● The variety of requirements for equipment which the States may provide in order to meet their air pollution needs underlines the importance of letting the Coast Guard license serve as authority for the vessel to use, in all our ports, the equipment which it certifies.

C.   Who May Be Sued

1.   Doctrine of Sovereign Immunity

(a) Federal Government

FEDERAL TORT CLAIMS ACT, 60 Stat. 842 (1946).

TITLE IV—FEDERAL TORT CLAIMS ACT

ADMINISTRATIVE ADJUSTMENT OF TORT CLAIMS AGAINST THE
UNITED STATES

CLAIMS OF $1,000 OR LESS

SEC. 403. (a) Subject to the limitations of this title, authority is hereby conferred upon the head of each Federal agency, or his designee for the purpose, acting on behalf of the United States, to consider, ascertain, adjust, determine, and settle any claim against the United States for money only, accruing on and after January 1, 1945, on account of damage to or loss of property or on account of personal injury or death, where the total amount of the claim does not exceed $1,000, caused by the negligent or wrongful act or omission of any employee of the Government while acting within the scope of his office or employment, under circumstances where the United States, if a private person, would be liable to the claimant for such damage, loss, injury, or death, in accordance with the law of the place where the act or omission occurred.

(b) Subject to the provisions of part 3 of this title, any such award or determination shall be final and conclusive on all officers of the Government, except when procured by means of fraud, notwithstanding any other provision of law to the contrary.

(c) Any award made to any claimant pursuant to this section, and any award, compromise, or settlement of any claim cognizable under this title made by the Attorney General pursuant to section 413, shall be paid by the head of the Federal agency concerned out of appropriations that may be made therefor, which appropriations are hereby authorized.

(d) The acceptance by the claimant of any such award, compromise, or settlement shall be final and conclusive on the claimant, and shall constitute a complete release by the claimant of any claim against the United States and against the employee of the Government whose act or omission gave rise to the claim, by reason of the same subject matter.

● ● ●

PART 3—SUITS ON TORT CLAIMS AGAINST THE UNITED STATES

JURISDICTION

SEC. 410. (a) Subject to the provisions of this title, the United States district court for the district wherein the plaintiff is resident or wherein the act or omission complained of occurred, including the

FEDERAL TORT CLAIMS ACT

United States district courts for the Territories and possessions of the United States, sitting without a jury, shall have exclusive jurisdiction to hear, determine, and render judgment on any claim against the United States, for money only, accruing on and after January 1, 1945, on account of damage to or loss of property or on account of personal injury or death caused by the negligent or wrongful act or omission of any employee of the Government while acting within the scope of his office or employment, under circumstances where the United States, if a private person, would be liable to the claimant for such damage, loss, injury, or death in accordance with the law of the place where the act or omission occurred. Subject to the provisions of this title, the United States shall be liable in respect of such claims to the same claimants, in the same manner, and to the same extent as a private individual under like circumstances, except that the United States shall not be liable for interest prior to judgment, or for punitive damages. Costs shall be allowed in all courts to the successful claimant to the same extent as if the United States were a private litigant, except that such costs shall not include attorneys' fees.

(b) The judgment in such an action shall constitute a complete bar to any action by the claimant, by reason of the same subject matter, against the employee of the Government whose act or omission gave rise to the claim. No suit shall be instituted pursuant to this section upon a claim presented to any Federal agency pursuant to part 2 of this title unless such Federal agency has made final disposition of the claim: *Provided*, That the claimant may, upon fifteen days' notice given in writing, withdraw the claim from consideration of the Federal agency and commence suit thereon pursuant to this section: *Provided further*, That as to any claim so disposed of or so withdrawn, no suit shall be instituted pursuant to this section for any sum in excess of the amount of the claim presented to the Federal agency, except where the increased amount of the claim is shown to be based upon newly discovered evidence not reasonably discoverable at the time of presentation of the claim to the Federal agency or upon evidence of intervening facts, relating to the amount of the claim. Disposition of any claim made pursuant to part 2 of this title shall not be competent evidence of liability or amount of damages in proceedings on such claim pursuant to this section.

ADMINISTRATIVE PROCEDURE ACT, 5 U.S.C. 701-706.

● ● ●

§ 701. Application; definitions.

(a) This chapter applies, according to the provisions thereof, except to the extent that—

(1) statutes preclude judicial review; or

(2) agency action is committed to agency discretion by law.

(b) For the purpose of this chapter—

(1) "agency" means each authority of the Government of the United States, whether or not it is within or subject to review by another agency, but does not include—

(A) the Congress;

(B) the courts of the United States;

(C) the governments of the territories or possessions of the United States;

(D) the government of the District of Columbia;

(E) agencies composed of representatives of the parties or of representatives of organizations of the parties to the disputes determined by them;

(F) courts martial and military commissions;

(G) military authority exercised in the field in time of war or in occupied territory; or

(H) functions conferred by sections 1738, 1739, 1743, and 1744 of title 12; chapter 2 of title 41; or sections 1622, 1884, 1891–1902, and former section 1641(b)(2), of title 50, appendix; and

(2) "person", "rule", "order", "license", "sanction", "relief", and "agency action" have the meanings given them by section 551 of this title.

§ 702. Right of review.

A person suffering legal wrong because of agency action, or adversely affected or aggrieved by agency action within the meaning of a relevant statute, is entitled to judicial review thereof. (Pub. L. 89–554, Sept. 6, 1966, 80 Stat. 392.)

● ● ●

§ 703. Form and venue of proceeding.

The form of proceeding for judicial review is the special statutory review proceeding relevant to the subject matter in a court specified by statute or, in the absence or inadequacy thereof, any applicable form of legal action, including actions for declaratory judgments or writs of prohibitory or mandatory injunction or habeas corpus, in a court of competent jurisdiction. Except to the extent that prior, adequate, and exclusive opportunity for judicial review is provided by law, agency action is subject to judicial review in civil or criminal proceedings for judicial enforcement. (Pub. L. 89–554, Sept. 6, 1966, 80 Stat. 392.) ● ● ●

§ 704. Actions reviewable.

Agency action made reviewable by statute and final agency action for which there is no other adequate remedy in a court are subject to judicial review. A preliminary, procedural, or intermediate agency action or ruling not directly reviewable is subject to review on the review of the final agency action. Except as otherwise expressly required by statute, agency action otherwise final is final for the purposes of this section whether or not there has been presented or determined an application for a declaratory order, for any form of reconsiderations, or, unless the agency otherwise requires by rule and provides that the action meanwhile is inoperative, for an appeal to superior agency authority. (Pub. L. 89–554, Sept. 6, 1966, 80 Stat. 392.) ● ● ●

§ 705. Relief pending review.

When an agency finds that justice so requires, it may postpone the effective date of action taken by it, pending judicial review. On such conditions as may be required and to the extent necessary to prevent irreparable injury, the reviewing court, including the court to which a case may be taken on appeal from or on application for certiorari or other writ to a reviewing court, may issue all necessary and appropriate process to postpone the effective date of an agency action or to preserve status or rights pending conclusion of the review proceedings. (Pub. L. 89–554, Sept. 6, 1966, 80 Stat. 393.)

● ● ●

§ 706. Scope of review.

To the extent necessary to decision and when presented, the reviewing court shall decide all relevant questions of law, interpret constitutional and statutory provisions, and determine the meaning or applicability of the terms of an agency action. The reviewing court shall—

(1) compel agency action unlawfully withheld or unreasonably delayed; and

(2) hold unlawful and set aside agency action, findings, and conclusions found to be—

(A) arbitrary, capricious, an abuse of discretion, or otherwise not in accordance with law;

(B) contrary to constitutional right, power, privilege, or immunity;

(C) in excess of statutory jurisdiction, authority, or limitations, or short of statutory right;

(D) without observance of procedure required by law;

(E) unsupported by substantial evidence in a case subject to sections 556 and 557 of this title or otherwise reviewed on the record of an agency hearing provided by statute; or

(F) unwarranted by the facts to the extent that the facts are subject to trial de novo by the reviewing court.

In making the foregoing determinations, the court shall review the whole record or those parts of it cited by a party, and due account shall be taken of the rule of prejudicial error. (Pub. L. 89–554, Sept. 6, 1966, 80 Stat. 393.)

. . . .

LITTEL v. MORTON, 445 F. 2d 1207 (1971).

WINTER, Circuit Judge:

This case involves close questions of application of the doctrine of sovereign immunity and permissible judicial review under the Administrative Procedure Act, 5 U.S.C.A. §§ 701, et seq. They are raised by litigation instituted by Norman M. Littell, Esq., a member of the bar, who was formerly counsel for the Navajo Tribe of Indians. Littell sought judicial review by mandamus of a determination of a previous Secretary of the Interior disallowing his claims for compensation for professional services rendered to the Tribe. The district court concluded that it lacked jurisdiction under the doctrine of sovereign immunity and, alternatively, that the Secretary, in disapproving Littell's claim, exercised a discretionary power not subject to review under the APA by application for mandamus. We conclude otherwise. We reverse the order dismissing the action and remand it for trial.

● ● ●

Littell's services as counsel were performed under a written contract, which was renewed and modified from time to time. He acted as general counsel, for which he received a fixed annual retainer, and he also acted as claims counsel. As claims counsel he was to be paid a contingent fee based upon an agreed percentage of any moneys or the value of any lands which he recovered for the Tribe in actions against the United States Government. To assist him in performing his function as general counsel, Littell was provided with legal assistants paid by the Tribe, but the contract explicitly provided that the legal assistants paid by the Tribe were not to participate in claims work. Any associates of Littell who worked on claims cases were to be paid by Littell personally. The contract, its renewals and modifications were all routinely approved by the Secretary pursuant to 25 U.S.C.A. § 81.

After the contract and its various renewals had been in existence for over sixteen years, the Secretary notified Littell, on November 1, 1963, that his contract *as general counsel* would be terminated effective December 1, 1963, unless Littell adduced evidence refuting specific charges that he had been guilty of misconduct in his relations with the Tribe. Although afforded an opportunity to present his defense to the Secretary administratively, Littell chose to institute an action to enjoin the Secretary from terminating the contract. At first Littell obtained a preliminary injunction restraining the Secretary from terminating the contract, and the order was affirmed on appeal. Udall v. Littell, 119 U.S.App.D.C. 197, 338 F.2d 537 (1964). After trial on the merits, the district court made the injunction permanent, but on appeal this order was reversed, and the prayer for relief dismissed. Udall v. Littell, 125 U.S.App.D.C. 89, 366 F.2d 668 (1966), cert. den., 385 U.S. 1007, 87 S.Ct. 713, 17 L.Ed.2d 545, reh. den., 386 U.S. 939, 87 S.Ct. 952, 17 L.Ed. 2d 812 (1967). In the second appeal, the Court of Appeals concluded that Littell had used Tribal staff attorneys on claims cases in violation of the contract and that the breach constituted adequate grounds for cancelling his contract as general counsel. 366 F.2d at 677.

Thereafter, Littell filed a claim for compensation with the Secretary. He sought payment for services as general counsel for the period prior to the final determination of his litigation with the Secretary, and he sought his contingent fee with respect to five claims cases in which he had allegedly obtained substantial benefits for the Tribe. The Secretary denied his claim for payment for services as general counsel, ruling that notwithstanding that termination of the contract by the Secretary had been enjoined for a substantial period of time, the effective date of termination was December 1, 1963, so that Littell was not entitled to payment for services rendered thereafter. Littell's claims for compensation for claims cases were also rejected for a variety of reasons. ● ● ●

Littell then sued the Secretary in the district court asserting jurisdiction under 28 U.S.C.A. §§ 1331 and 1391 (e). Since special statutory provisions to review the Secretary's determination do not exist, mandamus was sufficient to obtain judicial review of the Secretary's determination under the APA, 5 U.S.C.A. § 703, if the APA is otherwise applicable and if suit is not barred by sovereign immunity. ● ● ●

We consider first if the APA is applicable, because if it is not, manifestly, we need not consider the question of sovereign immunity. ● ● ●

we conclude that, while § 82 commits the decision to deny compensation to an Indian attorney to the discretion of the Secretary, the APA provides limited judicial review to determine if there was an abuse of that discretion. ● ● ●

Thus, the Secretary's decision here would be an abuse of discretion "if it were made without a rational explanation, inexplicably departed from established policies, or rested * * * on other 'considerations that Congress could not have intended to make relevant.'" 360 F.2d at 719 (citations omitted). ● ● ●

We turn then to the question of whether the doctrine of sovereign immunity precludes the application of the APA. It must be recognized at the outset that an effort to establish logical consistency in the decisions dealing with sovereign immunity is bound to be frustrating. The authorities are not reconcilable, and there are conceptual conflicts in the various holdings with which an intermediate appellate court must grapple. Our task is magnified because we have been unable to find any case in which the Supreme Court has sought to reconcile the notion of sovereign immunity with the fundamental concept of the APA that a person adversely affected by administrative action is presumptively entitled to judicial review of its correctness.

Two Courts of Appeals have sought to resolve the problem by holding that the APA, where applicable, constitutes a waiver by the government of sovereign immunity. ● ● ●

On the other hand, at least four have now specifically rejected the waiver theory. ● ● ●

The waiver theory is attractive for several reasons. First, it possesses the virtues of simplicity and ease of application. Secondly, the exceptions to judicial review found in § 10(a) of the APA (5 U.S.C.A. § 701(a)) to a large degree protect the policy reasons underlying the doctrine of sovereign immunity. In other words, where sovereign immunity would normally seem appropriate, the "statutes preclude judicial review" and "committed to agency discretion by law" exceptions would prevent or limit judicial review under the APA.

Despite the attractiveness of the waiver theory, we do not consider ourselves free to adopt it. The judicial review provisions of the APA were adopted in 1946 in substantially the same form as exist today. Yet between 1946 and 1963, the Supreme Court decided at least five cases dealing with attempts to review administrative decisions in which sovereign immunity was applied. ● ● ●

In none of these cases was mention made of the judicial review provisions of the APA, although, because they dealt with final administrative decisions, some discussion of the APA would have seemed to have been appropriate. In still another case, Blackmar v. Guerre, 342 U.S. 512, 516, 72 S.Ct. 410, 96 L.Ed. 534 (1952), there is the following dictum "[s]till less is the Act [APA] to be deemed an implied waiver of all governmental immunity from suit." As a source of further confusion, the Supreme Court has recently decided a number of cases dealing with final administrative decisions in which judicial review was permitted under the APA without any mention of the doctrine of sovereign immunity. ● ● ●

Perhaps all these cases may be reconciled with the waiver theory by saying that in each of the sovereign immunity cases, review was not available under the APA; and in each of the APA cases, that sovereign immunity was not applicable. But the fact remains that the Supreme Court has made no such attempt at reconciliation. As Mr. Justice Stewart said in Malone v. Bowdoin, *supra:* "While it is possible to differentiate many of these cases upon their individual facts, it is fair to say that to reconcile completely all the decisions of the Court in this field prior to 1949 would be a Procrustean task." 369 U.S. at 646, 82 S.Ct. at 983. That "Procrustean task," as we have mentioned, still remains to be accomplished.

Thus, we are constrained to concede that the doctrine of sovereign immunity applies independently of the judicial review provisions of APA. A court may thus be compelled under some circumstances to dismiss a case on the ground of sovereign immunity even though judicial review would seem to be available under the APA. The problem, of course, is to decide in what sorts of circumstances such a result will obtain. In this regard, we accept the formulation of the Ninth Circuit, which directly faced the identical issue in State of Washington v. Udall, *supra:* "In any case wherein the immunity doctrine is so transcending as to require dismissal of the suit, the Act [APA] does not provide for Administrative Review." 417 F.2d at 1320.

Therefore, having decided that the APA does provide for limited judicial review here, we are left to consider two questions: First, does the doctrine of sovereign immunity appear applicable? And secondly, if sovereign immunity appears applicable, are the reasons for its application so compelling as to require dismissal of the case despite the APA?

It appears to us that the doctrine of sovereign immunity, as formulated by the Supreme Court, is applicable here.

In Dugan v. Rank, *supra*, the Supreme Court defined the general circumstances in which the doctrine is to be applied:

> The general rule is that a suit is against the sovereign if "the judgment sought would expend itself on the public treasury or domain, or interfere with the public administration," * * * or if the effect of the judgment would be "to restrain the Government from acting, or to compel it to act." (citations omitted.)

372 U.S. at 620, 83 S.Ct. at 1006. Here, Littell is seeking to compel the Secretary to act and to require the government, as well as the Navajo Tribe, to pay money. It would be hard to imagine a case more literally within the general rule.

The Court in *Dugan*, however, went on to describe exceptions to this general rule: "Those exceptions are (1) action by officers beyond their statutory powers and (2) even though within the scope of their authority, the powers themselves or the manner in which they are exercised are constitutionally void." 372 U.S. at 621–622, 83 S.Ct. at 1007. It is clear here that the Secretary's actions were within the authority conferred on him by § 82, and it is extremely doubtful that the Secretary's exercise of this authority was unconstitutional. If Littell's allegation that the Secretary arbitrarily denied him compensation under the contract is true, then the government would have deprived Littell of property without due process in violation of the Fifth Amendment, so that it might be argued that the second exception to the sovereign immunity doctrine is operative. However, that argument has been precluded by the Supreme Court by its decision in Larson v. Domestic and Foreign Commerce Corp., *supra*. ● ● ●

We do not think, however, that the underlying policies of the doctrine of sovereign immunity are so strong here as to require dismissal of this suit. In the first place, the doctrine of sovereign immunity is presently under attack from many sides. In his treatise, Professor Davis advocates its complete abolition. K. Davis, Administrative Law Treatise, §§ 27.00–27.00–8 (Supp.1970). We consider his arguments highly persuasive. The American Bar Association in 1969 adopted a proposal to amend the APA to eliminate sovereign immunity where the Act is otherwise applicable. See K. Davis, *supra*, § 27.00–8, at 916. Against a weakening of general faith in the validity of the doctrine, we are persuaded that the justifications for the doctrine are not compelling here. In Larson v. Domestic and Foreign Commerce Corp., *supra*, the Court articulated the doctrine's rationale:

> There are the strongest reasons of public policy for the rule that such relief cannot be had against the sovereign. The Government, as representative of the community as a whole, cannot be stopped in its tracks by any plaintiff who presents a disputed question of property or contract right. As was early recognized, "the interference of the Courts with the performance of the ordinary duties of the executive departments of the government, would be productive of nothing but mischief. * * *" (footnote omitted.)

337 U.S. at 704, 69 S.Ct. at 1468. The rationale for sovereign immunity essentially boils down to substantial bothersome interference with the operation of government. It can be said with some justification that both Congress, through the enactment of the APA, and the courts, through liberal application of the APA and silence as to sovereign immunity, have largely rejected this rationale.

LITTELL v. MORTON

However, to the extent that it is still viable, it is only tangentially present here. In no way will this case cause the Department of the Interior to be "stopped in its tracks" in its supervision of Indian affairs. Littell has been replaced by a new attorney to represent the Navajos; representation of the Tribe continues uninterruptedly. The issue involved here is strictly between the government, the Tribe and Littell, and there is no premium on a quick administrative decision which judicial review would prevent. This is not a case where an important government project is halted pending litigation, although the Supreme Court does not seem inclined to prevent judicial review even when this is the case. See Citizens to Preserve Overton Park v. Volpe, *supra*. The sovereign immunity of the Tribe is not seriously impugned. If in fact Littell effected substantial recoveries for it, it was benefited. Certainly it contracted with knowledge of the statutes and approval of the Secretary, to pay a not ex-cessive contingent fee for professional services which advanced its interests. We are not inclined to apply sovereign immunity to provide the Tribe with free legal services in the face of an allegation that payment has been refused arbitrarily.

Finally, we are constrained to add that this would appear to be a most appropriate case for judicial review. The essential issues in this case are ones of contract interpretation and appropriate remedies if breach of contract is established. There is certainly no compelling agency expertise in this area of the law. These are questions always considered to have been within the special competence of the courts. The notion that the government can administratively give a unilateral and final interpretation to a contract under which it may be obligated to pay, and thereby avoid payment, is one that should not be encouraged.

Reversed and remanded.

· ·

See also DUGAN v. RANK, 372 U.S. 609 (1963) in which the United States Supreme Court held that a suit against the United States seeking to prevent the storing and diverting of water for a dam was beyond the jurisdiction of the courts because the United States had not consented to be sued.

(b) State Government

NEW JERSEY TORT CLAIMS ACT, N.J.S.A. 59:1-1 to 14-4.

TITLE 59

CLAIMS AGAINST PUBLIC ENTITIES

SUBTITLE 1. NEW JERSEY TORT CLAIMS ACT

59:1-2. Legislative declaration

The Legislature recognizes the inherently unfair and inequitable results which occur in the strict application of the traditional doctrine of sovereign immunity. On the other hand the Legislature recognizes that while a private entrepreneur may readily be held liable for negligence within the chosen ambit of his activity, the area within which government has the power to act for the public good is almost without limit and therefore government should not have the duty to do everything that might be done. Consequently, it is hereby declared to be the public policy of this State that public entities shall only be liable for their negligence within the limitations of this act and in accordance with the fair and uniform principles established herein. All of the provisions of this act should be construed with a view to carry out the above legislative declaration. L.1972, c. 45, § 59:1-2. ● ● ●

59:2-1. Immunity of public entity generally

a. Except as otherwise provided by this act, a public entity is not liable for an injury, whether such injury arises out of an act or omission of the public entity or a public employee or any other person.

b. Any liability of a public entity established by this act is subject to any immunity of the public entity and is subject to any defenses that would be available to the public entity if it were a private person. L.1972, c. 45, § 59:2-1. ● ● ●

59:2-2. Liability of public entity

a. A public entity is liable for injury proximately caused by an act or omission of a public employee within the scope of his employment in the same manner and to the same extent as a private individual under like circumstances.

b. A public entity is not liable for an injury resulting from an act or omission of a public employee where the public employee is not liable. L.1972, c. 45, § 59:2-2. ● ● ●

59:2-3. Discretionary activities

a. A public entity is not liable for an injury resulting from the exercise of judgment or discretion vested in the entity;

b. A public entity is not liable for legislative or judicial action or inaction, or administrative action or inaction of a legislative or judicial nature;

c. A public entity is not liable for the exercise of discretion in determining whether or to seek or whether to provide the resources necessary for the purchase of equipment, the construction or maintenance of facilities, the hiring of personnel and, in general, the provision of adequate governmental services;

d. A public entity is not liable for the exercise of discretion when, in the face of competing demands, it determines whether and how to utilize or apply existing resources, including those allocated for equipment, facilities and personnel unless a court concludes that the determination of the public entity was palpably unreasonable. Nothing in this section shall

exonerate a public entity for negligence arising out of acts or omissions of its employees in carrying out their ministerial functions.
L.1972, c. 45, § 59:2-3.

● ● ●

59:2-4. Adoption or failure to adopt or enforce a law

A public entity is not liable for an injury caused by adopting or failing to adopt a law or by failing to enforce any law.
L.1972, c. 45, § 59:2-4.

Effective date, see § 59:14-4.

59:2-5. Issuance, denial, suspension or revocation of permit, license, etc.

A public entity is not liable for an injury caused by the issuance, denial, suspension or revocation of, or by the failure or refusal to issue, deny, suspend or revoke, any permit, license, certificate, approval, order, or similar authorization where the public entity or public employee is authorized by law to determine whether or not such authorization should be issued, denied, suspended or revoked.
L.1972, c. 45, § 59:2-5.

● ● ●

59:2-6. Failure to inspect, or negligent inspection of, property

A public entity is not liable for injury caused by its failure to make an inspection, or by reason of making an inadequate or negligent inspection of any property; provided, however, that nothing in this section shall exonerate a public entity from liability for negligence during the course of, but outside the scope of, any inspection conducted by it, nor shall this section exonerate a public entity from liability for failure to protect against a dangerous condition as provided in chapter 4.[1]
L.1972, c. 45, § 59:2-6.

● ● ●

59:2-7. Recreational facilities

A public entity is not liable for failure to provide supervision of public recreational facilities; provided, however, that nothing in this section shall exonerate a public entity from liability for failure to protect against a dangerous condition as provided in chapter 4.[1]
L.1972, c. 45, § 59:2-6.

● ● ●

59:2-8. Public assistance programs—termination of benefits

A public entity is not liable for injuries caused by the termination or reduction of benefits under a public assistance program.
L.1972, c. 45, § 59:2-8.

● ● ●

59:2-9. Slander of title

A public entity is not liable for its acts or omissions resulting in a slander on the title of any property.
L.1972, c. 45, § 52:2-9.

● ● ●

59:2-10. Public employee conduct—limitation on entity liability

A public entity is not liable for the acts or omissions of a public employee constituting a crime, actual fraud, actual malice, or willful misconduct.
L.1972, c. 45, § 52:2-10.

● ● ●

● ●

See STEIFFER v. KANSAS CITY, 175 Kan. 794, 267 P.2d 474 (1954) involving an action to enjoin the City of Kansas City from operating and maintaining a public dump where the court held that the immunity of a municipality from liability does not apply where the municipality creates a nuisance.

2. The Federal Government as the Polluter

(a) NATIONAL ENVIRONMENTAL POLICY ACT OF 1969, 42 U.S.C. sec. 4321 (1969)

Chapter 55.—NATIONAL ENVIRONMENTAL POLICY

§ 4321. Congressional declaration of purpose.

The purposes of this chapter are: To declare a national policy which will encourage productive and enjoyable harmony between man and his environment; to promote efforts which will prevent or eliminate damage to the environment and biosphere and stimulate the health and welfare of man; to enrich the understanding of the ecological systems and natural resources important to the Nation; and to establish a Council on Environmental Quality. (Pub. L. 91-190, § 2, Jan. 1, 1970, 83 Stat. 852.)

* * *

SUBCHAPTER I.—POLICIES AND GOALS

SUBCHAPTER REFERRED TO IN OTHER SECTIONS

This subchapter is referred to in sections 4342, 4344 of this title.

§ 4331. Congressional declaration of national environmental policy.

(a) The Congress, recognizing the profound impact of man's activity on the interrelations of all components of the natural environment, particularly the profound influences of population growth, high-density urbanization, industrial expansion, resource exploitation, and new and expanding technological advances and recognizing further the critical importance of restoring and maintaining environmental quality to the overall welfare and development of man, declares that it is the continuing policy of the Federal Government, in cooperation with State and local governments, and other concerned public and private organizations, to use all practicable means and measures, including financial and technical assistance, in a manner calculated to foster and promote the general welfare, to create and maintain conditions under which man and nature can exist in productive harmony, and fulfill the social, economic, and other requirements of present and future generations of Americans.

(b) In order to carry out the policy set forth in this chapter, it is the continuing responsibility of the Federal Government to use all practicable means, consistent with other essential considerations of national policy, to improve and coordinate Federal plans, functions, programs, and resources to the end that the Nation may—

(1) fulfill the responsibilities of each generation as trustee of the environment for succeeding generations;

(2) assure for all Americans safe, healthful, productive, and esthetically and culturally pleasing surroundings;

(3) attain the widest range of beneficial uses of the environment without degradation, risk to health or safety, or other undesirable and unintended consequences;

(4) preserve important historic, cultural, and natural aspects of our national heritage, and maintain, wherever possible, an environment which supports diversity and variety of individual choice;

(5) achieve a balance between population and resource use which will permit high standards of living and a wide sharing of life's amenities; and

(6) enhance the quality of renewable resources and approach the maximum attainable recycling of depletable resources.

(c) The Congress recognizes that each person should enjoy a healthful environment and that each person has a responsibility to contribute to the preservation and enhancement of the environment.

EXECUTIVE ORDER NO. 11,514, 35 Fed. Reg. 4247 (1970).

Executive Order 11514
PROTECTION AND ENHANCEMENT OF ENVIRONMENTAL QUALITY

By virtue of the authority vested in me as President of the United States and in furtherance of the purpose and policy of the National Environmental Policy Act of 1969 (Public Law No. 91–190, approved January 1, 1970), it is ordered as follows:

SECTION 1. *Policy.* The Federal Government shall provide leadership in protecting and enhancing the quality of the Nation's environment to sustain and enrich human life. Federal agencies shall initiate measures needed to direct their policies, plans and programs so as to meet national environmental goals. The Council on Environmental Quality, through the Chairman, shall advise and assist the President in leading this national effort.

SEC. 2. *Responsibilities of Federal agencies.* Consonant with Title I of the National Environmental Policy Act of 1969, hereafter referred to as the "Act", the heads of Federal agencies shall:

(a) Monitor, evaluate, and control on a continuing basis their agencies' activities so as to protect and enhance the quality of the environment. Such activities shall include those directed to controlling pollution and enhancing the environment and those designed to accomplish other program objectives which may affect the quality of the environment. Agencies shall develop programs and measures to protect and enhance environmental quality and shall assess progress in meeting the specific objectives of such activities. Heads of agencies shall consult with appropriate Federal, State and local agencies in carrying out their activities as they affect the quality of the environment.

(b) Develop procedures to ensure the fullest practicable provision of timely public information and understanding of Federal plans and programs with environmental impact in order to obtain the views of interested parties. ● ● ●

(c) Insure that information regarding existing or potential environmental problems and control methods developed as part of research, development, demonstration, test, or evaluation activities is made available to Federal agencies, States, counties, municipalities, institutions, and other entities, as appropriate.

(d) Review their agencies' statutory authority, administrative regulations, policies, and procedures, including those relating to loans, grants, contracts, leases, licenses, or permits, in order to identify any deficiencies or inconsistencies therein which prohibit or limit full compliance with the purposes and provisions of the Act. ● ● ●

(e) Engage in exchange of data and research results, and cooperate with agencies of other governments to foster the purposes of the Act.

(f) Proceed, in coordination with other agencies, with actions required by section 102 of the Act.

SEC. 3. *Responsibilities of Council on Environmental Quality.* The Council on Environmental Quality shall:

(a) Evaluate existing and proposed policies and activities of the Federal Government directed to the control of pollution and the enhancement of the environment and to the accomplishment of other objectives which affect the quality of the environment. This shall include continuing review of procedures employed in the development and enforcement of Federal standards affecting environmental quality. Based upon such evaluations the Council shall, where appropriate, recommend to the President policies and programs to achieve more

EXECUTIVE ORDER NO. 11,514

effective protection and enhancement of environmental quality and shall, where appropriate, seek resolution of significant environmental issues.

(b) Recommend to the President and to the agencies priorities among programs designed for the control of pollution and for enhancement of the environment.

(c) Determine the need for new policies and programs for dealing with environmental problems not being adequately addressed.

(d) Conduct, as it determines to be appropriate, public hearings or conferences on issues of environmental significance.

(e) Promote the development and use of indices and monitoring systems (1) to assess environmental conditions and trends, (2) to predict the environmental impact of proposed public and private actions, and (3) to determine the effectiveness of programs for protecting and enhancing environmental quality.

(f) Coordinate Federal programs related to environmental quality.

● ● ●

(k) Foster investigations, studies, surveys, research, and analyses relating to (i) ecological systems and environmental quality, (ii) the impact of new and changing technologies thereon, and (iii) means of preventing or reducing adverse effects from such technologies.

● ● ●

THE WHITE HOUSE,
March 5, 1970.

(b) FEDERAL-AID HIGHWAY ACT, 23 U.S.C. sec. 138.

§ 138. Preservation of parklands.

It is hereby declared to be the national policy that special effort should be made to preserve the natural beauty of the countryside and public park and recreation lands, wildlife and waterfowl refuges, and historic sites. The Secretary of Transportation shall cooperate and consult with the Secretaries of the Interior, Housing and Urban Development, and Agriculture, and with the States in developing transportation plans and programs that include measures to maintain or enhance the natural beauty of the lands traversed. After the effective date of the Federal-Aid Highway Act of 1968, the Secretary shall not approve any program or project which requires the use of any publicly owned land from a public park, recreation area, or wildlife and waterfowl refuge of national, State, or local significance as determined by the Federal, State, or local officials having jurisdiction thereof, or any land from an historic site of national, State, or local significance as so determined by such officials unless (1) there is no feasible and prudent alternative to the use of such land, and (2) such program includes all possible planning to minimize harm to such park, recreational area, wildlife and waterfowl refuge, or historic site resulting from such use. (Added Pub. L. 89–574, § 15(a), Sept. 13, 1966, 80 Stat. 771, and amended Pub. L. 90–495, § 18(a), Aug. 23, 1968, 82 Stat. 823.)

. . . .

(c) DEPARTMENT OF TRANSPORTATION ACT, 49 U.S.C. sec. 1651.

§ 1651. Congressional declaration of purpose.

(b)

(2) It is hereby declared to be the national policy that special effort should be made to preserve the natural beauty of the countryside and public park and recreation lands, wildlife and waterfowl refuges, and historic sites. (Pub. L. 89–670, § 2, Oct. 15, 1966, 80 Stat. 931.) ● ● ●

§ 1653. General provisions.

(f) Maintenance and enhancement of natural beauty of land traversed by transportation lines.

It is hereby declared to be the national policy that special effort should be made to preserve the natural beauty of the countryside and public park and recreation lands, wildlife and waterfowl refuges, and historic sites. The Secretary of Transportation shall cooperate and consult with the Secretaries of the Interior, Housing and Urban Development, and Agriculture, and with the States in developing transportation plans and programs that include measures to maintain or enhance the natural beauty of the lands traversed. After August 23, 1968, the Secretary shall not approve any program or project which requires the use of any publicly owned land from a public park, recreation area, or wildlife and waterfowl refuge of national, State, or local significane as determined by the Federal, State, or local officials having jurisdiction thereof, or any land from an historic site of national, State, or local significance as so determined by such officials unless (1) there is no feasible and prudent alternative to the use of such land, and (2) such program includes all possible planning to minimize harm to such park, recreational area, wildlife and waterfowl refuge, or historic site resulting from such use.

3. Action Against Public Officials

(a) No Action for Discretionary Acts

ROY v. FARR, 258 A. 2d 799 (Vt. 1969).

KEYSER, Justice.

This is a petition for a writ of mandamus by which the petitioner seeks to compel the board of health of the town of Richmond to abate an unhealthful condition existing on land adjacent to the residential property of both the petiti~ner and other persons as provided by 18 V.S.A. § 609.

The petition was brought on February 28, 1969. At that time defendants Farr, Conant and Palermo were the selectmen of the town of Richmond. Selectman Farr was the appointed health officer of the town. 18 V.S.A. § 601. The selectmen, together with the health officer, constitute the local board of health. 18 V.S.A. § 604.

The record shows that defendant Farr's term of office expired on town meeting day, March 4, 1969. At that time one Gordon B. Stensrud was elected selectman to fill this vacancy. ● ● ●

In order to have the proper and necessary parties before the court, an interlocutory order and summons was issued and served on the present members of the Richmond Board of Health not named in the original petition shown by the public records to be Dr. John Lantman, Health Officer, and Selectmen Willard Conant and Gordon Stensrud. ● ● ●

The board of health resists the petition on two grounds—(1) it claims the removal of the unhealthful condition by the board under 18 V.S.A. § 609 is not mandatory duty for the reason that such action requires the exercise of its judgment and discretion and is not a ministerial act, and (2) it contends that the petitioner has an adequate remedy by an action for abatement of a public nuisance against the offending landowner.

The following facts which appear in the petition and answer are undisputed. The petitioner is a resident and owner of certain real estate located on Lemroy Court in the town of Richmond. In 1966 an unhealthful condition existed on land adjacent to petitioner's residential property on Lemroy Court and to other lands which he had developed into residential properties. This condition resulted from the discharge of raw sewage by one George Dutil into an open gully southeast of petitioner's residence. The defendants were notified of this unhealthful condition by the Vermont Department of Health in March 1967, and were advised that the discharge of the sewage was considered to be a public health hazard. On June 27, 1967, defendant Farr, as the town health officer, notified the offending property owner, George Dutil, that the unhealthful condition was due to the discharge of raw sewage from his disposal facilities and that in the event he, Dutil, failed to comply with the order of the defendants requiring him to remove the unhealthful condition within thirty days, the defendant would order the removal of the condition pursuant to 18 V.S.A. § 609 and charge him, Dutil, with the expense of the same. Dutil failed to comply with the order and the unhealthful condition still exists.

The critical question to be first decided is whether mandamus will lie on the facts shown in this case.

The duties of the health officer regarding sanitary inspections are prescribed by 18 V.S.A. § 606 as follows:

The health officer shall make sanitary inspections when and where he has reason to suspect that anything exists which may be detrimental to the public health. He may enter any house or other building or place for the purpose of making such inspections. By written order he shall direct the destruction or removal within a specified time of unhealthful conditions or causes of sickness; and shall in all things conform to the rules and regulations of the board.

The facts show a compliance with the mandate of this statute. The inspection was made and a written order was given to the offending party, George Dutil. He was directed by said order to remove the condition, failing which the board of health

ROY v. FARR

would do so at his expense ● ●●

The local board took no remedial steps to enforce its order by having the condition prevented or removed. The petitioner claims that since Dutil did not comply with the order, the board, under Section 609, supra, must take action to have the condition eliminated. The defendant contends that its duty under the statute is discretionary and requires the exercise of its judgment which, if true, will supersede mandamus since the writ does not lie to enforce the performance of judicial or quasi-judicial acts. Under such circumstances, this Court will not order the board to act. ● ● ●

On the other hand, mandamus will lie to compel a public officer to perform an official act which is merely ministerial. Town of Bennington v. Booth, 101 Vt. 24, 27, 140 A. 157, 57 A.L.R. 156; Town of Glover v. Anderson, 120 Vt. 153, 155, 134 A.2d 612. So here, in order to justify the issuance of a writ of mandamus, it must be made to appear that the duty of the local board of health to remove the public health hazard is a ministerial one. Barber v. Chase, 101 Vt. 343, 351, 143 A. 302, and that the right sought to be enforced is certain and clear. Glover v. Anderson, supra.

However, there is a well-recognized exception to these general propositions depending upon whether the facts make it a proper case to come within the exception. Where such facts show, in some manner, an arbitrary abuse of the power vested by law in an administrative officer or board which amounts to a virtual refusal to act or to perform a duty imposed by law, mandamus may be resorted to in the absence of other adequate legal remedy. ● ● ●

The petitioner has a clear right not to be subjected to the unhealthful condition determined by the State Department of Health to be a public health hazard. The defendant admits that the discharge of raw sewage as shown is a condition which has existed for many years. The situation ostensibly developed to such a serious and hazardous unhealthful condition that the State health authorities acted in 1967. It is evident that the local health officer likewise determined that such condition existed or else the order of removal would not have been issued. The right which the petitioner seeks to be enforced is adequately shown to be certain and clear.

The defendant argues that the action of the board of health is the performance of a discretionary act and involves an inquiry of fact.

The general supervision of the public health of the town is committed to the local health officer and board of health. Their authority to act in such matters is expressly granted by 18 V.S.A., Chapter 11. The state board of health and commissioner in their discretion may exercise similar powers. 18 V.S.A. § 109.

The health officer chose to act by making an inspection of the situation after which the removal order was given Dutil. This required a determination based on his inquiry that the condition was detrimental to public health and created an unhealthful condition. It was at this point that the judgment and discretionary action came into play and was exercised. After the decision was made to issue the order of removal there remained only the action of the board to have the condition removed upon non-compliance with the order. This required neither an inquiry of fact nor exercise of judgment or discretion. Each had already been exercised.

We think the dangerous public health hazard was a compelling reason for the board to exercise its powers under the statute and required it to cause the condition to be eliminated or removed in accordance with the order to Dutil and the applicable statute. The failure and neglect of the board to take such action amounted to an arbitrary abuse of its lawful authority.

We turn to the remaining question of whether a writ of mandamus is the only fully adequate and complete remedy available to the petitioner.

While it is true that the writ will not issue where the right is doubtful, it will not be refused because of the existence of another remedy unless that remedy is clear and adequate. Town of Bennington v. Booth, supra. The remedy here suggested by the defendants is an action by the petitioner for the abatement of a public nuisance.

Mandamus affords a plain, speedy and adequate remedy. It is practical, efficient and prompt in its administration toward the result sought to be accomplished. In order to supersede mandamus, the other remedy must be competent to afford relief on the very subject matter in question, and be equally convenient, beneficial and effective. Glover v. Anderson, supra, 120 Vt. at page 160, 134 A.2d 612.

It is well settled that a person who suffers special damage from the erection and maintenance of a public nuisance is entitled to relief in his own right; but, it must appear that the injury is distinct from that suffered by the general public.

● ● ●

It is manifestly clear from the facts before us that the injury is not a personal one peculiar only to the petitioner but is one suffered by the public as well. To require the petitioner to bring a petition to abate a nuisance which affects the public health would cause him to bear all of the expense and delay which are involved in personal litigation. We are persuaded by the facts in the case that an action by the petitioner to abate a public nuisance does not meet the test laid down by this Court in Glover v. Anderson, supra, and would not afford him such a clear, speedy and fully adequate remedy as the law provides. Town of Bennington v. Booth, supra.

Judgment that the prayer of the petition is granted, and that a mandamus issue directing the Board of Health of the Town of Richmond, namely, Dr. John Lantman, Vincent Palermo, Willard Conant and Gordon Stensrud, to forthwith remove, or cause to be removed, the health hazard resulting from the open discharge of raw sewage by one George Dutil on land adjacent to the residential property of the petitioner, Louis G. Roy, all in accordance with the order given to said Dutil and the statutes in such case made and provided, with actual costs of this proceeding to the petitioner.

. . . .

(b) Tort Liability

For information relating to the liability of public officials for wrongful acts, see:

Jennings, "Tort Liability of Administrative Officers," 21 Minn. L. Rev. 263 (1937).

1. Balancing of Equities

PEOPLE EX REL. STREAM CONTROL COMMISSION v. CITY OF
PORT HURON, 305 Mich. 153, 9 N.W. 2d 41 (1943)

BUSHNELL, J. The stream control commission, created by Act No. 245, Pub. Acts 1929 (1 Comp. Laws 1929, § 278 *et seq.* [Stat. Ann. § 3.521 *et seq.*]), issued an order on February 11, 1936, requiring the city of Port Huron to "proceed to the construction of a sewage treatment plant, and the necessary collecting and intercepting sewers, pumping stations, force mains and other appurtenances, in connection therewith, all when and as approved by the Michigan department of health, to permit treatment for the sewage of the city before its discharge to State waters." The city having failed to comply with this order, the commission filed a bill of complaint on December 9, 1939, for the purpose of enforcing its order and restraining the city from discharging untreated sewage into the Black or St. Clair rivers.

The trial judge held that the grounds of public necessity as disclosed by the testimony were insufficient to warrant "the present interference" by the court. He denied the relief sought, until further order, on the principle that:

"A court of equity will refuse to grant an injunction when it appears that greater injury and inconvenience will be caused to the defendant by granting the injunction than will be caused to the complainant by refusing it."

An appeal was taken by the State from a decree in favor of the city. ● ● ●

The city of Port Huron takes its water from the St. Clair river near Lake Huron, which is connected with Lake St. Clair by the St. Clair river, and discharges its raw sewage into the St. Clair river, which borders it on the east, and into the Black river, a tributary of the St. Clair, which runs through the city. The city of Sarnia and the village of Point Edward, which are situated almost directly opposite the city of Port Huron on the east bank of the St. Clair river in the Province of Ontario, also discharge raw sewage into this river, as does a large oil refinery. During the years 1937, 1938 and 1939, a total of 45,168 vessels passed Port Huron, which added to the pollution of these waters.

The city argues that the construction of a sewage disposal plant will not materially reduce the pollution in the rivers, and insists that its present method of sewage disposal does not create a health hazard amounting to a public nuisance to the people residing along the river and those in the cities of Marysville, St. Clair, Marine City and Algonac, located within 30 miles below Port Huron.

The record contains sufficient testimony to substantiate the State's contention that the present raw sewage disposal method is a constant menace to the health and well-being of the downriver communities, as well as to tourists. This evidence clearly justifies the commission's order. Under the authority of the *City of Niles Case, supra,* where similar arguments were advanced, it is no defense to a statutory charge of river-water pollution that others have or are contributing to that condition. This court said:

"In order to stop pollution of the river it was necessary for the commission to take action against the city of Niles inasmuch as it was the first city in the State, on the course of the river, below the Indiana cities and thus open the way for suit to compel the Indiana cities to stop pollution of the waters of the river. It is an instance where the State must clean up its own dooryard before being in a position to ask or seek to compel its neighbor to clean up. This was not an arbitrary exercise of power by the commission but a practical movement toward accomplishment of a most desirable end."

Even if we should concur with the trial judge in his conclusion that "a balancing of equities" favors the city, this is not a proper case for the application of that doctrine. The doctrine of "comparative injury" should be confined to those situations where the plaintiff can be substantially compensated. This principle is distinguished in *City of Harrisonville* v. *W. S. Dickey Clay Manfg. Co.,* 289 U. S. 334, 337 (53 Sup. Ct. 602, 77 L. Ed. 1208), where Mr. Justice Brandeis said:

"The discharge of the effluent into the creek is a tort; and the nuisance, being continuous or recurrent, is an injury for which an injunction may be granted. Thus, the question here is not one of equitable jurisdiction. The question is whether, upon the facts found, an injunction is the appropriate remedy. For an injunction is not a remedy which issues as of course. Where substantial redress can be afforded by the payment of money and issuance of an injunction would subject the defendant to grossly disproportionate hardship, equitable relief may be denied although the nuisance is indisputable. This is true even if the conflict is between interests which are primarily private." * * *

The doctrine of "comparative injury" should not be invoked to justify the continuance of an act that tends to impair public health. In *Board of Commissioners of the County of Ohio* v. *Elm Grove Mining Co.,* 122 W. Va. 442, 451 (9 S. E. [2d] 813), the court said:

"Notwithstanding a business be conducted in the regular manner, yet if in the operation thereof, it is shown by facts and circumstances to constitute a nuisance affecting public health 'no measure of necessity, usefulness or public benefit will protect it from the unflinching condemnation of the law.' 1 Wood on Nuisances (3d Ed.), § 19. * * * There is extremely narrow basis for undertaking to balance conveniences where people's health is involved." ● ● ●

The act creating the commission was under the police power vested in the State, and the order in question was not arbitrary or unreasonable but became necessary by reason of the previous refusal of the city of Port Huron to stop pollution of the St. Clair and Black rivers. The evidence justified the order of the commission, and the decree entered below must be vacated. ● ● ●

The decree is vacated and one will be entered here in conformity with this opinion. A public question being involved, no costs will be allowed. It is so ordered.

. . . .

For additional discussion of the balancing of equities as a defense in environmental suites see Coase, "The Problem of Social Cost," 3 J. Law & Econ. 1 (1960).

2. State of the Art: (I did all that could be done).

RENKEN v. HARVEY ALUMINUM, 226 F. Supp. 169 (D. Ore. 1963).

KILKENNY, District Judge.

Each of the plaintiffs, since 1958, and in many instances prior to that year, has been in continuous possession of land in Wasco County, Oregon, which land was and is used principally for agricultural and horticultural purposes, in growing and production, for home and commercial purposes, of certain fruit consisting of cherries, prunes, peaches and apricots.

Plaintiffs seek to enjoin the defendant from operating its plant in such a manner as to permit the escape therefrom of excessive quantities of the element, fluorine, which is carried by air currents to plaintiffs' lands. Defendant is a corporation, incorporated under the laws of the State of California. ● ● ●

Defendant's plant was constructed, and is being operated, pursuant to the Defense Production Act of 1950, as amended. Its original cost, and subsequent additions, is in excess of $40,000,000.00. The plant annually produces approximately 80,000 tons of aluminum, which is used by the defendant, and others, throughout the United States for industrial and National Defense purposes. Approximately 550 persons, living in the area of The Dalles, are employed in said plant. It has a gross annual payroll of $3,500,000.00.

The plant produces primary aluminum, by the use of what is known as the vertical stud soderberg elecrolytic cells. At present 300 cells are in operation. The basic process employed at the plant is the same as that employed the world over. in making aluminum, the process being precisely described by Judge East in his opinion in Fairview Farms, Inc. v. Reynolds Metals Company, 176 F.Supp. 178 (D.C.Or.1959). The vertical stud soderberg cells employed by Harvey were not used in the Reynolds plant. The essential difference between the cells, or pots, used in the Reynolds plant is, inso-

far as the escape of particulates and gasses is concerned, that Reynold uses a hood, with a controlling air system, which captures most of the stray gasses, affluents and particulates which might escape into the open area around the pots. The vertical type, employed by Harvey, has an apron which collects approximately 80% of these gasses and particulates, but the remaining 20% escapes from the area where the hoods would be located, mixes with other air in the building and then drifts upward into the water spray controls in the roof. It is conceded that in the production of aluminum there is inevitably a release, from the cells, of some gasses and particulates, including fluorides.

The initial fume control apparatus at the Harvey plant consisted of a cast iron skirt surrounding the anode, which collected a portion of the fumes at the source and directed them to burners mounted at both ends of each anode. To these burners were connected fume exhaust ducts which lead the fumes to a main collector pipe carrying them to the dust collector and a fan. The fan created a suction which pulled the fumes from the cells and the burners, through the ducts. From the fans the fumes are directed to a humidifying and bubbling chamber before entering the scrubber tower. The fumes are washed in the tower by multiple layers of water sprayers placed 10 feet apart. At the top of the towers is a mist eliminator.

Tests made, from time to time, indicate that the fume control system, thus described, operated at 95% efficiency, or better, during the test periods on the portion of the fumes caught and delivered to the system. The amount of equivalent fluoride ion leaving the scrubbing towers into the atmosphere from this control apparatus is calculated at 300 pounds per day. This system treats approximately 80% of the fumes released from the cells. The remaining 20% of the fumes escape into the open building, and rise to the top where they pass into roof monitors located at the top of each of the buildings housing the cells. In the spring of 1962, a system of sprayers and screens were installed in the roof monitor and this system has been operating at full capacity since the beginning of 1963. These sprayers and screens collect a portion of the fluorides reaching the roof monitor. Since this latest installation the roof monitor sprays and screens have been between 67 and 70% effective in collecting the fluorides reaching the roof monitors. The amount of equivalent fluoride ion leaving the roof monitors into the atmosphere is calculated at 1,000 pounds per day. Overall, the combination of the original fume control system, as it has been added to and improved from time to time, and the roof monitor sprays and screens has achieved approximately 90% effectiveness with respect to collecting the fluorides released from the aluminum cells.

The record is undisputed that approximately 1,300 pounds of fluoride ion escape from the roof monitors and scrubbing towers into the atmosphere each day. Although the prevailing wind is southwesterly, the record clearly shows that on numerous days each month and on many hours of each day, the area is without measurable wind. At such times, a blanket of smoke from defendant's plant, covers the area, including plaintiffs' lands and orchards. This blanket was observed by the Court, not only on the day of inspection of the plant, but also on many occasions since that time. There is no doubt in my mind but that better controls can be exercised over the escape of the material in question. No sound reason has been advanced by defendant why hoods, similar to those employed by Reynolds, should not be installed. While it is true that a substantial portion of the gasses and particulates escape at the time when the new aluminum ore is being introduced into the pot or the liquid metal is removed,

I am convinced that such an escape could be prevented by a properly designed hood over the open area. I agree with the expert, that after the installation of the hood, the small amount of gasses which might escape on the introduction of ore or the removal of liquid metal would be inconsequential.

Likewise, the record convinces me of the feasability of the introduction of electrostatic precipitators for the removal of the minute or small particulates which are not removed by the other processes. The multi-cyclone dust collector now used in the plant at The Dalles is efficient in collecting the large or heavy particulates, but is of little value in removing the smaller variety. All of the experts agree that this is the field in which the electrostatic precipitators are at their best. The great weight of the evidence points to the conclusion that the installation of the cell hoods and the employment of electrostatic precipitators would greatly reduce, if not entirely eliminate, the escape of the excessive material now damaging the orchards of the plaintiffs.

While the cost of the installations of these additional controls will be a substantial sum, the fact remains that effective controls must be exercised over the escape of these noxious fumes. Such expenditures would not be so great as to substantially deprive defendant of the use of its property. While we are not dealing with the public as such, we must recognize that air pollution is one of the great problems now facing the American public. If necessary, the cost of installing adequate controls must be passed on to the ultimate consumer. The heavy cost of corrective devices is no reason why plaintiffs should stand by and suffer substantial damage. ● ● ●

Defendant concedes that plaintiffs repeatedly warned it of the emissions, damages to and alleged trespasses on plaintiffs' property. The evidence supports, and I find, that the emissions from defendant's plant continued to settle on plaintiffs' land and orchards to and including the time of the trial. That the continued settling of the fluorides from

RENKEN v. HARVEY ALUMINUM (INCORPORATED)

defendant's plant on plaintiffs' property constituted a continuing trespass, as a matter of law, is beyond question. ● ● ●

That equity will intervene to prevent a continuing trespass is well recognized. ● ● ●

Plaintiffs rely on Fairview Farms, Inc. v. Reynolds Metals Co., supra, and in particular on that portion of the opinion in which it is indicated that an award of compensatory damages for past trespasses and future trespasses would adequately compensate the plaintiffs. The basic reason the Court did not grant an injunction in the Fairview case was that there was no evidence the acts or conduct of Reynolds were reasonably certain to be repeated in the future. Here, of course, the evidence is entirely to the contrary. Here, Harvey has taken the position that it has done everything possible to eliminate the problem, and that it must continue to operate with its present control system. The 1962-1963 improvement by Harvey was of no particular significance ● ● ●

Frankly stated, there is no good reason why the defendant company, like other companies similarly situated, should not make a reasonable expenditure in the erection of hoods, or like devices, over or around its pots or cells. To require less would be placing a premium on air pollution. What's good for Reynolds should be good for Harvey, even though the cost of the new system might exceed $2,000,000.00, as it did in the case of Reynolds. ● ● ●

The defendant will be required to install proper hoods around the cells and electrostatic precipitators in usual, advantageous and proper places in the plant, within one year of the date of the decree. Otherwise, an injunction will issue as prayed for by plaintiffs.

There is no room for application of the doctrine of balancing of the equities at this time. The required improvements should entirely eliminate the problem.

McELWAIN v. GEORGIA-PACIFIC, 245 Ore. 247, 421 P. 2d 957 (1967).

McALLISTER, Chief Justice.

This is an action brought by the plaintiffs, Ross and Edith McElwain, against the defendant, Georgia-Pacific Corporation, to recover both compensatory and punitive damages for injury to plaintiffs' real property caused by the operation of defendant's paper mill in Toledo.

Plaintiffs own two and one-half acres of land, improved with a dwelling house and garage, located directly east of defendant's mill. The complaint alleged that since defendant commenced operation of its plant on or about January 1, 1958, plaintiffs' property was damaged by "certain noxious and toxic gases, fumes and smoke and particles" blown and deposited thereon by defendant's mill. It is further alleged that the effluents from defendant's mill killed the trees and vegetation on plaintiffs' property and otherwise depreciated the value of the property. Plaintiffs prayed for $35,000 in compensatory damages and $20,000 in punitive damages. The court withdrew the issue of punitive damages, and the jury returned a verdict of $2,000, compensatory damages. The plaintiffs appeal.

Plaintiffs assign as error the withdrawal by the trial court of plaintiffs' claim for punitive damages.

Although this court has on occasion indulged in the dictum that punitive damages are not "favored in the law," it has, nevertheless, uniformly sanctioned the recovery of punitive damages whenever there was evidence of a wrongful act done intentionally, with knowledge that it would cause harm to a particular person or persons. Hodel, The Doctrine of Exemplary Damages in Oregon, 44 Or.L.Rev. 175 (1965). Malice is the term most frequently used in our decisions to define a state of mind that will justify the imposition of punitive damages. Malice, as a basis for punitive damages, signifies nothing more than a wrongful act done intentionally, without just cause or excuse. ●●●

The intentional disregard of the interest of another is the equivalent of legal malice, and justifies punitive damages for trespass. Allison v. Hodo, 84 Ga.App. 790, 67 S.E.2d 606, 608 (1951). Where there is proof of an intentional, unjustifiable infliction of harm with deliberate disregard of the social consequences, the question of award of punitive damages is for the jury.

● ● ●

It is abundantly clear from the record that defendant knew when it decided to construct its kraft mill in Toledo, that there was danger, if not a probability, that the mill would cause damage to adjoining property. This is disclosed by defendant's evidence that the plans for the mill included, as an integral part thereof, certain air pollution control devices designed to minimize the damage caused by the mill to surrounding property.

The record is equally clear that, almost from the day it began to operate, the effluents from defendant's mill were a source of concern to the State Board of Health, and its successor, the State Sanitary Authority, and to the owners of the adjacent property. Although the trial judge excluded most of the relevant evidence offered by plaintiffs to show the extent and nature of the effluents deposited on their property, the defendant's evidence discloses that it was required to keep and furnish records to the state regulating authorities concerning the fallout of effluents on the neighboring properties. ● ● ●

When defendant's mill was constructed the following air control equipment was installed therein:

McELWAIN v. GEORGIA-PACIFIC CORPORATION

Date	Equipment	Function
12/57	No. 1 Electrostatic Precipitator	Remove dust from Recovery Furnace gases
12/57	No. 1 Peabody Scrubber	Remove dust from kiln gases
12/57	No. 1 Black Liquor Oxidation Tower	Stabilize liquor and minimize release of odors
12/57	Blow Heat Accumulator	Condense all digester gases so that non-condensables can be vented to oxidation tower for re-absorption

In about June, 1960 the capacity of defendant's mill was increased from about 240 tons to 600 tons of paper per day. In connection with that expansion program two additional pieces of pollution control equipment were installed, as follows:

3/60	No. 2 Peabody Scrubber	Remove dust from kiln gases
5/60	No. 2 Electrostatic Precipitator	Remove dust from Recovery Furnace gases

In 1961 a Turpentine Recovery System was installed "to remove turpentine vapors," and in 1962 two Lagoon Surface Aerators and other oxidation equipment was installed to "reduce odor release from liquid streams." According to defendant the equipment described above is all the pollution control equipment which had been installed prior to the filing of the complaint in this action. There is no contention by defendant that the fallout of effluents on plaintiffs' property was eliminated or even alleviated by its efforts at control.

Defendant contends that it should not be liable for punitive damages if it did everything reasonably possible to eliminate or minimize the damage caused by its mill to the neighboring properties. We need not pause to determine whether there is merit in defendant's contention. It is sufficient to call attention to the substantial evidence from which the jury could have found that during the period involved in this action the defendant had not done everything reasonably possible to eliminate or minimize the damage to adjoining properties by its mill. That evidence was introduced by defendant itself. Its expert in charge of its pollution control program, Dr. Taylor, testified that between the filing of plaintiffs' complaint and the time of the trial the defendant had installed or was in process of installing the following additional pollution control equipment:

4/63	Rebuild #1 Precipitator	Replace internal units and increase electrical capacity
11/63	No. 2 Black Liquor Oxidation System	Stabilize liquor and minimize release of odors
3/64	#3 Electrostatic Precipitator	Remove dust from Recovery furnace gases (Expansion)
3/64	#3 Peabody Scrubber	Remove dust from kiln gases (Expansion)
3/64	290–ft Stack	High level discharge of all three recovery furnace gases
4 to 6/64	Three wet scrubber systems for three Recovery Furnaces	Wash residual salt from recovery furnace gases and reduce odor
5/64	Relocate #2 stack at kilns	High level discharge of kiln gases

———◆———

Dr. Taylor testified that the increase in the height of the stack and the other controls were designed to minimize particulate fallout. ● ● ●
Except as to the three "wet scrubbers" installed from April to June, 1964, there is no contention that the additional controls could not have been installed either (a) when the mill was built, or (b) as soon as it became apparent that the mill pollution was damaging the adjoining properties. It was admitted that the increase of the stack height to 290 feet would decrease the fallout on plaintiffs' property. The failure to increase the stack height earlier is not explained.

The evidence also discloses that the defendant's efforts to control pollution were influenced by the cost factor. ● ● ●
There was an abundance of evidence sufficient by any standard to support an award of punitive damages. We conclude that the trial court erred in withdrawing the issue of punitive damages from the jury.

The case is remanded for a new trial.

DENECKE, Justice (dissenting).

The majority holds that the fact the defendant did not install all the possible air pollution controls at the beginning of the plant's operation is evidence defendant did not do everything reasonably possible to eliminate or minimize the damage to plaintiffs and, therefore, the jury may punish the defendant by awarding plaintiffs punitive damages. I disagree that the facts permit this inference. ● ● ●

There was no witness who expressed an opinion that a reasonably prudent mill operator would have proceeded any differently than did the defendant. It appears from the testimony of both parties that the control of air pollution from a Kraft mill is as difficult for lay understanding as some portions of the practice of medicine. As in medical malpractice cases, it is appropriate to require opinion testimony whether the defendant has or has not observed the ap-

McELWAIN v. GEORGIA-PACIFIC CORPORATION

plicable standard of care. As in a medical malpractice case, I do not believe it is evidence of negligence merely to show that the defendant used procedures later which he could have used initially. The question is, did reasonable prudence require that such procedures be used initially? There was no testimony that it did.

My principal difference with the majority, however, is concerning the legal basis for permitting the jury, in its discretion, to award punitive damages.

The majority bases its decisions upon the state of mind of the defendant at the time the tortious acts were committed. This is an accepted thesis. They apparently have selected alternate states of mind, proof of which would permit a jury to award punitive damages. According to the majority, punitive damages are awardable "whenever there was evidence of a wrongful act done intentionally, with knowledge that it would cause harm to a particular person or persons" and punitive damages are awardable in this case because there is "substantial evidence from which the jury could have found that during the period involved in this action the defendant had not done everything reasonably possible to eliminate or minimize the damage to adjoining properties by its mill."

I construe the first basis, stripped to its essentials, to state the principle that punitive damages are awardable for all intentional torts. I do not interpret our past decisions to so hold.

We have previously decided that punitive damages could not be awarded in cases in which there was an intentional trespass to land, but the trespasser's motive was deemed not "malicious." ● ● ●

The other ground upon which the majority rests its decision that punitive damages are awardable is upon the proposition that defendant has not done everything reasonably possible to prevent or minimize damage to plaintiffs, i.e., on the state-of-mind scale,—negligence.

In certain malpractice cases we have permitted the award of punitive damages although the defendant was at most guilty of a high degree of negligence. However, we have regarded these cases as a separate category. ● ● ●

Reynolds Metals Company v. Lampert, 316 F.2d 272; 324 F.2d 465 (9th Cir. 1963), relied upon by plaintiffs, does not hold, in my opinion, that punitive damages can be assessed against an industrial concern that a jury finds did not do everything reasonably possible to prevent damage by air pollution. I base this particularly on the evidence in that case that the defendant had conscious knowledge that it could do more to prevent or reduce pollution than it was doing, but it continued to pollute at the same or greater rate because it was cheaper to continue to damage plaintiffs' property and pay compensatory damages than to install available and feasible air pollution equipment. There was no such evidence or inference in the present case. The State Sanitary Authority Director of Air Pollution testified that Georgia-Pacific was proceeding in the only feasible manner,—trial and error—trying, testing, revising, reversing and repeating the sequence.

In my opinion a negligent state of mind should not be sufficient to enable the jury to award punitive damages. ● ● ●

Many times this court has stated: "[P]unitive damages are not favored in the law." ● ● ●

The purpose of punitive damages is to deter the defendant and others in like circumstances from committing the intentional act which has injured the plaintiffs. Van Lom v. Schneiderman, 187 Or. 89, 107, 210 P.2d 461, 11 A.L.R.2d 1195 (1949). It is not to provide additional compensation to damaged parties. See Clarence Morris, Punitive Damages in Tort Cases, 44 Harv. L.Rev. 1173 (1931).

Punitive damages is an oddity in the law of damages. An award of punitive damages is not to compensate for injury, but to penalize, with the object of deterring. To deter by means of punitive damages was an integral part of the ancient English tort law when public purpose and private compensation were intermingled. When a clear division was made between criminal law, with the object of protection to the public at large, and civil tort law, with the object of compensating injured persons, punishment as a deterrent was left to the state acting through the criminal law. Today, the sole remaining vestige in civil law which provides for punishment is the awarding of punitive damages.

We have never sought to deter defendants from future negligent conduct by awarding of punitive damages, with the exceptions stated above. Negligent vehicle drivers are a much more serious menace than negligent papermill operators; however, we have never intimated we would permit a jury to assess punitive damages against a negligent motorist to deter negligent driving. Permitting a jury to award punitive damages to deter a negligent industry is a change in direction in the law of punitive damages.

Turning to the other bases for the majority opinion, I am also of the opinion that granting the jury the power of deterrence to prevent an intentional trespass is not warranted.

The witnesses called by both parties agree that with the present state of knowledge the defendant cannot prevent its plant from polluting the air in some degree and damaging plaintiffs' property. Therefore, the only way in which an award of punitive damages can deter defendant from intentionally operating its plant knowing it will cause a trespass or continue a nuisance to plaintiffs' damage is if the award is large enough in amount so that the defendant cannot continue profitably to operate its plant. Any lesser award would be only for the private profit of the parties plaintiff and would not accomplish the public purpose.

In my opinion the granting to a jury of the power to award punitive damages is not a suitable vehicle to decide whether or not an industry should continue to operate.

The jury in the award of punitive damages "acts something like a judge in passing sentence on the defendant in a criminal case." ● ● ●

It also seems anomalous to me that we would permit juries to close down industries by punitive damage awards when there may be factors present which would cause an equity court to refuse to close down the same industry when asked to issue an injunction. ● ● ●

We are committed to the doctrine in considering injunctions that an industry will not be closed down if it is merely proven that the operator is knowingly and continuously committing a trespass or nuisance to the damage of the adjoining landowner; the equities must be "balanced." I cannot understand why we should adopt a contrary view by permitting a jury to award punitive damages in order to accomplish the same end, closing down the operation. ● ● ● if a court sitting in equity would not shut down the defendant's operation, a jury should not be given the discretion to bring about a contrary result.

O'CONNELL, Justice (dissenting).

The only justification for the imposition of punitive damages is to deter wrongful conduct in those circumstances where other legal sanctions are not available to effect deterrence.[1] ● ● ●

PERRY, J., joins in this dissent.

3. Government Approval of Activity

See HURON CEMENT COMPANY v. DETROIT, supra, I,B,4 (b) page 85.

4. Exhaustion of Administrative Remedies and Primary Administrative Jurisdiction

FEDERAL ADMINISTRATIVE PROCEDURE ACT, 5 U.S.C. sections 701-706, P.L. 89-554, 80 STAT. 378 (1966).

§ 701. Application; definitions.

(a) This chapter applies, according to the provisions thereof, except to the extent that—

(1) statutes preclude judicial review; or

(2) agency action is committed to agency discretion by law. ● ● ●

§ 702. Right of review.

A person suffering legal wrong because of agency action, or adversely affected or aggrieved by agency action within the meaning of a relevant statute, is entitled to judicial review thereof. ● ● ●

§ 703. Form and venue of proceeding.

The form of proceeding for judicial review is the special statutory review proceeding relevant to the subject matter in a court specified by statute or, in the absence or inadequacy thereof, any applicable form of legal action, including actions for declaratory judgments or writs of prohibitory or mandatory injunction or habeas corpus, in a court of competent jurisdiction. Except to the extent that prior, adequate, and exclusive opportunity for judicial review is provided by law, agency action is subject to judicial review in civil or criminal proceedings for judicial enforcement. ● ● ●

§ 704. Actions reviewable.

Agency action made reviewable by statute and final agency action for which there is no other adequate remedy in a court are subject to judicial review. A preliminary, procedural, or intermediate agency action or ruling not directly reviewable is subject to review on the review of the final agency action. Except as otherwise expressly required by statute, agency action otherwise final is final for the purposes of this section whether or not there has been presented or determined an application for a declaratory order, for any form of reconsiderations, or, unless the agency otherwise requires by rule and provides that the action meanwhile is inoperative, for an appeal to superior agency authority. ● ● ●

§ 705. Relief pending review.

When an agency finds that justice so requires, it may postpone the effective date of action taken by it, pending judicial review. On such conditions as may be required and to the extent necessary to prevent irreparable injury, the reviewing court, including the court to which a case may be taken on appeal from or on application for certiorari or other writ to a reviewing court, may issue all necessary and appropriate process to postpone the effective date of an agency action or to preserve status or rights pending conclusion of the review proceedings. ● ● ●

§ 706. Scope of review.

To the extent necessary to decision and when presented, the reviewing court shall decide all relevant questions of law, interpret constitutional and statutory provisions, and determine the meaning or applicability of the terms of an agency action. The reviewing court shall—

(1) compel agency action unlawfully withheld or unreasonably delayed; and

(2) hold unlawful and set aside agency action, findings, and conclusions found to be—

(A) arbitrary, capricious, an abuse of discretion, or otherwise not in accordance with law;

(B) contrary to constitutional right, power, privilege, or immunity;

(C) in excess of statutory jurisdiction, authority, or limitations, or short of statutory right;

(D) without observance of procedure required by law;

(E) unsupported by substantial evidence in a case subject to sections 556 and 557 of this title or otherwise reviewed on the record of an agency hearing provided by statute; or

(F) unwarranted by the facts to the extent that the facts are subject to trial de novo by the reviewing court.

In making the foregoing determinations, the court shall review the whole record or those parts of it cited by a party, and due account shall be taken of the rule of prejudicial error.

NOR-AM AGRICULTURAL PRODUCTS, INC. v. HARDIN, 435 F. 2d 1151 (Ct. App. 7th Cir. 1970).

CUMMINGS, Circuit Judge.

This is an appeal from a preliminary injunction granted by the district court which effectually restrains the Secretary of Agriculture and other personnel of the Department of Agriculture from continuing the suspension of the registration of 17 Panogenic compounds as "economic poisons" under the Federal Insecticide, Fungicide and Rodenticide Act. 7 U.S.C. § 135 et seq. A three-judge panel of this Court, one judge dissenting, upheld the preliminary injunction. 435 F.2d 1133. Subsequently, the Government's petition for a rehearing *en banc* was granted.

Plaintiff Morton International, Inc. manufactures seventeen types of cyano (methylmercuri) guanadine known as Panogens. Plaintiff Nor-Am Agricultural Products, Inc. distributes Morton's Panogens. These mercury compounds are used as fungicides in treating seeds intended for planting. They were duly registered as "economic poisons" with the Secretary of Agriculture, as required by Section 4(a) of the Federal Insecticide, Fungicide and Rodenticide Act. 7 U.S.C. § 135b(a).

Pursuant to Section 4(c) of the Act (7 U.S.C. § 135b(c)), on February 18, 1970, the Department of Agriculture telegraphed plaintiff Nor-Am that its Panogen registrations had been suspended "in view of the recent accident involving the ingestion of pork from hog feed seed treated with cyano (methylmercuri) guanadine." ● ● ●

On March 9, 1970, the registrations of similar products of other manufacturers were suspended. The suspensions prevent the shipment of these products until their registration is again permitted. Plaintiffs and the other distributors and manufacturer were not, however, required to recall existing stocks from their customers.

Administrative review of the Secretary's order was initiated on March 27, 1970, when Nor-Am requested an expedited administrative hearing as provided by Section 4(c) of the Act.[1] Instead of awaiting such a hearing, however, plaintiffs filed this suit on April 9, 1970, and quickly sought a preliminary injunction. Thereupon defendants moved to dismiss the proceeding. They claimed that the district court lacked jurisdiction to review the suspension order in advance of the hearing established by the statute; that plaintiffs had not exhausted the administrative procedures established by the Act; that the Secretary's order was a non-reviewable, discretionary act; and that the Secretary had not acted arbitrarily or capriciously. ● ● ●

At the hearing on the motion for the preliminary injunction, two Nor-Am employees and the general manager of a seed improvement association testified that Panogen products had been marketed for 20 years as a very useful fungicide seed treatment. ● ● ●

After the hearing, the district judge found that the court had jurisdiction over the subject matter of the dispute pursuant to the provisions of 28 U.S.C. § 1331, 28 U.S.C. § 1337, 28 U.S.C. §§ 2201–2202, Section 10 of the Administrative Procedure Act, 5 U.S.C. §§ 701–706, and the "general equity powers of this Court." The district judge also determined that unless preliminary injunctive relief were granted, plaintiffs would suffer irreparable harm for which they had no adequate administrative or legal remedy, although they were "likely to prevail on the merits." The judge further concluded that preliminary relief was "consistent with the public interest." Accordingly, he held the suspension of the Panogen registrations to have been arbitrary, capricious, and contrary to law, and defendants were enjoined from taking action against plaintiffs or the Panogens in reliance on the suspension order. Defendants were also ordered to give notice that the Panogens may again be distributed and sold in interstate commerce. Finally, the preliminary injunction permitted defendants to issue notices of cancellation of the registrations of these "economic poisons" effective only after the public hearing permitted by Section 4(c) of the Act.[4] Upon consideration of this cause by the entire Court, we are of the opinion that the district court lacked power to grant this relief because the plaintiffs have not exhausted their administrative remedy.

The fundamental provisions regulating judicial review of administrative actions are contained in the 1946 Administrative Procedure Act. 5 U.S.C. § 701 et seq. Section 10(c) of that Act governs which agency actions shall be reviewable:

"Agency action made reviewable by statute and final agency action for which there is no other adequate remedy in a court are subject to judicial review. A preliminary, procedural, or intermediate agency action or ruling not directly reviewable is subject to review on the review of the final agency action. * * *" 5 U.S.C. § 704. ● ● ●

In determining the status of the instant suspension in the light of the Administrative Procedure Act, we must turn first to the pertinent provisions of the Federal Insecticide, Fungicide and Rodenticide Act. 7 U.S.C. § 135 et seq. The 1964 amendments to Section 4 of that Act (Pub.L. 88–305, 88th Cong., 2nd Sess.) greatly strengthened the ability of the Secretary of Agriculture to take affirmative action protecting the public from hazardous and mislabeled commodities. Congress enacted new powers to deny, suspend, and cancel registrations where the Secretary had previously been compelled to accede to registration under protest should he be faced with an adamant demand. In Section 4(c), Congress also added hearing procedures guiding the exercise of these new powers. ● ● ●

these statutory provisions do not expressly or impliedly contemplate immediate review of emergency suspensions by either district or appellate courts. ● ● ●

Equally unacceptable is the contention that an emergency suspension order is a "final order" of the Secretary made reviewable by Section 4(c). That limitation on judicial review serves to avoid delay and interference with agency proceedings by confining review to orders effectively terminating administrative adjudication. ● ● ●

We conclude that Congress intended to confine judicial review of registration disputes under Section 4(c) of the Act to final orders of the Secretary culminating administrative adjudication. Under this Act, the emergency suspension of registration preceding such adjudication does not constitute such a final order and is therefore not "reviewable by statute" within Section 10(c) of the Administrative Procedure Act, *supra*, p. 1155. ● ● ●

Plaintiffs contend that this order should nevertheless entitle them to review under the "final agency action" provision of Section 10(c) of the Administrative Procedure Act. They argue that suspension of registration by the Secretary possesses sufficient "finality" as an administrative action to warrant immediate recourse to the courts despite its status as a preliminary act within the framework of Section 4(c) of the Federal Insecticide, Fungicide and Rodenticide Act. Suspension, they urge, immediately and drastically affects their rights and interests as greatly as formally finalized cancellation. They suggest that neither subsequent agency proceedings nor judicial review established by Section 4(d) adequately test the Secretary's determination of "imminent hazard to the public." Unless they are permitted this exceptional remedy, they claim that the Secretary's findings amount to autonomous discretion.

Under Section 10(c) of the Administrative Procedure Act, the concept of finality of administrative action encompasses a complex array of considerations which may vary in accordance with the character and activities of the administrative agency, and with the nature and role of the agency action from which judicial review is sought. See Abbott Laboratories v. Gardner, 387 U.S. 136, 148–156, 87 S.Ct. 1507, 18 L.Ed.2d 681.[5] The flexibility of the finality concept does not, however, permit facile disregard of the purposes of congressional delegation of power and of the clear procedural scheme delineated in this particular statute. ● ○ ●

The function of the Secretary's emergency power, as well as the practical exigencies of coordinating administrative and judicial machinery, militates against avoiding the prescribed procedures. The emergency suspension of registration of an economic poison under Section 4(c) involves highly discretionary administrative action with deeply rooted antecedents in the realm of public health and safety. In subtle areas of regulation, summary emergency action frequently precedes formal administrative or judicial adjudication. See, e. g., Ewing v. Mytinger & Casselberry, Inc., 339 U.S. 594, 599–600, 70 S.Ct. 870, 94 L.Ed. 1088; cf. Phillips v. Commissioner of Internal Revenue, 283 U.S. 589, 596–597, 51 S.Ct. 608, 75 L.Ed. 1289; Bowles v. Willingham, 321 U.S. 503, 64 S.Ct. 641, 88 L.Ed. 892; Fahey v. Mallonee, 332 U.S. 245, 67 S.Ct. 1552, 91 L.Ed. 2030. Where, as here, Congress follows discretionary preliminary or interlocutory agency action with specially fashioned adjudicative machinery, strict observance of the prescribed procedure prior to judicial intervention is compellingly indicated.

Precipitous judicial review of this tentative judgment would at best be a difficult matter of dubious social benefit. Moreover, it strains administrative resources at a stage in the process which is most delicate and to a degree which may ultimately be rendered unnecessary by ordinary agency operations, both formal and informal. Even the limited review here contemplated nullifies the need or utility of the further agency action desired by Congress. The administrative process is interrupted before issues have been crystalized and narrowed and without affording opportunity for application of technical expertise and informed judgment. As this record demonstrates, judicial review at this stage requires factual elaboration by the district court. Such bifurcation and duplication of governmental resources and efforts demonstrates the wisdom of judicial restraint,

since once the district court has inserted itself into the process, it becomes wasteful or pointless to return the matter to the agency. ● ○ ●

Judicial review of the Secretary's suspension order is inconsistent with the procedural remedies created by Congress for such an occasion. It is also at odds with the restraint courts have long exercised in dealing with preventive measures available to agencies charged with protecting such sensitive areas of public welfare. Here the plaintiffs have not yet exhausted their statutorily prescribed administrative remedies and there has as yet been no "final agency action" within Section 10(c) of the Administrative Procedure Act. ● ○ ●

In addition to the statutory avenues of review, plaintiffs urge that the equity powers of the court have been properly invoked to prevent irreparable injury caused by the suspension order.

The circumvention of clearly prescribed administrative procedures by awarding equitable relief is an exceptional practice. As explained in Aircraft & Diesel Equipment Corp. v. Hirsch, 331 U.S. 752, 773–774, 67 S.Ct. 1493, 1503–1504, 91 L.Ed. 1796, the rule that administrative remedies may occasionally be by-passed to protect strong private interests from irreparable harm

"is not one of mere convenience or ready application. Where the intent of Congress is clear to require administrative determination, either to the exclusion of judicial action or in advance of it, a strong showing is required, both of inadequacy of the prescribed procedure and of impending harm, to permit shortcircuiting the administrative process. Congress' commands for judicial restraint in this respect are not lightly to be disregarded."

Plaintiffs have failed to establish such an irremediable threat to sufficiently strong interests to warrant equitable intercession at this juncture.

We cannot accept the verdict of the judge below that the administrative remedies are inadequate. ● ○ ●

The primary interests threatened in this case are not public but private. They are interests of property rather than of life or liberty. Although plaintiffs claim danger to farmers and consumers from removal of their products, their direct and immediate concern is the impact of suspension upon their businesses. ● ● ●

We do not demean plaintiffs' possible losses when noting moreover, that the temporary suspension affects business profits, not the very existence of the commodities plaintiffs seek to purvey. Where public health and safety demand emergency removal of a commodity from the market, even unrecoverable financial losses incurred *pendente lite* must be deemed an expense of the litigation itself. See Ewing v. Mytinger & Casselberry, Inc., 339 U.S. 594, 70 S.Ct. 870, 94 L.Ed. 1088; cf. Fahey v. Mallonee, 332 U.S. 245, 67 S.Ct. 1552, 91 L.Ed. 2030.

Congress was not bound to supply the optimal protection to registrants affected by emergency suspensions. Congress balanced the public and private interests when it fashioned not only the Secretary's discretionary power but also the administrative procedures to follow exercise of that power. ● ● ●

If this preliminary injunction were approved, other litigants could obtain district court threshold review by parroting plaintiffs' claim that the Secretary had acted arbitrarily and capriciously in suspending their registrations, even though Sections 4(c) and 4(d) specify that review shall only be in the courts of appeals after action by the advisory committee and then by the Secretary. We should not countenance such an evasion of the review procedure provided by Congress in this statute.[6] In reaching this conclusion, we express no opinion on the merits of the controversy between these parties concerning the registration of Panogens.

The preliminary injunction is dissolved and the case is remanded to the district court with instructions to dismiss the complaint.

Reversed.

PELL, Circuit Judge (dissenting).

. . . .

See: REYNOLDS METALS COMPANY v. MARTIN, supra, I, A,3 in which the court held that a nuisance action is an exception to the requirement of review by the state Sanitary Authority before a court action may be brought.

<u>HIGH VOLTAGE ENGINEERING CORP. v. PIERCE</u>, 359 F. 2d 33
(Ct. App. 10th Cir. 1966).

MURRAH, Chief Judge.

This appeal is from a judgment on a jury verdict in an action by appellee Pierce against appellant High Voltage for personal injuries caused by a radioactive beam from an electron accelerator manufactured and supplied by High Voltage to the intervenor Sandia Corporation,[1] Pierce's employer.

The Van deGraaff two million volt accelerator was designed and used to propel electron beams at target material for nuclear experimental purposes. This is accomplished by spraying electrons on a moving belt for transmission to a high voltage terminal. From the terminal they flow to a cathode for emission into the accelerator tube and propulsion to the experiment target at the end of the tube. Four switches control the accelerator's operation. One switch turns on the power and another controls the belt and its drive motor. A third switch determines the amount of voltage on the terminal. Another, the beam switch, allows the electrons to be emitted as a beam from the cathode into the accelerator tube. The electron beam causes radiation and potential human danger in the target area.

The accelerator is housed in a concrete chamber or "target room". On the date of the accident, a Sandia Corporation employee, trained by appellant, was operating the drive motor and belt to dispel a 1,700,000 volt "self-charge" on the voltage terminal. The beam switch was off. The appellee-Pierce asked the operator if it was safe to enter the accelerator chamber to set up an experiment. After being told it was safe because the beam switch was off, Pierce entered the chamber despite the blinking of warning lights and a sounding horn indicating that the drive motor was operating. Two minutes later he left the room and discovered the injuries complained of.

The theory of appellees' case as correctly submitted to the jury is that a radioactive beam referred to as "dark current phenomenon" was emitted from the accelerator tube while the beam switch was off and the accelerator was in a condition of self-charge at high voltage. The court defined the issues by telling the jury that the accelerator was a dangerous instrumentality when emitting an electron beam; that it could and did emit an electron beam under the conditions prevailing at the time the appellee was injured; and that High Voltage knew that this phenomenon could occur. The issues were further sharpened by stating the contention of appellees to the effect that they did not know of the phenomenon and High Voltage was, therefore, under a duty to give adequate warning of the attendant danger. The trial court then succinctly stated the appellant's contention to the effect that it was under no duty to warn the appellees of the particular danger because as scientists they knew or should have known of it. Moreover, if they did not know, they had been given adequate warning of the particular hazard, and entry into the chamber under the prevailing circumstances was contributorily negligent.

The trial court then proceeded to state the applicable law of the case to the effect that as the supplier of a dangerous instrumentality the appellant was under a legal duty to warn prospective users of dangers which it knew or should know, and that such warning should be commensurate with the degree of danger involved, i. e. the warning must be directed to the specific danger and sufficient to cause a reasonable man acting under similar circumstances with the same knowledge and background to know the potential danger involved in the exercise of reasonable care.

The appellant makes no objection to the statement of the issues or the law of the case as stated in the trial court's instructions. It takes the position, however, that the trial court should have followed the law and the ruling in Marker v. Universal Oil Products Co., 10 Cir., 250 F.2d 603, and directed a verdict on the grounds that the evidence conclusively shows that the peculiar danger causing the injury was equally within the knowledge of the parties and the appellant was, therefore, under no duty to warn or inform. Alternatively, it contends that as a matter of law its legal duty was fulfilled by complete and adequate instructions to any user of the accelerator and that the harm in this case resulted from an unanticipated misuse by an adequately informed user.

 The directed verdict in Marker was sustained on the conclusiveness of the proof that the dangerous condition was equally within the technical knowledge of both parties and that the harm, therefore, resulted from an unanticipated misuse. If the appellee had equal knowledge of the danger involved, or if he was adequately informed of it, his subsequent entry into the chamber would constitute unanticipated misuse or contributory negligence, both barring recovery. See Marker v. Universal Oil Products Co., supra; Parkinson v. California Co., 10 Cir., 255 F.2d 265.

 The court in our case gave no equal knowledge instruction, and the appellant does not complain of its failure to do so. But, if, as in Marker, the evidence conclusively shows equal technical knowledge of the danger, High Voltage was entitled to a directed verdict under applicable law. Unlike Marker, however, we do not think the proof in our case conclusively shows equal technical knowledge of the dark current phenomenon which admittedly caused the danger and consequent harm. ● ● ● The Director of Physical Research at Sandia, who was completely familiar with accelerators, testified that he was aware of the principle of dark current phenomenon, but that he was not aware of the scientific fact that it could occur in this particular accelerator.[2] Appellee Pierce testified he did not know about it; the operator denied he knew of it; another scientist who had been similarly injured testified that he did not know of it or of anyone who did. The issue of equal scientific knowledge was well within the realm of fact.

Alternatively, High Voltage cites seven specific instances of unanticipated gross misuse of the accelerator based upon adequate notice, any one of which would bar recovery. Five of the cited instances are based upon failure to heed specific warnings contained in the manual of instructions accompanying delivery of the accelerator. ● ● ●

The fifth asserted warning contained in the manual under the heading "Radiation Hazard" stated that "The output from the high voltage accelerator tube of this apparatus can produce radiation effects with serious and possibly fatal consequences to personnel. ● ● ●

Another misuse was claimed for failure of Pierce to take a hand survey meter (a geiger-counter) into the target room with him in accordance with the safety instructions promulgated by Sandia. The testimony was to the effect that the hand survey meter was required and that the operator of the accelerator had been instructed to always take the meter into the room when doing maintenance work on the accelerator, whether the beam switch was on or off. There was also evidence to the effect that Pierce knew of the hand meter and its purpose and that he did not take it into the target room with him and was not instructed to do so by the operator. The operator first indicated that if Pierce had taken the hand meter into the target room the accident would not have happened. Upon reflection, he indicated that because of the time it took the meter to register radiation the accident might have happened in any event. Pierce testified that if there had been any question of safety, he would not have gone into the target room or would have taken a meter with him; that he did not realize the danger under the circumstances because he knew the beam switch was off.

High Voltage takes the position that even if Pierce was not guilty of misuse or contributory negligence, Sandia was negligent and such negligence was the sole cause of the injury, first, for failure to promulgate proper safety rules for the operation of the machine and, second, failure to observe and enforce the safety rules it did promulgate, namely the proper use of both the remote metering system and the hand survey meter.

Judge Payne thought these defenses presented questions of fact under the evidence and told the jury that the warnings, if any, in the instruction manual would be binding upon Pierce only if he knew about them or should have known in the exercise of due care, but if the warnings were adequate they were binding upon Sandia in any event and it was under a duty to pass them on to its employees, including Pierce; that the jury should determine whether the instructions did contain warnings and, if so, whether they were adequate and whether Sandia passed them on to Pierce; that they should make this determination in determining whether Sandia was negligent and whether its negligence, if any, was the sole and proximate cause of the accident.

The seventh claimed misuse of the machine has to do with Dr. Pierce's entry into the target room in disregard of the door interlocks and the audible, visual warnings, i. e. flashing lights and sounding horn. The horn blows for forty-five seconds after entry into the target room when the power is on even though the beam switch is off, and the lights continue to flash as long as the drive motor is in operation. When Pierce went to the operator in the console room outside the target room, the drive motor was in operation, the beam switch was off and the lights were flashing. ● ● ●

High Voltage contends that Pierce was negligent in entering the room in these circumstances and that in any event Sandia was solely negligent by failing to prohibit Pierce from entering the target room under prevailing conditions; that the interlocking doors, horn and flashing lights were clear warning to anyone.

Judge Payne submitted this issue to the jury instructing them to determine from all the evidence and surrounding circumstances whether these warnings were sufficient to adequately warn a reasonable man in the exercise of ordinary care. On both the motion for directed verdict and motion for judgment n. o. v. Judge Payne was deeply disturbed and perplexed concerning whether as a matter of law the warning signals were adequate in and of themselves to inform Sandia and Pierce of the peculiar danger which prevailed at the time of the accident and which caused the harm. He was impressed with the significance of the words on the console panel: "Radiation Beam" "On" "Off" and seemed to think the operator may have been lulled into the belief that with the radiation beam switch off the target chamber was safe from radiation despite the warning signals. Considered in the light of all the circumstances, the court could not say as a matter of law that the warnings were sufficient to constitute unanticipated misuse or contributory negligence.

● ● ●

It is, of course, the function of the trial court to analyze the evidence and appraise its sufficiency in the first instance. Judge Payne did analyze and appraise the evidence with extreme care, and we should not superimpose our judgment on that of the trial court unless we can say from our objective appraisal of all of the facts and circumstances that his judgment on the adequacy of notice was clearly wrong. When all of the evidence is considered in the light most favorable to appellees, we cannot say that the trial court erroneously submitted it to the jury.

● ● ●

The judgment is affirmed.

MAHONEY v. U.S., 220 F. Supp. 823 (D.C. Tenn. 1963) aff'd 339 F. 2d 605.

ROBERT L. TAYLOR, Chief Judge.

These cases, three in number, are actions to recover damages under the Federal Tort Claims Act, Title 28 U.S.C. § 1346(b) [1] and Section 2674.

The Act makes the Government liable "respecting * * * tort claims * * * in the same manner and to the same extent as a private individual under like circumstances." 28 U.S.C. § 2674. Discretionary functions or duties are excepted. § 2680(a). [2]

The Government, through the Atomic Energy Commission, hereinafter sometimes called AEC, is engaged in a program of production and development of atomic energy at Oak Ridge, Tennessee. Plaintiffs were employees of Union Carbide Nuclear Corporation, an operating division of Union Carbide Corporation, hereinafter sometimes called Carbide, that operates the production facilities at Oak Ridge at the instance of AEC under a cost type Government contract with the United States.

This Court has previously held that Carbide is an independent contractor in the operation of the Government plants at Oak Ridge. (Mahoney v. United States, D. C., 216 F.Supp. 523.)

Plaintiff Mahoney claims that the disease which renders him permanently and totally disabled and the other two plaintiffs claim that the deaths of their respective intestates were caused by the negligence of the Government in the operation of the Oak Ridge Gaseous Diffusion Plant K–25 in that the living plaintiff and the two decedents in the course of their employment were exposed to radioactive substances or toxic gases. That the defendant failed to provide adequate safeguards, failed to furnish a safe place to work, failed to provide adequate medical supervision, proper equipment, proper protective clothing, particularly respirators or gas masks necessary to screen out any toxic gases or radioactive materials to prevent the employees from breathing them. ● ● ●

Plaintiffs likewise claim that their conditions were either caused or accelerated from toxic gases and radioactive materials to which they were subjected and that as a result plaintiff's intestate Wilson Kirk Beckham died on April 24, 1962 from Hodgkin's disease, which is a type of blood cancer, and plaintiff's intestate Howard N. Pierce died on January 13, 1961 from acute granulocytic [5] leukemia and plaintiff Mahoney is presently suffering from chronic lymphatic leukemia.

Plaintiffs also claim that the operation of the K–25 plant constituted an ultrahazardous activity and that the United States had a non-delegable duty to assure its operation in such a manner as to avoid injury to plaintiff or plaintiffs' decedents.

The Government denies all acts of negligence and also denies plaintiffs (plaintiffs will be used hereafter at times as if Pierce and Beckham were living) were engaged in inherently dangerous or ultrahazardous activities. The Government further denies that there was any causal relation between plaintiffs' diseases and their employment.

Contributory negligence is pleaded as a bar to the actions. ● ● ●

The controlling issues in the case are:

(a) Was the Government guilty of any act of negligence that proximately caused the disability of the living plaintiff and the disabilities and deaths of plaintiffs' intestates?

(b) If the Government was guilty of proximate negligence, were plaintiffs guilty of proximate contributory negligence or remote contributory negligence? (Proximate contributory negligence would bar a recovery under Tennessee law and remote contributory negligence would mitigate the damages.)

(c) Was there a causal relation between the work of plaintiffs as employees of Carbide and their physical condition and deaths. ● ● ●

The Government cannot be charged with negligence of the employees of an independent contractor under the non-delegable rule of local law. ● ● ●

An employer ordinarily is not liable for injuries resulting from the performance of work given over by him to an independent contractor unless the work was unlawful itself or the injury was a necessary consequence of executing the work in the manner provided for in the contract, or subsequently prescribed by the employer, or was caused by the violation of some absolute non-delegable duty which the employer was bound at his peril to discharge, or was due to some specific negligence of the employer himself. International Harvester Co. v. Sartain, 32 Tenn.App. 425, 451, 222 S.W.2d 854. One exception to the rule is that if the location and condition and the nature of the work to be done are such that in the natural course of things mischievous consequences may be expected to arise unless means are adopted by which such consequences may be prevented the owner is under the non-delegable duty to see that appropriate preventative measures are adopted. Another exception is where the work is intrinsically dangerous and the performance of the contract would probably result in injury to third persons or the public. Ibid, 32 Tenn.App. 451, 452, 456, 222 S.W.2d 854.

Under the Tennessee rule, an owner of property is required to use reasonable care to provide a safe place for an independent contractor and his employees to work. Shell Oil Co. v. Blanks, 46 Tenn.App. 539, 330 S.W.2d 569 (1959).

If the owner retains general control of his premises, an employee of an independent contractor who performs work on the premises is an invitee and the owner owes him the duty of exercising reasonable care to have the premises in a reasonably safe condition for use in a manner consistent with the purpose of the invitation. The duty requiring the owner to keep the premises reasonably safe for a contractor and his employees does not apply where the work itself is of an unsafe nature. ● ● ●

The burden of proving which of the causes created the disease or injury is upon plaintiff where there are a number of causes for such disease or injury. Willis et al. v. Heath, 21 Tenn.App. 179, 107 S.W.2d 228.

We proceed to briefly summarize the testimony of the witnesses with these general rules in mind.

Summary of Testimony of Each Witness ● ● ●
Statistics

Plaintiffs contend that the statistical odds are 10,000 to 1 in favor of the probability that there is causal connection between the radiation to which the plaintiffs were exposed and their resulting disabilities. It is argued that four cases, two of leukemia and two Hodgkin's disease, is a high ratio among 800 employees in the Oak Ridge plants. ● ● ●

Carbide, by permitting men to cut into the pipes before purging them of all pockets of gas showed casualness in the enforcement of its safety practices. Proper purging would have eliminated all gas from the pipes that were disconnected from the system. There is evidence that dust was permitted to accumulate in portions of the building which was at various times contaminated to some extent, and which was on occasions swept with brooms. Good practice required the removal of the dust by mops or vacuum cleaners. There is also testimony that numerous complaints were made by employees that the gas masks and respirators were insufficient to protect them from gas. On the basis of their testimony, many of the employees of Carbide were permitted to smell too much gas. This indicated that there was a certain casualness or carelessness that grew up in the plants among the employees and their supervisors in the face of uncertain dangers. But in spite of this claimed laxity in the enforcement of safety standards, the preponderance of the proof fails to show that plaintiffs' exposures to radiation or toxic gases were sufficient to cause leukemia or Hodgkin's disease. Plaintiffs' exposures were well below the marginal limits for human safety. ● ● ●

The Court is of the opinion and holds that plaintiffs failed to establish a causal relation between their work for Carbide and their resulting diseases or injuries by a preponderance of the evidence. The Court is further of the opinion and finds that plaintiffs failed to show by a preponderance of the evidence that the Government was guilty of any act of negligence that proximately caused their diseases or injuries. The Court, therefore, concludes that plaintiffs have failed to establish a case of liability against the Government under the Federal Tort Claims Act.

The remaining questions raised by the parties have been considered, but in view of the conclusions reached, it is not deemed necessary to pass upon them.

Present order in conformity with the views here expressed.

. . . .

The Court never reached the question of contributory negligence because of its finding that there was insufficient evidence to show a causal relationship between radiation exposure and leukemia.

Suppose that there had been sufficient evidence to establish the causal relationship but there was also evidence to show that the deceased workers had repeatedly ignored instructions to wear a gas mask in specified areas. Should the defendant be liable?

. . . .

HENRIKSON v. KOPPERS CO., INC. 11 N.J. 600, 95 A2d 7 10 (1953).

VANDERBILT. C. J.

• • • The second question is whether there was as a matter of law contributory negligence or assumption of risk on plaintiff's part that bars his recovery. Although there is an obvious difference between contributory negligence and assumption of risk there is a tendency to treat them as identical. The former involves the notion of some fault or breach of duty on the part of an individual. His actions are such as to constitute a failure to use such care for his safety as the ordinarily prudent man in similar circumstances would use. On the other hand assumption of risk, though usually applied to the relationship of master and servant, may be used in other fields. No matter where applied, the doctrine may involve no fault or negligence, but rather entails the undertaking of a risk of a known danger. Seaboard Air Line Railway v. Horton, 233 U.S. 492, 502, 34 S.Ct. 635, 58 L.Ed. 1062, 1069 (1914); Cetola v. Lehigh Valley Railroad Co., 89 N.J.L. 691, 99 A. 310 (E. & A.1916). But, as stated by Mr. Justice Holmes, "Assumption of risk in this broad sense obviously shades into negligence as commonly understood. Negligence consists in conduct which common experience or the special knowledge of the actor shows to be so likely to produce the result complained of, under the circumstances known to the actor, that he is held answerable for that result, although it was not certain, intended, or foreseen. He is held to assume the risk upon the same ground. * * *" Schlemmer v. Buffalo, R. & P. Railway Co., 205 U.S. 1, 12, 27 S.Ct. 407, 409, 51 L.Ed. 681 (1906).

Here the testimony was conflicting as to whether the plaintiff had knowledge of the danger. • • •

As we stated in Paolercio v. Wright, 2 N.J. 412, 418, 67 A.2d 168, 170 (1949), "the rule is that unless it is clearly established beyond fair debate that the plaintiff was negligent and that the negligence proximately contributed to his injury, a motion for a nonsuit or to direct a verdict will be denied." A jury question was presented here. • • •

6. Assumption of Risk

POTTER v. BRITTAN, 286 F2d 521 (1961).

GOODRICH, Circuit Judge

● ● ●

The one point left in the case on this appeal involves the plaintiffs' insistence that the trial judge incorrectly charged the jury. The defenses of assumption of risk and contributory negligence were both made by the defendants. The trial judge charged on each and his clear statement of the rule of contributory negligence is not challenged. As to assumption of risk the judge said: "Assumption of risk is so closely identified with contributory negligence that a practical distinction is difficult when considered in relation to the facts in a particular case. * * * The tendency is to treat assumption of risk and contributory negligence as convertible terms so that they are now virtually identical concepts."

This did not satisfy plaintiffs' counsel and in colloquy on exceptions to the court's charge he said: "My request is really that they shouldn't get the impression that assumption of risk and contributory negligence are two separate defenses. * * * The pleading makes them two, but the law does not. * * * It's a contributory negligence defense which one judge will call assumption of risk and one will call contributory negligence." ◑ ● ●

The position of the legal scholars on the subject is perfectly clear. At the risk of tiresome repetition a few quotations are in order because the subject seems to be one on which there is a good deal of confusion. The first quotation is from a very famous tort scholar, Francis H. Bohlen, and it was written in 1926:

"The defense of contributory negligence is quite distinct. Negligence involves the idea of misconduct, a failure to measure up to the standard of that ideal personage, the normal social man; assumption of risk does not. A risk while obvious may not be so imminently dangerous that a prudent man would necessarily avoid it, yet if it shall be freely encountered it will in general be held to be so far assumed that no recovery for the consequent injury is possible. Voluntary conscious action may be negligent if the known danger be great and imminent, but it is not negligent because voluntary. By contributory negligence a plaintiff is barred from recovery by his own misconduct, though the defendant has been guilty of an act admittedly wrongful as to him. Voluntary subjection to a known risk negatives the existence of any duty on the defendant's part by the breach of which he could be a wrongdoer.

"It is essential that the two ideas should be kept quite distinct. * *" (Footnotes omitted.)[3]

The same point is made by current writers. Prosser on Torts, for example, talks about the situation where the two defenses overlap. He says:

"Ordinarily it makes little difference which the defense is called. The distinction may become important, however, under such statutes as the Federal Employers' Liability Act, which has now abrogated the defense of assumption of risk entirely, but has left, contributory negligence as a partial defense reducing the amount of recovery. In working out the distinction, the courts have arrived at the conclusion that assumption of risk is a matter of knowledge of the danger and intelligent acquiescence in it, while contributory negligence is a matter of some fault or departure from the standard of reasonable conduct, however unwilling or protesting the plaintiff may be. The two may co-exist, or either may exist without the other." (Footnotes omitted.)[4]

Finally, in the last work on the subject, Harper and James on Torts, 1956, the authors say:

"*Assumption of risk.* Contributory negligence has sometimes been thought to be no more than an aspect of assumption of risk, so that plaintiff is barred from recovery under the maxim volenti non fit injuria. This explanation, too, would warrant the rule in its present form, as a complete bar to plaintiff's action. The two notions, however, do not cover the same ground and in many situations do not even overlap, though they may. Assumption of risk involves the negation of defendant's duty; contributory negligence is a defense to a breach of such duty. Assumption of risk may involve perfectly reasonable conduct on plaintiff's part; contributory negligence never does." (Footnotes omitted.)[5]

It would be hard to find any point on which scholarly discussion is so completely unanimous. ● ● ●

. . . .

7.   Statute of Limitations

(a)   Actions Against Private Persons: E.g. N.J.S.A. 2A:14-1

2A:14–1.   6 years

Every action at law for trespass to real property, for any tortious injury to real or personal property, for taking, detaining, or converting personal property, for replevin of goods or chattels, for any tortious injury to the rights of another not stated in sections 2A:14–2 and 2A:14–3 of this title, or for recovery upon a contractual claim or liability, express or implied, not under seal, or upon an account other than one which concerns the trade or merchandise between merchant and merchant, their factors, agents and servants, shall be commenced within 6 years next after the cause of any such action shall have accrued.

(b)   Actions Against the State: E.g. N.J.S.A. 59:13-5

● ● ●

In all contract claims against the State, the claimant shall be forever barred from recovering against the State if:

a. he fails to notify the appropriate contracting agency within 90 days of accrual of his claim except as otherwise provided in section 6 hereof; or

b. he fails to file suit within 2 years of accrual of his claims or within 1 year after completion of the contract giving rise to paid claim, whichever may be later; or

c. the claimant accepts personally or through his agent or legal representative any award, compromise or settlement made by the State of New Jersey.

8. Pre-emption by Federal Government

CITY OF BURBANK v. LOCKHEED AIR TERMINAL INC., 93 S. Ct. 1854 (1973).

Mr. Justice DOUGLAS delivered the opinion of the Court.

The Court in Cooley v. Board of Wardens, 12 How. 299, 13 L.Ed. 996, first stated the rule of pre-emption which is the critical issue in the present case. Speaking through Justice Curtis, it said:

"Now the power to regulate commerce, embraces a vast field, containing not only many, but exceedingly various subjects, quite unlike in their nature; some imperatively demanding a single uniform rule, operating equally on the commerce of the United States in every port; and some, like the subject now in question, as imperatively demanding that diversity, which alone can meet the local necessities of navigation. . . . Whatever subjects of this power are in their nature national, or admit only of one uniform system, or plan of regulation, may justly be said to be of such a nature as to require exclusive legislation by Congress." Id., at 319.

This suit brought by appellees asked for an injunction against the enforcement of an ordinance adopted by the City Council of Burbank, California, which made it unlawful for a so-called pure jet aircraft to take off from the Hollywood-Burbank Airport between 11 p. m. of one day and 7 a. m. the next day, and making it unlawful for the operator of that airport to allow any such aircraft to take off from that airport during such periods.[1] ● ● ●

The District Court found the ordinance to be unconstitutional on both Supremacy Clause and Commerce Clause grounds. 318 F.Supp. 914. The Court of Appeals affirmed on the grounds of the Supremacy Clause both as respects pre-emption and as respects conflict.[2] 457 F.2d 667. The case is here on appeal. ● ● ●

The Federal Aviation Act of 1958, 72 Stat. 737, 49 U.S.C. § 1301 et seq., as amended by the Noise Control Act of 1972, 86 Stat. 1234, and the regulations under it, 14 CFR Pts. 71–77, 91–97, are central to the question of pre-emption.

Section 1508 provides in part, "The United States of America is declared to possess and exercise complete and exclusive national sovereignty in the airspace of the United States . . . ." By § 1348 the Administrator of the Federal Aeronautics Act (FAA) has been given broad authority to regulate the use of the navigable airspace, "in order to insure the safety of aircraft and the efficient utilization of such airspace . . . ." and "for the protection of persons and property on the ground. . . ."[3]

The Solicitor General, though arguing against pre-emption, concedes that as respects "airspace management" there is pre-emption. ● ● ●

Curfews, such as Burbank has imposed, would according to the testimony at the trial and the District Court's findings increase congestion, cause a loss of efficiency, and aggravate the noise problem. FAA has occasionally operated curfews. See Virginians for Dulles v. Volpe, D. C., 344 F.Supp. 573. But the record shows that FAA has consistently opposed curfews, unless managed by it, in the interests of its management of the "navigable airspace."
● ● ●

The Noise Control Act of 1972, 86 Stat. 1234, which was approved October 27, 1972, provides that the Administrator "after consultation with appropriate Federal, State, and local agencies and interested persons" shall conduct a study of various facets of the aircraft "noise" problems and report to the Congress within nine months,[4] i. e., by July 1973. The 1972 Act by amending § 611 of the Federal Aviation Act,[5] also involves the

Environmental Protection Agency (EPA) in the comprehensive scheme of federal control of the aircraft noise problem. Under the amended § 611(b)(1) the FAA, after consulting with EPA, shall provide "for the control and abatement of aircraft noise and sonic boom, including the application of such standards and regulations in the issuance, amendment, modification, suspension or revocation of any certificate authorized by this title." [6] Section 611(b)(2) as amended provides that future certificates for aircraft operations shall not issue unless the new aircraft noise requirements are met.[7] Section 611(c)(1) as amended provides that not later than July 1973 EPA shall submit to FAA proposed regulations to provide such "control and abatement of aircraft noise and sonic boom" as EPA determines is "necessary to protect the public health and welfare." The FAA is directed within 30 days to publish the proposed regulations in a notice of proposed rule making. Within 60 days after that publication FAA is directed to commence a public hearing on the proposed rules. Section 611(c)(1). That subsection goes on to provide that within "a reasonable time after the conclusion of such hearing and after consultation with EPA," FAA is directed either to prescribe the regulations substantially as submitted by EPA; or prescribe them in modified form, or publish in the Federal Register a notice that it is not prescribing any regulation in response to EPA's submission together with its reasons therefor.

Section 611(c)(2) as amended also provides that if EPA believes that FAA's action with respect to a regulation proposed by EPA "does not protect the public health and welfare from aircraft noise or sonic boom," EPA shall consult with FAA and may request FAA to review and report to EPA on the advisability of prescribing the regulation originally proposed by EPA. That request shall be published in the Federal Register; FAA shall complete the review requested and report to EPA in the time specified together with a detailed statement of FAA's findings and the reasons for its conclusion and shall identify any impact statement filed under § 102(2)(C) of the National Environmental Policy Act of 1969,[8] 83 Stat. 853, 42 U.S.C. § 4332, with respect to FAA's action. FAA's action, if adverse to EPA's proposal, shall be published in the Federal Register. ● ● ●

There is to be sure no express provision of pre-emption in the 1972 Act. That, however, is not decisive. As we stated in Rice v. Santa Fe Elevator Corp., 331 U.S. 218, 230, 67 S.Ct. 1146, 1152, 91 L.Ed. 1447:

"Congress legislated here in a field which the States have traditionally occupied. . . . So we start with the assumption that the historic police powers of the States were not to be superseded by the Federal Act unless that was the clear and manifest purpose of Congress. . . . Such a purpose may be evidenced in several ways. The scheme of federal regulation may be so pervasive as to make reasonable the inference that Congress left no room for the States to supplement it. . . . Or the Act of Congress may touch a field in which the federal interest is so dominant that the federal system will be assumed to preclude enforcement of state laws on the same subject. . . . Likewise, the object sought to be obtained by the federal law and the character of obligations imposed by it may reveal the same purpose. . . . Or the state policy may produce a result inconsistent with the objective of the federal statute."

It is the pervasive nature of the scheme of federal regulation of aircraft noise that leads us to conclude that there is pre-emption. ● ● ●

"Federal control is intensive and exclusive. Planes do not wander about in the sky like vagrant clouds. They move only by federal permission, subject to federal inspection, in the hands of federally certified personnel and under an intricate system of federal commands. The moment a ship taxis onto a runway it is caught up in an elaborate and detailed system of controls."

Both the Senate and House Committees included in their Reports clear statements that the bills would not change the existing pre-emption rule.
● ● ●
The Senate Report stated: [10] "States and local governments are preempted from establishing or enforcing noise emission standards for aircraft unless such standards are identical to standards prescribed under this bill.
● ● ●
When the blended provisions of the present Act were before the House, Congressman Staggers, Chairman of the House Commerce Committee, in urging the House to accept the amended version, said: [18]

"I cannot say what industry's intention may be, but I can say to the gentleman what my intention is in trying to get this bill passed. We have evidence that across America some cities and States are trying to do [sic] pass noise regulations. Certainly we do not want that to happen. It would harass industry and progress in America. That is the reason why I want to get this bill passed during this session."

When the House approved the blended provisions of the bill, Senator Tunney moved that the Senate concur. He made clear[19] that the regulations to be considered by EPA for recommendation to FAA would include:

". . . proposed means of reducing noise in airport environments through the application of emission controls on aircraft, the regulation of flight patterns and aircraft and airport operations, and modifications in the number, frequency, or scheduling of flights [as well as] . . . the imposition of curfews on noisy airports,
● ● ●

When the President signed the bill he stated that "many of the most significant sources of noise move in interstate commerce and can be effectively regulated only at the federal level."[20]

Our prior cases on pre-emption are not precise guidelines in the present controversy, for each case turns on the peculiarities and special features of the federal regulatory scheme in question. Cf. Hines v. Davidowitz, 312 U.S. 52, 61 S.Ct. 399, 85 L.Ed. 581; Huron Portland Cement Co. v. Detroit, 362 U.S. 440, 80 S.Ct. 813, 4 L.Ed.2d 852. Control of noise is of course deep-seated in the police power of the States. Yet the pervasive control vested in EPA and in FAA under the 1972 Act seems to us to leave no room for local curfews or other local controls. What the ultimate remedy for aircraft noise which plagues many communities and tens of thousands of people is not known. The procedures under the 1972 Act are underway.[21] In addition, the Administrator has imposed a variety of regulations relating to takeoff and landing procedures and runway preferences. The Federal Aviation Act requires a delicate balance between safety and efficiency, 49 U.S.C. § 1348(a), and the protection of persons on the ground. 49 U.S.C. § 1348(c). Any regulations adopted by the Administrator to control noise pollution must be consistent with the "highest degree of safety." 49 U.S. C. § 1431(d)(3). The interdependence of these factors requires a uniform and exclusive system of federal regulation if the congressional objectives underlying the Federal Aviation Act are to be fulfilled.

If we were to uphold the Burbank ordinance and a significant number of municipalities followed suit, it is obvious that fractionalized control of the timing of takeoffs and landings would severely limit the flexibility of the FAA in controlling air traffic flow.[22] The difficulties of scheduling flights to avoid congestion and the concomitant decrease in safety would be compounded ● ● ●

We are not at liberty to diffuse the powers given by Congress to FAA and EPA by letting the States or municipalities in on the planning. If that change is to be made, Congress alone must do it.

Affirmed.

Mr. Justice REHNQUIST, with whom Mr. Justice STEWART, Mr. Justice WHITE, and Mr. Justice MARSHALL join, dissenting.

The Court concludes that congressional legislation dealing with aircraft noise has so "pervaded" that field that Congress has *impliedly* pre-empted it, and therefore the ordinance of the city of Burbank here challenged is invalid under the Supremacy Clause of the Constitution. The Court says that the 1972 "Act reaffirms and reinforces the conclusion that FAA, now in conjunction with EPA, has full control over aircraft noise, pre-empting state and local control." *Ante* at 1859. Yet the House and Senate committee reports explicitly state that the 1972 Act to which the Court refers was *not* intended to alter the balance between state and federal regulation which had been struck by earlier congressional legislation in this area.

● ● ●

Appellees do not contend that the noise produced by jet engines could not reasonably be deemed to affect adversely the health and welfare of persons constantly exposed to it; control of noise, sufficiently loud to be classified as a public nuisance at common law, would be a type of regulation well within the traditional scope of the police power possessed by States and local governing bodies. Because noise regulation has traditionally been an area of local, not national, concern, in determining whether congressional legislation has, by implication, foreclosed remedial local enactments "we start with the assumption that the historic police powers of the States were not to be superseded by the Federal Act unless that was the clear and manifest purpose of Congress." *Rice v. Santa Fe Elevator Corp.*, 331 U.S. 218, 230, 67 S.Ct. 1146, 1152, 91 L.Ed. 1447 (1947). ● ● ●

Since Congress' intent in enacting the 1972 Act was clearly to retain the status quo between the federal regulation and local regulation, a holding of *implied* pre-emption of the field depends upon whether two earlier congressional enactments, the Federal Aviation Act of 1958, 72 Stat. 737, 49 U.S.C. § 1301 et seq., and the 1968 Noise Abatement Amendment to that Act, 49 U.S.C. § 1431, manifested the clear intent, to preclude local regulations, that our prior decisions require. ● ● ●

Considering the language Congress enacted into law, the available legislative history, and the light shed by these on the congressional purpose, Congress did not intend either by the 1958 Act or the 1968 Amendment to oust local governments from the enactment of regulations such as that of the city of Burbank. The 1972 Act quite clearly intended to maintain the status quo between federal and local authorities. The legislative history of the 1972 Act, quite apart from its concern with avoiding additional pre-emption, discloses a primary focus on the alteration of procedures within the Federal Government for dealing with problems of aircraft noise already entrusted by Congress to federal competence. The 1972 Act set up procedures by which the Administrator of the Environmental Protection Agency would have a role to play in the formulation and review of standards promulgated by the Federal Aviation Administration dealing with noise emissions of jet aircraft. ● ● ●

The history of congressional action in this field demonstrates, I believe, an affirmative congressional intent to allow local regulation. But even if it did not go that far, that history surely does not reflect "the clear and manifest purpose of Congress" to prohibit the exercise of "the historic police powers of the States" which our decisions required before a conclusion of implied preemption is reached. Clearly Congress could preempt the field to local regulation if it chose ● ● ● But neither Congress nor the Administrator has chosen to go that route. Until they do, the ordinance of the city of Burbank is a valid exercise of its police power.

9. Prescriptive Right to Continue Nuisance

WEST KENTUCKY COAL CO. v. RUDD, 328 S.W. 2d 156 (Ky. 1959).

CULLEN, Commissioner.

C. B. Moore, owner of a 528-acre farm lying on Pond River, in Hopkins and Muhlenberg Counties, brought action against eight coal mining companies who operate in the Pond River drainage area, alleging that the companies were casting and discharging from their properties large quantities of coal slack, copperas waters and other deleterious substances which were carried into the waters of Pond River and were deposited on his land during overflow periods, causing damage to the productivity and fertility of his land. He sought a permanent injunction, and damages. ● ● ●

The court entered judgment granting a permanent injunction, and an order transferring the damage phase of the case to the common law docket, for a jury trial. The coal companies have appealed from the judgment. ● ● ●

As to one of the appellants alone, the W. G. Duncan Coal Company, it is contended that a *prescriptive* right has been acquired to discharge pollutants into Pond River, by reason of continued use of the stream for such purposes by that company for more than 15 years before commencement of the action. Reliance is placed upon W. G. Duncan Coal Company v. Jones, Ky., 254 S.W.2d 720, 721, 723, wherein such a right was recognized. The Jones case, however, limits such a right to use "for the same purpose, to the same extent, and under the same circumstances and conditions." The evidence in the instant case would warrant the conclusion that there had been a substantial change in the operations of the W. G. Duncan Coal Company in the Pond River area in recent years, in that a washing process had been instituted, and in that there had been a material increase in the quantity of coal produced. So we cannot say that the chancellor erred in determining that the present operations of the Duncan Company were not within the scope of a prescriptive right. ● ● ●

The judgment is affirmed.

. . . .

AUBELE v. A. B. GALETOVICH, INC., 83 Ohio L. Abs. 200, 165 N.E. 683 (Ct. App. 1960).

HUNSICKER, Presiding Judge

On March 31, 1958, Garthe Aubele and several of his neighbors, residents of the village of Seven Hills, Cuyahoga County, Ohio, filed an action in the Common Pleas Court of Cuyahoga County against A. B. Galetovich, Inc. ● ● ●

The petition asks that the parties defendant be enjoined from casting surface waters and effluent from septic tanks into a watercourse which passes through the property of the plaintiffs. The petition also asks that the village be enjoined from granting any further building permits to the developers, and that the village "declare to be null and void those permits already issued for the construction of dwellings on the tract of land described in the petition."

The answers of the defendants admit that a housing development along Justo Lane is being made. The answers also say that houses in this development, as in all other houses of the village, have septic tanks which discharge therefrom an effluent. The answers deny that surface water has been diverted or increased in the natural water course which drains the developed area; and further deny that such surface waters cause serious erosion on the lands of the plaintiffs, or that the effluent is a cause of any injury to the premises.

As in most cases of this type, there is a great conflict in the evidence, and the claims of the parties cannot easily be reconciled. There are, however, certain facts that cannot be disputed; among which are that there is a combination sanitary and storm sewer along Justo Lane, which crosses certain lands over which an easement has been obtained, and which sewer then empties into the small watercourse that crosses the lands of the plaintiffs. This watercourse is the natural drainage point for nearly all of the watershed area covered by the housing development.

* * *

The septic tanks of the 16 houses now found in the proposed 62-house development, and all of the septic tanks that will be constructed in the future along Justo Lane, will connect by lateral sewers to the main or combination sewer that eventually empties into the watercourse which traverses the lands of the plaintiffs (appellants in this court). * * *

Much of the argument advanced by the defendants (appellees in this court) seeks to justify all acts of the parties: first, upon the fact that everyone else in the village uses septic tanks, and the effluent therefrom is either cast upon the ground or into a watercourse; and, second, that the appellants are also contributing to the conditions about which they complain, by the use of their own septic tanks.

The village of Seven Hills could not give consent to any of its inhabitants to cast sewage upon the lands of another, nor could it, as a municipal corporation, cast sewage upon the lands of another without incurring liability therefor.

As we view the matter raised by this action, we must first determine whether the appellants have established a case with that degree of proof which is required to grant the extraordinary relief sought herein. * * *

To say that an owner of land may never improve such lands or develop it to its highest and best use without being subject to a claim for damages or injunction, by reason of the resulting natural increase in the flow of water into a watercourse, such as we have herein, is to take a position that would prevent the progress that results from a growing industrial and commercial area. A lower riparian owner, along a watercourse, must expect that, as the upper lands are built up with homes and stores, much of the water which was absorbed by the land will now run off of hard-surfaced streets and the roofs of buildings, to seek its natural outlet in the channel developed with the contour of the land. * * *

The matter of the effluent which is being passed over the lands of the appellants presents a different problem than the surface waters from a natural watershed. * * *

It is clear to the members of this court that one may not obtain by prescription, or otherwise than by purchase, a right to cast sewage upon the lands of another without his consent. * * *

The difficulty we have in this case, however, is that the appellants have failed to establish their claims by that degree of proof necessary to warrant this court, in this appeal on questions of law and fact, to order the relief sought by the claimants. What may occur in the future in this development, or what proof of acts on the part of the appellees and others may warrant either an action in injunction or an action for damages, is not for this court to conjecture. The appellees are not absolved by the action we take herein, but the petition of the appellants is dismissed only because they have failed to establish their claims. * * *

Petition dismissed at the costs of the appellants. The parties will prepare and file the necessary and proper journal entry.

Petition dismissed.

E.   Judicial Remedies

1.   Compensatory Damages

See: BOOMER v. ATLANTIC CEMENT CO., supra, I,A,1.

. . . .

HARRISONVILLE v. DICKEY CLAY COMPANY, 289 U.S. 334
    (1932).

MR. JUSTICE BRANDEIS delivered the opinion of the Court.

W. S. Dickey Clay Manufacturing Company, a Delaware Corporation, owns a stock farm of 300 acres lying near the sewage disposal plant of the City of Harrisonville, Missouri. A small, meandering, intermittent stream called Town Creek flows through a detached portion of the farm, consisting of 100 acres, devoted solely to pasturage. Since 1923, a drain pipe has discharged into the creek, at a point in the pasture, the effluent from the disposal plant of the City's general sewage system. In 1928, the Company brought, in the federal court for western Missouri, this suit against the City, alleging injury to the property through drainage of the effluent from the disposal plant and seeking both damages and an injunction. ● ● ●

The District Court found that the detached portion of the Company's land used for pasturage is seriously affected by the pollution of Town Creek; that the aggregate loss in rental for the five years during which it owned the land had been $500; and that it would cost $3500 to restore the creek to the condition existing prior to the nuisance. The court, therefore, awarded damages in the sum of $4000. It held, also, that the Company was entitled to an injunction; but allowed the City six months within which to abate the nuisance by introducing some method that would prevent the discharge of putrescible sewage into the creek. Upon an appeal by the City, the Circuit Court of Appeals modified the decree by eliminating therefrom the item of $3500 damages. As so modified the decree was affirmed. 61 F. (2d) 210. The Company acquiesced in the modification; and in this Court the City did not question the propriety of the award of $500 damages. But, on the ground that the injunction should have been denied, it petitioned for a writ of certiorari, which was granted. 288 U.S. 594. ● ● ●

HARRISONVILLE v. DICKEY CLAY CO.

The discharge of the effluent into the creek is a tort; and the nuisance, being continuous or recurrent, is an injury for which an injunction may be granted. Thus, the question here is not one of equitable jurisdiction. The question is whether, upon the facts found, an injunction is the appropriate remedy. For an injunction is not a remedy which issues as of course. Where substantial redress can be afforded by the payment of money and issuance of an injunction would subject the defendant to grossly disproportionate hardship, equitable relief may be denied although the nuisance is indisputable. This is true even if the conflict is between interests which are primarily private. Compare *Parker* v. *Winnipiseogee Lake Cotton & Woolen Co.*, 2 Black 545, 552–553.[1] Where an important public interest would be prejudiced, the reasons for denying the injunction may be compelling.[2] See *Osborne* v. *Missouri Pacific Ry. Co.*, 147 U.S. 248, 258, 259; *New York City* v. *Pine*, 185 U.S. 93, 97; *Cubbins* v. *Mississippi River Commission*, 204 Fed. 299, 307.[3] Such we think is the situation in the case at bar.

If an injunction is granted the courses open to the City are (a) to abandon the present sewage disposal plant, erected at a cost of $60,000, and leave the residents to the primitive methods theretofore employed, if the State authorities should permit; or (b) to erect an auxiliary plant at a cost of $25,000 or more, if it should be legally and practically possible to raise that sum. That expenditure would be for a desirable purpose; but the City feels unable to make it. On the other hand, the injury to the Company is wholly financial. The pasture land affected by the effluent would be worth, it was said, $50 or $60 an acre if the stream were freed from pollution. Denial of the injunction would subject the Company to a loss in value of the land amounting, on the basis of the trial court's findings, to approximately $100 per year. That loss can be measured by the reduction in rental or the depreciation in the market value of the farm, assuming the nuisance continues; and can be made good by the payment of money. The compensation payable would obviously be small as compared with the cost of installing an auxiliary plant, for the annual interest on its cost would be many times the annual loss resulting to the Company from the nuisance. Complete monetary redress may be given in this suit by making denial of an injunction conditional upon prompt payment as compensation of an amount equal to the depreciation in value of the farm on account of the nuisance complained of. We require this payment not on the ground that the nuisance is to be deemed a permanent one as contended,[4] but because to oblige the Company to bring, from time to time, actions at law for its loss in rental would be so onerous as to deny to it adequate relief.

Second. By the Company it is contended that the City should be enjoined because it had the power to condemn the land or its use for sewage purposes. The City questions the existence of that power. We have no occasion to determine this issue of Missouri law. Possession of the right of condemnation would afford added reason why compensation should be substituted for an injunction.[5]

* * *

The decree is reversed and the cause remanded to the District Court for further proceedings to determine the depreciation in value of the property on account of the nuisance, and to enter a decree withholding an injunction if such sum be paid within the time to be fixed by that court.

Reversed.

[4] Where a nuisance to real property results from a structure which is in character relatively enduring and not likely to be abated either voluntarily or by order of a court, it is frequently held that the nuisance is a permanent one; and if the prospective damages resulting therefrom can be estimated with reasonable certainty, the diminution in the value of the property is immediately recoverable as damages.

2. Injunctions

See: HULBERT v. CALIFORNIA PORTLAND CEMENT CO., supra, I,A,1.

. . . .

COSTAS v. CITY OF FOND DU LAC, 24 Wis. 2d 409, 129 N.W. 2d 217 (1964).

HALLOWS, Justice.

The defendant claims it has not created a nuisance by the operation of its sewage disposal plant; the plaintiffs have suffered no irreparable injury; the condition of the injunction is impossible of performance; and the court may not direct the details and the manner in which a nuisance is to be abated. ● ● ●

The city of Fond du Lac since 1913 has operated a sewage disposal plant in the north end of the city not far from Lake Winnebago. The plaintiffs are owners of valuable real estate located a short distance south and somewhat to the east of the sewage disposal plant. Plaintiffs' property consists of an outdoor-movie theater and an outdoor restaurant; a large motel with an outdoor swimming pool is in the process of being constructed. Construction of this motel was undertaken upon the assurances the offensive odors emanating from the sewage disposal plant would be corrected.

For some years and more specifically since 1956 or 1957, the problem of obnoxious and offensive odors from the sewage disposal plant has existed. It is established by the evidence that these strong and obnoxious odors, developed at the plant, were carried by the wind over the plaintiffs' premises and over a large part of the city. There is some testimony the odors were noticeable as far as two miles out in Lake Winnebago. The odors have made life extremely annoying and unbearable to people subjected to them, and particularly the evidence shows the plaintiffs' business, customers, and employees were affected by the odors. Plaintiffs' theater is subject to a lease which permits the lessee during the term of the lease to purchase the premises at its then market value. ● ● ●

The city's contention that it is not causing a nuisance in the operation of its sewage disposal plant can hardly be taken seriously. The argument, in effect, is that the nuisance, if any, is a public nuisance and not a private one as to the plaintiffs and, therefore, the plaintiffs have no cause of action. A nuisance may be both public and private in character. Mitchell Realty Co. v. West Allis (1924), 184 Wis. 352, 199 N.W. 390, 35 A.L.R. 396; 4 Restatement, Torts, p. 215, ch. 40. A public nuisance which causes a particular injury to an individual different in kind and degree from that suffered by the public constitutes a private nuisance. Such injury is usually a material and unreasonable impairment of the right of enjoyment or the individual's right to the reasonable use of his property or the impairment of its value. Stadler v. City of Milwaukee (1874), 34 Wis. 98; Schneider v. Fromm Laboratories (1952), 262 Wis. 21, 53 N.W.2d 737.[1] This concept is expressed in sec. 280.01, Stats., by providing any person may maintain an action to recover damages for or to abate a private nuisance and any person, county, city, village or town, may maintain an action to recover damages or to abate a public nuisance from which injuries peculiar to the complainant are suffered.

A private nuisance to an individual may also be a private nuisance to other individuals in their capacity other than as members of the public. The test is not the number of persons injured but the character of the injury and of the right impinged upon. One may be especially affected although others are similarly affected. Anstee v. Monroe Light & Fuel Co. (1920), 171 Wis. 291, 177 N.W. 26. Conversely, the fact the nuisance may or may not be enjoined as a public nuisance has no effect upon the right to abate a private nuisance.

The city contends the plaintiffs had not been injured in relation to their property because they have not lost money in their business and point to an advertisement of the outdoor restaurant in the daily paper thanking the public for a most successful season in 1963. There is no requirement the plaintiffs must go broke in their business in order to establish irreparable damages as a ground for abating a nuisance. If the damages cannot be adequately compensated in money or are impossible of determination, an injunction is the appropriate relief to abate a nuisance unless there are other intervening considerations which require the denial of the injunctional relief or at least its delay. The court's finding that the plaintiffs were substantially injured in their use and enjoyment of their property and that the value of the property was affected is not against the great weight and clear preponderance of the evidence and will not be disturbed.

Relying on Hasslinger v. Hartland (1940), 234 Wis. 201, 290 N.W. 647, the defendant contends the nuisance was caused by the operation of the plant approved by a state agency and, therefore, was not actionable. In Hasslinger it is observed but not held, "It may be that if the claim of the adjoining landowner is that the manner of operation is such as to constitute a nuisance, the fact that the plant was built according to specifications of the State Board of Health and is being operated in accordance with their orders and regulations may conclusively establish that there is no nuisance arising out of design or operation of the plant." This misleading language is overruled because of the implication that operation of the sewage disposal plant in accordance with specifications and orders and regulations of the state board of health cannot constitute a nuisance.

This court does not subscribe to the doctrine that the state board of health by virtue of sec. 144.03, Stats., is given exclusive jurisdiction over the determination of nuisance so as to foreclose a judicial determination of whether the operation of a sewage disposal plant results in creating a nuisance. ● ● ●

In Hasslinger we held the approval by the state board of health of the plans which involved the location of the sewage disposal plant did not foreclose a judicial determination of whether the plant was a nuisance by reason of its location; the same may be said of the method of its operation. ● ● ●

It is contended the trial court has imposed an impossible condition upon the city. This argument centers upon the fact the order enjoins the city absolutely after June 15th from permitting gases to escape from the sewage disposal plant without deodorizing and purifying them so as to avoid the creation of a nuisance. ● ● ●

Attached to the back of the order was a memorandum in which the court stated the order contemplated the city would attempt to comply in a bona fide way with the order and take immediate steps to place the plant in a businesslike working and operating condition and to deodorize and purify gases by the use of in-plant chlorination and of deodorizing chemicals. The court stated it recognized that 100 percent success might not always be obtainable but such efforts on the part of the city would be a basis for the city temporarily being relieved from the strict compliance with the order.

By this manner of enjoining the city and although the injunction is absolute in form, the city is not required to do the impossible. The city has not shown that to maintain the plant in a businesslike working and operating condition is impossible or that the use of in-plant chlorination and the use of deodorizing chemicals is likewise impossible. The position of the defendant-city is it should not be hurried or nudged along in abating this nuisance because it has existed so long now there is no need to hurry and the city will eventually take care of the problem. Essentially, the attitude is that the city because it is a city is not subject to the law. It is quite apparent from the record and so believed by the trial court that the city was not inclined to take the nuisance seriously or to do much about it. The reasons advanced for the delay in solving this problem by the city officials did not justify, in the trial court's opinion, the city's inaction. We cannot say on the evidence presented the trial court was in error in considering the city was dragging its feet in providing new digesters and in abating the nuisance. We approve the form of the order made by the trial court. It is substantially what was approved in Briggson v. Viroqua (1953), 264 Wis. 47, 58 N.W.2d 546, and in Winchell v. City of Waukesha, supra.

The city argues the order directs the manner in which it must abate the nuisance and this a court of equity cannot do. ● ● ●
However, there are situations in which the balancing of convenience or equities is attempted by the court and the decree does provide in detail how the nuisance shall be abated or partially controlled. It is recognized the court may require the defendant to adopt methods and appliances where their adoption will avoid the conditions complained of. 39 Am.Jur., Nuisances, p. 443, sec. 172, Form and Scope of Injunction. The issue of whether the form of the decree should be affirmative and mandatory in requiring specific acts to abate the nuisance or should be prohibitive is not a question of the court's powers but whether a need exists for the exercise of equitable power in requiring affirmative acts to reach a desired result. Many prohibitory orders require only desisting for compliance but when a nuisance results from the omission of an act the prohibitory form of the order necessarily requires the doing, in fact, of an act. ● ● ●

Any act which will abate the nuisance will comply with the order. The memorandum is not an order requiring the performance of the acts therein contemplated by the court. The performance of such methods of abating the nuisance is a condition or as the court states a basis for relief if such methods are tried and bona fide performance does not eliminate the nuisance.

The order is not broader, and should not be, than necessary to give the plaintiffs the relief to which they are entitled. We do not condemn its manner of coercion. It is the very nature of an injunction to be coercive. While the injunction may fit the facts snuggly and be embarrassing to the city officials, no reason appears why it is unjust or how the city will be harmed or why the city should be relieved from showing good faith in respecting the private rights of its citizens.

Order affirmed.

3. Punitive Damages

See: McELWAIN v. GEORGIA-PACIFIC CORPORATION, supra. I,D,2.

. . . .

REYNOLDS METALS v. LAMPART, 324 F2d 465 (1963).

CROCKER, District Judge.

Appellants, Reynolds Metals Co. and Henry W. Shoemaker, petitioned for rehearing in banc, and were granted a rehearing limited to the question of punitive damages before the panel which heretofore acted in this case.

To bring this case into proper focus, it should be reiterated: ● ● ●

(2) That the settling of fluorides from appellants' plant on appellees' property constituted trespass as a matter of law in the State of Oregon. Martin v. Reynolds Metals Co. (1959), 221 Or. 86, 342 P.2d 790.

(3) That the Supreme Court of Oregon has said that the jury may award punitive damages if " * * * the injury was done maliciously or willfully and wantonly or committed with bad motive or recklessly so as to imply a disregard of social obligations." Fisher v. Carlin (1959), 219 Or. 159, 346 P.2d 641.

In addition, it should be noted:

(1) That in Oregon a jury may award punitive damages if there was "evidence of malice or wilfull wanton disregard of the property rights of plaintiff or other aggravating circumstances." Hall v. Work (1960), 223 Or. 347, 354 P.2d 837, 366 P.2d 533.

(2) That Alvarez v. Retail Credit Ass'n of Portland, Oregon, Inc. (1963), 76 Or.Adv.Sh. 671, 381 P.2d 499, cited by appellants, does not overrule Fisher v. Carlin. In fact, it recognizes that there may be "other improper motives" than ill will "that make the aggravated wrong one for which punitive damages may be allowed."

(3) That the Oregon legislature has not spoken on this subject.

The decision in this case is that under the law of the State of Oregon and the particular facts in this case the question of punitive damages should have been submitted to the jury, as the jury could reasonably have found that appellants had acted with wanton disregard of the property rights of appellees or other aggravating circumstances, or recklessly so as to imply a disregard of social obligations or other improper motive.

The particular facts that lead to this conclusion are,

(1) That appellants had knowledge that fluorides from their plant had caused injury every year since 1949 to gladiolus grown on appellees' property.

(2) That in 1957 appellants increased their production by putting more electricity into reduction cells which almost doubled the amount of escaping fluorides.

(3) That Paul R. Martin testified that on April 23, 1959, Mr. Shoemaker, Manager of appellants' plant, when asked why he didn't use better fluoride controls, said: "It is cheaper to pay claims than it is to control fluorides." The trial court erroneously instructed the jury to disregard this testimony but only after withdrawing the question of punitive damages from them. The credibility of this testimony was for the jury.

● ● ●

After rehearing the question of punitive damages, the original decision in this case that the judgment of the trial court be reversed and the case remanded to the District Court for retrial not inconsistent with the opinion remains the decision of this court.

4. Mandamus

DAVISON v. PATTERSON, 110 A. 827, 94 NJL 345.

it seems well to add a few observations on the function of the writ of mandamus. It was remarked by the writer in Newark v. Lewis, 82 N. J. Law, 281, 282, 81 Atl. 1072, that the office of the writ, as directed to a public officer, is to compel him to do something that he is required by law to do, and has failed or refused to do, rather than to compel him to do in a different way what he has already done. If he is vested by law with discretionary power or with the jurisdiction to decide questions of law or to ascertain matters of fact, the court will not, by proceedings by mandamus, usurp the power to dictate how the discretion shall be exercised, or to decide what conclusions of law or of fact shall be reached.

. . . .

SMITH v. UNITED STATES, 333 F. 2d 70 (1964).

BREITENSTEIN, Circuit Judge.

This action was brought by the settlers on an ill-fated federal reclamation project to recover their losses. Recovery is sought by way of mandamus [1] and the Federal Tort Claims Act. [2] The trial court sustained a motion to dismiss [3] and this appeal followed.

The plaintiffs-appellants are the members of the Board of Commissioners of the Third Division Irrigation District, Riverton Project, Wyoming, who sue on their own behalf and on behalf of other individuals similarly situated. The defendants-appellees are the United States, Department of Interior, Bureau of Reclamation, Secretary of the Interior, and the Commissioner of Reclamation.

The first claim is for mandamus under 28 U.S.C. §§ 1361 and 1391(e). In substance the allegations are: In 1917 a government engineer, in reporting on the project lands, called attention to the danger of seepage and the necessity of drainage to maintain irrigability. In spite of this report the Department in 1948 published a circular and notices describing the project lands as potentially productive for agricultural purposes. Relying thereon and on representations of the Bureau of Reclamation that a living could be made on the land, the plaintiffs applied for, and each was awarded, a farm unit in the Third Division Irrigation District of the project. They entered on the land in 1950 and 1951, invested their life savings, and attempted to farm. The doubt of reasonable opportunity for success soon became apparent. A series of studies and reports began in 1952 and continued to 1961. These pointed out the drainage problems and recommended substantial and continuing reductions in the irrigable acreage. The 1961 report of a board of consultants said that "drainability of some lands in the Third Division is questionable, if not entirely lacking, and their rehabilitation in the foreseeable future seems economically unfeasible." There was no compliance with 43 U.S.C. § 412 which provides that no new project or new division of a project shall be approved for construction until the Secretary makes a finding "that it is feasible, that it is adaptable for actual settlement and farm homes, and that it will probably return the cost thereof to the United States." The plaintiffs were induced to enter the Third Division without knowledge of the conditions and in reliance upon the representations that a living could be made on the family units. Although the complete inadequacy of the project and its development had been described in various surveys, the agents of the United States induced plaintiffs to

SMITH v. UNITED STATES

enter the lands. The plaintiffs are destitute; they have asked defendants to correct the mistakes; and they "have been advised by agents of the United States Government that the project is to be closed."

The relief, in the nature of mandamus, sought by the first claim is that (1) the defendants "provide adequate recompense for the losses sustained by the plaintiffs"; (2) the defendants make a determination of the lack of economic feasibility of the project, and (3) the defendants request Congress to give such relief "as will provide equity" to the plaintiffs. ● ● ●

For a variety of reasons the first claim cannot be sustained. The courts have no power to control or influence the judgment of an officer or to direct the performance of a discretionary duty.[4] Any effort by a court to compel the Secretary to find lack of feasibility would violate this established principle. The courts have no control over the decisions of the individual defendants with respect to the feasibility or lack of feasibility of a reclamation project.[5]

The concept that the court should order the individual defendants to request Congress to give equitable relief to the plaintiffs violates the well established principle of separation of powers. We agree with the trial court that it "would thwart every constitutional canon for this court to order an arm of the Executive Department to demand action by the Legislative Department."[6]

Plaintiffs rely on the 1962 Act[7] relating to mandamus against federal officers and employees. Prior thereto the review of decisions of the Secretary of the Interior and similar officers was in the District of Columbia courts, in terms of mandamus to force them to perform ministerial duties. The 1962 Act provides a remedy by which the same jurisdiction can be exercised throughout the country.[8] It did not enlarge the scope of permissible mandamus relief.

The claim that the court should order that the plaintiffs be compensated for their losses is an effort to obtain a money judgment against the United States because of the failure of a federal reclamation project. The United States has never waived sovereign immunity to permit recovery in such circumstances.

In any event Congress has acted to alleviate the plight of the plaintiffs. Since the entry of judgment in the trial court, relief has been afforded by the Act of March 10, 1964, Public Law 88–278, 78 Stat. 156. This Act authorizes the Secretary of the Interior to negotiate with the entrymen on the Third Division of the Riverton Project for the purchase of their lands at an appraised value determined without reference to deterioration in irrigability because of seepage or inadequate drainage and appropriates $2,000,000 for such acquisitions and other purposes. Water deliveries are to continue for the period 1964–1966. Before January 1, 1967, the Secretary is to determine the economic feasibility of described areas in the Third Division and report his findings to Congress.

Congress has acted, required the determination of economic feasibility, and provided for recompense. Plaintiffs say that there should be a judicial determination of value. This is no more than criticism of the Act, which in substance grants the relief sought by the first claim. ● ● ●

Affirmed.

II. Air Pollution

    A. Private Law Suits

        1. Nuisance Doctrine

See: BOOMER v. ATLANTIC CEMENT CO., supra, I,A,1.

           . . . .

        2. Negligence

See: REYNOLDS METALS v. YTURBIDE, supra, I,A,2.

           . . . .

        3. Trespass

See: REYNOLDS METALS COMPANY v. MARTIN, supra, I,A,3.

           . . . .

        4. Ultrahazardous Activities

See: LUTHRINGER v. MOORE, supra, I,A,4.

           . . . .

See: Juerensmeyer, "Control of Air Pollution Through
the Assertion of Private Rights," 1967 Duke L. J.
1126 (1967).

B. FEDERAL CONTROL: THE CLEAN AIR ACT 42 U.S.C. sec. 1857 et seq. (1967).

1. Purposes of the Act

SUBCHAPTER I.—AIR POLLUTION PREVENTION AND CONTROL

§ 1857. Congressional findings; purposes of subchapter.

(a) The Congress finds—

(1) that the predominant part of the Nation's population is located in its rapidly expanding metropolitan and other urban areas, which generally cross the boundary lines of local jurisdictions and often extend into two or more States;

(2) that the growth in the amount and complexity of air pollution brought about by urbanization, industrial development, and the increasing use of motor vehicles, has resulted in mounting dangers to the public health and welfare, including injury to agricultural crops and livestock, damage to and the deterioration of property, and hazards to air and ground transportation;

(3) that the prevention and control of air pollution at its source is the primary responsibility of States and local governments; and

(4) that Federal financial assistance and leadership is essential for the development of cooperative Federal, State, regional, and local programs to prevent and control air pollution.

(b) The purposes of this subchapter are—

(1) to protect and enhance the quality of the Nation's air resources so as to promote the public health and welfare and the productive capacity of its population;

(2) to initiate and accelerate a national research and development program to achieve the prevention and control of air pollution;

(3) to provide technical and financial assistance to State and local governments in connection with the development and execution of their air pollution prevention and control programs; and

(4) to encourage and assist the development and operation of regional air pollution control programs. ● ● ●

AMENDMENTS

1967—Subsec. (b)(1). Pub. L. 90–148 inserted "and enhance the quality of" following "to protect".

1965—Subsec. (b). Pub. L. 89–272 substituted "this title" for "this Act", which for purposes of codification has been changed to "this subchapter."

. . . .

2. Designation of Air Quality Control Regions

§ 1857c-2. Air quality control regions.

(a) Responsibility of State for air quality; submission of implementation plan.

Each State shall have the primary responsibility for assuring air quality within the entire geographic area comprising such State by submitting an implementation plan for such State which will specify the manner in which national primary and secondary ambient air quality standards will be achieved and maintained within each air quality control region in such State.

(b) Designated regions.

For purposes of developing and carrying out implementation plans under section 1857c-5 of this title—

(1) an air quality control region designated under this section before December 31, 1970, or a region designated after such date under subsection (c) of this section, shall be an air quality control region; and

(2) the portion of such State which is not part of any such designated region shall be an air quality control region, but such portion may be subdivided by the State into two or more air quality control regions with the approval of the Administrator.

(c) Authority of Administrator to designate regions; notification of Governors of affected States.

The Administrator shall, within 90 days after December 31, 1970, after consultation with appropriate State and local authorities, designate as an air quality control region any interstate area or major intrastate area which he deems necessary or appropriate for the attainment and maintenance of ambient air quality standards. The Administrator shall immediately notify the Governors of the affected States of any designation made under this subsection. (July 14, 1955, ch. 360, title I, § 107, as added Dec. 31, 1970, Pub. L. 91–604, § 4(a), 84 Stat. 1678.)

3. Issuance of air quality criteria and control techniques

§ 1857c–3. Air quality criteria and control techniques.

(a) Air pollutant list; publication and revision by Administrator; issuance of air quality criteria for air pollutants.

(1) For the purpose of establishing national primary and secondary ambient air quality standards, the Administrator shall within 30 days after December 31, 1970, publish, and shall from time to time thereafter revise, a list which includes each air pollutant—

(A) which in his judgment has an adverse affect on public health or welfare;

(B) the presence of which in the ambient air results from numerous or diverse mobile or stationary sources; and

(C) for which air quality criteria had not been issued before December 31, 1970 but for which he plans to issue air quality criteria under this section.

(2) The Administrator shall issue air quality criteria for an air pollutant within 12 months after he has included such pollutant in a list under paragraph (1). Air quality criteria for an air pollutant shall accurately reflect the latest scientific knowledge useful in indicating the kind and extent of all identifiable effects on public health or welfare which may be expected from the presence of such pollutant in the ambient air, in varying quantities. The criteria for an air pollutant, to the extent practicable, shall include information on—

(A) those variable factors (including atmospheric conditions) which of themselves or in combination with other factors may alter the effects on public health or welfare of such air pollutant;

(B) the types of air pollutants which, when present in the atmosphere, may interact with such pollutant to produce an adverse effect on public health or welfare; and

(C) any known or anticipated adverse effects on welfare.

(b) Issuance by Administrator of information on air pollution control techniques; standing consulting committees for air pollutants; establishment; membership.

(1) Simultaneously with the issuance of criteria under subsection (a) of this section, the Administrator shall, after consultation with appropriate advisory committees and Federal departments and agencies, issue to the States and appropriate air pollution control agencies information on air pollution control techniques, which information shall include data relating to the technology and costs of emission control. Such information shall include such data as are available on available technology and alternative methods of prevention and control of air pollution. Such information shall also include data on alternative fuels, processes, and operating methods which will result in elimination or significant reduction of emissions.

(2) In order to assist in the development of information on pollution control techniques, the Administrator may establish a standing consulting committee for each air pollutant included in a list published pursuant to subsection (a) (1) of this section, which shall be comprised of technically qualified individuals representative of State and local governments, industry, and the academic community. Each such committee shall submit, as appropriate, to the Administrator information related to that required by paragraph (1).

(c) Review, modification, and reissuance by Administrator.

The Administrator shall from time to time review, and, as appropriate, modify, and reissue any criteria or information on control techniques issued pursuant to this section.

(d) Publication in Federal Register; availability of copies for general public.

The issuance of air quality criteria and information on air pollution control techniques shall be announced in the Federal Register and copies shall be made available to the general public. (July 14, 1955, ch. 360, title I, § 108, as added Dec. 31, 1970, Pub. L. 91–604, § 4(a), 84 Stat. 1678.)

4. Issuance of national ambient air quality standards

§ 1857c–4. National primary and secondary ambient air quality standards; promulgation; procedure.

(a)(1) The Administrator—

(A) within 30 days after December 31, 1970, shall publish proposed regulations prescribing a national primary ambient air quality standard and a national secondary ambient air quality standard for each air pollutant for which air quality criteria have been issued prior to such date; and

(B) after a reasonable time for interested persons to submit written comments thereon (but no later than 90 days after the initial publication of such proposed standards) shall by regulation promulgate such proposed national primary and secondary ambient air quality standards with such modifications as he deems appropriate. •

(2) With respect to any air pollutant for which air quality criteria are issued after December 31, 1970, the Administrator shall publish, simultaneously with the issuance of such criteria and information, proposed national primary and secondary ambient air quality standards for any such pollutant. The procedure provided for in paragraph (1)(B) of this subsection shall apply to the promulgation of such standards.

(b)(1) National primary ambient air quality standards, prescribed under subsection (a) of this section shall be ambient air quality standards the attainment and maintenance of which in the judgment of the Administrator, based on such criteria and allowing an adequate margin of safety, are requisite to protect the public health. Such primary standards may be revised in the same manner as promulgated.

(2) Any national secondary ambient air quality standard prescribed under subsection (a) of this section shall specify a level of air quality the attainment and maintenance of which in the judgment of the Administrator, based on such criteria, is requisite to protect the public welfare from any known or anticipated adverse effects associated with the presence of such air pollutant in the ambient air. Such secondary standards may be revised in the same manner as promulgated. (July 14, 1955, ch. 360, title I, § 109, as added Dec. 31, 1970, Pub. L. 91–604, § 4(a), 84 Stat. 1679.)

. . . .

5. Federal Enforcement

§ 1857c–8. Federal enforcement procedures.

(a) Determination of violation of applicable implementation plan or standard; notification of violator; issuance of compliance order or initiation of civil action upon failure to correct; effect of compliance order; contents of compliance order.

(1) Whenever, on the basis of any information available to him, the Administrator finds that any person is in violation of any requirement of an applicable implementation plan, the Administrator shall notify the person in violation of the plan and the State in which the plan applies of such finding. If such violation extends beyond the 30th day after the date of the Administrator's notification, the Administrator may issue an order requiring such person to comply with the requirements of such plan or he may bring a civil action in accordance with subsection (b) of this section.

(2) Whenever, on the basis of information available to him, the Administrator finds that violations of an applicable implementation plan are so widespread that such violations appear to result from a failure of the State in which the plan applies to enforce the plan effectively, he shall so notify the State. If the Administrator finds such failure extends beyond the 30th day after such notice, he shall give public notice of such finding. During the period beginning with such public notice and ending when such State satisfies the Administrator that it will enforce such plan (hereafter referred to in this section as "period of federally assumed enforcement"), the Administrator may enforce any requirement of such plan with respect to any person—

(A) by issuing an order to comply with such requirement, or

(B) by bringing a civil action under subsection (b) of this section.

(3) Whenever, on the basis of any information available to him, the Administrator finds that any person is in violation of section 1857c–6(e) of this title (relating to new source performance standards) or section 1857c–7 (c) of this title (relating to standards for hazardous emissions), or is in violation of any requirement of section 1857c–9 of this title (relating to inspections, etc.), he may issue an order requiring such person to comply with such section or requirement, or he may bring a civil action in accordance with subsection (b) of this section.

(4) An order issued under this subsection (other than an order relating to a violation of section 1857c–7 of this title) shall not take effect until the person to whom it is issued has had an opportunity to confer with the Administrator concerning the alleged violation. A copy of any order issued under this subsection shall be sent to the State air pollution control agency of any State in which the violation occurs. Any order issued under this subsection shall

state with reasonable specificity the nature of the violation, specify a time for compliance which the Administrator determines is reasonable, taking into account the seriousness of the violation and any good faith efforts to comply with applicable requirements. In any case in which an order under this subsection (or notice to a violator under paragraph (1) is issued to a corporation, a copy of such order (or notice) shall be issued to appropriate corporate officers.

(b) Civil action for appropriate relief; jurisdiction; venue; notice to appropriate State agency.

The Administrator may commence a civil action for appropriate relief, including a permanent or temporary injunction, whenever any person—

(1) violates or fails or refuses to comply with any order issued under subsection (a) of this section; or

(2) violates any requirement of an applicable implementation plan during any period of Federally assumed enforcement more than 30 days after having been notified by the Administrator under subsection (a) (1) of this section of a finding that such person is violating such requirement; or

(3) violates section 1857c–6(e) or section 1857c–7(c) of this title; or

(4) fails or refuses to comply with any requirement of section 1857c–9 of this title.

Any action under this subsection may be brought in the district court of the United States for the district in which the defendant is located or resides or is doing business, and such court shall have jurisdiction to restrain such violation and to require compliance. Notice of the commencement of such action shall be given to the appropriate State air pollution control agency.

(c) Penalties.

(1) Any person who knowingly—

(A) violates any requirement of an applicable implementation plan during any period of Federally assumed enforcement more than 30 days after having been notified by the Administrator under subsection (a) (1) of this section that such person is violating such requirement, or

(B) violates or fails or refuses to comply with any order issued by the Administrator under subsection (a) of this section, or

(C) violates section 1857c–6(e) or section 1857c–7(c) of this title.

shall be punished by a fine of not more than $25,000 per day of violation, or by imprisonment for not more than one year, or by both. If the conviction is for a violation committed after the first conviction of such person under this paragraph, punishment shall be by a fine of not more than $50,000 per day of violation, or by imprisonment for not more than two years, or by both.

(2) Any person who knowingly makes any false statement, representation, or certification in any application, record, report, plan, or other document filed or required to be maintained under this chapter or who falsifies, tampers with, or knowingly renders inaccurate any monitoring device or method required to be maintained under this chapter, shall upon conviction, be punished by a fine of not more than $10,000, or by imprisonment for not more than six months, or by both. (July 14, 1955, ch. 360, title I, § 113, as added Dec. 31, 1970, Pub. L. 91–604, § 4(a), 84 Stat. 1686.)

. . . .

6.   Emergency Powers

§ 1857h–1. Emergency powers.

Notwithstanding any other provision of this chapter, the Administrator, upon receipt of evidence that a pollution source or combination of sources (including moving sources) is presenting an imminent and substantial endangerment to the health of persons, and that appropriate State or local authorities have not acted to abate such sources, may bring suit on behalf of the United States in the appropriate United States district court to immediately restrain any person causing or contributing to the alleged pollution to stop the emission of air pollutants causing or contributing to such pollution or to take such other action as may be necessary. (July 14, 1955, ch. 360, title III, § 303, as added Dec. 31, 1970, Pub. L. 91–604, § 12(a), 84 Stat. 1705.)

7. Citizen Suits

§ 1857h-2. Citizen suits.

(a) Establishment of right to bring suit.

Except as provided in subsection (b) of this section, any person may commence a civil action on his own behalf—

(1) against any person (including (i) the United States, and (ii) any other governmental instrumentality or agency to the extent permitted by the Eleventh Amendment to the Constitution) who is alleged to be in violation of (A) an emission standard or limitation under this chapter or (B) an order issued by the Administrator or a State with respect to such a standard or limitation, or

(2) against the Administrator where there is alleged a failure of the Administrator to perform any act or duty under this chapter which is not discretionary with the Administrator.

The district courts shall have jurisdiction, without regard to the amount in controversy or the citizenship of the parties, to enforce such an emission standard or limitation, or such an order, or to order the Administrator to perform such act or duty, as the case may be.

(b) Notice.

No action may be commenced—

(1) under subsection (a) (1) of this section—

(A) prior to 60 days after the plaintiff has given notice of the violation (i) to the Administrator, (ii) to the State in which the violation occurs, and (iii) to any alleged violator of the standard, limitation, or order, or

(B) if the Administrator or State has commenced and is diligently prosecuting a civil action in a court of the United States or a State to require compliance with the standard, limitation, or order, but in any such action in a court of the United States any person may intervene as a matter of right.

(2) under subsection (a) (2) of the section prior to 60 days after the plaintiff has given notice of such action to the Administrator.

except that such action may be brought immediately after such notification in the case of an action under this section respecting a violation of section 1857c-7 (c)(1)(B) of this title or an order issued by the Administrator pursuant to section 1857c-8(a) of this title. Notice under this subsection shall be given in such manner as the Administrator shall prescribe by regulation.

(c) Venue; intervention by Administrator.

(1) Any action respecting a violation by a stationary source of an emission standard or limitation or an order respecting such standard or limitation may be brought only in the judicial district in which such source is located.

(2) In such action under this section, the Administrator, if not a party, may intervene as a matter of right.

(d) Award of costs; security.

The court, in issuing any final order in any action brought pursuant to subsection (a) of this section, may award costs of litigation (including reasonable attorney and expert witness fees) to any party, whenever the court determines such award is appropriate. The court may, if a temporary restraining order or preliminary injunction is sought, require the filing of a bond or equivalent security in accordance with the Federal Rules of Civil Procedure.

(e) Non-restriction of other rights.

Nothing in this section shall restrict any right which any person (or class of persons) may have under any statute or common law to seek enforcement of any emission standard or limitation or to seek any other relief (including relief against the Administrator or a State agency).

(f) Definition.

For purposes of this section, the term "emission standard or limitation under this chapter" means—

(1) a schedule or timetable of compliance, emission limitation, standard of performance or emission standard, or

(2) a control or prohibition respecting a motor vehicle fuel or fuel additive,

which is in effect under this chapter (including a requirement applicable by reason of section 1857f of this title or under an applicable implementation plan. (July 14, 1955, ch. 360, title II, § 304, as added Dec. 31, 1970, Pub. L. 91-604, § 12(a), 84 Stat. 1706.)

8. Retention of State Authority

§ 1857d–1. Retention of State authority.

Except as otherwise provided in sections 1857f–6a, 1857f–6c(c)(4) and 1857f–11 of this title (preempting certain State regulation of moving sources) nothing in this chapter shall preclude or deny the right of any State or political subdivision thereof to adopt or enforce (1) any standard or limitation respecting emissions of air pollutants or (2) any requirement respecting control or abatement of air pollution; except that if an emission standard or limitation is in effect under an applicable implementation plan or under section 1857c–6 or section 1857c–7 of this title, such State or political subdivision may not adopt or enforce any emission standard or limitation which is less stringent than the standard or limitation under such plan or section. (July 14, 1955, ch. 360, title I, § 116, formerly § 109, as added Nov. 21, 1967, Pub. L. 90–148, § 2, 81 Stat. 497, renumbered and amended Dec. 31, 1970, Pub. L. 91–604, § 4(a), (c), 84 Stat. 1678, 1689.)

AMENDMENTS

1970—Pub. L. 91-604, § 4(c), substituted provisions which authorized any State or political subdivision thereof to adopt or enforce, except as otherwise provided, emission standards or limitations under the specified conditions, or any requirement respecting control or abatement of air pollution, for provisions which authorized any State, political subdivision, or intermunicipal or interstate agency to adopt standards and plans to achieve a higher level of air quality than approved by the Secretary.

. . . .

9. Non Degradation of Existing Air Quality

FRI v. SIERRA CLUB, ___U.S.___, 41 L. W. 4825 (1973)

The United States Supreme Court, in a divided, 4-4 decision, upheld a lower court ruling requiring state implementation plans under the Clean Air Act to prevent substantial degradation of existing air quality.

In response to the court decision, EPA has promulgated regulations designed to prevent "significant deterioration" of air quality in areas where the air is cleaner than required by federal standards. The regulations (Federal Register 38:18986, July 16, 1973) offer four options:

1. Air Quality Increment Plan

2. Emission Limitation Plan

3. Local Definition Plan

4. Area Classification Plan

See: Note, "The Clean Air Act and the Concept of Non-Degradation: Sierra v. Ruckelshaus," 2 Ecology L. Q. 801 (1972).

C. State Control

As a result of the provision in the Clean Air
Act (42 U.S.C. 1857d) by which states retain authority
to regulate air quality, all 50 states have adopted air
pollution control legislation. For a discussion of
state legislation see Grad, Treatise On Environmental
Law 2-97.

D. Municipal Control

NORTHWESTERN LAUNDRY v. DES MOINES, 239 U.S.
486 (1916).

The City of Des Moines adopted an ordinance prohibiting the emission of dense smoke as a
nuisance. The ordinance required the remodeling of
practically all furnaces within the city to meet new
standards. The United States Supreme Court held that
the ordinance does not violate the due process or equal
protection clauses of the Fourteenth Amendment.

SITTNER v. SEATTLE, 62 Wash. 2d 834, 384 P.
2d 859 (1963).

The City of Seattle adopted an ordinance
regulating the emission of smoke of prescribed opacity
as measured by the Ringelmann Smoke Chart. The court
upheld the ordinance and rejected the argument that the
ordinance was unreasonable, discriminatory or vague.

VERONA v. SHALIT, 92 N.J. Super. 65, 222 A.
2d 145 (1966).

The Borough of Verona adopted an ordinance making it a criminal offense "to allow noxious
fumes to escape ... and any ... foul or obnoxious odors...
"The court held the ordinance invalid because it was too
vague and indefinite for enforcement."

E. Emission Standards for Moving Sources (Federal Automobile Exhaust Emission Control), 42 U.S.C. sec. 1857f.

1. Establishment of Standards

§ 1857f-1. Establishment of standards.

(a) Air pollutant emissions.

Except as otherwise provided in subsection (b) of this section—

(1) The Administrator shall by regulation prescribe (and from time to time revise) in accordance with the provisions of this section, standards applicable to the emission of any air pollutant from any class or classes of new motor vehicles or new motor vehicle engines, which in his judgment causes or contributes to, or is likely to cause or to contribute to, air pollution which endangers the public health or welfare. Such standards shall be applicable to such vehicles and engines for their useful life (as determined under subsection (d) of this section), whether such vehicles and engines are designed as complete systems or incorporated devices to prevent or control such pollution.

(2) Any regulation prescribed under this subsection (and any revision thereof) shall take effect after such period as the Administrator finds necessary to permit the development and application of the requisite technology, giving appropriate consideration to the cost of compliance within such period.

. . . .

2. Prohibited Acts

§ 1857f-2. Prohibited acts.

(a) Manufacture, sale, or importation of vehicles or engines not in conformity with regulations; failure to make reports or provide information; removal of devices installed in conformity with regulations; prohibited sale or lease of vehicles or engines.

The following acts and the causing thereof are prohibited—

(1) in the case of a manufacturer of new motor vehicles or new motor vehicle engines for distribution in commerce, the sale or the offering for sale, or the introduction, or delivery for introduction, into commerce ● ● ● unless such vehicle or engine is covered by a certificate of conformity issued (and in effect) under regulations prescribed under this part ● ● ●

(2) for any person to fail or refuse to permit access to or copying of records or to fail to make reports or provide information, required under section 1857f-6 of this title;

(3) for any person to remove or render inoperative any device or element of design installed on or in a motor vehicle or motor vehicle engine in compliance with regulations under this subchapter prior to its sale and delivery to the ultimate purchaser ● ● ●

(b) Authority of Administrator to make exemptions; refusal to admit vehicle or engine into United States; vehicles or engines intended for export.

(1) The Administrator may exempt any new motor vehicle or new motor vehicle engine, from subsection (a) of this section, upon such terms and conditions as he may find necessary for the purpose of research, investigations, studies, demonstrations, or training, or for reasons of national security.

(2) A new motor vehicle or new motor vehicle engine offered for importation or imported by any person in violation of subsection (a) of this section shall be refused admission into the United States, but the Secretary of the Treasury and the Administrator may, by joint regulation, provide for deferring final determination as to admission ● ● ●

(c) Exemptions; annual report of exemptions to Congress.

Upon application therefor, the Administrator may exempt from subsection (a)(3) of this section any vehicles (or class thereof) manufactured before the 1974 model year from subsection (a)(3) of this section [1] for the purpose of permitting modifications to the emission control device or system of such vehicle in order to use fuels other than those specified in certification testing under section 18571-5(a)(1) of this title

3. Injunction Proceedings

§ 1857f–3. Jurisdiction of district court to restrain violations; actions brought by or in name of United States; territorial scope of subpenas for witnesses.

(a) The district courts of the United States shall have jurisdiction to restrain violations of paragraph (1), (2), (3), or (4) of section 1857f–2(a) of this title.

(b) Actions to restrain such violations shall be brought by and in the name of the United States. In any such action, subpenas for witnesses who are required to attend a district court in any district may run into any other district. (July 14, 1955, ch. 360, title II, § 204, as added Oct. 20, 1965, Pub. L. 89–272, title I, § 101(8), 79 Stat. 994, and amended Nov. 21, 1967, Pub. L. 90–148, § 2, 81 Stat. 500; Dec. 31, 1970, Pub. L. 91–604, § 7(b), 84 Stat. 1694.)

AMENDMENTS

1970—Subsec. (a). Pub. L. 91–604 inserted reference to par. (4) of section 1857f–2(a) of this title.

1967—Pub. L. 90–148 reenacted section without change.

. . . .

4. Penalties

§ 1857f–4. Penalties for violations; separate offenses.

Any person who violates paragraph (1), (2), (3) or (4) of section 1857f–2(a) of this title shall be subject to a civil penalty of not more than $10,000. Any such violation with respect to paragraph (1), (2), or (4) of section 1857f–2(a) of this title shall constitute a separate offense with respect to each motor vehicle or motor vehicle engine. (July 14, 1955, ch. 360, title I, § 205, as added Oct. 20, 1965. Pub. L. 89–272, title I, § 101(8), 79 Stat. 994, and amended Nov. 21, 1967, Pub. L. 90–148, § 2, 81 Stat. 500; Dec. 31, 1970, Pub. L. 91–604, § 7(c), 84 Stat. 1694.)

AMENDMENTS

1970—Pub. L. 91–604 increased the upper limit of the allowable fine from "$1,000" to "$10,000".

1967—Pub. L. 90–148 reenacted section without change.

. . . .

5. Regulation of Fuels

§ 1857f–6c. Regulation of fuels.

(a) Authority of Administrator to regulate.

The Administrator may by regulation designate any fuel or fuel additive and, after such date or dates as may be prescribed by him, no manufacturer or processor of any such fuel or additive may sell, offer for sale, or introduce into commerce such fuel or additive unless the Administrator has registered such fuel or additive in accordance with subsection (b) of this section.

. . . .

6. State Standards

§ 1857f–6a. State standards.

(a) No State or any political subdivision thereof shall adopt or attempt to enforce any standard relating to the control of emissions from new motor vehicles or new motor vehicle engines subject to this part. No State shall require certification, inspection, or any other approval relating to the control of emissions from any new motor vehicle or new motor vehicle engine as condition precedent to the initial retail sale, titling (if any), or registration of such motor vehicle, motor vehicle engine, or equipment.

(b) The Administrator shall, after notice and opportunity for public hearing, waive application of this section to any State which has adopted standards (other than crankcase emission standards) for the control of emissions from new motor vehicles or new motor vehicle engines prior to March 30, 1966, unless he finds that such State does not require standards more stringent than applicable Federal standards to meet compelling and extraordinary conditions or that such State standards and accompanying enforcement procedures are not consistent with section 1857f–1(a) of this title.

(c) Nothing in this part shall preclude or deny to any State or political subdivision thereof the right otherwise to control, regulate, or restrict the use, operation, or movement of registered or licensed motor vehicles.

III. WATER POLLUTION

A. Private Rights and Remedies

1. In General

Rose, THE LEGAL ADVISER ON HOME OWNERSHIP, pp. 238-242.

A. Riparian Rights, in General

Riparian rights are the various rights which belong to the owners of land adjoining a body of water. Technically, "riparian" is used to describe land adjoining a river or stream and "littoral" is used for land on a lake or ocean. But in this discussion "riparian" will be used to describe both situations. The important distinction is that these rights do not belong to the public at large, but are incidental to the ownership of land adjoining water. Following are some of the riparian rights of interest to a homeowner.

You have a right to the continued flow of water in its natural course, which restricts the right of an upstream riparian owner to divert or redirect the course of a stream or river before it reaches the downstream owners. You also have a right to the continued flow of water in its natural height and volume, which also influences the right of riparian owners to dam or control the volume of flow. The right to a continuation of the natural purity of the water also is yours, despite the many problems of pollution. You have the right to use the water for fishing, swimming, and boating. And you have incidental rights of ownership, including some degree of title to the bed, the right to enclose, and the right to exclude.

As a riparian owner, you are entitled to all of these rights. Your riparian neighbors upstream, downstream, and across the stream are entitled to these same rights. In fact, equality of riparian rights is the essence of law on this subject—each riparian owner has an equal right to reasonable use of the body of water. The nature and extent of each of these rights depend, in many ways, upon whether the body of water is a lake, a stream, or a navigable river or ocean.

B. Lakes and Ponds

A lake or pond is distinguished from a river or stream in that a river or stream has a current or movement of water, whereas in a lake or pond the water is at rest. A private lake is distinguished from a public lake in that the general public has certain rights to boat, swim, and fish in a public lake, but only the owners are entitled to use a private lake. The difference between a public or private lake depends upon whether the lake is navigable or unnavigable. (The definition of "navigable" is covered in this section, Subsection D.(1).)

(1) NAVIGABLE LAKES. In most states, if the lake is navigable the state owns the bed of the lake and holds it for the benefit and use of the public. In other states ownership of the bed of a navigable lake may be held privately, but nevertheless the public is free to use any part of the lake and the riparian owners have no greater privileges or rights to the water.

However, riparian owners still retain their exclusive rights to the shore.

(2) UNNAVIGABLE LAKES. If the lake is not navigable, then title to the bed of the lake may be privately owned. If a lake or pond is entirely within the boundaries of your land, then you also own the lake and have all the rights of private ownership, including the right to fence it in and to exclude all others. If you own only a part of the bed of a lake and one or more persons owns the balance of the bed of the lake, then your right to'the use of the whole lake varies in different states.

In some states the owner of only a portion of the bed of a lake does not have the right to use the whole lake for boating, fishing, etc. In these states each owner has exclusive use of the water within his boundaries but may not go beyond his boundaries. If you own part of a lake bed in one of these states, you may put up a fence or other obstruction to prevent your neighbors from trespassing onto your part of the lake. In other states the owner of only a part of the bed of a lake may use the entire lake as long as he does not interfere with the reasonable use of his riparian co-owners.

Whether the lake is navigable or unnavigable, every riparian owner is limited to a reasonable use of the water. The owner of lakeside property may not discard or discharge into the lake anything which pollutes or contaminates the water and thereby deprives other riparian owners of its use. Nor may a riparian owner lower the level of the lake by draining or pumping the water elsewhere.

C. Streams and Rivers

For the purpose of this discussion, a river or stream will be defined as a body of water with a current flowing in a definite direction in a bed, with banks and a permanent source of supply. It is this flow or movement of water which creates the relationship betwen a riparian owner and his upstream and downstream neighbors.

(1) RELATIONSHIP WITH UPSTREAM AND DOWNSTREAM NEIGHBORS.

(a) Different Laws Govern Your Right to Continued Flow. The right of a riparian owner along a river or stream to the continued flow of water varies in different states. In most states a riparian owner is entitled to the continuation of the natural flow of water in its natural course and its natural volume and purity, subject to the reasonable use of the upstream owners. In a number of the arid Western states, the rule is entirely different. These states are governed by the rule of "prior appropriation," which means that the first person to use the water gets superior rights to all others. In these states the upstream owner who first diverts the water for his own use is entitled to its exclusive use, and persons who later acquire downstream property have no rights to the continued flow of the water. Other Western states now have statutes which modify this rule and now give downstream owners limited rights to continued flow of the water.

(b) The Right to Divert and Obstruct. In most of the states which follow the natural flow and reasonable use principle, the owner of property may change the course of a stream running through his property, but must redirect it back to its natural course before it reaches its downstream owners. Furthermore, an upstream owner may not unreasonably increase or decrease the velocity or volume of the water, nor may he increase the amount of mud or debris carried by the flow. In most states the upstream owner has only a limited right to obstruct or dam the flow of water—the test is one of reasonableness. If the state or Federal government decides to build a dam for public use, the downstream owners must be compensated, in condemnation proceedings, for the taking of their riparian rights.

(c) The Right to Accretions. If the current of the stream carries soil away from an upstream owner and deposits it downstream, these deposits, called accretions, become the property of the downstream owner. If an island is formed by this accretion, the island belongs to the owner of the bed where it forms.

(2) RELATIONSHIP WITH ACROSS-THE-STREAM NEIGHBORS.

(a) Ownership of the Bed. The law which governs the ownership of the bed of a stream is the same as the law relating to lakes—if the stream is navigable, title to the bed belongs to the state; if the stream is unnavigable, title to the bed belongs to the riparian owners.

(b) Division Line. The riparian owner on each side of an unnavigable stream is entitled to exclusive rights up to the middle of the stream. However, courts have held that each owner must be reasonable and cannot be so picayune as to object, for example, to a fishing line carried across the middle of the stream.

(c) Diversion of Water. A riparian owner is liable for injury or damage to his neighbor across the stream from flooding caused by filling in the banks on his side. He may not divert the water away from his neighbor by deepening or dredging his side.

D. Navigable Waters: Public Waters

There are many homes on the banks of major rivers, navigable lakes, and the seashore. The riparian rights of these homeowners are subject to the public use of the public waters. In most cases the test of whether a body of water is public water is whether the water is "navigable."

(1) WHAT WATERS ARE "NAVIGABLE"? A body of water is legally "navigable" if it is navigable in fact. One court has held that water is navigable if it can be used as a highway for commerce. In one case a stream was held to be navigable because it could be used to float logs to a mill. A stream can be navigable even though parts are obstructed or unsuitable for navigation.

(2) RIGHTS TO NAVIGABLE WATERS. Navigable waters are public waters. The rights of riparian owners are subordinated to the rights of the public to use the water for navigation. All of the public has equal rights to make reasonable use of public waters. The rights of riparian owners are no greater than the rights of the general public, except that the banks and shore line of navigable waters remain private property.

2. Common Law Riparian Rights-Eastern States

(a) Natural Flow Doctrine

WESTON PAPER CO. v. POPE, 155 Ind. 394, 57 N.E. 719 (1900).

HADLEY, J. Appellees sued the appellant, a corporation, for damages, and for an injunction forbidding the discharge into Brandywine creek of the putrescible, fermentable, and otherwise deleterious waste from the appellant's strawboard works, situate on the border of said creek, near the city of Greenfield, in Hancock county. Appellees own a farm of 160 acres located on both sides of the creek, at a point three miles below appellant's works, upon which for 30 years they have resided, and engaged in the business of farming and stock-raising. The lands contiguous to the stream are used for grazing farm animals, and so arranged in fields that live stock have ready access to the stream, where the large number kept therein always found plenty of water, which water privilege was of great value, and enhanced the value of appellees' farm. Prior to the use of the stream by appellant the stream contained fish suitable for food, with which appellees supplied their table. In 1894 appellant completed its said mill to manufacture paper and other products from straw, and has continuously, since completion to this date, operated said mill in the manufacture of paper ● ● ●
If the said pollution of the stream by appellant shall be permitted, it will lessen the value of appellees' farm $5 to $10 per acre. By reason of the pollution of said water by the appellant, the rental value of appellees' farm has been decreased, in the period prior to the commencement of this suit, the sum of $250, and the appellees have been damaged thereby $250. At the commencement of this suit appellant was discharging substantially all of said corruptible matter into said stream, and was then proposing and asserting its right to continue to do so. Appellant, since 1898, by the use of purifying devices, has diminished the amount of deleterious matter discharged into the stream, and has lessened the odors therefrom, but still continues, and will still continue, to discharge therein such quantities of said waste matter as will materially increase the pollution of said stream, and cause the accumulation of putrescible matter, and the emanation therefrom of strong, offensive, and noxious odors, to the injury of the plaintiffs. Said odors injuriously and materially affect the citizens and owners and occupants of lands along said stream, including the appellees, and materially lessen their comfort and happiness, and affect the appellees in a manner peculiar to themselves, and different from the general public. Said conditions constitute a nuisance, and the damages are immeasurable by a pecuniary standard. Appellant, in the construction of its plant in 1893, expended $90,000 in permanent structures, and before beginning the construction, and during its progress, appellees had knowledge that appellant proposed to expend a large sum of money in the erection and fitting of its mill, and that it proposed to manufacture paper from straw, but appellees made no objection to such structures and contemplated business, and donated a quantity of straw to appellant to induce such location and business. But appellees were not informed, and did not know or believe, that the business would pollute the waters of the stream. Appellant operates its mill in a careful and skillful manner, and the use of said stream as an outlet for part of the waste water is a necessary use of said stream, and conducted in a skillful manner, and the consequent pollution of the stream is without malice or desire to injure the plaintiffs or other persons; but it is reasonably practicable for appellant to still further largely reduce the amount of deleterious matter carried into the stream. To deprive appellant altogether from the use of said stream for drainage from its mill would compel appellant to abandon the business of paper-making, and thus render its plant of but little value. The defendant owns no land bordering on said stream. Its factory and land are situated a short distance away, and its said waste water is discharged into said stream through pipes laid across lands leased for that purpose. The foregoing are, in substance, the facts specially found, and upon which the court concluded the law to be "(1) that the plaintiffs should recover from the defendant $250 as damages up to the commencement of this action, together with costs herein expended; and (2) that the defendant should be enjoined from discharging into Brandywine creek the putrescible and fermentable or otherwise deleterious waste from its said strawboard works at Greenfield in such quantities as to have any material deleterious effect upon the waters of said stream." ● ● ● In the discussion it is not denied that the defendant's pollution of the waters of Brandywine creek has injured the plaintiffs in the enjoyment of their homes and property, but it is denied that the plaintiffs are entitled to injunction, or to damages for such injuries, however actual and substantial, for the reason that the defendant's strawpaper-making is a lawful business, conducted skillfully and without negligence or malice, and a discharge of its waste into Brandywine creek—the only practicable, natural drainage channel—is abso-

lutely necessary to the operation of the mill. It is urged that such use of the stream, under like circumstances, is the lawful right of the superior properietor, and that detriment to the lower lands from the incidental corruption of the waters of the stream is damnum absque injuria. We think it is universally held that land on a lower level owes a natural servitude to that on a higher level, in respect to receiving the waters that naturally flow down to it in such state of increased impurity as is imposed by upper inhabitants from the ordinary use of their lands for domestic purposes. Every owner is entitled to the free use and enjoyment of his property, within reasonable bounds. He may do by his own land, in its use and development, as he pleases, and is not answerable for the elements and forces of nature that may by natural processes affect an inferior estate. And he is not confined to the surface. He may, with a careful regard for the rights of his neighbors, develop and utilize the natural resources of his land. ● ● ●　　　　　The same rule recognizes the right of cities located upon the banks of a stream to discharge therein the city sewage, to the defilement of the water, when such discharge is necessary, as the only practicable means of dispatching the sewage. City of Richmond v. Test, 18 Ind. App. 482, 48 N. E. 610; City of Valparaiso v. Hagen, 153 Ind. 337, 54 N. E. 1062. The principle underlying this class of cases is that the public has a general interest in the business carried on, as in being cured of diseases by mineral water, baths, and in procuring coal for fuel, and, in promoting city sanitation, and since the business is of a character that it cannot be conducted at any other place than where nature has located it, or where public necessity requires it to be, individual rights must yield to the public good.

The principle of these cases, however, is not applicable to the case before us. Here appellant is not engaged in the development of any natural resource, or in any usual or ordinary use of its own land. Its sole business is the manufacture of articles of commerce for its own profit. It is engaged in a business that may be carried on elsewhere less injuriously to the rights of others. It is engaged in bringing to its mill, not from its own premises, but from elsewhere, materials from which, by artificial means, it evolves putrescent matter, which it casts into Brandywine creek, to the serious and substantial injury of lower proprietors. This appellant has no right to do. No court, so far as we have observed, has gone so far as to recognize the right of a manufacturer to establish his plant upon the banks of a nonnavigable stream, and pollute its waters by a business wholly brought to the place, entirely disconnected with any use of the land itself, and which he may just as well conduct elsewhere, without responding in damages to those injured thereby, and to injunction if the injury done is substantial and continuing. ● ● ●

The fact that appellant has expended a large sum of money in the construction of its plant, and that it conducts its business in a careful manner and without malice, can make no difference in its rights to the stream.

● ● ●

It is no defense that the city of Greenfield empties its sewage into the stream, whereby it is polluted. The fact that a water course is already contaminated from various causes does not entitle others to add thereto, nor preclude persons through whose land the water flows from obtaining relief by injunction against its further pollution. ● ● ●

Judgment affirmed.

(b) Reasonable Use Doctrine (Balancing of Interests)

WESTVILLE v. WHITNEY HOME BUILDERS, INC. 40 N.J. Super. 62, 122 A. 2d 233 (1956)

CONFORD, J. A. D.

The plaintiff, Borough of Westville, is a municipality in Gloucester County. It is situated on the outskirts of Camden, near the Delaware River. The Township of Deptford adjoins it on the south. The defendant, Whitney Home Builders, Inc., has been engaged in the construction of a one-family residential development in Deptford, near the Westville line. ● ● ●

Under plans approved by the State Board of Health in the summer of 1954, the defendant sewerage company has constructed in Deptford, near the Westville boundary, a sewage treatment plant geared to handle and treat the sewage from 300 homes. The plant went into operation the latter part of December 1954. At the time of the trial of this cause in April and May 1955, some 30 homes were being serviced. The gravamen of this action concerns the disposition of the liquid effluent of the treated sewage. It is discharged into a small natural stream or ditch which traverses the property of the defendants and flows thence in a northeasterly direction through Westville somewhat less than a mile and then empties into a pond, which, with part of the ditch, is situated in the borough's principal park. The park land was acquired by the borough by tax foreclosure in 1939. The pond drains over a spillway on its easterly bank into an outlet to the waters of Big Timber Creek, some 1,000 feet away, a tributary of the nearby Delaware.

Both the ditch and the pond originate in natural watercourses fed by surface waters. In 1940 the pond was improved in the course of a federal W. P. A. project for conversion of the foreclosed land into a park. The pond averages two to three feet in depth and is now about 500 feet in length. It has been used for many years by the public for skating in winter and by boys for fishing and, occasionally, wading in summer. Wading in recent years has apparently been infrequent. Since the construction of the park it has been a recreational center of the borough. There are benches around the pond and basketball and baseball play areas. It is the locale for all public patriotic exercises and the situs of memorials for veterans of both world wars. A newly erected schoolhouse is situated west of the park, near the pond. ● ● ●

The plaintiffs named in the complaint, which was filed August 2, 1954, were the borough and the local board of health. They alleged the impending construction of the sewerage system, the proposed discharge of the sewage effluent into the ditch and its consequent flow from the ditch into and through the park pond. The threatened use of the ditch was described as "deleterious" and plaintiffs charged:

"(a) that they have a right that the surface waters which heretofore have flowed through said ditch shall not be contaminated or polluted by the discharge of the effluent from said proposed sewerage disposal plant; and

"(b) that the discharge of said effluent, if permitted, would create a public nuisance and be productive of a hazard to the public health."

and demanded judgment of injunction and damages. ● ● ● a pretrial conference produced a pretrial order, filed February 18, 1955, wherein the remaining count of the complaint is paraphrased as a cause of action by the borough, "as lower riparian proprietor, to restrain defendants, as upper riparian proprietors, from unreasonably contaminating or polluting, or further unreasonably contaminating or polluting, the waters" of the ditch * * * "by the discharge of sewage effluent into said ditch." The trial court concluded that there had been no showing of contamination as it defined the term—"increase of bacteria and organisms," or of any "appreciable pollution." The showing as to prospective "putrescence" and decay from increased vegetation in the pond was found "too speculative" to found a claim for relief. The plaintiff's grievance was assessed as one solely "psychological or esthetic" in nature, and not, as such, the appropriate subject of injunctive relief. Judgment was entered on the merits for defendants. ● ● ●

Plaintiff purports at the opening of its argument to rely solely for its right to injunctive relief upon the asserted inherent offensiveness and loathesomeness of the sewage effluent, no matter how efficient defendants' treatment plant and relatively free from impurities the effluent, analytically speaking. It urges that the flow into the ditch and pond *ipso facto* introduces a self-evident "noisome substance" into the common watercourse, Worthen & Aldrich v. White Spring Paper Co., 74 N.J.Eq. 647, 654, 70 A. 468 (Ch.1908), affirmed 75 N.J. Eq. 624, 78 A. 1135 (E. & A.1909), this amounting to an invasion of its property rights in its status as a riparian owner, which entitles it to relief without regard to the existence of damages in any other sense. ● ● ●

Water pollution is generally measured in important degree in terms of bacteria count and index of coliform micro-organisms (B coli), the latter reflecting the degree of animal (including human) excrement. Analysis of the waters of the ditch and pond by an expert for defendants prior to the construction of the plant, on July 27, 1954, showed "gross pollution" at points above and below the proposed site of the sewage plant and in the pond, in terms both of bacteria and B coli. The measure of dissolved oxygen at the mouth of the pond was 1.9 parts per million in July, 1954, an indication of the beginning of putrefaction. All the witnesses testified that the polluted condition of the ditch and pond stemmed from the normal floatage of impurities on surface waters in such a semi-urban area. ● ● ●

The only other tangible, rather than psychological, objection advanced by plaintiff was to the possibilities of odor or stench. There was some evidence that when the plant operates at full capacity and there is simultaneously a period of low natural flow in the ditch, the volume of effluent may be expected to exceed that of the natural stream flow. Corson stated that at such times there would be stench in the pond, attributable to depletion of dissolved oxygen in the sewage. But this is seen to be without warrant ● ● ● The conclusion of the trial court that the evidence of potential odors from vegetation or putrescence is speculative seems to us a fair characterization, on the present record. ● ● ●

Defendants contend that, in effect, this is an action to enjoin a public nuisance, a remedy assertedly granted but rarely, and then only at the suit of the Attorney-General. But see Mayor, etc., of Alpine v. Brewster, 7 N.J. 42, 52, 80 A.2d 297 (1951), as to cases where an individual has also sustained special damage over and above the public injury. We need not pursue that legal inquiry, as it is not now claimed by the plaintiff borough or apparent to us that it is here sought to enjoin a public nuisance. We take it that plaintiff seeks only to vindicate its proprietary right as a riparian owner to have abated what it conceives to be a misuse to its detriment by another riparian proprietor of the common watercourse. The maintenance of such an action is clearly its right notwithstanding its status as a municipal corporation. 11 McQuillin, Municipal Corporations (3rd ed. 1950) § 31.19, p. 215; cf. Paterson v. East Jersey Water Co., 74 N.J.Eq. 49, 70 A. 472 (Ch.1908), affirmed 77 N.J.Eq. 588, 78 A. 1134 (E. & A.1910). Its ownership of the land in the park and its use of the pond for recreational purposes supports its authority to apply to the courts for relief against such actions as it conceives to be wrongful and injurious to the public in its enjoyment of the facilities maintained by the municipality. ● ● ●

We thus come to a consideration of the law governing the mutual rights and obligations of riparian owners, *inter sese*, in respect to the use of the water flow. It will be seen that this subject, in New Jersey as elsewhere in this country, is in a state of some doctrinal confusion. The early history of this field is summarized by the American Law Institute in the Restatement, Torts, chapter 41, scope note, pp. 341, 342:

"In the early English Common Law there was little litigation over the private use of water. The uses for water were limited mainly to use for domestic purposes and for running small grist mills, and the law in respect to such uses was relatively simple: 'First come, first served.' Each landowner was regarded as having the privilege of using the water on his land for his own ordinary purposes irrespective of the effect on others, but this was not as harsh a rule as it might seem, for the simple reason that such use seldom had any material effect on others. There was water enough for all because there were no such things as public waterworks, sewage disposal systems, large factories, and power plants.

"With the beginning of the industrial revolution, however, the situation changed. There arose many new uses for water which either consumed large quantities of it or polluted it to such an extent that it was of little use to others. The resulting conflict of interests in the use of water demanded a more equitable rule than 'first come, first served.' Story and Kent, with their knowledge of Roman Law, seized upon the law of Riparian Rights and applied it to these new and 'extraordinary' uses. In brief, that theory of law embodied the principle that all riparian proprietors on a watercourse or lake have equal rights in respect to the use of the water, and that none can use to the extent of depriving others of an equal opportunity to use. ● ● ●

While the "first come, first served" concept referred to above became firmly imbedded in a doctrine of "prior appropriation" in many western states, by decision and statute, because of the geography of aridity and the incidents of frontier history, Comment, 19 Mo.L.Rev. 138, 139 (1954), it has been customary to say that most of the American states transmuted the philosophy of "equal rights" into one or the other of two particular rationales, the "natural flow" theory and the "reasonable use" doctrine.

The natural flow theory, long held in England, contemplates that it is the right of every riparian proprietor to have the flow of water across his land maintained in its natural state, not sensibly diminished in quantity or impaired in quality. Each may use the water for "natural purposes," or for extraordinary needs when there is no material effect upon the water and the use is on or in connection with the use of the riparian land. ● ● ●

The reasonable use doctrine does not concern itself with the impairment of the natural flow or quality of the water but allows full use of the watercourse in any way that is beneficial to the riparian owner provided only it does not unreasonably interfere with the beneficial uses of others, the court or jury being the arbiter as to what is unreasonable. ● ● ●

The American Law Institute has said:

"Most courts, either not realizing that there are two distinct theories [natural flow and reasonable use] or not fully grasping their fundamental differences, attempt to apply both theories, with results that are not only illogical but weirdly inconsistent at times," Restatement, Torts, chapter 41, scope note, p. 346.

The Acquackanonk Water Co. case, supra, is a good example of such a mixture of concepts. After referring conventionally to the equal right of flow "without diminution or alteration" (29 N.J.Eq. at page 369), the opinion goes on (at page 370):

"The owner must so use and apply the water as to work no *material* injury or annoyance to his neighbor below him, who has an equal right to the subsequent use of the same water. * * * All that the law requires of the party by or over whose land a stream passes is, that he should use the water in a *reasonable* manner, and so as not to destroy or render useless, or *materially diminish or affect* the application of the water by the proprietors above or below on the stream." (Emphasis added.)

This excerpt is substantially the reasonable use rule, and it clearly reflects the court's philosophy in the particular case. There may be "alteration" of the natural state of the water if the use is reasonable and there is no material effect upon the reasonable use of another. ● ● ●

See also the discussion in 93 C.J.S., Waters, where, in successive asseverations, a riparian owner is said to have a "natural easement" "to have the water flow pure and undefiled", and that right is nevertheless stated to be "subject to the right of each riparian proprietor to use the stream to a reasonable extent, and whether or not a pollution of the waters of a stream is an actionable injury to a lower riparian proprietor depends on whether it is the result of such a reasonable use of the stream as the upper owner is entitled to make or of an unreasonable use in excess of his rights." § 43, p. 688, citing many cases exemplifying the reasonable use doctrine.

An illuminating variant of the reasonable use doctrine is its expression in terms of "fair participation" between riparian owners. In Sandusky Portland Cement Co. v. Dixon Pure Ice Co., 221 F. 200, L.R.A. 1915E, 1210 (7th Cir.1915), certiorari denied 238 U.S. 630, 35 S.Ct. 793, 59 L.Ed. 1497 (1915), a lower owner who manufactured ice from river water was held entitled to an injunction against the heating of the water by an upper proprietor to an extent which materially retarded the formation of ice. The court said (221 F. at page 204):

"Complainant may not insist on such a use of the water by the defendant as will deprive the latter of any use thereof which may be necessary for its business purposes, provided complainant can by reasonable diligence and effort make the flowing water reasonably answer its own purposes. There must be a fair participation between them. * * * But where, as in the present case, it is shown by the evidence that defendant's use of the river water, while essential for its own purposes, entirely destroys the right of complainant thereto, there can be no claim by defendant that its use thereof is reasonable. In other words, the emergency of defendant's needs is not the measure of its rights in the water." ● ● ●

On principle, we conclude that the interests of a changing, complex and technologically mushrooming society call for the application of the "reasonable use" doctrine in this field; a rule which enables judicial arbitration, in the absence of controlling legislation, of the fair participation in common waters of those who have a right of property therein on the basis of what all of the attendant circumstances shows to be reasonable. ● ● ●

It remains to apply the foregoing principles to the special problem presented here. We have already taken notice of the plea of plaintiff that the effluent flowing into the ditch and pond is "noisome" and necessarily a pollutant because its origin in association with human *excreta* and *secreta* engenders such revulsion in the average person as assertedly must substantially impair the use of the pond as an important part of the public recreational and park area. The synthesis of the evidence set out in II, supra, cannot help but lead to the fair conclusion that the effluent is not reasonably to be regarded as a threat to health, nor offensive, now or in fair prospect, to the senses of sight or smell. No user of the park not knowing of the discharge of the effluent is ever apt to suffer lessened enjoyment ascribable to its flow. Indeed the contrary may be true in times of drought. As recognized by trial court and counsel the question is substantially one of psychological impairment of the recreational function of the park.

We by no means make light of plaintiff's grievance. The problem presented has impressed us as of considerable import. As conceded by the trial court the people of Westville cannot be expected to be happy over the continuous presence of sewage effluent in their park pond, no matter how relatively pure. However, as will be more particularly developed presently, it cannot be said that the discharge of treated sewage effluent into a running stream is *per se* an unreasonable riparian use in today's civilization. Under the reasonable use approach we are called upon to counterweigh social uses and harms.

And this we must do in a realistic rather than a theoretical way, and on the basis of the evidence of record, rather than on emotion or runaway imagination.

At the time of the trial the plant had been in operation almost five months. Only two citizens of Westville testified as witnesses, one the borough clerk and the other the borough attorney. Neither gave any evidence of actually lessened use or enjoyment of the park by the citizenry in a recreational sense. We recognize, of course, that the five-month period did not include the summer months, when the height of recreational use is reached. We entertain no doubt that an actual impairment of the use of the pond for psychological reasons associated with defendants' operations would call for serious consideration by the court. But we cannot deal with a different record than that before us. The "'state of a man's mind is as much a fact as the state of his digestion.'" Rubenstein v. Rubenstein, 20 N.J. 359, 368, 120 A.2d 11, 15 (1956). We cannot assume, without evidence to the contrary, that, whatever the extent of public knowledge in Westville of the existence of the effluent, a pond and ditch not sensibly different in any apparent respect from what it has always been will not constitute substantially the same setting for park and recreational purposes that it has in the past. Initial public revulsion, if present, may or may not give way to acceptance of a situation which eventualities prove to involve no unpleasantness or actual harm. On the contrary, unpleasantness or harm may arise. ● ● ●

On the other scale of the balance, we find the defendant sewerage company, certificated as a public utility pursuant to legislation, serving a function plainly essential to the public health, and by an instrumentality expressly approved, both as to plant and outlet, by the State Board of Health, pursuant to R.S. 58:12–3, N.J.S.A.

● ● ●

On the basis of the entire case we cannot conclude that the denial of injunctive relief by the trial court was erroneous. We do not rest our conclusion on the premise, which plaintiff has properly been at pains to dissipate, that there is required a showing of any particular kind of damages or injury other than psychological where there has, indeed, been the invasion of a property right. See Holsman v. Boiling Spring Bleaching Co., supra (14 N.J.Eq., at pages 342, 343). Our conception is, rather, that a determination as to the existence of an actionable invasion of the unquestionable property right of a riparian owner in the flow of a watercourse depends upon a weighing of the reasonableness, under all the circumstances, of the use being made by the defendant and of the materiality of the harm, if any found to be visited by such use upon the reasonable uses of the water by the complaining owner. For all of the reasons we have set out, we do not consider that the balance of uses and harms reflected by this record points to an injunction. We trust that what we have said will not be read in anywise to impugn the appropriateness of plaintiff's use of the ditch and pond for recreational and park purposes as a riparian owner. If defendants' future operation of the treatment plant is ever shown to be such, in fact, as unreasonably to affect the use and enjoyment by the people of Westville of their park and pond, nothing herein determined upon the basis of the present record will, of course, preclude appropriate relief.

Judgment affirmed.

4 <u>Restatement Torts</u> sec. 853 (1939).

§ 853. UTILITY OF USE—FACTORS CONSIDERED.

In determining the utility of a use of water causing intentional harm to another riparian proprietor through a non-trespassory invasion of his interest in the use of water in a watercourse or lake, the following factors are to be considered:

(a) the social value which the law attaches to the primary purpose for which the use is made;

(b) the suitability of the use to the watercourse or lake, and to the customs and usages existing with respect to it;

(c) the impracticability of preventing or avoiding the harm; and

(d) the classification of the use as riparian or non-riparian (§ 855).

● ● ●

Comment on Clause (a):

c. Primary purpose of the use. By primary purpose of the use of water is meant the actor's main or predominant objective in making it when he knows that it is interfering or will interfere with another's use. ● ● ●

Comment on Clause (b):

f. Suitability of use to watercourse or lake. The water in a watercourse or lake is a common asset of all the riparian proprietors thereon, and each is entitled to a fair share in its use. ● ● ●

Comment on Clause (c):

g. Impracticability of preventing or avoiding the harm. When a riparian proprietor knows to a substantial certainty that his use of water will interfere with another's use of water, his use lacks utility unless he has taken all practicable steps to avoid or minimize the harm. ● ● ●

h. Other factors. The factors stated in this Section are not intended to be exhaustive. They are the most important, but in some cases where the harmful use has considerable utility but the gravity of the harm is also great, other factors may be considered. For example, the fact that the stream or lake is the only source of water available to the particular proprietor may make the utility of his use greater than it would be if he could obtain water without too much difficulty from a spring, well or other source.

● ● ●

3. Appropriative Water Rights-Western States

WATERS AND WATER RIGHTS, Okla. Stat. Ann. 82:26 (1952).

§ 26. Engineer to issue license

On or before the date set for the application of the water to a beneficial use, the State Engineer[1] shall cause the works to be inspected, after due notice to the owner of the permit. Upon the completion of such inspection, the State Engineer shall issue a license to appropriate water to the extent and under the conditions of the actual application thereof to a beneficial use, but in no manner extending the rights described in the permit: Provided, that the inspection to determine the amount of water applied to a beneficial use shall be made at the same time as that of the constructed work, if requested by the owner, and if such action is deemed proper by the State Engineer.

R.L.1910, § 3653.

. . . .

COLO. CONST. art. XVI, sec. 6.

Section 6. Diverting unappropriated water—priority preferred uses.— The right to divert the unappropriated waters of any natural stream to beneficial uses shall never be denied. Priority of appropriation shall give the better right as between those using the water for the same purpose; but when the waters of any natural stream are not sufficient for the service of all those desiring the use of the same, those using the water for domestic purposes shall have the preference over those claiming for any other purpose, and those using the water for agricultural purposes shall have preference over those using the same for manufacturing purposes.

4. Public or Private Nuisance

FREITAS v. CITY OF ATWATER, 196 Cal. App. 2d 289, 16
    Cal. Rptr. 393 (1961).

SCHOTTKY, J.—The city of Atwater, the Foremost Food
and Chemical Company, Inc., a corporation, and the Davis
Canning Company, a corporation, have appealed from an
order granting plaintiffs an injunction which restrained the
appellants as follows:
1. The city of Atwater was permanently enjoined from
(a) delivering to the Atwater Main any more water than the
capacity of its three pipelines into it, or delivering any cannery waste or any sewage effluent from the city's new sewer
treatment plant; and (b) enlarging in any way the size of
its three pipelines or increasing the burden on the Atwater
Main.
2. The Davis Canning Company was permanently enjoined
from conveying any water, cannery waste or other substance
from its cannery or ponds into the Atwater Main situated
on the plaintiffs' property.
3. The Foremost Food and Chemical Company, Inc. (The
Blue Dairy Products Company) was permanently enjoined
from conveying water or other substance into any portion
of the Atwater Main situated on the plaintiffs' property.
● ● ●
        The plaintiffs, who are primarily dairymen, live
in the vicinity of the Atwater Main, which is south of the
city of Atwater. The object of the plaintiff was to prevent
the three appealing defendants and one other from continuing
to use the Atwater Main for the disposal of their waste water
and to prevent the city from discharging the chlorinated
effluent from its new sewage treatment plant (which was
under construction at the time this action was being tried)
into the Atwater Main. ● ● ●
The evidence introduced at the trial disclosed that the
Atwater Main was built in 1916 through the lands the plaintiffs now own by a drainage improvement district, which subsequently conveyed the easement for the ditch to the Merced
Irrigation District, a public corporation. The Merced Irrigation District is not a party to the action.
Commencing with its incorporation in 1922, the city has
used the Atwater Main for the discharge of waters from its
storm drainage system and from its municipal swimming pool.
This discharge, which is directly into the Atwater Main, has
increased as the population of the city has increased. At no
time has the city ever obtained permission from anyone to
use the Atwater Main.
The cannery and its predecessor have used the Atwater
Main since 1940 for disposal of its waste water. In that year

the Merced Irrigation District entered into an agreement with the Ripon Canning Company, Inc., whereby the latter was granted a license to dispose of 1,000 gallons of clear water per minute into the Atwater Main. In 1945 a contract was entered into by the Merced Irrigation District and the Scientific Nutrition Corporation whereby the latter was granted a license to discharge 2,000 gallons per minute of clear uncontaminated water into the Atwater Main. In 1950 a similar agreement was made with the predecessor of the Davis Canning Company, Atwater Packing Corporation. The record also discloses that in 1957 the Merced Irrigation District terminated the license after complaints were received. ● ● ●

According to the testimony introduced by the plaintiffs, the pollution of the water in the Atwater Main first became objectionable in 1956. Obnoxious odors emanated from the water of the Atwater Main. In addition, there was evidence that the gases emanating from the Atwater Main burned the eyes. The trial judge, upon stipulation by all parties, made a personal examination of the Atwater Main and found dead fish.

The court found substantially as follows:

That the city of Atwater had established a limited prescriptive right to drain storm water and surface water from a portion of the city through three pipelines into the Atwater Main because of the fact that the pipelines were constructed openly at a considerable expense without objection and the city had used the pipelines for many years.

That the city had not acquired a right to dispose of any additional amount of water either from its new sewer plant or any other source, nor had it acquired the right to dispose of cannery waste or sewer effluent into the Atwater Main.

That Davis Canning Company had not established a prescriptive right to put any cannery waste or water into the Atwater Main; that the only right it ever had was a permissive right obtained from the Merced Irrigation District.

That the Davis Canning Company had been conveying a part of its waste through pipelines into totally inadequate settling ponds, which resulted in odors offensive to the senses.

That the remaining waste from the canning company, which consisted of fruit and vegetable juices and portions of fruits and vegetables, passed directly into the Atwater Main; that part of the waste material from the cannery attaches to the banks of the Atwater Main and there decays, causing a slimy substance which produces a strong offensive odor.

That the method used by the canning company in disposing of the waste matter from the cannery constituted a public and private nuisance.

That the Foremost Food and Chemical Company, Inc., had not created a nuisance during the time it had used the Atwater Main; that its right to use the Atwater Main was only a permissive right which had been terminated; and that the creamery had not established a prescriptive right to use the Atwater Main. ● ● ●

In arguing for a reversal of the judgment appellant canning company contends that it had established a prescriptive right to dispose of its cooler water into the Atwater Main.

• • •

Since the question of adverse use is one of fact, the question before this court is whether there is substantial evidence in the record to support the decision of the trial court that the cannery did not acquire a prescriptive right to use the Atwater Main as against the plaintiffs. There is evidence in the record that the cannery's predecessors in interest obtained permission from the Merced Irrigation District to discharge water into the Atwater Main. A fee was paid for the license, both by Davis and its predecessors. Under such circumstances the court could well find that Davis Canning Company did not have the proper state of mind to create an adverse use. Here there was evidence of submission to the right of the Merced Irrigation District. This was sufficient to support the finding of the trial court that the use was not adverse to anyone.

The canning company also contends that it obtained a claim of right to put its wash water into the Atwater Main (water used to wash the fruit and carry off any unprocessable substance from the fruit). The evidence most favorable to the respondents discloses that the manner in which the settling pond was used constituted a public and private nuisance. The evidence also shows that permission to use the Atwater Main had been obtained from the Merced Irrigation District. If the use were permissive and not adverse, which would be a question of fact, no prescriptive right was obtained and any discussion of nuisance is moot. In any event, the cannery could not obtain a prescriptive right to maintain a public nuisance. (*Wright* v. *Best*, 19 Cal.2d 368 [121 P.2d 702].)

"[A] public nuisance may also be a private one, when it interferes with the enjoyment of land, . . ." (Prosser on Torts (2d ed.), p. 391.)   There was evidence that the effluent from the settling pond killed fish in the Atwater Main. This would be a public nuisance. (Prosser on Torts (2d ed.), p. 402.) There was also evidence that the pollution of the Atwater Main caused injury to plaintiffs' cattle and that the gases exuded were injurious to health. One disinterested witness testified the odors reminded him "of stepping into a chemical lab, like sulphuric acid. It burned your nose. It actually burned, and it made your eyes water. It was terrific." Another witness who lived approximately 500 feet from the Atwater Main described the odors as "like something decaying." He also testified that the gases caused a person's eyes, nose, throat and ears to burn. There was additional testimony to the same effect. This also would be a nuisance, but probably only a private one. (See Prosser on Torts (2d ed.), p. 402, where he states that the pollution of a stream which merely inconveniences a number of riparian owners is a private nuisance.) The respondents contended that the pollution of the Atwater Main first became bad in 1956 or 1957, so the right to pollute the stream had not ripened into a prescriptive right at the time this suit was instituted. Respondents, of course, could seek equitable relief to enjoin the private nuisance.

Appellant city of Atwater contends that its prescriptive right to use the drain for the disposal of its waste water includes the right to dispose of the purified effluent from its new municipal sewage treatment plant. First it should be pointed out that effluent from the old sewage plant never was a part of the prescriptive right the city obtained in the Atwater Main. The city's prescriptive right was to use the Atwater Main for the disposal of storm drainage waters and water from the municipal swimming pool. This would not be true even under section 479 of the Restatement of Property, which reads: "In ascertaining whether a particular use is permissible under an easement appurtenant created by prescription there must be considered, in addition to the factors enumerated in section 478, the needs which result from a normal evolution in the use of the dominent tenement and the extent to which the satisfaction of those needs increases the burden on the servient tenement."

In comment (c) of section 479 of the Restatement of Property it is stated that "prescriptive interests do not include the privilege to make uses necessitated by a development of the dominent tenement not foreseeable during the prescriptive period as a normal development of that tenement."

Here the foreseeable use was storm drainage waters. Effluent from a sewage treatment plant was not foreseeable, particularly since the effluent from the old sewage plant did not flow into the Atwater Main. ● ● ●

Both the city and the cannery contend that the trial court erred in issuing a permanent injunction. We do not agree with this contention.   A permanent injunction will issue to prevent a wrongful act if its continuance may ripen into an easement in favor of a defendant which will deprive plaintiff of the use and enjoyment of his property or take from him the substance of his estate. (27 Cal.Jur.2d 157.)

The injunction was proper to prevent both the cannery and the city from acquiring a prescriptive right to use the Atwater Main. The injunction only enjoined the city from discharging its sewage effluent into the Atwater Main. It was proper to prevent the threatened injury under the facts of the instant case. If the city by the exercise of the right of eminent domain obtains the land, the city will be free to use the Atwater Main for the discharge of the effluent from its new plant and the injunction issued in the instant case would be moot. ● ● ●

The judgment is affirmed.

174

B. Federal Regulation

1. The Federal Water Pollution Control Act Amendments of 1972, 33 U.S.C. sec 1151, P.L. 92-500 92nd Cong., 2nd Sess. (1972).

(a) Declaration of Goals and Policy

"TITLE I—RESEARCH AND RELATED PROGRAMS

"DECLARATION OF GOALS AND POLICY

"Sec. 101. (a) The objective of this Act is to restore and maintain the chemical, physical, and biological integrity of the Nation's waters. In order to achieve this objective it is hereby declared that, consistent with the provisions of this Act—

"(1) it is the national goal that the discharge of pollutants into the navigable waters be eliminated by 1985;

"(2) it is the national goal that wherever attainable, an interim goal of water quality which provides for the protection and propagation of fish, shellfish, and wildlife and provides for recreation in and on the water be achieved by July 1, 1983;

"(3) it is the national policy that the discharge of toxic pollutants in toxic amounts be prohibited;

"(4) it is the national policy that Federal financial assistance be provided to construct publicly owned waste treatment works;

"(5) it is the national policy that areawide waste treatment management planning processes be developed and implemented to assure adequate control of sources of pollutants in each State; and

"(6) it is the national policy that a major research and demonstration effort be made to develop technology necessary to eliminate the discharge of pollutants into the navigable waters, waters of the contiguous zone, and the oceans.

"(b) It is the policy of the Congress to recognize, preserve, and protect the primary responsibilities and rights of States to prevent, reduce, and eliminate pollution, to plan the development and use (including restoration, preservation, and enhancement) of land and water resources, and to consult with the Administrator in the exercise of his authority under this Act. It is further the policy of the Congress to support and aid research relating to the prevention, reduction, and elimination of pollution, and to provide Federal technical services and financial aid to State and interstate agencies and municipalities in connection with the prevention, reduction, and elimination of pollution.

"(c) It is further the policy of Congress that the President, acting through the Secretary of State and such national and international organizations as he determines appropriate, shall take such action as may be necessary to insure that to the fullest extent possible all foreign countries shall take meaningful action for the prevention, reduction, and elimination of pollution in their waters and in international waters and for the achievement of goals regarding the elimination of discharge of pollutants and the improvement of water quality to at least the same extent as the United States does under its laws.

"**(d)** Except as otherwise expressly provided in this Act, the Administrator of the Environmental Protection Agency (hereinafter in this Act called 'Administrator') shall administer this Act.

"**(e)** Public participation in the development, revision, and enforcement of any regulation, standard, effluent limitation, plan, or program established by the Administrator or any State under this Act shall be provided for, encouraged, and assisted by the Administrator and the States. The Administrator, in cooperation with the States, shall develop and publish regulations specifying minimum guidelines for public participation in such processes.

"**(f)** It is the national policy that to the maximum extent possible the procedures utilized for implementing this Act shall encourage the drastic minimization of paperwork and interagency decision procedures, and the best use of available manpower and funds, so as to prevent needless duplication and unnecessary delays at all levels of government.

. . . .

(b)   Grants for Construction of Treatment Works

i.   Purpose

"TITLE II—GRANTS FOR CONSTRUCTION OF
TREATMENT WORKS

"PURPOSE

"**Sec. 201.**   (a) It is the purpose of this title to require and to assist the development and implementation of waste treatment management plans and practices which will achieve the goals of this Act.

"**(b)** Waste treatment management plans and practices shall provide for the application of the best practicable waste treatment technology before any discharge into receiving waters, including reclaiming and recycling of water, and confined disposal of pollutants so they will not migrate to cause water or other environmental pollution and shall provide for consideration of advanced waste treatment techniques.

"**(c)** To the extent practicable, waste treatment management shall be on an areawide basis and provide control or treatment of all point and nonpoint sources of pollution, including in-place or accumulated pollution sources.

"**(d)** The Administrator shall encourage waste treatment management which results in the construction of revenue producing facilities providing for—

"(1) the recycling of potential sewage pollutants through the production of agriculture, silviculture, or aquaculture products, or any combination thereof;

"(2) the confined and contained disposal of pollutants not recycled;

"(3) the reclamation of wastewater; and

"(4) the ultimate disposal of sludge in a manner that will not result in environmental hazards.

"(e) The Administrator shall encourage waste treatment management which results in integrating facilities for sewage treatment and recycling with facilities to treat, dispose of, or utilize other industrial and municipal wastes, including but not limited to solid waste and waste heat and thermal discharges. Such integrated facilities shall be designed and operated to produce revenues in excess of capital and operation and maintenance costs and such revenues shall be used by the designated regional management agency to aid in financing other environmental improvement programs.

"(f) The Administrator shall encourage waste treatment management which combines 'open space' and recreational considerations with such management.

"(g) (1) The Administrator is authorized to make grants to any State, municipality, or intermunicipal or interstate agency for the construction of publicly owned treatment works.

"(2) The Administrator shall not make grants from funds authorized for any fiscal year beginning after June 30, 1974, to any State, municipality, or intermunicipal or interstate agency for the erection, building, acquisition, alteration, remodeling, improvement, or extension of treatment works unless the grant applicant has satisfactorily demonstrated to the Administrator that—

"(A) alternative waste management techniques have been studied and evaluated and the works proposed for grant assistance will provide for the application of the best practicable waste treatment technology over the life of the works consistent with the purposes of this title; and

"(B) as appropriate, the works proposed for grant assistance will take into account and allow to the extent practicable the application of technology at a later date which will provide for the reclaiming or recycling of water or otherwise eliminate the discharge of pollutants.

"(3) The Administrator shall not approve any grant after July 1, 1973, for treatment works under this section unless the applicant shows to the satisfaction of the Administrator that each sewer collection system discharging into such treatment works is not subject to excessive infiltration.

"(4) The Administrator is authorized to make grants to applicants for treatment works grants under this section for such sewer system evaluation studies as may be necessary to carry out the requirements of paragraph (3) of this subsection. Such grants shall be made in accordance with rules and regulations promulgated by the Administrator. Initial rules and regulations shall be promulgated under this paragraph not later than 120 days after the date of enactment of the Federal Water Pollution Control Act Amendments of 1972.

ii. Federal Share

"FEDERAL SHARE

"Sec. 202. (a) The amount of any grant for treatment works made under this Act from funds authorized for any fiscal year beginning after June 30, 1971, shall be 75 per centum of the cost of construction thereof (as approved by the Administrator). Any grant (other than for reimbursement) made prior to the date of enactment of the Federal Water Pollution Control Act Amendments of 1972 from any funds authorized for any fiscal year beginning after June 30, 1971, shall, upon the request of the applicant, be increased to the, applicable percentage under this section.

· · · · · · · · · · · · · · · · · ·

(c) Standards and Enforcement

i. Effluent Limitations

"TITLE III—STANDARDS AND ENFORCEMENT
"EFFLUENT LIMITATIONS

"Sec. 201. (a) Except as in compliance with this section and sections 302, 306, 307, 318, 402, and 404 of this Act, the discharge of any pollutant by any person shall be unlawful.

"(b) In order to carry out the objective of this Act there shall be achieved—

"(1) (A) not later than July 1, 1977, effluent limitations for point sources, other than publicly owned treatment works, (i) which shall require the application of the best practicable control technology currently available as defined by the Administrator pursuant to section 304(b) of this Act, or (ii) in the case of a discharge into a publicly owned treatment works which meets the requirements of subparagraph (B) of this paragraph, which shall require compliance with any applicable pretreatment requirements and any requirements under section 307 of this Act; and

"(B) for publicly owned treatment works in existence on July 1, 1977, or approved pursuant to section 203 of this Act prior to June 30, 1974 (for which construction must be completed within four years of approval), effluent limitations based upon secondary treatment as defined by the Administrator pursuant to section 304(d) (1) of this Act; or,

"(C) not later than July 1, 1977, any more stringent limitation, including those necessary to meet water quality standards, treatment standards, or schedules of compliance, established pursuant to any State law or regulations (under authority preserved by section 510) or any other Federal law or regulation, or required to implement any applicable water quality standard established pursuant to this Act.

"(2) (A) not later than July 1, 1983, effluent limitations for categories and classes of point sources, other than publicly owned treatment works, which (i) shall require application of the best available technology economically achievable for such category or class, which will result in reasonable further progress toward the national goal of eliminating the discharge of all pollutants, as determined in accordance with regulations issued by the Administrator pursuant to section 304(b) (2) of this Act, which such effluent limitations shall require the elimination of discharges of all pollutants if the Administrator finds, on the basis of information available to him (including information developed pursuant to section 315), that such elimination is technologically and economically achievable for a category or class of point sources as determined in accordance with regulations issued by the Administrator pursuant to section 304(b) (2) of this Act, or (ii) in the case of the introduction of a pollutant into a publicly owned treatment works which meets the requirements of subparagraph (B) of this paragraph, shall require compliance with any applicable pretreatment requirements and any other requirement under section 307 of this Act; and

"(B) not later than July 1, 1983, compliance by all publicly owned treatment works with the requirements set forth in sec-

. . . .

ii.   Toxic and Pretreatment Effluent Standards

"TOXIC AND PRETREATMENT EFFLUENT STANDARDS

"Sec. 307. (a) (1) The Administrator shall, within ninety days after the date of enactment of this title, publish (and from time to time thereafter revise) a list which includes any toxic pollutant or combination of such pollutants for which an effluent standard (which may include a prohibition of the discharge of such pollutants or combination of such pollutants) will be established under this section. The Administrator in publishing such list shall take into account the toxicity of the pollutant, its persistence, degradability, the usual or potential presence of the affected organisms in any waters, the importance of the affected organisms and the nature and extent of the effect of the toxic pollutant on such organisms.

* * *

"(d) After the effective date of any effluent standard or prohibition or pretreatment standard promulgated under this section, it shall be unlawful for any owner or operator of any source to operate any source in violation of any such effluent standard or prohibition or pretreatment standard.

WATER POLLUTION CONTROL

iii. Penalties

"Sec. 309.

● ● ●

"(b) The Administrator is authorized to commence a civil action for appropriate relief, including a permanent or temporary injunction, for any violation for which he is authorized to issue a compliance order under subsection (a) of this section. Any action under this subsection may be brought in the district court of the United States for the district in which the defendant is located or resides or is doing business, and such court shall have jurisdiction to restrain such violation and to require compliance. Notice of the commencement of such action shall be given immediately to the appropriate State.

"(c) (1) Any person who willfully or negligently violates section 301, 302, 306, 307, or 308 of this Act, or any permit condition or limitation implementing any of such sections in a permit issued under section 402 of this Act by the Administrator or by a State, shall be punished by a fine of not less than $2,500 nor more than $25,000 per day of violation, or by imprisonment for not more than one year, or by both. If the conviction is for a violation committed after a first conviction of such person under this paragraph, punishment shall be by a fine of not more than $50,000 per day of violation, or by imprisonment for not more than two years, or by both.

2. Rivers and Harbors Act of 1899, 33 U.S.C. sections 403-04, 406-09, 411-16, 418 (1964).

§ 403. Obstruction of navigable waters generally; wharves; piers, etc.; excavations and filling in.

The creation of any obstruction not affirmatively authorized by Congress, to the navigable capacity of any of the waters of the United States is prohibited; and it shall not be lawful to build or commence the building of any wharf, pier, dolphin, boom, weir, breakwater, bulkhead, jetty, or other structures in any port, roadstead, haven, harbor, canal, navigable river, or other water of the United States, outside established harbor lines, or where no harbor lines have been established, except on plans recommended by the Chief of Engineers and authorized by the Secretary of the Army; and it shall not be lawful to excavate or fill, or in any manner to alter or modify the course, location, condition, or capacity of, any port, roadstead, haven, harbor, canal, lake, harbor or refuge, or inclosure within the limits of any breakwater, or of the channel of any navigable water of the United States, unless the work has been recommended by the Chief of Engineers and authorized by the Secretary of the Army prior to beginning the same. (Mar. 3, 1899, ch. 425, § 10, 30 Stat. 1151.)

● ● ●

§ 404. Establishment of harbor lines; conditions to grants for extension of piers, etc.

Where it is made manifest to the Secretary of the Army that the establishment of harbor lines is essential to the preservation and protection of harbors he may, and is, authorized to cause such lines to be established, beyond which no piers, wharves, bulkheads, or other works shall be extended or deposits made, except under such regulations as may be prescribed from time to time by him: *Provided,* That whenever the Secretary of the Army grants to any person or persons permission to extend piers, wharves, bulkheads, or other works, or to make deposits in any tidal harbor or river of the United States beyond any harbor lines established under authority of the United States, he shall cause to be ascertained the amount of tidewater displaced by any such structure or by any such deposits, and he shall, if he deem it necessary, require the parties to whom the permission is given to make compensation for such displacement either by excavating in some part of the harbor, including tidewater channels between high and low water mark, to such an extent as to create a basin for as much tidewater as may be displaced by such structure or by such deposits, or in any other mode that may be satisfactory to him. (Mar. 3, 1899, ch. 425, § 11, 30 Stat. 1151.)

● ● ●

§ 406. Penalty for wrongful construction of bridges, piers, etc.; removal of structures.

Every person and every corporation that shall violate any of the provisions of sections 401, 403, and 404 of this title or any rule or regulation made by the Secretary of the Army in pursuance of the provisions of section 404 of this title shall be deemed guilty of a misdemeanor, and on conviction thereof shall be punished by a fine not exceeding $2,500 nor less than $500, or by imprisonment (in the case of a natural person) not exceeding one year, or by both such punishments, in the discretion of the court. And further, the removal of any structures or parts of structures erected in violation of the provisions of the said sections may be enforced by the injunction of any district court exercising jurisdiction in any district in which such structures may exist, and proper proceedings to this end may be instituted under the direction of the Attorney General of the United States. (Mar. 3, 1899, ch. 425, § 12, 30 Stat. 1151; Feb. 20, 1900, ch. 23, § 2, 31 Stat. 32; Mar. 3, 1911, ch. 231, § 291, 36 Stat. 1167.) ● ● ●

§ 407. Deposit of refuse in navigable waters generally.

It shall not be lawful to throw, discharge, or deposit, or cause, suffer, or procure to be thrown, discharged, or deposited either from or out of any ship, barge, or other floating craft of any kind, or from the shore, wharf, manufacturing establishment, or mill of any kind, any refuse matter of any kind or description whatever other than that flowing from streets and sewers and passing therefrom in a liquid state, into any navigable water of the United States, or into any tributary of any navigable water from which the same shall float or be washed into such navigable water; and it shall not be lawful to deposit, or cause, suffer, or procure to be deposited material of any kind in any place on the bank of any navigable water, or on the bank of any tributary of any navigable water, where the same shall be liable to be washed into such navigable water, either by ordinary or high tides, or by storms or floods, or otherwise, whereby navigation shall or may be impeded or obstructed ● ● ●

§ 408. Taking possession of, use of, or injury to harbor or river improvements.

It shall not be lawful for any person or persons to take possession of or make use of for any purpose, or build upon, alter, deface, destroy, move, injure, obstruct by fastening vessels thereto or otherwise, or in any manner whatever impair the usefulness of any sea wall, bulkhead, jetty, dike, levee, wharf, pier, or other work built by the United States, or any piece of plant, floating or otherwise, used in the construction of such work under the control of the United States, in whole or in part, for the preservation and improvement of any of its navigable waters or to prevent floods, or as boundary marks, tide gauges, surveying stations, buoys, or other established marks, nor remove for ballast or other purposes any stone or other material composing such works: *Provided,* That the Secretary of the Army may, on the recommendation of the Chief of Engineers, grant permission for the temporary occupation or use of any of the aforementioned public works when in his judgment such occupation or use will not be injurious to the public interest. (Mar. 3, 1899, ch. 425, § 14, 30 Stat. 1152.) ● ● ●

§ 409. Obstruction of navigable waters by vessels; floating timber; marking and removal of sunken vessels.

It shall not be lawful to tie up or anchor vessels or other craft in navigable channels in such a manner as to prevent or obstruct the passage of other vessels or craft; or to voluntarily or carelessly sink, or permit or cause to be sunk, vessels or other craft in navigable channels; or to float loose timber and logs, or to float what is known as "sack rafts of timber and logs" in streams or channels actually navigated by steamboats in such manner as to obstruct, impede, or endanger navigation. And whenever a vessel, raft or other craft is wrecked and sunk in a navigable channel, accidentally or otherwise, it shall be the duty of the owner of such sunken craft to immediately mark it with a buoy or beacon during the day and a lighted lantern at night, and to maintain such marks until the sunken craft is removed or abandoned, and the neglect or failure of the said owner so to do shall be unlawful; and it shall be the duty of the owner of such sunken craft to commence the immediate removal of the same, and prosecute such removal diligently, and failure to do so shall be considered as an abandonment of such craft, and subject the same to removal by the United States as provided for in sections 411 to 416, 418, and 502 of this title. (Mar. 3, 1899, ch. 425, § 15, 30 Stat. 1152.)

● ● ●

§ 411. Penalty for wrongful deposit of refuse; use of or injury to harbor improvements, and obstruction of navigable waters generally.

Every person and every corporation that shall violate, or that shall knowingly aid, abet, authorize, or instigate a violation of the provisions of sections 407, 408, and 409 of this title shall be guilty of a misdemeanor, and on conviction thereof shall be punished by a fine not exceeding $2,500 nor less than $500, or by imprisonment (in the case of a natural person) for not less than thirty days nor more than one year, or by both such fine and imprisonment, in the discretion of the court, one-half of said fine to be paid to the person or persons giving information which shall lead to conviction. (Mar. 3, 1899, ch. 425, § 16, 30 Stat. 1153.) ● ● ●

§ 412. Liability of masters, pilots, and so forth, and of vessels engaged in violations.

Any and every master, pilot, and engineer, or person or persons acting in such capacity, respectively, on board of any boat or vessel who shall knowingly engage in towing any scow, boat, or vessel loaded with any material specified in section 407 of this title to any point or place of deposit or discharge in any harbor or navigable water, elsewhere than within the limits defined and permitted by the Secretary of the Army, or who shall willfully injure or destroy

any work of the United States contemplated in section 408 of this title, or who shall willfully obstruct the channel of any waterway in the manner contemplated in section 409 of this title, shall be deemed guilty of a violation of sections 401, 403, 404, 406, 407, 408, 409, 411 to 416, 418, 502, 549, 686, and 687 of this title, and shall upon conviction be punished as provided in section 411 of this title, and shall also have his license revoked or suspended for a term to be fixed by the judge before whom tried and convicted. And any boat, vessel, scow, raft, or other craft used or employed in violating any of the provisions of sections 407, 408, and 409 of this title shall be liable for the pecuniary penalties specified in section 411 of this title, and in addition thereto for the amount of the damages done by said boat, vessel, scow, raft, or other craft, which latter sum shall be placed to the credit of the appropriation for the improvement of the harbor or waterway in which the damage occurred, and said boat, vessel, scow, raft, or other craft may be proceeded against summarily by way of libel in any district court of the United States having jurisdiction thereof. (Mar. 3, 1899, ch. 425, § 16, 30 Stat. 1153.) ● ● ●

§ 413. Duty of United States attorneys and other Federal officers in enforcement of provisions; arrest of offenders.

The Department of Justice shall conduct the legal proceedings necessary to enforce the provisions of sections 401, 403, 404, 406, 407, 408, 409, 411, 549, 686, and 687 of this title; and it shall be the duty of United States attorneys to vigorously prosecute all offenders against the same whenever requested to do so by the Secretary of the Army or by any of the officials hereinafter designated, and it shall furthermore be the duty of said United States attorneys to report to the Attorney General of the United States the action taken by him against offenders so reported, and a transcript of such reports shall be transmitted to the Secretary of the Army by the Attorney General; and for the better enforcement of the said provisions and to facilitate the detection and bringing to punishment of such States in charge of river and harbor improvements, and the assistant engineers and inspectors employed under them by authority of the Secretary of the Army, and the United States collectors of customs and other revenue officers shall have power and authority to swear out process, and to arrest and take into custody, with or without process, any person or persons who may commit any of the acts or offenses prohibited by the said sections, or who may violate any of the provisions of the same: *Provided,* That no person committed in the presence of some one of the aforesaid officials: *And provided further,* That whenever any arrest is made under such sections, the person so arrested shall be brought forthwith before a commissioner, judge, or court of the United States for examination of the offenses alleged against him; and such commissioner, judge, or court shall proceed in respect thereto as authorized by law in case of crimes against the United States. (Mar. 3, 1899, ch. 425, § 17, 30 Stat. 1153; June 25, 1948, ch. 646, § 1, 62 Stat. 909, eff. Sept. 1, 1948.)

§ 414. Removal by Secretary of the Army of sunken water craft generally.

Whenever the navigation of any river, lake, harbor, sound, bay, canal, or other navigable waters of the United States shall be obstructed or endangered by any sunken vessel, boat, water craft, raft, or other similar obstruction, and such obstruction has existed for a longer period than thirty days, or whenever the abandonment of such obstruction can be legally established in a less space of time, the sunken vessel, boat, water craft, raft, or other obstruction shall be subject to be broken up, removed, sold, or otherwise disposed of by the Secretary of the Army at his discretion, without liability for any damage to the owners of the same: *Provided,* That in his discretion, the Secretary of the Army may cause reasonable notice of such obstruction of not less than thirty days, unless the legal abandonment of the obstruction can be established in a less time, to be given by publication, addressed "To whom it may concern," in a newspaper published nearest to the locality of the obstruction, requiring the removal thereof: *And provided also,* That the Secretary of the Army may, in his discretion, at or after the time of giving such notice, cause sealed proposals to be solicited by public advertisement, giving reasonable notice of not less than ten days, for the removal of such obstruction as soon as possible after the expiration of the above specified thirty days' notice, in case it has not in the meantime been so removed, these proposals and contracts, at his discretion, to be conditioned that such vessel, boat, water craft, raft, or other obstruction, and all cargo and property contained therein, shall become the property of the contractor, and the contract shall be awarded to the bidder making the proposition most advantageous to the United States: *Provided,* That such bidder shall give satisfactory security to execute the work: *Provided further,* That any money received from the sale of any such wreck, or from any contractor for the removal of wrecks, under this paragraph shall be covered into the Treasury of the United States. (Mar. 3, 1899, ch. 425, § 19, 30 Stat. 1154.) ● ● ●

§ 415. Summary removal of water craft obstructing navigation.

Under emergency, in the case of any vessel, boat, water craft, or raft, or other similar obstruction, sinking or grounding, or being unnecessarily delayed in any Government canal or lock, or in any navigable waters mentioned in section 414 of this title, in such manner as to stop, seriously interfere with, or specially endanger navigation, in the opinion of the Secretary of the Army, or any agent of the United States to whom the Secretary may delegate proper authority, the Secretary of the Army or any such agent shall have the right to take immediate possession of such boat, vessel, or other water craft, or raft, so far as to remove or to destroy it and to clear immediately the canal, lock, or navigable waters aforesaid of the obstruction thereby caused, using his best judgment to prevent any unnecessary injury; and no one shall interfere with or prevent such removal or destruction: *Provided,* That the officer or agent charged with the removal or destruction of an obstruction under this section may in his discretion give notice in writing to the owners of any such obstruction requiring them to remove it: *And provided further,* That the expense of removing any such obstruction as aforesaid shall be a charge against such craft and cargo; and if the owners thereof fail or refuse to reimburse the United States for such expense within thirty days after notification, then the officer or agent aforesaid may sell the craft or cargo, or any part thereof that may not have been destroyed in removal, and the proceeds of such sale shall be covered into the Treasury of the United States. (Mar. 3, 1899, ch. 425, § 20, 30 Stat. 1154.)

● ● ●

§ 416. Appropriation for removal of sunken water craft.

. . . .

See: UNITED STATES v. REPUBLIC STEEL CORP., 362 U.S. 482 where the Supreme Court held that discharge of industrial solid wastes was an "obstruction".

See: UNITED STATES v. STANDARD OIL, 384 U.S. 224 (1966) and UNITED STATES v. ESSO STANDARD OIL CO. OF PUERTO RICO, 357 F. 2d 621 (3d Cir. 1967) for an expansive definition of "refuse".

C. Interstate Compacts

See: Note, "Water Pollution Control Through Interstate Agreement," 1 U.C.D. L. Rev. 43 (1969).

See: Hines, "Nor Any Drop to Drink: Public Regulation of Water Quality. Interstate Agreements for Pollution Control," 52 Iowa L. Rev. 432 (1966).

. . . .

D. State Regulation

VERMONT WOOLEN CORP. v. WACKERMAN , 122 Vt. 219, 167 A. 2d 533 (1961).

BARNEY, Justice.

The Vermont State Water Conservation Board on December 12, 1957, held a hearing in connection with classification of the waters of a certain Kingsbury Branch watercourse as authorized by 10 V.S.A. §§ 905 and 907. The plaintiff corporation, a riparian property owner and user of the waters of Kingsbury Branch in its operations, was notified of the hearing and appeared, objecting to the proposed classification. Thereafter, plaintiff received in the mail an order from the board defining the present condition of Kingsbury Branch as below Class D and setting up a classification to be reached by pollution abatement of Class C. ● ● ●

In 10 V.S.A. § 902 are defined, in terms of purity, the various water classifications used in the statutes relating to water pollution. By the language of the definitions Class D is water so polluted as to fail as a habitat for wildlife and common food and game fishes indigenous to the region; waters polluted beyond a Class D status contain sewage or industrial waste to the point of nuisance. Class D waters are so impure as to be unsuitable for irrigation of crops or other agricultural uses. Class C, while a suitable habitat for fish and wildlife, is too polluted for recreational bathing or for public water supply even with filtration and disinfection. Its only acceptable agricultural use is for irrigation of crops that are cooked prior to consumption. Class B is free enough of pollution to allow its use for bathing and aquatic recreation, for general irrigation and agricultural purposes and, with filtration and disinfection, for public water supply. Class A is water so free from any pollution as to be suitable for all purposes including public water supply.

The legislature itself has determined the classification of certain waters by the provisions of 10 V.S.A. § 903. All waters used as public reservoirs and waters flowing into them are Class A. Natural lakes and ponds of twenty acres or more wholly within the state and the waters flowing into them shall be Class B, unless such classification is objected to by ten property owners on such a pond or lake, in which case the board may, after hearing, classify it differently. The statute goes on to make classification of the remaining waters of the state, including determination of what degree of purity ought to apply and be maintained, the function of the water conservation board. ● ● ●

The plaintiff attacks the constitutionality of these water pollution statutes on several grounds. ● ● ●

The legislation in question here is concerned with promoting the public welfare (10 V.S.A. § 915) by providing the maximum of beneficial use and enjoyment of the waters of the state to its people. 10 V.S.A. § 903(3). Reference to the classifications of water purity previously described demonstrate that pollution abatement is to be carried out in furtherance of public health and for the protection of fish and game. Both of these purposes have already been recognized as areas appropriate for the exercise of the police power. See State v. Quattropani, 99 Vt. 360, 133 A. 352; and State v. Theriault, 70 Vt. 617, 41 A. 1030, 43 L.R.A. 290.

As is said in the Quattropani case, the police power is not limitless, even though it be but another name for sovereignty itself. It is subject to judicial review to test the reasonableness and appropriateness of the legislation to accomplish the result intended without oppression or discrimination. State v. Morse, 84 Vt. 387, 394, 80 A. 189, 34 L.R.A.,N.S., 190. Except for this limitation, it is for the legislature to determine what measures are appropriate and necessary to conserve and safeguard the public safety, health and welfare. State v. Quattropani, supra, 99 Vt. 360, 363, 133 A. 352. As that case states, all contracts entered into, all charters granted, all rights possessed and all property held are subject to the proper exercise of this police power, and must submit to its valid regulations and restrictions. The determination of validity is the function of the courts.

The specific objective is to require those who contribute to pollution in our streams to take steps to reduce or bring to an end such pollution as they may be responsible for. Nothing brought forward by the plaintiff disputes the clear and reasonable relationship of the statutory program in question to the legislative objectives. Nor has there been a demonstration of an infringement upon constitutional rights by the requirements of the statutes. The claim of the plaintiff is that if it is

required to correct its sewage and industrial waste problem, the cost of doing so will be so high as to be confiscatory of its whole business operation. Whether that circumstance, if true, invalidates the exercise of police power in this kind of situation is not now before us, but see Aitken v. Village of Wells River, 70 Vt. 308, 40 A. 829, 41 L.R.A. 566, and Anchor Hocking Glass Corp. v. Barber, 118 Vt. 206, 215, 105 A.2d 271.

The statutory provisions which could order plaintiff to undertake such a pollution reducing program have not yet been brought into play. They are 10 V.S.A. §§ 911 and 912; they call for the fact of pollution to be proved by evidence introduced at a hearing for that purpose with an opportunity for the plaintiff to defend. In addition, these sections provide that pollution abatement measures will not be required if the cost of installation, maintenance and operation thereof are unreasonable or inequitable. Not only would it appear that plaintiff is raising these issues of confiscation prematurely, but also that the legislature has foreseen the problems of difficult pollution situations and taken steps to avoid unreasonably burdensome enforcement of these statutes.

As a related point, plaintiff complains that it is unfair discrimination and a burdensome inequality to require it to pay the full cost of abating its own pollution when other members of the community and other riparian owners will share the benefits. To state the proposition is to expose its weakness. Manifestly, there is nothing unfair in requiring one who contributes to the creation of a detrimental situation to be responsible for its correction to the extent of his contribution. See Western Union Tel. Co. v. Burlington Traction Co., 90 Vt. 506, 99 A. 4; Bacon v. Boston & Maine R. R., 83 Vt. 421, 76 A. 128; and Thorpe v. Rutland & Burlington R. Co., 27 Vt. 140.

This Court recognizes that riparian rights constitute property and has said so in State v. Morse, 84 Vt. 387, 392,

80 A. 189, 34 L.R.A.,N.S., 190. However, the claim that such rights can become by prescription invulnerable to regulation cannot be allowed to pass unchallenged. It is a proposition that runs counter to the doctrine of the primacy of the police power or sovereignty for the protection of the welfare of the public expressed in State v. Quattropani, supra, 99 Vt. 360, 363, 133 A. 352. Without the consent of the legislature, the interests of the State in all of its waters cannot be defeated by long user, for prescription cannot be allowed to overcome public welfare. ● ● ●

The plaintiff objects to the provision of the order that requires it to install septic tanks for the houses it owns and the provision requiring the submission of plans and specifications of treatment facilities for its industrial wastes. Alleging that the expense of all this would be burdensome to the plaintiff, it claims that the expenses of furnishing plans and specifications would, by themselves, amount to thousands of dollars. This, says the plaintiff, clearly establishes the unreasonableness of the order as applied to it. Therefore, even as an application of the police power, says the plaintiff, the order is unconstitutional. ● ● ●

Burdensome cost is a factor to be considered in weighing the reasonableness of legislation and orders made under it when testing them for constitutionality. However, when the legislation is, as here, supported by strongly favored policy considerations, neither legislation nor orders will be struck down as unreasonable solely because a financial hardship is necessarily worked on a particular individual, even to the point of being destructive of his business. Anchor Hocking Glass Corp. v. Barber, supra.

The order is also attacked by the plaintiff as being arbitrary and uncertain; and as furnishing no standard whereby the plaintiff can determine the differences between the several classifications referred to in the order. ● ● ●

Plaintiff has no responsibilities with respect to determining the classification of Kingsbury Branch waters, and its subjective understanding or lack of it concerning the different classes of water purity is immaterial. The classifications relate to the purity of the stream water generally as measured by the board, not to the waste water discharged by plaintiff's operation, and are sufficiently reasonable and definite for that purpose. ● ● ●

There is a suggestion in the argument made in plaintiff's brief that the construction we have approved would have the effect of forever prohibiting any alteration of the disposition of all wastes with respect to a classified stream, even though circumstances might change. There are two factors that overrule this contention. The first is that provision is made under 10 V.S.A. § 910 for petitioning the board with respect to projected changes in the sources of pollution. The second is the use of the permissive word "may" in lieu of some mandatory term in connection with the enforcement provisions of 10 V.S.A. § 909. Taken together, these two factors demonstrate an intent on the part of the legislature to leave the statutory mandate to the board flexible enough to permit it to adjust its enforcement to altering circumstances. ● ● ●

Plaintiff has demonstrated no constitutional deficiency in either the relevant statutes or the order of the board, nor has any error been made to appear in the proceedings. Its bill was properly dismissed.

Judgment affirmed.

· · · · · · · · · · · · · · · · · ·

See also CITY OF NEWARK v. NEW JERSEY DEPT. OF HEALTH, 109 N.J. Super. 166, 262 A. 2d 718 (1970) upholding the validity of state Department of Health regulations dealing with potable water standards.

E. Local Regulation

STATE v. FINNEY, 65 Idaho 630, 150 P. 2d 130 (1944).

DUNLAP, Justice.

Appellant Finney was convicted in the Police Court of the City of Coeur d'Alene on the charge of maintaining within the limits of the City of Coeur d'Alene upon a certain section of Coeur d'Alene Lake, a houseboat used as a residence, in violation of Ordinance No. 762 of said City. Upon appeal to the District Court of the Eighth Judicial District, in and for Kootenai County, and after trial by the court without a jury, the learned judge of said court sustained the prior conviction by adjudging the defendant guilty as charged, and ordered him to pay a fine of $1.

The case is before us on appeal from this judgment. ● ♥ ●

A number of assignments of error are alleged, mainly based upon the contention the ordinance is unconstitutional, in that it violates the 14th Amendment of the Federal Constitution; Article 1, Section 1, Article 1, Section 13 and Article 1, Section 14, of the State Constitution.

Section 2 of the ordinance is pertinent here. It reads in part as follows: "Section 2. No person, persons or corporations shall moor, anchor or maintain upon the waters of Lake Coeur d'Alene * * * any houseboat or craft used as a residence or for living purposes * * * and the mooring, anchoring or maintaining of such houseboat or structure in city waters is hereby declared to be a public nuisance."

Appellant attacks the sufficiency of the complaint, contending it states merely the conclusion and not the acts constituting the nuisance.

The charge as contained in the complaint is very much in the words as used in Section 2 of the ordinance, and is to effect that appellant, in violation of the ordinance, maintained upon the waters of the Lake a houseboat used as a residence, and for living purposes, and thereby maintained a public nuisance. The complaint sets forth the offense, with such particulars as time, place, person and property, as to enable the person charged to understand distinctly the character of the offense complained of, and to answer the same, and is sufficient. Section 19-4001, I.C.A.; State v. Ashby, 40 Idaho 1, 230 P. 1013, 46 C.J. 818, Section 481.

The portion of the Lake involved here, was taken into and made a part of the City of Coeur d'Alene by Ordinance No. 759 passed and approved April 18, 1938, and its enactment was pursuant to and authorized by Section 49-1149, I.C.A.

It was undoubtedly the intention of the Legislature in thus expressly authorizing incorporated cities and villages situated on navigable streams and lakes, to include portions thereof within their respective boundaries, as authorized by the Act, for the purpose of enabling the municipalities to exercise control over this included and added territory, to the same extent and for the same purpose as it is generally empowered with respect to other territory within the corporate boundaries.

Among the powers specifically granted to the municipalities by the Legislature, is the power "to make regulations to secure the general health of the city and to prevent and remove nuisances, and to provide the city with water." Sec. 49-313, Subdiv. 4.

The undisputed evidence in this case shows Coeur d'Alene to be a congested, growing city. It is a popular summer resort and its beaches and parks adjoining this section of the Lake are widely used, with Sunday crowds of from ten to twenty-five thousand enjoying these facilities; its business and residential sections are in close proximity to that part of the waters involved here, and the City's place of intake of its water supply from this Lake is also within this section.

The evidence in this case is undisputed that defendant's houseboat was used for living purposes at the time and place charged in the complaint. Its place of moorage, and its use for that purpose was prohibited by the ordinance in question, and while construing enactments of this nature, and in considering the effect of their operation, regard must be had to constitutional provisions intended to secure the liberty and to protect the rights of citizens to the end that no citizen shall be deprived of life, liberty or property without due process of law (State v. Frederic, 28 Idaho 709, 155 P. 977) it is at once apparant the enactment and enforcement of the ordinance was in the interest of general health and welfare, and the right of a municipality to so act for the welfare of the whole is no longer open to question. State ex rel. Euclid-Doan Bldg. Co. v. Cunningham, 97 Ohio St. 130, 119 N.E. 361 L.R.A.1918D, 700.

Conceding appellant has, under license from the reparian owner, long used that portion of the Lake involved here, for moorage of his boat, and thus acquired a vested right so to do, still this right must yield to the police power, as exercised by the City in this instance. ● ● ●

The due process and equal protection provisions of these Constitutions are not intended to interfere with the power of the State in the exercise of the police powers to prescribe regulations for the protection and promotion of the welfare of the people. It is only subject to the qualification that the measure adopted for the purpose of regulating the exercise of the rights of liberty and the use and enjoyment of property must be designed to effect some public object which the government may legally accomplish, and it must be reasonable and have some direct, real and substantial relation to the public object sought to be accomplished. ● ● ●

It is also contended by appellant in effect that the city could not by ordinance make it a nuisance to maintain in the prohibited area, a houseboat used for living purposes, if as a matter of fact such act did not constitute a nuisance. In other words, that a general power of a city to declare a nuisance does not include the power to declare anything a nuisance which is not one in fact nor one per se. With this contention we are in accord, and so held in the cases of City of Twin Falls v. Harlan, 27 Idaho 769, 151 P. 1191, and Porter v. City of Lewiston, 41 Idaho 324, 238 P. 1014, 1016.

However, in the latter case, this Court,

speaking through Mr. Justice Givens, said: "A city council in passing an ordinance, declaring what things may constitute a nuisance, is acting in its legislative capacity, and, in the absence of an abuse of the discretion lodged in such body, it may declare what are nuisances, and, if the conditions and circumstances surrounding and attaching to the things so declared to be nuisances warrant such action on the part of the city council, such ordinances will be sustained. State v. Superior Court, 103 Wash. 409, 174 P. 973; State v. Morse, 84 Vt. 387, 80 A. 189, 34 L.R.A.,N.S., 190, Ann.Cas.1913B, 218; Kirk v. Wyman, 83 S.C. 372, 65 S.E. 387 [23 L.R.A.,N.S., 1188]."

And, in the more recent case of City of Idaho Falls v. Grimmett, 63 Idaho 90, 117 P.2d 461, the holding of this Court on this point is expressed in syllabus 6, as follows: "Where a given situation admittedly presents a proper field for exercise of police power by a municipality, the extent of its invocation and application is a matter lying largely in legislative discretion, and every presumption is to be indulged in favor of exercise of such discretion, unless arbitrary action is clearly disclosed."

In view of the statutory provision herein referred to (Subdivision 4, Section 49-313, I.C.A.) and of the circumstances of this case herein related, it would appear the City was not only empowered, but was fully justified in the exercise of its police power, as expressed in the ordinance, in forbidding the use of houseboats for living purposes in the section of the Lake affected thereby, and that the regulation thus adopted was reasonable and not arbitrary and fully justified as a public health measure. ● ● ●

Judgment affirmed.
No costs awarded.

BROWN v. CLE ELUM, 143 Wash. 606, 255 P. 961 (1927), rev'd per curiam, 145 Wash. 588, 261 P. 112 (1927).

PER CURIAM. This case was originally heard before Department 2 of this court, and the opinion written appears in 255 P. 961, to which reference is made for the facts upon which the action is based. That opinion contains the following statement:

"There looms in the horizon of this controversy a question of far-reaching importance; that is, as to whether or not the Legislature can constitutionally delegate to a city authority to exercise police power beyond its territorial limits and outside the boundaries of property it may own beyond its territorial limits, by the passing and enforcing of ordinances assuming to regulate the conduct of citizens beyond such limits and boundaries. No argument has been presented to us here touching that question, and we purposely refrain from expressing any views thereon. The city's power is here challenged only upon the two grounds we have noticed: (1) The United States ownership of the lands and waters; and (2) the reasonableness of the ordinance. No other question is here decided."

Upon a reargument of the case before the court en banc, the question referred to in the foregoing quotation was presented to the court, and after such presentation we are of the opinion that the ordinance in question is unconstitutional.

The ordinance provides for the punishment of persons who shall commit certain proscribed acts on property situated six miles beyond the corporate limits of the city of Cle Elum. The validity of the ordinance is attempted to be sustained under sections 9127 and 9473 of Remington's Compiled Statutes, which purport to give to the city the power to pass such an ordinance. Those sections of the Code can have no validity, however, in view of the constitutional provision, article 11, § 11, which provides that:

"Any county, city, town, or township, may make and enforce *within its limits* all such local, police, sanitary, and other regulations as are not in conflict with general laws." (Italics ours.)

This delegation of its police power by the state to various municipalities is strictly limited to the exercise of that power *within the limits* of such municipalities. ● ● ● In order for the appellant in this case to pass a valid ordinance under the sections of the Code relied on, it would be necessary for the court to read out of the constitutional provision the words, *"within its limits,"* and no case has been cited to us, and we have been unable to find one, where legislation similar to that here under consideration has been sustained where there also existed a constitutional provision such as ours. ● ● ●

The municipalities having only such legislative powers as are delegated to them, and the delegation by the Constitution containing a limitation as to the extent of that power, the Legislature is not empowered to exceed that limitation. It therefore must follow that the departmental decision be set aside and the judgment of the trial court affirmed.

The effect of holding this ordinance invalid will not be, of course, to render the municipalities powerless to protect property owned by them outside of their corporate limits from interference. The law provides several ways in which that protection can be secured; but without a constitutional amendment penal ordinances such as the one under consideration here cannot be given extraterritorial effect.

Judgment affirmed.

FULLERTON, J. (dissenting). The Legislature of the state, in the act providing for the incorporation of cities and towns, has sought to empower such cities and towns with the right to acquire, hold, and control real and personal property located outside of its corporate limits as a source for a water supply, and has by the same act sought to empower them to protect such supply from pollution by ordinance. The ordinance of the city here in question was enacted pursuant to this legislative grant of power, and is strictly within the power granted. It seems to me, therefore, that the question before the court is, Does the act of the Legislature violate any of the constitutional inhibitions?

The majority find the inhibition in the clause of the Constitution which they quote. In my opinion, this is a misapprehension of the purpose and meaning of the clause. ● ● ●

Its purpose was, as I conceive, to grant to the municipalities enumerated the power to enact ordinances for their local self-government, without the necessity of first receiving legislative sanction so to do. In other words, the powers granted are the powers they inherit in virtue of their creation as municipalities, and no legislation is necessary, other than the legislation by which they are created, to authorize them to exercise the granted powers, subject, of course, to the imposed limitation that the ordinance enacted under it shall not conflict with the general laws.

F.   Special Problems of Water Pollution

    1.   Thermal Pollution

See: Jost, "Cold Facts on Hot Water: Legal Aspects of Thermal Pollution," 1969 Wis. L. Rev. 253.

. . . .

    2.   Ocean Pollution

       (a)   The First Three Miles: State Control of Tidal Wetlands

SUBMERGED LANDS ACT of 1953, 43 U.S.C.A. sec. 1312.

§ 1312.   Seaward boundaries of States

The seaward boundary of each original coastal State is approved and confirmed as a line three geographical miles distant from its coast line or, in the case of the Great Lakes, to the international boundary. Any State admitted subsequent to the formation of the Union which has not already done so may extend its seaward boundaries to a line three geographical miles distant from its coast line, or to the international boundaries of the United States in the Great Lakes or any other body of water traversed by such boundaries. Any claim heretofore or hereafter asserted either by constitutional provision, statute, or otherwise, indicating the intent of a State so to extend its boundaries is approved and confirmed, without prejudice to its claim, if any it has, that its boundaries extend beyond that line. Nothing in this section is to be construed as questioning or in any manner prejudicing the existence of any State's seaward boundary beyond three geographical miles if it was so provided by its constitution or laws prior to or at the time such State became a member of the Union, or if it has been heretofore approved by Congress. May 22, 1953, c. 65, Title II, § 4, 67 Stat. 31.

STATE v. JOHNSON, 265 A. 2d 711 (Maine, 1970).

MARDEN, Justice.

On appeal from an injunction granted under the provisions of 12 M.R.S.A. §§ 4701–4709, inclusive, the Wetlands Act (Act),[1] originating in Chapter 348 P.L. 1967, which places restrictions upon the alteration and use of wetlands, as therein defined, without permission from the municipal officers concerned and the State Wetlands Control Board (Board). The Act is a conservation measure under the police power of the State to protect the ecology of areas bordering coastal waters.

● ● ●

The appellants own a tract of land about 220 feet wide and 700 feet long extending across salt water marshes between Atlantic Avenue on the east and the Webhannet River on the west in the Town of Wells. Westerly of the lots fronting on Atlantic Avenue the strip has been subdivided into lots for sale. The easterly 260 feet approximately of the strip has been filled and bears seasonal dwellings. Westerly of this 260 foot development is marsh-land flooded at high tide and drained, upon receding tide, into the River by a network of what our Maine historical novelist Kenneth E. Roberts called "eel runs," but referred to in the record as creeks. Similar marsh-land, undeveloped, lies to the north and south of appellants' strip, and westerly of the River, all of which makes up a substantial acreage (the extent not given in testimony, but of which we take judicial notice) of marsh-land known as the Wells Marshes. Appellants' land, by raising the grade above high water by the addition of fill, is adaptable to development for building purposes.

Following the effective date of the Act, an application to the municipal officers, with notice to the Wetlands Control Board, for permission to fill a portion of this land was denied by the Board, an administrative appeal was taken and the case reported to this Court, which appears sub nom. Johnson v. Maine Wetlands Control Board, Me., 250 A.2d 825 (Case No. 1) and in which the constitutionality of the Act was challenged. We held, by decision filed March 11, 1969 that absent a record of evidence as to the nature of the land involved and the benefits or harm to be expected from the denial of the permit, the case would have to be remanded.

Subsequent to March 11, 1969 fill was deposited on the land in question, as the result of which the State sought an injunction, the granting of which brings this case before us on appeal (Case No. 2). It is stipulated that the evidence in this case should be accepted as the evidence lacking in (Case No. 1) and that the two cases be consolidated for final determination of both.

The record establishes that the land which the appellants propose to build up by fill and build upon for sale, or to be offered for sale to be built upon, are coastal wetlands within the definition of the Act and that the refusal by the Board to permit the deposit of such fill prevents the development as proposed. The single Justice found that the property is a portion of a salt marsh area, a valuable natural resource of the State, that the highest and best use for the land, so filled, is for housing, and that unfilled it has no commercial value.

The issue is the same in both, namely, whether the denial of permit (Case No. 1) and the injunction (Case No. 2) so limit the use to plaintiffs of their land that such deprivation of use amounts to a taking of their property without constitutional due process and just compensation.[2]

Due Process

Due process of law has a dual aspect, procedural and substantive. 16 Am.Jur.2d, Constitutional Law § 548. ● ● ●

It is this substantive due process which is challenged in the Act. ● ● ●

The constitutional aspect of the current problem is to be determined by consideration of the extent to which appellants are deprived of their usual incidents of ownership,—for the conduct of the public authorities with relation to appellants' land is not a "taking" in the traditional sense. Our State has applied a strict construction of the constitutional provisions as to land.

60 A. 874, 876. The determination of unconstitutional deprivation is difficult and judicial decisions are diverse. Broadly speaking, deprivation of property contrary to constitutional guaranty occurs "if it deprives an owner of one of its essential attributes, destroys its value, restricts or interrupts its common necessary, or profitable use, hampers the owner in the application of it to the purposes of trade, or imposes conditions upon the right to hold or use it and thereby seriously impairs its value." 16 Am.Jur.2d Constitutional Law § 367. See also State v. Union Oil Company, 151 Me. 438, 446, 120 A.2d 708.

Conditions so burdensome may be imposed that they are equivalent to an outright taking, although the title to the property and some vestiges of its uses remain in the owner. East Coast Lumber Terminal, Inc. v. Town of Babylon, 174 F.2d 106, [5–7] 110 (2 CCA, 1949).

A guiding principle appears in the frequently cited case of Pennsylvania Coal Company v. Mahon et al., 260 U.S. 393, 413, 43 S.Ct. 158, 159–160, 67 L.Ed. 322 (1922) where Mr. Justice Holmes declared:

"Government hardly could go on if to some extent values incident to property could not be diminished without paying for every such change in the general law. As long recognized some values are enjoyed under an implied limitation and must yield to the police power. But obviously the implied limitation must have its limits or the contract and due process clauses are gone. One fact for consideration in determining such limits is the extent of the diminution. When it reaches a certain magnitude, in most if not in all cases there must be an exercise of eminent domain and compensation to sustain the act. So the question depends upon the particular facts." ● ● ●

Confrontation between public interests and private interests is common in the application of zoning laws, with which the Wetlands Act may be analogized, and the great majority of which, upon their facts, are held to be reasonable exercise of the police power. There are, however, zoning restrictions which have been recognized as equivalent to a taking of the property restricted. See Frankel v. City of Baltimore, 223 Md. 97, 162 A.2d 447, [2] 451 (1960); City of Plainfield v. Borough of Middlesex, 69 N.J.Super. 136, 173 A.2d 785, 788 (1961), and Arverne Bay Const. Co. v. Thatcher, 278 N.Y. 222, 15 N.E.2d 587, [10–13] 591 (N.Y.1938).

The same result has been reached as to zoning laws which identify their purposes as ones of conservation. See Dooley v. Town Plan and Zoning Commission of Town of Fairfield, 151 Conn. 304, 197 A.2d 770, [5, 6] 773 (1964, flood control); and Morris County Land Improvement Company v. Township of Parsippany-Troy Hills et al., 40 N.J. 539, 193 A.2d 232, [6, 7] 241 (1963, swampland preservation), and the rationale expressed in Commissioner of Natural Resources et al. v. S. Volpe & Co., Inc., 349 Mass. 104, 206 N.E.2d 666 (1965, involving "dredge and fill" Act); and MacGibbon et al. v. Board of Appeals of Duxbury, 347 Mass. 690, 200 N.E.2d 254 (1964) and 255 N.E.2d 347 (Mass.1970).

There has, as well, been restrictive conservation legislation which has been held not equivalent to taking. ● ● ● Between the public interest in braking and eventually stopping the insidious despoliation of our natural resources which have for so long been taken for granted, on the one hand, and the protection of appellants' property rights on the other, the issue is cast.

Here the single Justice has found that the area of which appellants' land is a part "is a valuable natural resource of the State of Maine and plays an important role in the conservation and development of aquatic and marine life, game birds and waterfowl," which bespeaks the public interest involved and the protection of which is sought by Section 4702 of the Act. With relation to appellants' interest the single Justice found that appellants' land absent the addition of fill "has no commercial value whatever." These findings are supported by the evidence and are conclusive. Danby v. Hanscom, 156 Me. 189, 191, 163 A.2d 372.

As distinguished from conventional zoning for town protection, the area of Wetlands representing a "valuable natural resource of the State," of which appellants' holdings are but a minute part, is of state-wide concern. The benefits from its preservation extend beyond town limits and are state-wide. The cost of its preservation should be publicly borne. To leave appellants with commercially valueless land in upholding the restriction presently imposed, is to charge them with more than their just share of the cost of this state-wide conservation program, granting fully its commendable purpose. In the phrasing of *Robb, supra,* their compensation by sharing in the benefits which this restriction is intended to secure is so disproportionate to their deprivation of reasonable use that such exercise of the State's police power is unreasonable.

The application of the Wetlands restriction in the terms of the denial of appellants' proposal to fill, and enjoining them from so doing deprives them of the reasonable use of their property and within Section 4704 is both an unreasonable exercise of police power and equivalent to taking within constitutional considerations. ● ● ●

Holding, as we do, that the prohibition against the filling of appellants' land, upon the facts peculiar to the case, is an unreasonable exercise of police power, it does not follow that the restriction as to draining sanitary sewage into coastal wetland is subject to the same infirmity. Additional considerations of health and pollution which are "separable from and independent of" the "fill" restriction may well support validity of the Act in those areas of concern. ● ● ●

Appeal sustained in both cases.

(b) Beyond the Three Mile Limits: Federal Control

UNITED STATES v. LOUISIANA, TEXAS, MISC., ET AL, 363 U.S. 1 (1960)

MR. JUSTICE HARLAN delivered the opinion of the Court.

The United States, invoking our original jurisdiction under Art. III, § 2, of the Constitution, brought this suit against the States of Louisiana, Texas, Mississippi, Alabama, and Florida, seeking a declaration that it is entitled to exclusive possession of, and full dominion and power over, the lands, minerals, and other natural resources underlying the waters of the Gulf of Mexico more than *three geographical miles* seaward from the coast of each State and extending to the edge of the Continental Shelf.[1] The complaint also asks that the States be enjoined from interfering with the rights of the United States in that area, and that they be required to account for all sums of money derived by them therefrom since June 5, 1950.[2] The case is now before us on the motions of the United States for judgment on the pleadings and for dismissal of Alabama's cross bill seeking to establish its rights to such submerged lands and resources within *three marine leagues* of its coast.

The controversy is another phase of the more than 20 years' dispute between the coastal States and the Federal Government over their respective rights to exploit the oil and other natural resources of offshore submerged lands. In 1947 this Court held that, as against California, the United States possessed paramount rights in such lands underlying the Pacific Ocean seaward of the low-water mark on the coast of California and outside of inland waters. *United States* v. *California*, 332 U. S. 19, 804. And on June 5, 1950, the Court, following the principles announced in the *California* case, made like holdings with respect to submerged lands in the Gulf of Mexico similarly lying off the coasts of Louisiana and Texas, and directed both States to account to the United States for all sums derived from natural resources in those areas after that date. *United States* v. *Louisiana*, 339 U. S. 699, 340

U. S. 899; *United States* v. *Texas,* 339 U. S. 707, 340 U. S. 900.[3]

On May 22, 1953, Congress, following earlier repeated unsuccessful attempts at legislation dealing with state and federal rights in submerged lands,[4] passed the Submerged Lands Act, 67 Stat. 29, 43 U. S. C. §§ 1301–1315. By that Act the United States relinquished to the coastal States all of its rights in such lands within certain geographical limits, and confirmed its own rights therein beyond those limits. The Act was sustained in *Alabama* v. *Texas,* 347 U. S. 272, as a constitutional exercise of Congress' power to dispose of federal property, Const. Art. IV, § 3, cl. 2. Since the Act concededly did not impair the validity of the *California, Louisiana,* and *Texas* cases, which are admittedly applicable to all coastal States, this case draws in question only the geographic extent to which the statute ceded to the States the federal rights established by those decisions.

The purposes of the Submerged Lands Act are described in its title as follows:

"To confirm and establish the titles of the States to lands beneath navigable waters within State boundaries and to the natural resources within such lands and waters, to provide for the use and control of said lands and resources, and to confirm the jurisdiction and control of the United States over the natural resources of the seabed of the Continental Shelf seaward of State boundaries."

To effectuate these purposes the Act, in pertinent part—

1. relinquishes to the States the entire interest of the United States in all lands beneath navigable waters within state boundaries (§ 3, 43 U. S. C. § 1311);[5]

2. defines that area in terms of state boundaries "as they existed at the time [a] State became a member of the Union, or as heretofore approved by the Congress," not extending, however, seaward from the coast of any State more than three marine leagues[6] in the Gulf of Mexico or more than three geographical miles in the Atlantic and Pacific Oceans (§ 2, 43 U. S. C. § 1301);[7]

3. confirms to each State a seaward boundary of three geographical miles, without "questioning or in any manner prejudicing the existence of any State's seaward boundary beyond three geographical miles if it was so provided by its constitution or laws prior to or at the time such State became a member of the Union, or if it has

been heretofore approved by Congress" (§ 4, 43 U. S. C. § 1312); [8] and

4. for purposes of commerce, navigation, national de-fense, and international affairs, reserves to the United States all constitutional powers of regulation and control over the areas within which the proprietary interests of the States are recognized (§ 6 (a), 43 U. S. C. § 1314); [9] and retains in the United States all rights in submerged lands lying beyond those areas to the seaward limits of the Continental Shelf (§ 9, 43 U. S. C. § 1302).[10]

The United States concedes that the statute grants to each of the defendant States submerged land rights in the Gulf of Mexico to the extent of three geographical miles, but contends that none of them is entitled to anything more. The States, conceding that three leagues is the limit of the statute's grant in the Gulf, contend that each of them is entitled to that much. The wide-ranging arguments of the parties, reflecting no doubt the magnitude of the economic interests at stake,[11] can be reduced to the following basic contentions:

The Government starts with the premise that the Act grants submerged land rights to a distance of more than three miles only to the extent that a Gulf State can show, in accordance with § 2 (b) of the Act, either that it had a legally established seaward boundary in excess of three miles at the time of its admission to the Union, or that such a boundary was thereafter approved for it by Congress prior to the passage of the Submerged Lands Act. It is contended that the Act did not purport to determine, fix, or change the boundary of any State, but left it to the courts to ascertain whether a particular State had a seaward boundary meeting either of these requirements. The Government then urges, as to any State relying on its original seaward boundary, that the Act contemplates as the measure of the grant a boundary which existed subsequent to a State's admission to the Union, and not one which existed only prior to admission—in other words, a boundary carrying the legal consequences of the event of admission. It reasons from this that since a State's seaward boundary cannot be greater than the national maritime boundary, and since the national boundary was at all relevant times never greater than three miles, no State could have had a seaward boundary in excess of three miles, regardless of what it may have claimed prior to admission. Further, the Government undertakes to show that, irrrespective of the

extent of the national maritime boundary, none of these
States ever had a valid seaward boundary in excess of three
miles, even prior to admission, and that no such boundary
was thereafter approved by Congress for any State.

The States, on the other hand, make several alternative
arguments. At one extreme, they contend that the Submerged Lands Act *ipso facto* makes a three-league grant
to all the Gulf States, or at least that the Act by its terms
establishes the seaward boundary of some States, notably
Texas and Florida, at three leagues. Alternatively, they
argue that if the extent of such state boundaries "at the
time" of admission was left to judicial determination,
then the controlling inquiry is what seaward boundary
each State had just prior to admission. If, however, the
Act contemplates a boundary as fixed by the event of
admission, each State contends that Congress fixed for it a
three-league Gulf boundary, and that whatever may have
been the extent of the national maritime boundary at the
time is an irrelevant factor. Florida further contends
that when it was readmitted to the Union in 1868, Congress approved for it a three-league Gulf boundary. And
finally the States argue that if the national boundary is in
any way relevant, it has at all material times in fact been
at three leagues in the Gulf of Mexico. • • •

In this opinion we consider the issues arising in common
between the Government and all the defendant States,
and the particular claims of Texas, Louisiana, Mississippi,
and Alabama, all of which depend upon their original
admission boundaries. The particular claims of Florida,
which involve primarily its readmission boundary, are
considered in a separate opinion. • • •

CONCLUSIONS.

On the basis of what has been said in this opinion, we
reach the following conclusions:

1. As to the States of Louisiana, Mississippi, and Alabama, a decree will be entered (1) declaring that the
United States is entitled, as against these States, to all the
lands, minerals, and other natural resources underlying the
Gulf of Mexico more than three geographical miles from
the coast of each such State, that is, from the line of ordinary low-water mark and outer limit of inland waters, and
extending seaward to the edge of the Continental Shelf;
(2) declaring that none of these States is entitled to any
interest in such lands, minerals, and resources; (3) enjoining these States from interfering with the rights of the

United States therein; (4) directing each such State appropriately to account to the United States for all sums of money derived therefrom subsequent to June 5, 1950; [140] and (5) dismissing the cross bill of the State of Alabama.[141]

2. As to the State of Texas, a decree will be entered (1) declaring that the State is entitled, as against the United States, to the lands, minerals, and other natural resources underlying the Gulf of Mexico to a distance of three leagues from Texas' coast, that is, from the line of ordinary low-water mark and outer limit of inland waters; (2) declaring that the United States is entitled, as against Texas, to no interest therein; (3) declaring that the United States is entitled, as against Texas, to all such lands, minerals, and resources lying beyond that area, and extending to the edge of the Continental Shelf; (4) enjoining the State from interfering with the rights of the United States therein; and (5) directing Texas appropriately to account to the United States for all sums of money derived since June 5, 1950, from the area to which the United States is declared to be entitled. ● ● ●

The parties may submit an appropriate form of decree giving effect to the conclusions reached in this opinion.

It is so ordered.

. . . .

See UNITED STATES v. RAY & ACME GENERAL CONTRACTORS, 423 F. 2d 16 (5th Cir., 1970) involving the claim of two private companies to a strip of reefs on the Continental Shelf, four and one half miles off the southeast coast of Florida on which they proposed to build a new soverign nation, to be named, Atlantis, Isle of Gold. The Circuit Court held that the United States has the exclusive right for purposes of exploration and exploitation of the reefs.

COASTAL ZONE MANAGEMENT ACT OF 1972, 16 U.S.C.A.
sections 1451 to 1464, P.L. 92-583, 86 STAT. 1280.

CONGRESSIONAL FINDINGS

Sec. 302. The Congress finds that—

(a) There is a national interest in the effective management, beneficial use, protection, and development of the coastal zone;

(b) The coastal zone is rich in a variety of natural, commercial, recreational, industrial, and esthetic resources of immediate and potential value to the present and future well-being of the Nation;

(c) The increasing and competing demands upon the lands and waters of our coastal zone occasioned by population growth and economic development, including requirements for industry, commerce, residential development, recreation, extraction of mineral resources and fossil fuels, transportation and navigation, waste disposal, and harvesting of fish, shellfish, and other living marine resources, have resulted in the loss of living marine resources, wildlife, nutrient-rich areas, permanent and adverse changes to ecological systems, decreasing open space for public use, and shoreline erosion;

(d) The coastal zone, and the fish, shellfish, other living marine resources, and wildlife therein, are ecologically fragile and consequently extremely vulnerable to destruction by man's alterations;

(e) Important ecological, cultural, historic, and esthetic values in the coastal zone which are essential to the well-being of all citizens are being irretrievably damaged or lost;

(f) Special natural and scenic characteristics are being damaged by ill-planned development that threatens these values;

(g) In light of competing demands and the urgent need to protect and to give high priority to natural systems in the coastal zone, present state and local institutional arrangements for planning and regulating land and water uses in such areas are inadequate; and

(h) The key to more effective protection and use of the land and water resources of the coastal zone is to encourage the states to exercise their full authority over the lands and waters in the coastal zone by assisting the states, in cooperation with Federal and local governments and other vitally affected interests, in developing land and water use programs for the coastal zone, including unified policies, criteria, standards, methods, and processes for dealing with land and water use decisions of more than local significance.

DECLARATION OF POLICY

Sec. 303. The Congress finds and declares that it is the national policy (a) to preserve, protect, develop, and where possible, to restore or enhance, the resources of the Nation's coastal zone for this and succeeding generations, (b) to encourage and assist the states to exercise effectively their responsibilities in the coastal zone through the development and implementation of management programs to achieve wise use of the land and water resources of the coastal zone giving full consideration to ecological, cultural, historic, and esthetic values as well as to needs for economic development, (c) for all Federal agencies engaged in programs affecting the coastal zone to cooperate and participate with state and local governments and regional agencies in effectuating the purposes of this title, and (d) to encourage the participation of the public, of Federal, state, and local governments and of regional agencies in the development of coastal zone management programs. With respect to implementation of such management programs, it is the national policy to encourage cooperation among the various state and regional agencies including establishment of interstate and regional agreements, cooperative procedures, and joint action particularly regarding environmental problems.

. . . .

MARINE PROTECTION, RESEARCH AND SANCTUARIES ACT OF 1972, 33 U.S.C.A. sec. 1401 et seq., P.L. 92-532, 86 STAT. 1052.

FINDING, POLICY, AND PURPOSE

Sec. 2. (a) Unregulated dumping of material into ocean waters endangers human health, welfare, and amenities, and the marine environment, ecological systems, and economic potentialities.

(b) The Congress declares that it is the policy of the United States to regulate the dumping of all types of materials into ocean waters and to prevent or strictly limit the dumping into ocean waters of any material which would adversely affect human health, welfare, or amenities, or the marine environment, ecological systems, or economic potentialities.

To this end, it is the purpose of this Act to regulate the transportation of material from the United States for dumping into ocean waters, and the dumping of material, transported from outside the United States, if the dumping occurs in ocean waters over which the United States has jurisdiction or over which it may exercise control, under accepted principles of international law, in order to protect its territory or territorial sea.

. . . .

(c) International Waters

See: Teclaff, "International Law and the Protection of the Oceans from Pollution," 40 Fordham L. Rev. 529 (1972).

IV. NOISE POLLUTION

A.   The Legal Consequences of Noise

1.   As a Detriment to Health

SHAWINSKI v. J.H. WILLIAMS & CO., 298 N.Y. 546,
81 N.E. 2d 93(1948).

Proceeding under the Workmen's Compensation Law, Consol. Laws, c. 67, by Matthew Slawinski, claimant, opposed by J. H. Williams & Company, employer, and the Fidelity & Casualty Company of New York, insurance carrier.

A schedule award of compensaton was made by the Workmen's Compensation Board for 45 per cent loss of hearing in claimant's left ear and 43.6 per cent loss of hearing in his right ear. The award was made upon the theory that the claimant had suffered from an occupational disease, tinnitus. It appeared that claimant worked in the forge department of the employer's factory on machine hammers of which there were approximately 100 in the room and that the noise was exceptionally heavy and sustained.

From the schedule award of compensation by the Board, the employer and insurance carrier appealed. The award was affirmed by the Appellate Division, 273 App. Div. 826, 76 N.Y.S.2d 888. Foster, J., dissented on the ground that there was no proof that claimant's wages were diminished by his partial deafness and that an employee who contracts an occupational disease without disability is not entitled to an award. From the order of affirmance by the Appellate Division, the employer and insurance carrier appeal.

Order affirmed with costs.

For additional information on the detrimental effect of noise on health see:

1. Council on Environmental Quality, Environmental Quality - First Annual Report 124-129 (1970).

2. American Speech and Hearing Association, Conference Proceedings, Noise as a Public Health Hazard (1968).

3. Report to the President and Congress on Noise, Report of the Administrator of EPA, Sen. Doc. No. 92-63 (1972).

See also:

1. Spater, "Noise and the Law," 63 Mich. L. Rev. 1373 (1965).

2. Hildebrand, "Noise Pollution: An Introduction to the Problem and An Outline for Future Legal Research," 70 Col. L. Rev. 652 (1970).

2. As a "Taking" of Property

GRIGGS v. ALLEGHENY COUNTY, 369 U.S. 84 (1962).

MR. JUSTICE DOUGLAS delivered the opinion of the Court.

This case is here on a petiti)n for a writ of certiorari to the Supreme Court of Pennsylvania which we granted (366 U. S. 943) because its decision (402 Pa. 411, 168 A. 2d 123) seemed to be in conflict with *United States* v. *Causby,* 328 U. S. 256. The question is whether respondent has taken an air easement over petitioner's property for which it must pay just compensation as required by the Fourteenth Amendment. *Chicago, B. & Q. R. Co.* v. *Chicago,* 166 U. S. 226, 241. The Court of Common Pleas, pursuant to customary Pennsylvania procedure, appointed a Board of Viewers to determine whether there had been a "taking" and, if so, the amount of compensation due. The Board of Viewers met upon the property; it held a hearing, and in its report found that there had been a "taking" by respondent of an air easement over petitioner's property and that the compensation payable (damages suffered) was $12,690. The Court of Common Pleas dismissed the exceptions of each party to the Board's report. On appeal, the Supreme Court of Pennsylvania decided, by a divided vote, that if there were a "taking" in the constitutional sense, the respondent was not liable.

Respondent owns and maintains the Greater Pittsburgh Airport on land which it purchased to provide airport and air-transport facilities. The airport was designed for public use in conformity with the rules and regulations of the Civil Aeronautics Administration within the scope of the National Airport Plan provided for in 49 U. S. C. § 1101 *et seq.* By this Act the federal Administrator is authorized and directed to prepare and continually revise a "national plan for the development of public airports."
● ● ●
The applications for projects must follow the standards prescribed by the Administrator. § 1108. ● ● ●

Respondent executed three agreements with the Administrator of Civil Aeronautics in which it agreed, among other things, to abide by and adhere to the Rules and Regulations of C. A. A. and to "maintain a master plan of the airport," including "approach areas." It was provided that the "airport approach standards to be followed in this connection shall be those established by the Administrator"; and it was also agreed that respondent "will acquire such easements or other interests in lands and air space as may be necessary to perform the covenants of this paragraph." The "master plan" laid out and submitted by respondent included the required "approach areas"; and that "master plan" was approved. One "approach area" was to the northeast runway. As designed and approved, it passed .over petitioner's home which is 3,250 feet from the end of that runway. The elevation at the end of that runway is 1,150.50 feet above sea level; the door sill at petitioner's residence, 1,183.64 feet; the top of petitioner's chimney, 1,219.64 feet. The slope gradient of the approach area is as 40 is to 3,250 feet or 81 feet, which leaves a clearance of 11.36 feet between the bottom of the glide angle and petitioner's chimney.

The airlines that use the airport are lessees of respondent; and the leases give them, among other things, the right "to land" and "take off." No flights were in violation of the regulations of C. A. A.; nor were any flights lower than   essary for a safe landing or take-off. ● ● ●

On take-off the noise of the planes is comparable "to the noise of a riveting machine or steam hammer." On the let-down the planes make a noise comparable "to that of a noisy factory." The Board of Viewers found that "The low altitude flights over plaintiff's property caused the plaintiff and occupants of his property to become nervous and distraught, eventually causing their removal therefrom as undesirable and unbearable for their residential use." ● ● ●

We start with *United States v. Causby, supra,* which held that the United States by low flights of its military planes over a chicken farm made the property unusable for that purpose and that therefore there had been a "taking," in the constitutional sense, of an air easement for which compensation must be made. ● ● ●

as we said in the *Causby* case, the use of land presupposes the use of some of the airspace above it. 328 U. S., at 264. Otherwise no home could be built, no tree planted, no fence constructed, no chimney erected. An invasion of the "superadjacent airspace" will often "affect the use of the surface of the land itself." 328 U. S., at 265.

It is argued that though there was a "taking," someone other than respondent was the taker—the airlines or the C. A. A. acting as an authorized representative of the United States. We think, however, that respondent, which was the promoter, owner, and lessor [2] of the airport, was in these circumstances the one who took the air easement in the constitutional sense. Respondent decided, subject to the approval of the C. A. A., where the airport would be built, what runways it would need, their direction and length, and what land and navigation easements would be needed. The Federal Government takes nothing; it is the local authority which decides to build an airport *vel non*, and where it is to be located. We see no difference between its responsibility for the air easements necessary for operation of the airport and its responsibility for the land on which the runways were built. Nor did the Congress when it designed the legislation for a National Airport Plan. ● ●●

That the instant "taking" was "for public use" is not debatable. For respondent agreed with the C. A. A. that it would operate the airport "for the use and benefit of the public," that it would operate it "on fair and reasonable terms and without unjust discrimination," and that it would not allow any carrier to acquire "any exclusive right" to its use.

The glide path for the northeast runway is as necessary for the operation of the airport as is a surface right of way for operation of a bridge, or as is the land for the operation of a dam. See *United States* v. *Virginia Electric Co.*, 365 U. S. 624, 630. As stated by the Supreme Court of Washington in *Ackerman* v. *Port of Seattle*, 55 Wash. 2d 401, 413, 348 P. 2d 664, 671, ". . . an adequate approach way is as necessary a part of an airport as is the ground on which the airstrip, itself, is constructed . . . ." Without the "approach areas," an airport is indeed not operable. Respondent in designing it had to acquire some private property. Our conclusion is that by constitutional standards it did not acquire enough.

Reversed.

MR. JUSTICE BLACK, with whom MR. JUSTICE FRANK-
FURTER concurs, dissenting.

In *United States* v. *Causby*,[1] the Court held that by
flying its military aircraft frequently on low landing and
takeoff flights over Causby's chicken farm the United
States had so disturbed the peace of the occupants and so
frightened the chickens that it had "taken" a flight easement from Causby for which it was required to pay "just
compensation" under the Fifth Amendment. Today the

Court holds that similar low landing and takeoff flights,
making petitioner Griggs' property "undesirable and
unbearable for . . . residential use," constitute a "taking" of airspace over Griggs' property—not, however, by
the owner and operator of the planes as in *Causby*, but by
Allegheny County, the owner and operator of the Greater
Pittsburgh Airport to and from which the planes fly.
Although I dissented in *Causby* because I did not believe
that the individual aircraft flights "took" property in the
constitutional sense merely by going over it and because
I believed that the complexities of adjusting atmospheric
property rights to the air age could best be handled by
Congress, I agree with the Court that the noise, vibrations and fear caused by constant and extremely low overflights in this case have so interfered with the use and
enjoyment of petitioner's property as to amount to a
"taking" of it under the *Causby* holding. I cannot agree,
however, that it was the County of Allegheny that did the
"taking." I think that the United States, not the Greater
Pittsburgh Airport, has "taken" the airspace over Griggs'
property necessary for flight.[2] While the County did
design the plan for the airport, including the arrange-
ment of its takeoff and approach areas, in order to comply
with federal requirements it did so under the supervision
of and subject to the approval of the Civil Aeronautics
Administrator of the United States.[3]

. . . .

See Munroe, "Aircraft Noise As A Taking of
Property," 13 N.Y.L.F. 476 (1967).

3. As a Nuisance

SMITH v. WESTERN WAYNE CO. CONSERVATION ASS'N.,
380 Mich. 526, 158 N.W.2d 463(1968).

PER CURIAM.

We adopt the following from the excellent opinion of the trial judge: *

"Plaintiffs' bill of complaint seeks injunctive relief. The main question presented for determination is whether the use of the rifle and pistol ranges (hereinafter referred to as 'Range') constructed on defendants' property and located in Section 19 of the northwest Plymouth Township is a nuisance in fact and should be enjoined. ● ● ●

"The Range is located in an area which is undeveloped, open agricultural country. ● ● ●

"In December 1961 defendants acquired a 62-acre tract of land, of which 40 acres are in northwest Plymouth Township and 22 acres in adjoining Salem Township, in Section 24. The land was purchased with proceeds of funds received by defendants from the Wayne County Road Commission as the result of eminent domain proceedings, whereby said commission had acquired (for park purposes) defendants' so-called Joy site, located in Nankin Township, on which defendants had a clubhouse and gun range. It is not disputed that defendants purchased the property in reliance on their right to use it for the purposes intended, inasmuch as the property was zoned agricultural, permitted gun clubs, and hunting in season had been allowed in the area for many years.[1] ● ● ●

"The Range was constructed in accordance with plans and specifications exceeding the requirements of the National Rifle Association. It is used by members and guests of the defendant association, as well as for competitive meets. The association has about 750 members, including doctors, lawyers, engineers, policemen, etc., membership being limited to persons over eighteen years of age of good character.

"The principal purposes of the association, as testified by its officers, are: to promote and further the conservation of wild life, game and natural resources of this state; to improve the relationships between farmer, owner and hunter, particularly in the western part of Wayne County; and to establish and improve social relationships between its members. To further its aims, the association became affiliated with the Michigan United Conservation Clubs (MUCC), the Director of Civilian Defense, the National Rifle Association, the Michigan Archers Association, and National Wild Life. ● ● ●

"The incident which ultimately led to the filing of plaintiffs' bill of complaint herein was the occurrence of what has been described in the testimony as a 'big-bore' meet, held on defendants' 200-yard rifle range on May 19–20, 1962, involving some 40 to 50 participants.[2] ● ● ●

"On May 21, 1962, a request was made upon defendants to reverse the range so that the shooting would not be in the general direction of the trailer court. The request was denied, because of defendants' investment in the already constructed range. Thereupon, on June 1, 1962, plaintiffs Smith and Oak Haven Trailer Court, Inc., joined with other property owners living on Ridge, North Territorial, Gottchalk and Napier Roads in filing a bill of complaint, seeking to enjoin defendants' use of the Range and praying for other relief hereinbefore noted.

"On the filing of the bill, plaintiffs obtained an order directing defendants to show cause why a temporary injunction should not issue, containing a restraining order enjoining defendants from using their lands, 'or any part thereof, for the service of food and beverages to themselves or others, or for the discharge of firearms, either individually or in rifle meets, or in similar contests.' On the hearing thereof, with the consent of the motion judge and approval of the executive judge of this circuit, the parties transformed the hearing to a trial on the merits.

"The trial involved 27 days of actual trial, extending over the period from June 25 to December 7, 1962, covering about 2000 pages of transcript, wherein 60 witnesses testified and 47 exhibits were received in evidence. In addition, with the parties' consent and their furnishing ground and air transportation, the Court personally inspected and viewed defendants' present and former (Joy, Nankin Township) sites, including the entire surrounding areas. Then, on August 5, 1962, the Court attended a meet staged to simulate the meet held on May 19–20. At that time, through prearranged signals, sound measurements were taken and tape recordings made by a qualified sound engineer at the homes of certain designated plaintiffs, including the closest and farthest from the range, the results of which were subsequently made a part of the testimonial record herein.

"During the trial, the original restraining order was first modified to permit defendants to serve food and beverages, and then modified to permit use of the Range for practice, but not for meets similar to the one held May 19–20. ● ● ●
"Thereafter, on October 11, 1963, an order was entered re-opening proofs, based on the written stipulation of the attorneys for all the parties. Pursuant thereto, a rifle-shooting demonstration of *eleven* riflemen (only 8 at a regular meet), using similar rifles and ammunition as used in the demonstration of August 5, 1962, was conducted on October 13, 1963, between 12 noon and 2 P.M., in the presence of the Court, attorneys, some plaintiffs, and interested spectators. Sound measurements of rapid fire were made at the homes of plaintiffs Rockwood and Evans ● ● ●

"In brief, it is the claim of plaintiffs that the noise from the use of defendants' range is so deafening that it impairs their rights 'to the peace, rest and comfort of their homes'; and that unless such use is abated, it will soon drive them out of their homes and result in irreparable damage to the owners of the trailer court, who will lose their tenants and be prevented from obtaining new tenants.

"It is recognized in Michigan, as well as in other jurisdictions, that under certain circumstances noise may constitute a nuisance and may be enjoined. In Borsvold v. United Dairies, 347 Mich. 672, at 680–681 [81 N.W.2d 378, 82 A.L.R.2d 406], the court gave the test for a nuisance: 'To render noise a nuisance, it must be of such a character as to be of actual physical discomfort to persons of ordinary sensibilities.' In applying this standard, the court states that consideration should be given to such additional factors as the character of the industry complained of, the character, volume, time and duration of the noise, and 'all the facts and circumstances of the case.'
● ● ●
"Though most of the Michigan cases wherein injunctions have been given have concerned noise which deprived people of sleep, there is no reason for claiming that one may be as noisy as one pleases as long as the noise stops before bedtime.
● ● ●
"The noise of the May 19–20 meet has been described by plaintiffs' witnesses as follows: 'Like the army had let loose over there'; 'There was a terrific uproar of guns, almost continuously, from daylight to dark'; 'It was like the Fourth of July':
● ● ●
"On the other hand, testimony of other witnesses, including a number of disinterested witnesses, is to the effect that the noise was not such as would disturb a normal, reasonable person. Thus, witness Nikkel, who was across the street from the trailer park, said he heard the shooting and that it was not shocking or disturbing. ● ● ●

There being a sharp dispute as to the effect, intensity, loudness and continuity of the noise produced by the firing, at the Court's suggestion, a simulated meet was held on August 5, 1962, as aforesaid, attended by the Court, attorneys, litigants, and an expert sound engineer. A maximum of 83 decibels (with 8 shooters) was recorded at Plaintiff Rowland's home, about one-half mile away. Other maximum readings were Webb, 52; trailer court, 63; and McClelland, 66½. No sound of firing could be recorded at some of the locations, because of background noises—i. e., birds, cars going by, etc. Thereafter, sound recordings were made in open court, with everyone quiet, and a reading of 48 decibels was obtained. Exhibit 37, 'Handbook of Measurements,' shows that normal conversation at three feet is 63 decibels and that 88 decibels is equivalent to the noise inside a sedan in city traffic. At the October 1963 simulated meet (with 11 riflemen), a maximum of 88¼ decibles was recorded at Plaintiff Evans' home, about one-quarter mile away, on Napier Road.

"Plaintiffs contend, however, that the noise made in the August 1962 demonstration was considerably less than that made in the meet of May 19, 20, which resulted in the filing of the bill. ● ● ●

"The noise of the shooting at the Range bears some relation to the types of weapons used, the number of shooters firing at approximately the same time, and the fact that the shooters are engaged in practice or are participating in a championship meet, calling for slow and rapid firing. Whether the noise is sufficient to constitute a nuisance depends upon its effect upon an ordinary reasonable man, that is, a normal person of ordinary habits and sensibilities. Relief cannot be based solely upon the subjective likes and dislikes of a particular plaintiff. To be workable, relief must be based upon an objective standard of reasonableness.

"It is urged by plaintiffs that the effect of noise upon human beings can not be measured in decibels and that the Court must not ignore 'phons' and 'sones,' which involve frequencies and subjective reactions on a measurable basis and psychological functions in relation to certain noises. Plaintiffs thus contend that 'it is not the decibel rating of the noise that is involved; it is how the noise affects the people in the neighborhood.'

"The Court having personally attended the demonstrations and having listened to the noise resulting from the use of defendants' range from the homes of various plaintiffs, the closest of which was about a quarter mile away and the farthest being about three quarters of a mile away, the Court does not find the noise to be such as would shock a person of ordinary sensibilities or cause actual physical discomfort. The Court finds that the noise is not of such character as to render it a nuisance, considering that the use of the Range is consistent with the character of the area, considering the location of plaintiffs' homes, and especially considering the very limited use of the Range during the year for competitive meets. The bigbore meet, which produces the highest decibel reading, is held only four or five times a year; the D.C.M. meet, a one-day affair, twice a year; sportsman rifle, twice a year; and pistol or small-arm meets on very infrequent occasions. ● ● ●

The trial judge, having carefully considered each of plaintiffs' claims, concluded, as do we, that none could be sustained on the basis of the proofs as to existing conditions or proposed future use of defendants' property. In denying relief to plaintiffs, his judgment carefully safeguarded their rights by imposing certain restrictions upon defendants' activities and providing for continued supervision by the court. The pertinent portion of the judgment reads as follows:

"It is further ordered and adjudged that the relief prayed for by plaintiffs in the complaints filed in the above entitled causes are hereby denied, and

"It is further ordered and adjudged that the defendants are free to use the Ranges and property in any normal manner subject to the following:

"a. The defendants shall install and maintain a forty (40) foot back stop with respect to its 200 yard range.

"b. That the noise level of shooting shall not exceed 88¼ decibels at one quarter mile distance.

"c. That the shooting hours shall be limited on week days between the hours of 9 A.M. and 6 P.M. and on Sundays between the hours of 10 A.M. and one hour after sunset. • • •

The judgment of the Court of Appeals is affirmed. Costs to appellees.

. . . .

B. Federal Regulation: Noise Control Act of 1972, 42 U.S.C.A. sec. 4901 et seq., P.L. 92-574, 86 STAT. 1234

1. Findings and Policy

FINDINGS AND POLICY

Sec. 2. (a) The Congress finds—

(1) that inadequately controlled noise presents a growing danger to the health and welfare of the Nation's population, particularly in urban areas;

(2) that the major sources of noise include transportation vehicles and equipment, machinery, appliances, and other products in commerce; and

(3) that, while primary responsibility for control of noise rests with State and local governments, Federal action is essential to deal with major noise sources in commerce control of which require national uniformity of treatment.

(b) The Congress declares that it is the policy of the United States to promote an environment for all Americans free from noise that jeopardizes their health or welfare. To that end, it is the purpose of this Act to establish a means for effective coordination of Federal research and activities in noise control, to authorize the establishment of Federal noise emission standards for products distributed in commerce, and to provide information to the public respecting the noise emission and noise reduction characteristics of such products.

2. Noise Emission Standards for Products Distributed in Commerce

NOISE EMISSION STANDARDS FOR PRODUCTS DISTRIBUTED
IN COMMERCE

Sec. 6. (a) (1) The Administrator shall publish proposed regulations, meeting the requirements of subsection (c), for each product—

(A) which is identified (or is part of a class identified) in any report published under section 5(b) (1) as a major source of noise,

(B) for which, in his judgment, noise emission standards are feasible, and

(C) which falls in one of the following categories:

(i) Construction equipment.

(ii) Transportation equipment (including recreational vehicles and related equipment).

(iii) Any motor or engine (including any equipment of which an engine or motor is an integral part).

(iv) Electrical or electronic equipment.

● ● ●

(c) (1) Any regulation prescribed under subsection (a) or (b) of this section (and any revision thereof) respecting a product shall include a noise emission standard which shall set limits on noise emissions from such product and shall be a standard which in the Administrator's judgment, based on criteria published under section 5, is requisite to protect the public health and welfare, taking into account the magnitude and conditions of use of such product (alone or in combination with other noise sources), the degree of noise reduction achievable through the application of the best available technology, and the cost of compliance. In establishing such a standard for any product, the Administrator shall give appropriate consideration to standards under other laws designed to safeguard the health and welfare of persons, including any standards under the National Traffic and Motor Vehicle Safety Act of 1966, the Clean Air Act, and the Federal Water Pollution Control Act. Any such noise emission standards shall be a performance standard. In addition, any regulation under subsection (a) or (b) (and any revision thereof) may contain testing procedures necessary to assure compliance with the emission standard in such regulation, and may contain provisions respecting instructions of the manufacturer for the maintenance, use, or repair of the product.

3. Aircraft Noise Standards

Sec. 7. (a) The Administrator, after consultation with appropriate Federal, State, and local agencies and interested persons, shall conduct a study of the (1) adequacy of Federal Aviation Administration flight and operational noise controls; (2) adequacy of noise emission standards on new and existing aircraft, together with recommendations on the retrofitting and phaseout of existing aircraft; (3) implications of identifying and achieving levels of cumulative noise exposure around airports; and (4) additional measures available to airport operators and local governments to control aircraft noise. ● ● ●

(b) Section 611 of the Federal Aviation Act of 1958 (49 U.S.C. 1431) [3] is amended to read as follows:

"CONTROL AND ABATEMENT OF AIRCRAFT NOISE AND SONIC BOOM

"Sec. 611. ● ● ●

"(b) (1) In order to afford present and future relief and protection to the public health and welfare from aircraft noise and sonic boom, the FAA, after consultation with the Secretary of Transportation and with EPA, shall prescribe and amend standards for the measurement of aircraft noise and sonic boom and shall prescribe and amend such regulations as the FAA may find necessary to provide for the control and abatement of aircraft noise and sonic boom
● ● ●

"(2) The FAA shall not issue an original type certificate under section 603(a) of this Act for any aircraft for which substantial noise abatement can be achieved by prescribing standards and regulations in accordance with this section, unless he shall have prescribed standards and regulations in accordance with this section which apply to such aircraft and which protect the public from aircraft noise and sonic boom, consistent with the considerations listed in subsection (d).

"(c) (1) Not earlier than the date of submission of the report required by section 7(a) of the Noise Control Act of 1972, EPA shall submit to the FAA proposed regulations to provide such control and abatement of aircraft noise and sonic boom ● ● ● the FAA shall—

"(A) in accordance with subsection (b), prescribe regulations (i) substantially as they were submitted by EPA, or (ii) which are a modification of the proposed regulations submitted by EPA, or

"(B) publish in the Federal Register a notice that it is not prescribing any regulation in response to EPA's submission of proposed regulations, together with a detailed explanation providing reasons for the decision not to prescribe such regulations.
● ● ●

"(d) In prescribing and amending standards and regulations under this section, the FAA shall—

"(1) consider relevant available data relating to aircraft noise and sonic boom, including the results of research, development, testing, and evaluation activities conducted pursuant to this Act and the Department of Transportation Act;

"(2) consult with such Federal, State, and interstate agencies as he deems appropriate;

"(3) consider whether any proposed standard or regulation is consistent with the highest degree of safety in air commerce or air transportation in the public interest;

"(4) consider whether any proposed standard or regulation is economically reasonable, technologically practicable, and appropriate for the particular type of aircraft, aircraft engine, appliance, or certificate to which it will apply; and

"(5) consider the extent to which such standard or regulation will contribute to carrying out the purposes of this section.

"(e) In any action to amend, modify, suspend, or revoke a certificate in which violation of aircraft noise or sonic boom standards or regulations is at issue, the certificate holder shall have the same notice and appeal rights as are contained in section 609, and in any appeal to the National Transportation Safety Board, the Board may amend, modify, or reverse the order of the FAA if it finds that control or abatement of aircraft noise or sonic boom and the public health and welfare do not require the affirmation of such order, or that such order is not consistent with safety in air commerce or air transportation."

. . . .

4. Railroad Noise Emission Standards

RAILROAD NOISE EMISSION STANDARDS

Sec. 17. (a) (1) Within nine months after the date of enactment of this Act, the Administrator shall publish proposed noise emission regulations for surface carriers engaged in interstate commerce by railroad. Such proposed regulations shall include noise emission standards setting such limits on noise emissions resulting from operation of the equipment and facilities of surface carriers engaged in interstate commerce by railroad which reflect the degree of noise reduction achievable through the application of the best available technology, taking into account the cost of compliance. These regulations shall be in addition to any regulations that may be proposed under section 6 of this Act.

5. Motor Carrier Noise Emission Standards

MOTOR CARRIER NOISE EMISSION STANDARDS

Sec. 18. (a) (1) Within nine months after the date of enactment of this Act, the Administrator shall publish proposed noise emission regulations for motor carriers engaged in interstate commerce. Such proposed regulations shall include noise emission standards setting such limits on noise emissions resulting from operation of motor carriers engaged in interstate commerce which reflect the degree of noise reduction achievable through the application of the best available technology, taking into account the cost of compliance. These regulations shall be in addition to any regulations that may be proposed under section 6 of this Act.

. . . .

6. Prohibited Acts

PROHIBITED ACTS

Sec. 10. (a) Except as otherwise provided in subsection (b), the following acts or the causing thereof are prohibited:

(1) In the case of a manufacturer, to distribute in commerce any new product manufactured after the effective date of a regulation prescribed under section 6 which is applicable to such product, except in conformity with such regulation.

(2) (A) The removal or rendering inoperative by any person, other than for purposes of maintenance, repair, or replacement, of any device or element of design incorporated into any product in compliance with regulations under section 6, prior to its sale or delivery to the ultimate purchaser or while it is in use, or (B) the use of a product after such device or element of design has been removed or rendered inoperative by any person.

(3) In the case of a manufacturer, to distribute in commerce any new product manufactured after the effective date of a regulation prescribed under section 8(b) (requiring information respecting noise) which is applicable to such product, except in conformity with such regulation.

(4) The removal by any person of any notice affixed to a product or container pursuant to regulations prescribed under section 8(b), prior to sale of the product to the ultimate purchaser.

(5) The importation into the United States by any person of any new product in violation of a regulation prescribed under section 9 which is applicable to such product.

(6) The failure or refusal by any person to comply with any requirement of section 11(d) or 13(a) or regulations prescribed under section 13(a), 17, or 18.

7. Enforcement

ENFORCEMENT

Sec. 11. (a) Any person who willfully or knowingly violates paragraph (1), (3), (5), or (6) of subsection (a) of section 10 of this Act shall be punished by a fine of not more than $25,000 per day of violation, or by imprisonment for not more than one year, or by both. If the conviction is for a violation committed after a first conviction of such person under this subsection, punishment shall be by a fine of not more than $50,000 per day of violation, or by imprisonment for not more than two years, or by both.

(b) For the purpose of this section, each day of violation of any paragraph of section 10(a) shall constitute a separate violation of that section.

. . . .

8. Citizen Suits

CITIZEN SUITS

Sec. 12. (a) Except as provided in subsection (b), any person (other than the United States) may commence a civil action on his own behalf—

(1) against any person (including (A) the United States, and (B) any other governmental instrumentality or agency to the extent permitted by the eleventh amendment to the Constitution) who is alleged to be in violation of any noise control requirement (as defined in subsection (e)), or

(2) against—

(A) the Administrator of the Environmental Protection Agency where there is alleged a failure of such Administrator to perform any act or duty under this Act which is not discretionary with such Administrator, or

(B) the Administrator of the Federal Aviation Administration where there is alleged a failure of such Administrator to perform any act or duty under section 611 of the Federal Aviation Act of 1958 which is not discretionary with such Administrator.

The district courts of the United States shall have jurisdiction, without regard to the amount in controversy, to restrain such person from violating such noise control requirement or to order such Administrator to perform such act or duty, as the case may be.

(b) No action may be commenced—

(1) under subsection (a) (1)—

(A) prior to sixty days after the plaintiff has given notice of the violation (i) to the Administrator of the Environmental Protection Agency (and to the Federal Aviation Administrator in the case of a violation of a noise control requirement under such section 611) and (ii) to any alleged violator of such requirement, or

(B) if an Administrator has commenced and is diligently prosecuting a civil action to require compliance with the noise control requirement, but in any such action in a court of the United States any person may intervene as a matter of right, or

NOISE CONTROL

(2) under subsection (a) (2) prior to sixty days after the plaintiff has given notice to the defendant that he will commence such action.

Notice under this subsection shall be given in such manner as the Administrator of the Environmental Protection Agency shall prescribe by regulation.

(c) In an action under this section, the Administrator of the Environmental Protection Agency, if not a party, may intervene as a matter of right. In an action under this section respecting a noise control requirement under section 611 of the Federal Aviation Act of 1958, the Administrator of the Federal Aviation Administration, if not a party, may also intervene as a matter of right.

(d) The court, in issuing any final order in any action brought pursuant to subsection (a) of this section, may award costs of litigation (including reasonable attorney and expert witness fees) to any party, whenever the court determines such an award is appropriate.

(e) Nothing in this section shall restrict any right which any person (or class of persons) may have under any statute or common law to seek enforcement of any noise control requirement or to seek any other relief (including relief against an Administrator).

(f) For purposes of this section, the term "noise control requirement" means paragraph (1), (2), (3), (4), or (5) of section 10(a), or a standard, rule, or regulation issued under section 17 or 18 of this Act or under section 611 of the Federal Aviation Act of 1958.

. . . .

C. State Regulation

1. Noise Control Standards in Building Codes

N.Y. MULT. DWELL. LAW, sec. 84.

§ 84. Construction standards for the control of noise

On or before January first, nineteen hundred sixty-nine, the department shall formulate, adopt, promulgate and thereafter from time to time amend standards of sound retardation for the walls, partitions and floors and ceilings between apartments and between apartments and public spaces situated therein based on the direct measurement of sound transmission loss determined in decibels for various frequencies or in accordance with the ASTM sound transmission class system or in accordance with such other recognized method or system for measuring reduction of sound transmission as the department may determine to be appropriate. Any construction of a multiple dwelling commenced after January first, nineteen hundred seventy shall comply with the standards promulgated pursuant to this section in effect at the time of commencement of such construction.

2. <u>Noise Control Regulation of Motor</u>
<u>Vehicles</u>

<u>CAL. VEHICLE CODE</u>, sec. 23130

§ 23130. Noise Limits

(a) No person shall operate either a motor vehicle or combination of vehicles of a type subject to registration at any time or under any condition of grade, load, acceleration or deceleration in such a manner as to exceed the following noise limit for the category of motor vehicle within the speed limits specified in this section:

	Speed limit of 35 mph or less	Speed limit of more than 35 mph
(1) Any motor vehicle with a manufacturer's gross vehicle weight rating of 6,000 pounds or more and any combination of vehicles towed by such motor vehicle:		
(A) Before January 1, 1973	88 dbA	90 dbA
(B) On and after January 1, 1973	86 dbA	90 dbA
(2) Any motorcycle other than a motor-driven cycle	82 dbA	86 dbA
(3) Any other motor vehicle and any combination of vehicles towed by such motor vehicle	76 dbA	82 dbA

(b) The noise limits established by this section shall be based on a distance of 50 feet from the center of the lane of travel within the speed limit specified in this section. ● ● ●

§ 23130.5. Vehicular Noise Limits: 35 m.p.h. or Less Speed Zone

(a) Notwithstanding the provisions of subdivision (a) of Section 23130, the noise limits, within a speed zone of 35 miles per hour or less on level streets, or streets with a grade not exceeding plus or minus 1 percent, for the following categories of motor vehicles, or combinations of vehicles, which are subject to registration, shall be:

(1) Any motor vehicle with a manufacturer's gross vehicle weight rating of 6,000 pounds or more and any combination of vehicles towed by such motor vehicle .... 82 dbA

(2) Any motorcycle other than a motor-driven cycle....... 77 dbA

(3) Any other motor vehicle and any combination of vehicles towed by such motor vehicle .... 74 dbA

No person shall operate such a motor vehicle or combination of vehicles in such a manner as to exceed the noise limits specified in this section. ● ● ●

(b) Measurements shall not be made within 200 feet of any intersection controlled by an official traffic control device, or within 200 feet of the beginning or end of any grade in excess of plus or minus 1 percent. Measurements shall be made when it is reasonable to assume that the vehicle flow is at a constant rate of speed, and measurement shall not be made under congested traffic conditions which require noticeable acceleration or deceleration. ● ● ●

(d) The noise limits established by this section shall be based on a distance of 50 feet from the center of the lane of travel within the speed limit specified in this section. ● ● ●

Vehicles equipped with at least two snowtread tires are exempt from this section.

. . . .

D. Municipal Regulation

1. Forms of Municipal Regulation

(a) To Preserve Peace and Tranquility

FETSCH v. POLICE JUSTICE COURT OF VILLAGE OF SANDS POINT, 9 Misc. 2d 25, 169 N.Y.S.2d 326(1957).

HILL, Justice.

This is an application for an order of prohibition against the Police Justice of a small incorporated village to prevent him from proceeding with the trial of a criminal charge against the defendants under a recently enacted anti-noise village ordinance.

Prohibition is an extraordinary remedy resting in the sound discretion of the court, not ordinarily available to a litigant, when the ordinary processes of the law offer an adequate remedy to redress his grievance. But this is rather an extraordinary case and while the petitioners indubitably will have a right to appeal after conviction, the question arises: Is such a remedy fully adequate, where a local ordinance attempts to proscribe conduct so innocuous and devoid of criminal proclivity as to make its interdiction preposterous?

To illustrate, section 3 of the ordinance provides:

"Section 3. It shall be unlawful for any person to make continue, or cause to be made or continued any loud, unnecessary or unusual noise or any noise which either annoys, disturbs, injures or endangers the comfort, repose, health, peace or safety to others, within the limits of the Village of Sands Point."

Thus the emitting of any noise whatever, which annoys or disturbs others is unlawful. This is so, since the disjunctive "or" is used in describing both the noise and its effect. This is not said by way of ap-

FETSCH v. POLICE JUSTICE COURT

proval, even if this sentence were not phrased in the alternative, but merely to show the extreme unreasonableness of the enactment. Audible belching, which some people find annoying in others, would qualify for criminal prosecution in this Village.

Section 4(2) provides that the "reproduction of sound at any time of the day or night on premises in the Village of Sands Point, as to be audible at the property line of adjoining premises shall be prima facie evidence of a violation of this section". It is a strange law indeed which can contemplate making operating a record player at 2 o'clock in the afternoon so that it can be heard at the property line, prima facie evidence of a crime.

Sounding of church bells to call people to religious service would be particularly objectionable, such sounds crossing as they do, property lines indiscriminately.

Enough has been said to describe this ordinance.

Petitioners, who operate a day school for children in the respondent Village claim that this ordinance has been passed for the sole purpose of putting them out of business, the Village having been unsuccessful in its previous attempts to do so, by legal proceedings which have been going on for years.

This might very well be true, but a cataloguing of these proceedings would be tedious and is unnecessary to this decision, which I prefer to rest on the ground that the Police Justice is without jurisdiction to try these alleged offenses (there are eight of them) since the conduct they charge is patently not criminal (People ex rel. Sampson v. Dunning, 113 App.Div. 35, 98 N.Y.S. 1067; People ex rel. Sandman v. Tuthill, 79 App.Div. 24, 79 N.Y.S. 905). The writ of prohibition is granted.

Settle order.

(b) To Abate Noise as a Nuisance

OLYMPIC DRIVE-IN THEATRE, INC. v. CITY OF PAGEDALE, 441 S.W.2d 5(Mo. 1969).

SEILER, Judge.

In 1961 plaintiff corporation built its drive-in theatre on a 10 or 11 acre tract in the southeast corner of St. Charles Rock Road and Kingsland Avenue in Pagedale, a city of the fourth class, population 5,106, in St. Louis County.[1] There is a residential area west of the drive-in. There is industrial property on the south and the Wabash Railway tracks are on the east and north. The 80 feet by 40 feet movie screen was located in the southeast corner of the tract, some 1,200 feet from the intersection.

● ● ●

The screen was visible from the front yards and porches of some of the residences on the west side of Kingsland, to varying degrees, depending upon the season and foliage. The city officials testified plaintiff's manager told them he was going to show first-run films, which they took to mean family-type movies, but that soon "adult" or "art" movies were being shown, with occasional westerns, horror shows and comedies.

The aldermen began receiving complaints, which reached a peak in 1965. There was one board of aldermen meeting attended by about 50 residents and a protest meeting in the high school attended by around 900 people. The board was under considerable pressure to do something about the drive-in. At the September 28, 1965 board meeting, the then mayor stated the city would do everything it could to build up a case against the drive-in, that "either they straighten up or go out of business". One alderman, who later became mayor, said as far as he was concerned, the theatre's current license would not be renewed upon expiration. There is a mass of testimony in the record about complaints, some based on personal knowledge and others not. Much of the testimony was received by the trial court on the theory that it rep-

resented legislative research done by the board in connection with the ordinances subsequently adopted. In summary, the complaints to the aldermen were from two groups: those living along the west side of Kingsland (and city officials who made observations for purposes of evidence) who complained about noise, dust, cars parked in front of their houses with the occupants watching the pictures and throwing beer cans in their yards, increased traffic, and instances of nudity or semi-nudity on the screen which they could see from their homes and which youngsters could see from the street or the yards. These people had personal knowledge of what they complained about. The other group was those who lived elsewhere, some outstate, and who attended meetings sponsored by committees and signed petitions protesting against the movies shown. Most of these had little or no personal knowledge of what they complained about. ● ● ●

In December 1965, and January 1966, Pagedale passed four ordinances which plaintiff attacked by the declaratory judgment proceeding now before us, contending the ordinances were designed to put it out of business and were unconstitutional in various respects.

The first ordinance, no. 317, was an amendment to the original drive-in theatre ordinance passed in 1951. The amendment provided that any drive-in theatre license could be revoked or suspended by the mayor, after notice and hearing, for several causes, including the one under attack here, to-wit, conduct of the business "so as to constitute a nuisance by reason of noise or immoral activity on the premises".

● ● ●

As to the first ordinance, no. 317, the portion under attack is too vague and indefinite to be valid. No one can tell by what standards the mayor is to decide whether activity on the premises was immoral. ● ● ●

As to the "noise" part of the ordinance, again the ordinance is too vague and indefinite. It does not set any standards as to how much noise or for how long continued, or any limits or areas where the noise is to be considered or state what persons are to be considered by the mayor in judging the effect of the noise. Again the determination is left entirely to the individual reactions and impressions of the mayor with no objective standard provided by which he is to test the noise or by which the operators may guide themselves in what they can and cannot do.

The ordinance is not saved by its reference to nuisance. Section 79.370, RS Mo 1959, gives the city the power to pass ordinances for the prevention of nuisances and their abatement, but the city has no power to declare that to be a nuisance which is not so at common law or by statute, City of Sturgeon v. Wabash Ry. Co., 223 Mo. App. 633, 17 S.W.2d 616, or which is not in fact a nuisance, Potashnick Truck Service v. City of Sikeston, 351 Mo. 505, 173 S.W. 2d 96, 100. The words "so as to constitute a nuisance" add nothing to the validity of the ordinance, because in order for the mayor to decide whether the conduct of the business constitutes a nuisance for which he may revoke the license, the only test is "noise or immoral activity on the premises", which as we have previously held, is too vague and indefinite to serve as a base for punitive action by the mayor. We hold the portion of ordinance no. 317 under consideration is invalid.[2] ● ● ●

Judgment is reversed as to Counts I and II and affirmed as to Count IV and the cause remanded for further proceedings consistent herewith.

All of the Judges concur.

. . . .

For additional information on noise as a nuisance see:

1. Lloyd, "Noise as Nuisance," U. Pa. L. Rev. 567 (1934).

2. Prosser, Handbook of the Law of Torts, 571 (4th ed. 1971).

(c) Zoning Ordinances

DUBE v. CITY OF CHICAGO, 7 Ill.2d 313, 131 N.E. 2d 9 (1955).

DAVIS, Justice.

By separate actions filed in the superior court of Cook County plaintiffs, Luella Dube, as owner, and others as lessees of a factory property located in the city of Chicago sought injunctions restraining the defendant, the city of Chicago, from prosecuting any action against them involving a violation of section 12 of the Chicago zoning ordinance and from prosecuting them under section 99-60 of the Chicago Municipal Code. The complaints alleged that both ordinances are unconstitutional as applied to plaintiffs or their property and are in violation of the due process provisions of the Fourteenth Amendment to the constitution of the United States and section 2 of article II of the constitution of Illinois; that they are discriminatory, permit the taking of private property for public use without just compensation and bear no substantial relation to the public health, safety, morals or general welfare. ● ● ●

The subject property is located at the northwest corner of the intersection of East Seventy-third Street and Kimbark Avenue in the city of Chicago, having a frontage of about 160 feet on East Seventy-third Street and a depth of 125 feet on Kimbark. The premises are bounded on the east by Kimbark Avenue, on the south by East Seventy-third Street, on the north by a public alley and on the west by the right of way of the Illinois Central Railroad on which are located tracks carrying the trains of that railroad, the South Shore electric and those of the Big Four Division and Michigan Central of the New York Central System. The premises are improved by a one-story brick factory building which occupies about the west half of the frontage on East Seventy-third Street. Plaintiffs also own the property north of the alley ● ● ● Both the original Dube property and the property to the north fronting on Seventy-second Place are located in an area designated by the Chicago zoning ordinance as a manufacturing district.

Section 12(2) of the Chicago zoning ordinance provides for certain uses in manufacturing districts in language in part as follows: "Manufacturing, processing, packing, bottling and distributing of cement products; ice; ink; metal and metal products (except smelting by employment of cupola, snap riveting and processes used in bending and shaping which produce noises disturbing the peace and comfort of occupants of adjacent premises); polishes from finished oil, fat and wax; products from plastics, rubber, shoddy and shoddy felt; soap from refined oils or fats, provided effective condensers or other appliances are used where necessary to prevent the escape of noxious odors, gases or fumes; woodwork (except sawmilling)." Section 19 of the same ordinance provides that any lawful use of property on the effective date of the ordinance, which by virtue of its provisions is a nonconforming use, is permitted after the ordinance becomes effective, subject to the limitations therein set forth. Section 99-60 of the Municipal Code of Chicago provides: "It shall be unlawful for any person to construct or maintain, within two hundred feet of any residence, a factory wherein are used pneumatic hammers or other apparatus which cause loud or unusual noises. Any person violating any of the provisions of this section shall be fined not less than twenty-five dollars nor more than one hundred dollars for each offense, and each day's violation shall be considered a separate and distinct offense." ● ● ●

Plaintiffs contend that the use to which the premises are now devoted is a legal nonconforming use in the pursuit of which they are protected under section 19 of the zoning ordinance; that as applied to them and their property the ordinances are unconstitutional for reasons already stated and that the trial court erred in dismissing their complaints for want of equity. ● ● ●

Upon the first question presented—that of legal nonconforming use· ● ● ●

The facts in the record clearly establish that the present use is not only a greatly expanded use but a different use. The manufacture of small items has given way to the fabrication of machinery and larger items. Operations formerly confined mostly to the building are now carried on outside and land not owned or used by the original proprietor is now utilized for this purpose. Heavier machinery than that formerly used is employed. The plant now employs about 45 men—more than twice the number ever employed by Dube. Therefore the present use is not only more extensive than the former but in fact more intensive and of a different character. Courts have recognized that the employment of new instrumentalities and methods may constitute an objectionable extension of an existing nonconforming use where they operate to change the original nature and purpose of the undertaking. De Felice v. Zoning Board of Appeals, 130 Conn. 156, 32 A.2d 635, 147 A.L.R. 161; 58 Am.Jur. 1030. So also an expansion of a use to land not formerly used may be an illegal extension or enlargement of the previous nonconforming use. Burmore Co. v. Champion, 124 N.J.L. 548, 12 A.2d 713; Annotation: 147 A.L.R. 167. Though the new use and the old may fall within the general category of "manufacturing" it is the particular use and not the general classification which governs. Wechter v. Board of Appeals, 3 Ill.2d 13, 119 N.E.2d 747. The fact therefore that the present use is a manufacturing use is not alone enough to afford it the protection of section 19 or establish its status as a legal nonconforming use. It may be, as plaintiffs contend, that a mere increase in the volume of business is not an expansion of a nonconforming use, but much more than an increase in volume is here involved and that factor is not determinative. The contention that plaintiffs are maintaining a legal nonconforming use must be rejected.

But plaintiffs also say that if section 12(2) of the Chicago zoning ordinance is enforced as to them and their property it would deprive the plaintiffs of the use to which the property was put before the enactment of the ordinance; that as applied to them the ordinance is unconstitutional as a denial of due process and a violation of the prohibition against taking private property for public use without just compensation. This contention stems from the particular provisions of section 12(2) which permit the manufacture of metal and metal products in the limited manufacturing districts involved but except therefrom "smelting by employment of cupola, snap riveting and processes used in bending and shaping which produce noises disturbing the peace and comfort of occupants of adjacent premises." ● ● ●

Provisions of the zoning laws prescribing conditions of business or manufacturing designed to avoid nuisance or annoyance have been held valid by the courts. ● ● ●

The cases hold that so long as such ordinances have as their object the protection of the public health, safety, comfort, morals and general welfare, are reasonably calculated to effect that purpose and are not arbitrary or unreasonable, they are to be upheld as a proper exercise of the police power. The tests applied are the same as those applied to zoning ordinances generally which must be justified, if at all, by the paramount interest of the public welfare and the realization that private interests must sometimes be subordinated to the public good. The constitutional declarations that private property shall not be taken for public use without just compensation or without due process of law are always subordinated to the interest of the public welfare as expressed through the exercise of the police power of the State. Trust Co. of Chicago v. City of Chicago, 408 Ill. 91, 96 N.E.2d 499; Ehrlich v. Village of Wilmette, 361 Ill. 213, 197 N.E. 567; Forbes v. Hubbard, 348 Ill. 166, 180 N.E. 767. Indeed, it is the nature of all zoning regulations that they invade or limit individual property rights to some extent, but notwithstanding that fact they are valid as a constitutional exercise of the police power so long as they are not arbitrary and bear a reasonable and substantial relation to the public health, safety, comfort, morals and general welfare.

While a city under its general power to define and abate nuisances has no power to declare that a nuisance which is not a nuisance in fact, Rosehill Cemetery Co. v. City of Chicago, 352 Ill. 11, 185

N.E. 170, 87 A.L.R. 742; Town of Cortland v. Larson, 273 Ill. 602, 113 N.E. 51, L.R.A.1917A, 314; People ex rel. Friend v. City of Chicago, 261 Ill. 16, 103 N.E. 609, 49 L.R.A.,N.S., 438, its power to enact regulations to prevent the endangering or impairment of public health is not limited to the regulation of such things as have already become nuisances or have been declared to be such by the judgment of a court, but where an act or thing is of such nature that it may become a nuisance, or may be injurious to the public health if not suppressed or regulated, it may be regulated though never injurious in the past and the legislation will be held valid though it may operate to deprive or limit property rights once it is shown that its exercise is proper and the method of its exercise within the meaning of due process. Sullivan v. City of Los Angeles Dept. of Bldg. & Safety, 116 Cal.App.2d 807, 254 P.2d 590; Laurel Hill Cemetery v. City and County of San Francisco, 216 U.S. 358, 30 S.Ct. 301, 54 L.Ed. 515; Hadacheck v. Sebastian, 239 U.S. 394, 36 S.Ct. 143, 60 L.Ed. 348. Though noise is not a nuisance *per se*, it may be of such a character as to constitute a nuisance in fact even though it arises from the operation of a factory, industrial plant or other lawful business or occupation. Phelps v. Winch, 309 Ill. 158, 140 N.E. 847, 28 A.L.R. 1169; 39 Am.Jur. 330. The test in such cases is " 'whether rights of property, of health or of comfort are so injuriously affected by the noise in question that the sufferer is subjected to a loss which goes beyond the reasonable limit imposed upon him by the condition of living, or of holding property, in a particular locality in fact devoted to uses which involve the emission of noise although ordinary care is taken to confine it within reasonable bounds; or in the vicinity of property of another owner who though creating a noise is acting with reasonable regard for the rights of those affected by it.' " City of Chicago v. Reuter Bros. Iron Works, Inc., 398 Ill. 202, 208, 75 N.E.2d 355, 359, quoting from the opinion in Tortorella v. H. Traiser & Co., 284 Mass. 497, 188 N.E. 254, 90 A.L.R. 1203. A zoning ordinance which delimits designated areas for the location of manufacturing industries or general business does not license the emission of every noise profitably attending the conduct of such businesses. Tortorella v. H. Traiser & Co., 284 Mass. 497, 188 N.E. 254, 90 A.L.R. 1203. In other words, no one, even in pursuing an otherwise lawful business, ever acquires a vested right to create or maintain a noisy nuisance in connection therewith. ● ● ●

We believe that the proof in the record before us is sufficient to show that plaintiffs have been guilty of maintaining a common-law nuisance in the manner in which they have operated their business. Six residents testified that the noise from the plant was such that it caused them serious discomfort. There was some testimony that the noise was attended by vibrations. One witness testified that when a certain heavy machine was used his house vibrated. Another testified that the dishes in his home rattled. Sometimes the operations carried on outside the plant are at night, though this does not happen all the time. All of these witnesses testified that the other noises in the neighborhood do not bother them; that the noises from Dube have been burdensome only since 1944 when operations were begun outside and that formerly the noises from Dube were not disturbing. Only one resident of the neighborhood testified that the noise from Dube did not disturb him. He was an employee of the plant. Plaintiffs introduced the testimony of two sound-testing engineers who had made certain tests with a sound-level meter, an instrument designed to measure the intensity of sound in decibels. Their testimony purports to show that the sounds and noises emanating from Dube are of no greater intensity than the other sounds in the neighborhood, including noises from trains, trucks and other vehicles. However reliable and accurate such devices may be in measuring intensity, they do not purport to measure the effect of particular sounds on human sensibilities. Nor do they account for differences of pitch or tone. The staccato beat of an air hammer on metal, though producing a sound of no greater intensity than the rumble of a truck, may produce a far more serious effect on the human being within hearing distance. Applying the test as laid down in the Tortorella case and adopted by this court in Reuter Bros. case, we conclude that the health and comfort of the residents of the neighborhood in this case are injuriously affected by the noises and vibrations in question and that they are subjected to discomforts which go beyond the reasonable limits imposed upon them because of living or of holding property in the vicinity of an industrial zone. It also appears that the operators of the factory have not used ordinary care to confine the noise within reasonable bounds.

Under the circumstances we cannot say that the ordinance as applied to plaintiffs and their property is unconstitutional. In challenging the constitutionality of the ordinance and seeking equitable relief against its enforcement plaintiffs assumed the burden of proving that, as applied to their property, the law was clearly arbitrary and unreasonable and bore no substantial relation to the public health, safety, comfort or general welfare. The trial court properly found that plaintiffs had not sustained their burden of proof. ● ● ●

The decree of the superior court of Cook County is affirmed.

Decree affirmed.

. . . .

For additional information on the use of zoning ordinances to control noise see:

"A Model Ordinance to Control Urban Noises Through Zoning Performance Standards," 8 Harv. Journal on Legislation, 613 (1971).

See also: Compilation of State and Local Ordinances on Noise Control, 115 Cong. Rec. 32178 (1969).

2. Limitations on Municipal Noise Regulation

(a) Constitutional Protection of Freedom of Speech

KOVACS v. COOPER, 336 U.S. 77(1949).

Mr. Justice REED announced the judgment of the Court and an opinion in which The CHIEF JUSTICE and Mr. Justice BURTON join.

This appeal involves the validity of a provision of Ordinance No. 430 of the City of Trenton, New Jersey. It reads as follows:

"4. That it shall be unlawful for any person, firm or corporation, either as principal, agent or employee, to play, use or operate for advertising purposes, or for any other purpose whatsoever, on or upon the public streets, alleys or thoroughfares in the City of Trenton, any device known as a sound truck, loud speaker or sound amplifier, or radio or phonograph with a loud speaker or sound amplifier, or any other instrument known as a calliope or any instrument of any kind or character which emits therefrom loud and raucous noises and is attached to and upon any vehicle operated or standing upon said streets or public places aforementioned."

The appellant was found guilty of violating this ordinance by the appellee, a police judge of the City of Trenton. His conviction was upheld by the New Jersey Supreme Court, Kovacs v. Cooper, 135 N.J.L. 64, 50 A.2d 451, and the judgment was affirmed without a majority opinion by the New Jersey Court of Errors and Appeals in an equally divided court. The dissents are printed. 135 N.J.L. 584, 52 A.2d 806.

We took jurisdiction[1] to consider the challenge made to the constitutionality of the section on its face and as applied on the ground that § 1 of the Fourteenth Amendment of the United States Constitution was violated because the section and the conviction are in contravention of rights of freedom of speech, freedom of assemblage and freedom to communicate information and opinions to others. The ordinance is also challenged as violative of the Due Process Clause of the Fourteenth Amendment on the ground that it is so obscure, vague, and indefinite as to be impossible of reasonably accurate interpretation. No question was raised as to the sufficiency of the complaint.

At the trial in the Trenton police court, a city patrolman testified that while on his post he heard a sound truck broadcasting music. Upon going in the direction of said sound, he located the truck on a public street near the municipal building. As he approached the truck, the music stopped and he heard a man's voice broadcasting from the truck. The appellant admitted that he operated the mechanism for the music and spoke into the amplifier. The record from the police court does not show the purpose of the broadcasting but the opinion in the Supreme Court suggests that the appellant was using the sound apparatus to comment on a labor dispute then in progress in Trenton.

The contention that the section is so vague, obscure and indefinite as to be unenforceable merits only a passing reference. This objection centers around the use of the words "loud and raucous." While these are abstract words, they have through daily use acquired a content that conveys to any interested person a sufficiently accurate concept of what is forbidden. ● ● ● We think the words of § 4 of this Trenton ordinance comply with the requirements of definiteness and clarity. ● ● ● The scope of the protection afforded by the Fourteenth Amendment, for the right of a citizen to play music and express his views on matters which he considers to be of interest to himself and others on a public street through sound amplification devices mounted on vehicles, must be considered. Freedom of speech, freedom of assembly and freedom to communicate information and opinion to others are all comprehended on this appeal in the claimed right of free speech. They will be so treated in this opinion.

The use of sound trucks and other peripatetic or stationary broadcasting devices for advertising, for religious exercises and for discussion of issues or controversies has brought forth numerous municipal ordinances. The avowed and obvious purpose of these ordinances is to prohibit or minimize such sounds on or near the streets since some citizens find the noise objectionable and to some degree an interference with the business or social activities in which they are engaged or the quiet that they would like to enjoy.[2] A satisfactory adjustment of the conflicting interests is difficult as those who desire to broadcast can hardly acquiesce in a requirement to modulate their sounds to a pitch that would not rise above other street noises nor would they deem a restriction to sparsely used localities or to hours after work and before sleep—say 6 to 9 p. m.—sufficient for the exercise of their claimed privilege. Municipalities are seeking actively a solution. National Institute of Municipal Law Officers, Report No. 123, 1948. Unrestrained use throughout a municipality of all sound amplifying devices would be intolerable. Absolute prohibition within municipal limits of all sound amplification, even though reasonably regulated in place, time and volume, is undesirable and probably unconstitutional as an unreasonable interference with normal activities. ● ● ● This ordinance ● ● ● is an exercise of the authority granted to the city by New Jersey "to prevent disturbing noises," N.J.Stat. Ann., tit. 40:48–1 (8), nuisances well within the municipality's power to control. The police power of a state extends beyond health, morals and safety, and comprehends the duty, within constitutional limitations, to protect the well-being and tranquility of a community.[4] A state or city may prohibit acts or things reasonably thought to bring evil or harm to its people.

In this case, New Jersey necessarily has construed this very ordinance as applied to sound amplification.[5] The Supreme Court said, 135 N.J.L. 64, 66, 50 A. 2d 451, 452:

"The relevant provisions of the ordinance apply only to (1) vehicles (2) containing an instrument in the nature of a sound amplifier or any other instrument emitting loud and raucous noises and (3) such vehicle operated or standing upon the public streets, alleys or thoroughfares of the city."

● ● ● We accept the determination of New Jersey that § 4 applies only to vehicles with sound amplifiers emitting loud and raucous noises. ● ● ● The question is ● ● ● whether or not there is a real abridgment of the rights of free speech.

Of course, even the fundamental rights of the Bill of Rights are not absolute. ● ● ●

"The hours and place of public discussion can be controlled." [11]   It was said decades ago in an opinion of this Court delivered by Mr. Justice Holmes, Schenck v. United States, 249 U.S. 47, 52, 39 S.Ct. 247, 249, 63 L.Ed. 470, that:

"The most stringent protection of free speech would not protect a man in falsely shouting fire in a theatre and causing a panic. It does not even protect a man from an injunction against uttering words that may have all the effect of force."

Hecklers may be expelled from assemblies and religious worship may not be disturbed by those anxious to preach a doctrine of atheism. The right to speak one's mind would often be an empty privilege in a place and at a time beyond the protecting hand of the guardians of public order.

While this Court, in enforcing the broad protection the Constitution gives to the dissemination of ideas, has invalidated an ordinance forbidding a distributor of pamphlets or handbills from summoning householders to their doors to receive the distributor's writings, this was on the ground that the home owner could protect himself from such intrusion by an appropriate sign "that he is unwilling to be disturbed." The Court never intimated that the visitor could insert a foot in the door and insist on a hearing. Martin v. City of Struthers, 319 U.S. 141, 143, 148, 63 S.Ct. 862, 863, 865, 87 L.Ed. 1313. We do not think that the Struthers case requires us to expand this interdiction of legislation to include ordinances against obtaining an audience for the broadcaster's ideas by way of sound trucks with loud and raucous noises on city streets. The unwilling listener is not like the passer-by who may be offered a pamphlet in the street but cannot be made to take it.[12] In his home or on the street he is practically helpless to escape this interference with his privacy by loud speakers except through the protection of the municipality.

City streets are recognized as a normal place for the exchange of ideas by speech or paper. But this does not mean the freedom is beyond all control. We think it is a permissible exercise of legislative discretion to bar sound trucks with broadcasts of public interest, amplified to a loud and raucous volume, from the public ways of municipalities. On the business streets of cities like Trenton, with its more than 125,000 people, such distractions would be dangerous to traffic at all hours useful for the dissemination of information, and in the residential thoroughfares the quiet and tranquility so desirable for city dwellers would likewise be at the mercy of advocates of particular religious, social or political persuasions. We cannot believe that rights of free speech compel a municipality to allow such mechanical voice amplification on any of its streets.

The right of free speech is guaranteed every citizen that he may reach the minds of willing listeners and to do so there must be opportunity to win their attention.

This is the phase of freedom of speech that is involved here. We do not think the Trenton ordinance abridges that freedom. It is an extravagant extension of due process to say that because of it a city cannot forbid talking on the streets through a loud speaker in a loud and raucous tone. Surely such an ordinance does not violate our people's "concept of ordered liberty" so as to require federal intervention to protect a citizen from the action of his own local government. ● ● ●

The preferred position [14] of freedom of speech in a society that cherishes liberty for all does not require legislators to be insensible to claims by citizens to comfort and convenience. To enforce freedom of speech in disregard of the rights of others would be harsh and arbitrary in itself. That more people may be more easily and cheaply reached by sound trucks, perhaps borrowed without cost from some zealous supporter, is not enough to call forth constitutional protection for what those charged with public welfare reasonably think is a nuisance when easy means of publicity are open. Section 4 of the ordinance bars sound trucks from broadcasting in a loud and raucous manner on the streets. There is no restriction upon the communication of ideas or discussion of issues by the human voice, by newspapers, by pamphlets, by dodgers. We think that the need for reasonable protection in the homes or business houses from the distracting noises of vehicles equipped with such sound amplifying devices justifies the ordinance.

Affirmed.

Mr. Justice MURPHY dissents.

(b) Federal Preemption of Aircraft Noise Regulation

AMERICAN AIRLINES, INC. v. TOWN OF HEMPSTEAD, 398 F.2d 369(2d Cir. 1968), cert. denied, 393 U.S. 1017(1969).

J. JOSEPH SMITH, Circuit Judge:

The Town of Hempstead appeals under 28 U.S.C. § 1292(a) (1) from an order of the District Court for the Eastern District of New York, John F. Dooling, Jr., Judge, granting a preliminary injunction against enforcement of its Unnecessary Noise Ordinance (No. 25), Article II, as amended March 10, 1964, so far as it applies to aircraft using John F. Kennedy International Airport. Judge Dooling's opinion appears at 272 F.Supp. 226. ● ● ●

The Town of Hempstead, primarily residential, is the largest town in New York State, with an estimated population in 1963 of nearly 806,000. It lies to the east of John F. Kennedy International Airport ("JFK"), and it is estimated that 150,000 people live in its incorporated villages which lie within three miles of the Airport. These people share with many others, inside and outside Hempstead and across the country, a severe aircraft noise problem which has developed in the years since the Second World War.

Because of the frequency with which jets fly in and out of JFK, the problem in Hempstead may be somewhat worse than in other communities. The District Court found that:

There is credible evidence that the noise of an aircraft overflight in Hempstead is frequently intense enough to interrupt sleep, conversation and the conduct of religious services, and to submerge for the duration of the maximum noise part of the overflight the sound of radio, phonograph and television. (Finding #127)

There is credible evidence that the noise of an aircraft overflight in Hempstead is frequently intense enough to interrupt classroom activities in schools and to be a source of discomfort to the ill and distraction to the well. (Finding #128)

It is a fair inference from the affidavits, the demonstration [in the courtroom] of the sound levels recorded in the Town and the evidence of frequency of overflights that airplane noise is a factor of moment affecting the decisions of people to acquire or dispose of interests in real property in the areas within the Town affected by the sound of airplane overflights. (Finding #129)

In an attempt to deal with the problem, the Town added a new article to its Unnecessary Noise Ordinance, forbidding anyone from operating a mechanism or device (including airplanes) which creates a noise within the Town exceeding either of two "limiting noise spectra." Claiming that the ordinance would prohibit airplanes using JFK from flying over the town, and thus would restrict the landing and take-off patterns and procedures normally adhered to by those airplanes, nine major American-flag air carriers, The Port of New York Authority, Charles H. Ruby as president of the Air Line Pilots Association, three air line pilots, individually and as representatives of their class, and the Administrator of the Federal Aviation Agency (as intervenor) sued to enjoin the enforcement of the ordinance against them.

The Town argued initially that aircraft could fly over the Town in compliance both with the ordinance and with the FAA regulations governing landing and take-off patterns and procedures. There was no question, however, but that at the time the suit was brought, take-offs and landings at JFK regularly produced noise exceeding the relevant limiting noise spectrum of the ordinance.

The District Court made crucial findings of fact which contradict the Town's initial argument that compliance with the ordinance is possible without alterations in flight patterns and procedures, and the Town has now shifted its ground, arguing in essence that the ordinance is not an undue burden on interstate commerce, because "the Town has unveiled a plan pursuant to which approximately 98% of all flights [to and from JFK] will avoid the Town while, at the same time, the present traffic capacity will be unaffected." (Town's brief, p. 22).

The crucial findings of fact are Nos. 281–294.[1] The court found that compliance with the ordinance would be determinative of the altitudes at which and flight paths by which commercial aircraft could fly into and out of JFK; that the flight requirements flowing from the ordinance would be in large part incompatible with existing traffic patterns and FAA procedures; that compliance would mean redesigning of the flight patterns for JFK, together with a reintegration of the redesigned patterns with those for the other New York City airports, and that the safety margins of the existing procedures could not be preserved without restricting the traffic handling capacity of JFK; and that there is no reliable evidence that a set of procedures could be devised for JFK in the present state of aviation development which could, without substantial sacrifice of the interest in flight safety, assure compliance with the ordinance. None of these findings have been attacked on this appeal, except that the Town still insists that its alternate plan, submitted to the District Court, could steer most flights away from the Town, thus assuring compliance with the ordinance. Apart from the lack of a showing that the District Court's finding to the contrary is clearly erroneous, it is clear that given the necessary determination of the legal issues in the case, the Town's alternate plan, even if it *were* feasible, would be irrelevant.

On the basis of his detailed and thorough findings of fact, Judge Dooling concluded: (1) that the ordinance is an unconstitutional burden on interstate commerce; (2) that the area in which the ordinance operates has been preempted by federal legislation and regulation; and (3) that the ordinance is in direct conflict with valid applicable federal regulation.

Any one of the District Court's three conclusions is enough, of course, to make the ordinance invalid. There is no need for determination of the validity of the first two grounds, since the third ground for the ordinance's invalidity (that it is in conflict with applicable federal regulation) is an ample basis for affirmance. ● ● ●

Before considering the grounds advanced by the District Court for the conclusion that the ordinance is invalid, we may point out that this case has nothing to do with questions of landowners' rights to compensation for overflights of their land which amount to a "taking" of their property. [See United States v. Causby, 328 U.S. 256, 66 S.Ct. 1062, 90 L.Ed. 1206 (1946), and Griggs v. Allegheny County, 369 U.S. 84, 82 S.Ct. 531, 7 L.Ed.2d 585 (1962).] All that is involved is the validity of the ordinance.

We consider first the point that the ordinance is in direct conflict with a valid applicable federal regulation. The Federal Aviation Act of 1958 provides, *inter alia:*

> There is recognized and declared to exist in behalf of any citizen of the United States a public right of freedom of transit through the navigable airspace of the United States. [49 U.S.C. § 1304]

> The Administrator is authorized and directed to develop plans for and formulate policy with respect to the use of the navigable airspace; and assign by rule, regulation, or order the use of the navigable airspace under such terms, conditions, and limitations as he may deem necessary in order to insure the safety of aircraft and the efficient utilization of such airspace. * * * [49 U.S.C. § 1348(a)]

> The Administrator is further authorized and directed to prescribe air traffic rules and regulations governing the flight of aircraft, for the navi-

gation, protection, and identification of aircraft, for the protection of persons and property on the ground, and for the efficient utilization of the navigable airspace, including rules as to safe altitudes of flight and rules for the prevention of collision * * *. [49 U.S.C. § 1348(c)]

As Judge Dooling found, the Administrator (Administrator of the Federal Aviation Agency, see 49 U.S.C. § 1301(1)) has promulgated extensive regulations under the Act, which unquestionably control the patterns and procedures of aircraft flying into and out of JFK.[2] The ordinance and these regulations are unquestionably in direct conflict. They are in conflict not because the regulations and the ordinance impose different standards for noise, but because the District Court has found, in view of the present state of development of noise suppression techniques, that compliance with the noise ordinance would require alterations in the flight patterns and procedures established by federal regulation. • • •

The Town also argues that *Cedarhurst* is irrelevant, because it regulated flight paths, while Hempstead's ordinance regulates noise. That ignores the essential point in the case, which is that some noise ordinances necessarily regulate flight paths, and the District Court found that Hempstead's is one of those.[4] In view of that finding, the injunction naturally followed. The order granting preliminary injunction is affirmed.

E.   Private Suits

See: <u>Smith v. Western Wayne Co. Conservation Ass'n</u>, <u>supra</u>, IV, A, 3

See: <u>Noise Control Act of 1972</u>, <u>supra</u>, IV, B, 8

. . . .

Additional References

See: Hildebrand, "Noise Pollution," 70 Colum L. Rev. 653 (1970)

See: Grad & Hack, "Noise Control in the Urban Environment," 1972 Urban Law Annual 3

V.   CONTROL OF POPULATION GROWTH AND DISTRIBUTION

> "The Liliputians think
> nothing can be more unjust, than
> that People, in Subservience to their
> own Appetites, should bring children
> into the World, and leave the
> (burdens) of supporting them on the
> Publick."
> J. Swift, Gulliver's Travels 43
> (R. Greenberg ed. 1961)

A.   Regulation of Population Control

1.   Involuntary Control: The Right to Propagate

(a). Compulsory Sterilization of Mentally Retarded

BUCK v. BELL, 274 U.S. 200(1927).

Mr. JUSTICE HOLMES delivered the opinion of the Court.

This is a writ of error to review a judgment of the Supreme Court of Appeals of the State of Virginia, affirming a judgment of the Circuit Court of Amherst County, by which the defendant in error, the superintendent of the State Colony for Epileptics and Feeble Minded, was ordered to perform the operation of salpingectomy upon Carrie Buck, the plaintiff in error, for the purpose of making her sterile. 143 Va. 310. The case comes here upon the contention that the statute authorizing the judgment is void under the Fourteenth Amendment as denying to the plaintiff in error due process of law and the equal protection of the laws.

Carrie Buck is a feeble minded white woman who was committed to the State Colony above mentioned in due form. She is the daughter of a feeble minded mother in the same institution, and the mother of an illegitimate feeble minded child. She was eighteen years old at the time of the trial of her case in the Circuit Court, in the latter part of 1924. An Act of Virginia, approved March

20, 1924, recites that the health of the patient and the welfare of society may be promoted in certain cases by the sterilization of mental defectives, under careful safeguard, &c.; that the sterilization may be effected in males by vasectomy and in females by salpingectomy, without serious pain or substantial danger to life; that the Commonwealth is supporting in various institutions many defective persons who if now discharged would become a menace but if incapable of procreating might be discharged with safety and become self-supporting with benefit to themselves and to society; and that experience has shown that heredity plays an important part in the transmission of insanity, imbecility, &c. The statute then enacts that whenever the superintendent of certain institutions including the above named State Colony shall be of opinion that it is for the best interests of the patients and of society that an inmate under his care should be sexually sterilized, he may have the operation performed upon any patient afflicted with hereditary forms of insanity, imbecility, &c., on complying with the very careful provisions by which the act protects the patients from possible abuse. ● ● ●

The attack is not upon the procedure but upon the substantive law. It seems to be contended that in no circumstances could such an order be justified. It certainly is contended that the order cannot be justified upon the existing grounds. The judgment finds the facts that have been recited and that Carrie Buck " is the probable potential parent of socially inadequate offspring, likewise afflicted, that she may be sexually sterilized without detriment to her general health and that her welfare and that of society will be promoted by her sterilization," and thereupon makes the order. In view of the general declarations of the legislature and the specific findings of the Court, obviously we cannot say as matter of law that the grounds do not exist, and if they exist they justify the result. We have seen more than once that the public welfare may call upon the best citizens for their lives. It would be strange if it could not call upon those who already sap the strength of the State for these lesser sacrifices, often not felt to be such by those concerned, in order to prevent our being swamped with incompetence. It is better for all the world, if instead of waiting to execute degenerate offspring for crime, or to let them starve for their imbecility, society can prevent those who are manifestly unfit from continuing their kind. The principle that sustains compulsory vaccination is broad enough to cover cutting the Fallopian tubes. *Jacobson* v. *Massachusetts,* 197 U. S. 11. Three generations of imbeciles are enough.

But, it is said, however it might be if this reasoning were applied generally, it fails when it is confined to the small number who are in the institutions named and is not applied to the multitudes outside. It is the usual last resort of constitutional arguments to point out shortcomings of this sort. But the answer is that the law does all that is needed when it does all that it can, indicates a policy, applies it to all within the lines, and seeks to bring within the lines all similarly situated so far and so fast as its means allow. Of course so far as the operations enable those who otherwise must be kept confined to be returned to the world, and thus open the asylum to others, the equality aimed at will be more nearly reached.

Judgment affirmed.

SKINNER v. OKLAHOMA, 316 U.S. 535(1942).

MR. JUSTICE DOUGLAS delivered the opinion of the Court.

This case touches a sensitive and important area of human rights. Oklahoma deprives certain individuals of a right which is basic to the perpetuation of a race—the right to have offspring. Oklahoma has decreed the enforcement of its law against petitioner, overruling his claim that it violated the Fourteenth Amendment. Because that decision raised grave and substantial constitutional questions, we granted the petition for certiorari.

The statute involved is Oklahoma's Habitual Criminal Sterilization Act. Okla. Stat. Ann. Tit. 57, §§ 171, *et seq.;* L. 1935, pp. 94 *et seq.* That Act defines an "habitual criminal" as a person who, having been convicted two or more times for crimes "amounting to felonies involving moral turpitude," either in an Oklahoma court or in a court of any other State, is thereafter convicted of such a felony in Oklahoma and is sentenced to a term of imprisonment in an Oklahoma penal institution. § 173. Machinery is provided for the institution by the Attorney General of a proceeding against such a person in the Oklahoma courts for a judgment that such person shall be rendered sexually sterile. §§ 176, 177. Notice, an opportunity to be heard, and the right to a jury trial are provided. §§ 177–181. The issues triable in such a proceeding are narrow and confined. If the court or jury finds that the defendant is an "habitual criminal" and that he "may be rendered sexually sterile without deteriment to his or her general health," then the court "shall render judgment to the effect that said defendant be rendered sexually sterile" (§ 182) by the operation of vasectomy in case of a male, and of salpingectomy in case of a female. § 174. Only one other provision of the Act is material here, and that is § 195, which provides that "offenses arising out of the violation of the prohibitory laws, revenue acts, embezzlement, or political offenses, shall not come or be considered within the terms of this Act."

Petitioner was convicted in 1926 of the crime of stealing chickens, and was sentenced to the Oklahoma State Reformatory. In 1929 he was convicted of the crime of robbery with firearms, and was sentenced to the reformatory. In 1934 he was convicted again of robbery with firearms, and was sentenced to the penitentiary. He was confined there in 1935 when the Act was passed. In 1936 the Attorney General instituted proceedings against him. Petitioner in his answer challenged the Act as unconstitutional by reason of the Fourteenth Amendment. A jury trial was had. The court instructed the jury that the crimes of which petitioner had been convicted were felonies involving moral turpitude, and that the only question for the jury was whether the operation of vasectomy could be performed on petitioner without detriment to his general health. The jury found that it could be. A judgment directing that the operation of vasectomy be performed on petitioner was affirmed by the Supreme Court of Oklahoma by a five to four decision. 189 Okla. 235, 115 P. 2d 123.

Several objections to the constitutionality of the Act have been pressed upon us. It is urged that the Act cannot be sustained as an exercise of the police power, in view of the state of scientific authorities respecting inheritability of criminal traits.[1] It is argued that due process is lacking because, under this Act, unlike the Act[2] upheld in *Buck* v. *Bell*, 274 U. S. 200, the defendant is given no opportunity to be heard on the issue as to whether he is the probable potential parent of socially undesirable offspring. See *Davis* v. *Berry*, 216 F. 413; *Williams* v. *Smith*, 190 Ind. 526, 131 N. E. 2. It is also suggested that the Act is penal in character and that the sterilization provided for is cruel and unusual punishment and violative of the Fourteenth Amendment. See *Davis* v. *Berry, supra.* Cf. *State* v. *Feilen*, 70 Wash. 65, 126 P. 75; *Mickle* v. *Henrichs*, 262 F. 687. We pass those points without intimating an opinion on them, for there is a feature of the Act which clearly condemns it. That is, its failure to meet the requirements of the equal protection clause of the Fourteenth Amendment.

We do not stop to point out all of the inequalities in this Act. A few examples will suffice. In Oklahoma, grand larceny is a felony. Okla. Stats. Ann. Tit. 21, §§ 1705, 5. Larceny is grand larceny when the property taken exceeds $20 in value. *Id.* § 1704. Embezzlement is punishable "in the manner prescribed for feloniously stealing property of the value of that embezzled." *Id.* § 1462. Hence, he who embezzles property worth more than $20 is guilty of a felony. A clerk who appropriates over $20 from his employer's till (*id.* § 1456) and a stranger who steals the same amount are thus both guilty of felonies. If the latter repeats his act and is convicted three times, he may be sterilized. But the clerk is not subject to the pains and penalties of the Act no matter how large his embezzlements nor how frequent his convictions. ● ● ●

the instant legislation runs afoul of the equal protection clause, though we give Oklahoma that large deference which the rule of the foregoing cases requires. We are dealing here with legislation which involves one of the basic civil rights of man. Marriage and procreation are fundamental to the very existence and survival of the race. The power to sterilize, if exercised, may have subtle, far-reaching and devastating effects. In evil or reckless hands it can cause races or types which are inimical to the dominant group to wither and disappear. There is no redemption for the individual whom the law touches. Any experiment which the State conducts is to his irreparable injury. He is forever deprived of a basic liberty. We mention these matters not to reëxamine the scope of the police power of the States. We advert to them merely in emphasis of our view that strict scrutiny of the classification which a State makes in a sterilization law is essential, lest unwittingly, or otherwise, invidious discriminations are made against groups or types of individuals in violation of the constitutional guaranty of just and equal laws. The guaranty of "equal protection of the laws is a pledge of the protection of equal laws." *Yick Wo* v. *Hopkins,* 118 U. S. 356, 369. When the law lays an unequal hand on those who have committed intrinsically the same quality of offense and sterilizes one and not the other, it has made as invidious a discrimination as if it had selected a particular race or nationality for oppressive treatment. *Yick Wo* v. *Hopkins, supra; Gaines* v. *Canada,* 305 U. S. 337. Sterilization of those who have thrice committed grand larceny, with immunity for those who are embezzlers, is a clear, pointed, unmistakable discrimination. ● ● ●

In *Buck* v. *Bell, supra,* the Virginia statute was upheld though it applied only to feeble-minded persons in institutions of the State. But it was pointed out that "so far as the operations enable those who otherwise must be kept confined to be returned to the world, and thus open the asylum to others, the equality aimed at will be more nearly reached." 274 U. S. p. 208. Here there is no such saving feature. Embezzlers are forever free. Those who steal or take in other ways are not. ● ● ●

Reversed.

DANDRIDGE v. WILLIAMS, 397 U.S. 471 (1970).

MR. JUSTICE STEWART delivered the opinion of the Court.

This case involves the validity of a method used by Maryland, in the administration of an aspect of its public welfare program, to reconcile the demands of its needy citizens with the finite resources available to meet those demands. Like every other State in the Union, Maryland participates in the Federal Aid to Families With Dependent Children (AFDC) program, 42 U.S.C. § 601 et seq. (1964 ed. and Supp. IV), which originated with ·the Social Security Act of 1935.[1] ● ● ●

The operation of the Maryland welfare system is not complex. By statute[2] the State participates in the AFDC program. It computes the standard of need for each eligible family based on the number of children in the family and the circumstances under which the family lives. In general, the standard of need increases with each additional person in the household, but the increments become proportionately smaller.[3] The regulation here in issue imposes upon the grant that any single family may receive an upper limit of $250 per month in certain counties and Baltimore City, and of $240 per month elsewhere in the State.[4] The appellees all have large families, so that their standards of need as computed by the State substantially exceed the maximum grants that they actually receive under the regulation. The appellees urged in the District Court that the maximum grant limitation operates to discriminate against them merely because of the size of their families, in violation of the Equal Protection Clause of the Fourteenth Amendment. They claimed further that the regulation is incompatible with the purpose of the Social Security Act of 1935, as well as in conflict with its explicit provisions.

In its original opinion the District Court held that the Maryland regulation does conflict with the federal statute, and also concluded that it violates the Fourteenth Amendment's equal protection guarantee. After reconsideration on motion, the court issued a new opinion resting its determination of the regulation's invalidity entirely on the constitutional ground.[5] Both the statutory and constitutional issues have been fully briefed and argued here, and the judgment of the District Court must, of course, be affirmed if the Maryland regulation is in conflict with either the federal statute or the Constitution.[6] We consider the statutory question first, because if the appellees' position on this question is correct, there is no occasion to reach the constitutional issues. *Ashwander* v. *TVA*, 297 U. S. 288, 346–347 (Brandeis, J., concurring); *Rosenberg* v. *Fleuti*, 374 U. S. 449.

The appellees contend that the maximum grant system is contrary to § 402 (a)(10) of the Social Security Act, as amended,[7] which requires that a state plan shall

> "provide . . . that all individuals wishing to make application for aid to families with dependent children shall have opportunity to do so, and that aid to families with dependent children shall be furnished with reasonable promptness to all eligible individuals."

The argument is that the state regulation denies benefits to the younger children in a large family. Thus, the appellees say, the regulation is in patent violation of the Act, since those younger children are just as "dependent" as their older siblings under the definition of "dependent child" fixed by federal law.[8] See *King* v. *Smith*, 392 U. S. 309. Moreover, it is argued that the regulation, in limiting the amount of money any single household may receive, contravenes a basic purpose of the federal law by encouraging the parents of large families to "farm out" their children to relatives whose grants are not yet subject to the maximum limitation.

It cannot be gainsaid that the effect of the Maryland maximum grant provision is to reduce the per capita benefits to the children in the largest families. Although the appellees argue that the younger and more recently arrived children in such families are totally deprived of aid, a more realistic view is that the lot of the entire family is diminished because of the presence of additional children without any increase in payments. ● ● ●

For
the reasons that follow, we have concluded that the
Maryland regulation is permissible under the federal law.

In *King* v. *Smith, supra,* we stressed the States' "undisputed power," under these provisions of the Social
Security Act, "to set the level of benefits and the standard of need." *Id.,* at 334. We described the AFDC
enterprise as "a scheme of cooperative federalism," *id.,* at
316, and noted carefully that "[t]here is no question
that States have considerable latitude in allocating their
AFDC resources, since each State is free to set its own
standard of need and to determine the level of benefits
by the amount of funds it devotes to the program." ● ● ●
Thus the starting point of the statutory analysis must
be a recognition that the federal law gives each State
great latitude in dispensing its available funds.

The very title of the program, the repeated references
to families added in 1962, Pub. L. 87–543, § 104 (a)(3),
76 Stat. 185, and the words of the preamble quoted above,
show that Congress wished to help children through the
family structure. The operation of the statute itself has
this effect. From its inception the Act has defined "dependent child" in part by reference to the relatives with
whom the child lives.[9] When a "dependent child" is
living with relatives, then "aid" also includes payments
and medical care to those relatives, including the spouse
of the child's parent. 42 U. S. C. § 606 (b) (1964 ed.,
Supp. IV). Thus, as the District Court noted, the
amount of aid "is . . . computed by treating the relative, parent or spouse of parent, as the case may be, of
the 'dependent child' as a part of the family unit." ● ● ●

The States must respond to this federal statutory concern for preserving children in a family environment.
Given Maryland's finite resources, its choice is either to
support some families adequately and others less adequately, or not to give sufficient support to any family.
We see nothing in the federal statute that forbids a
State to balance the stresses that uniform insufficiency
of payments would impose on all families against the
greater ability of large families—because of the inherent
economies of scale—to accommodate their needs to
diminished per capita payments. ● ● ●

For even if a parent should be inclined to increase his per capita family income by sending a child away, the federal law requires that the child, to be eligible for AFDC payments, must live with one of several enumerated relatives.[11] The kinship tie may be attenuated but it cannot be destroyed. ● ● ●

So long as some aid is provided to all eligible families and all eligible children, the statute itself is not violated.

This is the view that has been taken by the Secretary of Health, Education, and Welfare (HEW), who is charged with the administration of the Social Security Act and the approval of state welfare plans. The parties have stipulated that the Secretary has, on numerous occasions, approved the Maryland welfare scheme, including its provision of maximum payments to any one family, a provision that has been in force in various forms since 1947. Moreover, a majority of the States pay less than their determined standard of need, and 20 of these States impose maximums on family grants of the kind here in issue. ● ● ●

Although a State may adopt a maximum grant system in allocating its funds available for AFDC payments without violating the Act, it may not, of course, impose a regime of invidious discrimination in violation of the Equal Protection Clause of the Fourteenth Amendment. Maryland says that its maximum grant regulation is wholly free of any invidiously discriminatory purpose or effect, and that the regulation is rationally supportable on at least four entirely valid grounds. The regulation can be clearly justified, Maryland argues, in terms of legitimate state interests in encouraging gainful employment, in maintaining an equitable balance in economic status as between welfare families and those supported by a wage-earner, in providing incentives for family planning, and in allocating available public funds in such a way as fully to meet the needs of the largest possible number of families. The District Court, while apparently recognizing the validity of at least some of these state concerns, nonetheless held that the regulation "is invalid on its face for overreaching," 297 F. Supp., at 468—that it violates the Equal Protection Clause "[b]ecause it cuts too broad a swath on an indiscriminate basis as applied to the entire group of AFDC eligibles to which it purports to apply . . . ." 297 F. Supp., at 469.

If this were a case involving government action claimed'
to violate the First Amendment guarantee of free speech,
a finding of "overreaching" would be significant and
might be crucial. For when otherwise valid governmental regulation sweeps so broadly as to impinge upon
activity protected by the First Amendment, its very
overbreadth may make it unconstitutional. See, *e. g.*,
Shelton v. *Tucker*, 364 U. S. 479. But the concept of
"overreaching" has no place in this case. For here we
deal with state regulation in the social and economic field,
not affecting freedoms guaranteed by the Bill of Rights,
and claimed to violate the Fourteenth Amendment only
because the regulation results in some disparity in grants
of welfare payments to the largest AFDC families.[16] For
this Court to approve the invalidation of state economic
or social regulation as "overreaching" would be far too
reminiscent of an era when the Court thought the Fourteenth Amendment gave it power to strike down state
laws "because they may be unwise, improvident, or out
of harmony with a particular school of thought." *Wil-
liamson* v. *Lee Optical Co.*, 348 U. S. 483, 488. That
era long ago passed into history. *Ferguson* v. *Skrupa*,
372 U. S. 726.

In the area of economics and social welfare, a State
does not violate the Equal Protection Clause merely
because the classifications made by its laws are imperfect.
If the classification has some "reasonable basis," it does
not offend the Constitution simply because the classification "is not made with mathematical nicety or because
in practice it results in some inequality." ● ● ●
Under this long-established meaning of the Equal Protection Clause, it is clear that the Maryland maximum
grant regulation is constitutionally valid. We need not
explore all the reasons that the State advances in justification of the regulation. It is enough that a solid foundation for the regulation can be found in the State's
legitimate interest in encouraging employment and in
avoiding discrimination between welfare families and the
families of the working poor. By combining a limit on
the recipient's grant with permission to retain money
earned, without reduction in the amount of the grant,
Maryland provides an incentive to seek gainful employment. And by keying the maximum family AFDC
grants to the minimum wage a steadily employed head
of a household receives, the State maintains some sem-

blance of an equitable balance between families on welfare and those supported by an employed breadwinner.[19]

It is true that in some AFDC families there may be no person who is employable.[20] It is also true that with respect to AFDC families whose determined standard of need is below the regulatory maximum, and who therefore receive grants equal to the determined standard, the employment incentive is absent. But the Equal Protection Clause does not require that a State must choose between attacking every aspect of a problem or not attacking the problem at all. *Lindsley* v. *Natural Carbonic Gas Co.*, 220 U. S. 61. It is enough that the State's action be rationally based and free from invidious discrimination. The regulation before us meets that test.

We do not decide today that the Maryland regulation is wise, that it best fulfills the relevant social and economic objectives that Maryland might ideally espouse, or that a more just and humane system could not be devised. Conflicting claims of morality and intelligence are raised by opponents and proponents of almost every measure, certainly including the one before us. But the intractable economic, social, and even philosophical problems presented by public welfare assistance programs are not the business of this Court. The Constitution may impose certain procedural safeguards upon systems of welfare administration, *Goldberg* v. *Kelly, ante,* p. 254. But the Constitution does not empower this Court to second-guess state officials charged with the difficult responsibility of allocating limited public welfare funds among the myriad of potential recipients. Cf. *Steward Mach. Co.* v. *Davis,* 301 U. S. 548, 584–585; *Helvering* v. *Davis,* 301 U. S. 619, 644.

The judgment is reversed.

MR. JUSTICE DOUGLAS, dissenting.

2. Voluntary Control

(a). Dissemination of Contraceptive Devices and Information

GRISWOLD v. CONNECTICUT, 381 U.S. 479(1965).

MR. JUSTICE DOUGLAS delivered the opinion of the Court.

Appellant Griswold is Executive Director of the Planned Parenthood League of Connecticut. Appellant Buxton is a licensed physician and a professor at the Yale Medical School who served as Medical Director for the League at its Center in New Haven—a center open and operating from November 1 to November 10, 1961, when appellants were arrested.

They gave information, instruction, and medical advice to *married persons* as to the means of preventing conception. They examined the wife and prescribed the best contraceptive device or material for her use. Fees were usually charged, although some couples were serviced free.

The statutes whose constitutionality is involved in this appeal are §§ 53–32 and 54–196 of the General Statutes of Connecticut (1958 rev.). The former provides:

"Any person who uses any drug, medicinal article or instrument for the purpose of preventing conception shall be fined not less than fifty dollars or imprisoned not less than sixty days nor more than one year or be both fined and imprisoned."

Section 54–196 provides:

"Any person who assists, abets, counsels, causes, hires or commands another to commit any offense may be prosecuted and punished as if he were the principal offender."

The appellants were found guilty as accessories and fined $100 each, against the claim that the accessory statute as so applied violated the Fourteenth Amendment. The Appellate Division of the Circuit Court affirmed. The Supreme Court of Errors affirmed that judgment. 151 Conn. 544, 200 A. 2d 479. We noted probable jurisdiction. 379 U. S. 926. ● ● ●

Coming to the merits, we are met with a wide range of questions that implicate the Due Process Clause of the Fourteenth Amendment. ● ● ●

The association of people is not mentioned in the Constitution nor in the Bill of Rights. The right to educate a child in a school of the parents' choice—whether public or private or parochial—is also not mentioned. Nor is the right to study any particular subject or any foreign language. Yet the First Amendment has been construed to include certain of those rights. ● ● ●

In other words, the State may not, consistently with the spirit of the First Amendment, contract the spectrum of available knowledge. The right of freedom of speech and press includes not only the right to utter or to print, but the right to distribute, the right to receive, the right to read (*Martin* v. *Struthers,* 319 U. S. 141, 143) and freedom of inquiry, freedom of thought, and freedom to teach (see *Wieman* v. *Updegraff,* 344 U. S. 183, 195)—indeed the freedom of the entire university community. *Sweezy* v. *New Hampshire,* 354 U. S. 234, 249–250, 261–263; *Barenblatt* v. *United States,* 360 U. S. 109, 112; *Baggett* v. *Bullitt,* 377 U. S. 360, 369. Without those peripheral rights the specific rights would be less secure. And so we reaffirm the principle of the *Pierce* and the *Meyer* cases.

In *NAACP* v. *Alabama,* 357 U. S. 449, 462, we protected the "freedom to associate and privacy in one's associations," noting that freedom of association was a peripheral First Amendment right. ● ● ●

In other words, the First Amendment has a penumbra where privacy is protected from governmental intrusion. In like context, we have protected forms of "association" that are not political in the customary sense but pertain to the social, legal, and economic benefit of the members. ● ● ●

The right of "association," like the right of belief (*Board of Education* v. *Barnette,* 319 U. S. 624), is more than the right to attend a meeting; it includes the right to express one's attitudes or philosophies by membership in a group or by affiliation with it or by other lawful means. Association in that context is a form of expression of opinion; and while it is not expressly included in the First Amendment its existence is necessary in making the express guarantees fully meaningful.

The foregoing cases suggest that specific guarantees in the Bill of Rights have penumbras, formed by emanations from those guarantees that help give them life and substance. ● ● ●

The Fourth and Fifth Amendments were described in *Boyd* v. *United States*, 116 U. S. 616, 630, as protection against all governmental invasions "of the sanctity of a man's home and the privacies of life."* We recently referred in *Mapp* v. *Ohio*, 367 U. S. 643, 656, to the Fourth Amendment as creating a "right to privacy, no less important·than any other right carefully and particularly reserved to the people." See Beaney, The Constitutional Right to Privacy, 1962 Sup. Ct. Rev. 212; Griswold, The Right to be Let Alone, 55 Nw. U. L. Rev. 216 (1960).

We have had many controversies over these penumbral rights of "privacy and repose." See, *e. g., Breard* v. *Alexandria*, 341 U. S. 622, 626, 644; *Public Utilities Comm'n* v. *Pollak*, 343 U. S. 451; *Monroe* v. *Pape*, 365 U. S. 167; *Lanza* v. *New York*, 370 U. S. 139; *Frank* v. *Maryland*, 359 U. S. 360; *Skinner* v. *Oklahoma*, 316 U. S. 535, 541. These cases bear witness that the right of privacy which presses for recognition here is a legitimate one.

The present case, then, concerns a relationship lying within the zone of privacy created by several fundamental constitutional guarantees. And it concerns a law which, in forbidding the *use* of contraceptives rather than regulating their manufacture or sale, seeks to achieve its goals by means having a maximum destructive impact upon that relationship. Such a law cannot stand in light of the familiar principle, so often applied by this Court, that a "governmental purpose to control or prevent activities constitutionally subject to state regulation may not be achieved by means which sweep unnecessarily broadly and thereby invade the area of protected freedoms." *NAACP* v. *Alabama*, 377 U. S. 288, 307. Would we allow the police to search the sacred precincts of marital bedrooms for telltale signs of the use of contraceptives? The very idea is repulsive to the notions of privacy surrounding the marriage relationship.

We deal with a right of privacy older than the Bill of Rights—older than our political parties, older than our school system. Marriage is a coming together for better or for worse, hopefully enduring, and intimate to the degree of being sacred. It is an association that promotes a way of life, not causes; a harmony in living, not political faiths; a bilateral loyalty, not commercial or social projects. Yet it is an association for as noble a purpose as any involved in our prior decisions. ● ● ●   *Reversed.*

Mr. Justice Goldberg, whom The Chief Justice and
Mr. Justice Brennan join, concurring.

● ● ●   The language and history
of the Ninth Amendment reveal that the Framers of the
Constitution believed that there are additional fundamental rights, protected from governmental infringement,
which exist alongside those fundamental rights specifically
mentioned in the first eight constitutional amendments.

The Ninth Amendment reads, "The enumeration in
the Constitution, of certain rights, shall not be construed
to deny or disparage others retained by the people."   The
Amendment is almost entirely the work of James Madison.   It was introduced in Congress by him and passed
the House and Senate with little or no debate and virtually no change in language.   It was proffered to quiet
expressed fears that a bill of specifically enumerated
rights [3] could not be sufficiently broad to cover all essential rights and that the specific mention of certain
rights would be interpreted as a denial that others were
protected.[4] ● ● ● (See I,A.,6, supra.)

Mr. Justice Black, with whom Mr. Justice Stewart.
joins, dissenting.

I agree with my Brother Stewart's dissenting opinion.
And like him I do not to any extent whatever base my
view that this Connecticut law is constitutional on a
belief that the law is wise or that its policy is a good one.
In order that there may be no room at all to doubt why
I vote as I do, I feel constrained to add that the law is
every bit as offensive to me as it is to my Brethren of the
majority and my Brothers Harlan, White and Goldberg who, reciting reasons why it is offensive to them,
hold it unconstitutional.   There is no single one of the
graphic and eloquent strictures and criticisms fired at the
policy of this Connecticut law either by the Court's opinion or by those of my concurring Brethren to which I
cannot subscribe—except their conclusion that the evil
qualities they see in the law make it unconstitutional.
● ● ●

The Court talks about a constitutional "right of privacy" as though there is some constitutional provision or
provisions forbidding any law ever to be passed which
might abridge the "privacy" of individuals.   But there is
not. ● ● ●

(b). <u>Legislative Repeal of</u>
<u>Criminal Abortion Statutes</u>

<u>NEW YORK ABORTION LAW</u>, New York Penal Code sec.
125.05 (1970).

§ 125.05 Homicide, abortion and related offenses; definitions of terms

The following definitions are applicable to this article:

1. "Person," when referring to the victim of a homicide, means a human being who has been born and is alive.

2. "Abortional act" means an act committed upon or with respect to a female, whether by another person or by the female herself, whether she is pregnant or not, whether directly upon her body or by the administering, taking or prescription of drugs or in any other manner, with intent to cause a miscarriage of such female.

3. "Justifiable abortional act." An abortional act is justifiable when committed upon a female by a duly licensed physician acting under a reasonable belief that such is necessary to preserve the life of such female. A pregnant female's commission of an abortional act upon herself is justifiable when she acts upon the advice of a duly licensed physician that such is necessary to preserve her life. The submission by a female to an abortional act is justifiable when she believes that it is being committed by a duly licensed physician, and when she acts upon the advice of a duly licensed physician that such is necessary to preserve her life.

(c). Judicial Invalidity of Anti-Abortion Laws

ROE v. WADE, _____ U.S. _____ 93 S. Ct. 705(1973).

Mr. Justice BLACKMUN delivered the opinion of the Court.

This Texas federal appeal and its Georgia companion, Doe v. Bolton, *post*, — U.S. —, 93 S.Ct. 739, 34 L.Ed.2d —, present constitutional challenges to state criminal abortion legislation. The Texas statutes under attack here are typical of those that have been in effect in many States for approximately a century. ● ● ●

We forthwith acknowledge our awareness of the sensitive and emotional nature of the abortion controversy, of the vigorous opposing views, even among physicians, and of the deep and seemingly absolute convictions that the subject inspires. One's philosophy, one's experiences, one's exposure to the raw edges of human existence, one's religious training, one's attitudes toward life and family and their values, and the moral standards one establishes and seeks to observe, are all likely to influence and to color one's thinking and conclusions about abortion.

In addition, population growth, pollution, poverty, and racial overtones tend to complicate and not to simplify the problem.

Our task, of course, is to resolve the issue by constitutional measurement free of emotion and of predilection. We seek earnestly to do this, and, because we do, we have inquired into, and in this opinion place some emphasis upon, medical and medical-legal history and what that history reveals about man's attitudes toward the abortive procedure over the centuries. We bear in mind, too, Mr. Justice Holmes' admonition in his now vindicated dissent in Lochner v. New York, 198 U.S. 45, 76, 25 S.Ct. 539, 547, 49 L.Ed. 937 (1905):

"It [the Constitution] is made for people of fundamentally differing views, and the accident of our finding certain opinions natural and familiar, or novel, and even shocking, ought not to conclude our judgment upon the question whether statutes embodying them conflict with the Constitution of the United States." ● ● ●

The Texas statutes that concern us here are Arts. 1191–1194 and 1196 of the State's Penal Code,[1] Vernon's Ann.P.C.

"Article 1191. Abortion

"If any person shall designedly administer to a pregnant woman or knowingly procure to be administered with her consent any drug or medicine, or shall use towards her any violence or means whatever externally or internally applied, and thereby procure an abortion, he shall be confined in the penitentiary not less than two nor more than five years; if it be done without her consent, the punishment shall be doubled. By 'abortion' is meant that the life of the fetus or embryo shall be destroyed in the woman's womb or that a premature birth thereof be caused.

"Art. 1192. Furnishing the means

"Whoever furnishes the means for procuring an abortion knowing the purpose intended is guilty as an accomplice.

"Art. 1193. Attempt at abortion

"If the means used shall fail to produce an abortion, the offender is nevertheless guilty of an attempt to produce abortion, provided it be shown that such means were calculated to produce that result, and shall be fined not less than one hundred nor more than one thousand dollars.

"Art. 1194. Murder in producing abortion

"If the death of the mother is occasioned by an abortion so produced or by an attempt to effect the same it is murder.

"Art. 1196. By medical advice

"Nothing in this chapter applies to an abortion procured or attempted by medical advice for the purpose of saving the life of the mother."

The foregoing Articles, together with Art. 1195, comprise Chapter 9 of Title 15 of the Penal Code. Article 1195, not attacked here, reads:

"Art. 1195. Destroying unborn child

"Whoever shall during parturition of the mother destroy the vitality or life in a child in a state of being born and before actual birth, which child would otherwise have been born alive, shall be confined in the penitentiary for life or for not less than five years."

These make it a crime to "procure an abortion," as therein defined, or to attempt one, except with respect to "an abortion procured or attempted by medical advice for the purpose of saving the life of the mother." Similar statutes are in existence in a majority of the States.[2]

Texas first enacted a criminal abortion statute in 1854. Texas Laws 1854, c. 49, § 1, set forth in 3 Gammel, Laws of Texas, 1502 (1898). This was soon modified into language that has remained substantially unchanged to the present time. See Texas Penal Code of 1857, Arts. 531–536; Paschal's Laws of Texas, Arts. 2192–2197 (1866); Texas Rev.Stat., Arts. 536–541 (1879); Texas Rev.Crim.Stat., Arts. 1071–1076 (1911). The final article in each of these compilations provided the same exception, as does the present Article 1196, for an abortion by "medical advice for the purpose of saving the life of the mother." [3]

● ● ●

Jane Roe,[4] a single woman who was residing in Dallas County, Texas, instituted this federal action in March 1970 against the District Attorney of the county. She sought a declaratory judgment that the Texas criminal abortion statutes were unconstitutional on their face, and an injunction restraining the defendant from enforcing the statutes.

Roe alleged that she was unmarried and pregnant; that she wished to terminate her pregnancy by an abortion "performed by a competent, licensed physician, under safe, clinical conditions"; that she was unable to get a "legal" abortion in Texas because her life did not appear to be threatened by the continuation of her pregnancy; and that she could not afford to travel to another jurisdiction in order to secure a legal abortion under safe conditions. She claimed that the Texas statutes were unconstitutionally vague and that they abridged her right of personal privacy, protected by the First, Fourth, Fifth, Ninth, and Fourteenth Amendments. By an amendment to her complaint Roe purported to sue "on behalf of herself and all other women" similarly situated.

James Hubert Hallford, a licensed physician, sought and was granted leave to intervene in Roe's action. In his complaint he alleged that he had been arrested previously for violations of the Texas abortion statutes and that two such prosecutions were pending against him. He described conditions of patients who came to him seeking abortions, and he claimed that for many cases he, as a physician, was unable to determine whether they fell within or outside the exception recognized by Article 1196. He alleged that, as a consequence, the statutes were vague and uncertain, in violation of the Fourteenth Amendment, and that they violated his own and his patients' rights to privacy in the doctor-patient relationship and his own right to practice medicine, rights he claimed were guaranteed by the First, Fourth, Fifth, Ninth, and Fourteenth Amendments.

John and Mary Doe,[5] a married couple, filed a companion complaint to that of Roe. They also named the District Attorney as defendant, claimed like constitutional deprivations, and sought declaratory and injunctive relief. ● ● ●

The two actions were consolidated and heard together by a duly convened three-judge district court. The suits thus presented the situations of the pregnant single woman, the childless couple, with the wife not pregnant, and the licensed practicing physician, all joining in the attack on the Texas criminal abortion statutes. Upon the filing of affidavits, motions were made to dismiss and for summary judgment. The court held that Roe and Dr. Hallford, and members of their respective classes, had standing to sue, and presented justiciable controversies, but that the Does had failed to allege facts sufficient to state a present controversy and did not have standing. It concluded that, with respect to the requests for a declaratory judgment, abstention was not warranted. On the merits, the District Court held that the "fundamental right of single women and married persons to choose whether to have children is protected by the Ninth Amendment, through the Fourteenth Amendment," and that the

Texas criminal abortion statutes were void on their face because they were both unconstitutionally vague and constituted an overbroad infringement of the plaintiffs' Ninth Amendment rights. The court then held that abstention was warranted with respect to the requests for an injunction. It therefore dismissed the Doe complaint, declared the abortion statutes void, and dismissed the application for injunctive relief. 314 F.Supp. 1217 (N.D.Tex.1970).

The plaintiffs Roe and Doe and the intervenor Hallford, pursuant to 28 U. S.C. § 1253, have appealed to this Court from that part of the District Court's judgment denying the injunction. The defendant District Attorney has purported to cross appeal, pursuant to the same statute, from the court's grant of declaratory relief to Roe and Hallford. ● ● ●

We are next confronted with issues of justiciability, standing, and abstention. Have Roe and the Does established that "personal stake in the outcome of the controversy," Baker v. Carr, 369 U.S. 186, 204, 82 S.Ct. 691, 703, 7 L.Ed.2d 663 (1962), that insures that "the dispute sought to be adjudicated will be presented in an adversary context and in a form historically viewed as capable of judicial resolution," Flast v. Cohen, 392 U.S. 83, 101, 88 S.Ct. 1942, 1953, 20 L. Ed.2d 947 (1968), and Sierra Club v. Morton, 405 U.S. 727, 732, 92 S.Ct. 1361, 1364, 31 L.Ed.2d 636 (1972)? And what effect did the pendency of criminal abortion charges against Dr. Hallford in state court have upon the propriety of the federal court's granting relief to him as a plaintiff-intervenor?

A. *Jane Roe.* Despite the use of the pseudonym, no suggestion is made that Roe is a fictitious person. For purposes of her case, we accept as true, and as established, her existence; her pregnant state, as of the inception of her suit in March 1970 and as' late as May 21 of that year when she filed an alias affidavit with the District Court; and her inability to obtain a legal abortion in Texas.

Viewing Roe's case as of the time of its filing and thereafter until as late as May, there can be little dispute that it then presented a case or controversy and that, wholly apart from the class aspects, she, as a pregnant single woman thwarted by the Texas criminal abortion laws, had standing to challenge those statutes. ● ● ●

The usual rule in federal cases is that an actual controversy must exist at stages of appellate or certiorari review, and not simply at the date the action is initiated. ● ● ●

But when, as here, pregnancy is a significant fact in the litigation, the normal 266-day human gestation period is so short that the pregnancy will come to term before the usual appellate process is complete. If that termination makes a case moot, pregnancy litigation seldom will survive much beyond the trial stage, and appellate review will be effectively denied. Our law should not be that rigid. Pregnancy often 'comes more than once to the same woman, and in the general population, if man is to survive, it will always be with us. Pregnancy provides a classic justification for a conclusion of nonmootness. It truly could be "capable of repetition, yet evading review." ● ● ●

We therefore agree with the District Court that Jane Roe had standing to undertake this litigation, that she presented a justiciable controversy, and that the termination of her 1970 pregnancy has not rendered her case moot.

B. *Dr. Hallford.* The doctor's position is different. He entered Roe's litigation as a plaintiff-intervenor ● ● ●

Dr. Hallford is therefore in the position of seeking, in a federal court, declaratory and injunctive relief with respect to the same statutes under which he stands charged in criminal prosecutions simultaneously pending in state court. ● ● ●

We see no merit in that distinction. ● ● ●

Dr. Hallford's complaint in intervention, therefore, is to be dismissed.[7] He is remitted to his defenses in the state criminal proceedings against him. We reverse the judgment of the District Court insofar as it granted Dr. Hallford relief and failed to dismiss his complaint in intervention.

C. *The Does.* In view of our ruling as to Roe's standing in her case, the issue of the Does' standing in their case has little significance. The claims they assert are essentially the same as those of Roe, and they attack the same statutes. Nevertheless, we briefly note the Does' posture. ● ● ●

Their claim is that sometime, in the future, Mrs. Doe might become pregnant because of possible failure of contraceptive measures, and at that time in the future, she might want an abortion that might then be illegal under the Texas statutes.

This very phrasing of the Does' position reveals its speculative character. Their alleged injury rests on possible future contraceptive failure, possible future pregnancy, possible future unpreparedness for parenthood, and possible future impairment of health. Any one or more of these several possibilities may not take place and all may not combine. In the Does' estimation, these possibilities might have some real or imagined impact upon their marital happiness. But we are not prepared to say the the bare allegation of so indirect an injury is sufficient to present an actual case or controversy. ● ● ●

The Does therefore are not appropriate plaintiffs in this litigation. Their complaint was properly dismissed by the District Court, and we affirm that dismissal. ● ● ●

The principal thrust of appellant's attack on the Texas statutes is that they improperly invade a right, said to be possessed by the pregnant woman, to choose to terminate her pregnancy. Appellant would discover this right in the concept of personal "liberty" embodied in the Fourteenth Amendment's Due Process Clause; or in personal, marital, familial, and sexual privacy said to be protected by the Bill of Rights or its penumbras, see Griswold v. Connecticut, 381 U.S. 479, 85 S.Ct. 1678, 14 L.Ed.2d 510 (1965); Eisenstadt v. Baird, 405 U.S. 438 (1972); *id.,* at 460, 92 S.Ct. 1029, at 1042, 31 L.Ed.2d 349 (White, J., concurring); or among those rights reserved to the people by the Ninth Amendment, Griswold v. Connecticut, 381 U.S., at 486, 85 S.Ct., at 1682 (Goldberg, J., concurring). Before addressing this claim, we feel it desirable briefly to survey, in several aspects, the history of abortion, for such insight as that history may afford us, and then to examine the state purposes and interests behind the criminal abortion laws.

It perhaps is not generally appreciated that the restrictive criminal abortion laws in effect in a majority of States today are of relatively recent vintage. Those laws, generally proscribing abortion or its attempt at any time during pregnancy except when necessary to preserve the pregnant woman's life, are not of ancient or even of common law origin. Instead, they derive from statutory changes effected, for the most part, in the latter half of the 19th century.

1. *Ancient attitudes.* These are not capable of precise determination. We are told that at the time of the Persian Empire abortifacients were known and that criminal abortions were severely punished.[8] We are also told, however, that abortion was practiced in Greek times as well as in the Roman Era,[9] and that "it was resorted to without scruple." [10] The Ephesian, Soranos, often described as the greatest of the ancient gynecologists, appears to have been generally opposed to Rome's prevailing free-abortion practices. He found it necessary to think first of the life of the mother, and he resorted to abortion when, upon this standard, he felt the procedure advisable.[11] Greek and Roman law afforded little protection to the unborn. If abortion was prosecuted in some places, it seems to have been based on a concept of a violation of the father's right to his offspring. Ancient religion did not bar abortion.[12]

2. *The Hippocratic Oath.* ● ● ●

The Oath varies somewhat according to the particular translation, but in any translation the content is clear: "I will give no deadly medicine to anyone if asked, nor suggest any such counsel; and in like manner I will not give to a woman a pessary to produce abortion," [14] or "I will neither give a deadly drug to anybody if asked for it, nor will I make a suggestion to this effect. Similarly, I will not give to a woman an abortive remedy." [15]

Although the Oath is not mentioned in any of the principal briefs in this case or in Doe v. Bolton, post, — U.S. —, 93 S.Ct. 739, 34 L.Ed.2d —, it represents the apex of the development of strict ethical concepts in medicine, and its influence endures to this day. ● ● ●

3. *The Common Law.* It is undisputed that at the common law, abortion performed *before* "quickening"—the first recognizable movement of the fetus *in utero*, appearing usually from the 16th to the 18th week of pregnancy [20]—was not an indictable offense. [21] The absence of a common law crime for pre-quickening abortion appears to have developed from a confluence of earlier philosophical, theological, and civil and canon law concepts of when life begins. These disciplines variously approached the question in terms of the point at which the embryo or fetus became "formed" or recognizably human, or in terms of when a "person" came into being, that is, infused with a "soul" or "animated." ● ● ●

Whether abortion of a *quick* fetus was a felony at common law, or even a lesser crime, is still disputed. Bracton, writing early in the 13th century, thought it homicide. [23] But the later and predominant view, following the great common law scholars, has been that it was at most a lesser offense. In a frequently cited passage, Coke took the position that abortion of a woman "quick with childe" is "a great misprision and no murder." [24] Blackstone followed, saying that while abortion after quickening had once been considered manslaughter (though not murder), "modern law" took a less severe view. [25] A recent review of the common law precedents argues, however, that those precedents contradict Coke and that even post-quickening abortion was never established as a common law crime. [26] This is of some importance because while most American courts ruled, in holding or dictum, that abortion of an unquickened fetus was not criminal under their received common law, [27] others followed Coke in stating that abortion of a quick fetus was a "misprision," a term they translated to mean "misdemeanor." [28] That their reliance on Coke on this aspect of the law was uncritical and, apparently in all the reported cases, dictum (due probably to the paucity of common law prosecutions for post-quickening abortion), makes it now appear doubtful that abortion was ever firmly established as a common law crime even with respect to the destruction of a quick fetus.

4. *The English statutory law.* England's first criminal abortion statute, Lord Ellenborough's Act, 43 Geo. 3, c. 58, came in 1803. It made abortion of a quick fetus, § 1, a capital crime, but in § 2 it provided lesser penalties for the felony of abortion before quickening, and thus preserved the quickening distinction. ● ● ●

Recently Parliament enacted a new abortion law. This is the Abortion Act of 1967, 15 & 16 Eliz. 2, c. 87. The Act permits a licensed physician to perform an abortion where two other licensed physicians agree (a) "that the continuance of the pregnancy would involve risk to the life of the pregnant woman, or of injury to the physical or mental health of the pregnant woman or any existing children of her family, greater than if the pregnancy were terminated," or (b) "that there is a substantial risk that if the child were born it would suffer from such physical or mental abnormalities as to be seriously handicapped." The Act also provides that, in making this determination, "account may be taken of the pregnant woman's actual or reasonably foreseeable environment." It also permits a physician, without the concurrence of others, to terminate a pregnancy where he is of the good faith opinion that the abortion "is immediately necessary to save the life or to prevent grave permanent injury to the physical or mental health of the pregnant woman."

5. *The American law.* In this country the law in effect in all but a few States until mid-19th century was the pre-existing English common law. Connecticut, the first State to enact abortion legislation, adopted in 1821 that part of Lord Ellenborough's Act that related to a woman "quick with child." [29] The death penalty was not imposed. Abortion before quickening was made a crime in that State only in 1860.[30] In 1828 New York enacted legislation [31] that, in two respects, was to serve as a model for early anti-abortion statutes. First, while barring destruction of an unquickened fetus as well as a quick fetus, it made the former only a misdemeanor, but the latter second-degree manslaughter. Second, it incorporated a concept of therapeutic abortion by providing that an abortion was excused if it "shall have been necessary to preserve the life of such mother, or shall have been advised by two physicians to be necessary for such purpose." ● ● ●

It was not until after the War Between the States that legislation began generally to replace the common law. Most of these initial statutes dealt severely with abortion after quickening but were lenient with it before quickening. ● ● ●

Gradually, in the middle and late 19th century the quickening distinction disappeared from the statutory law of most States and the degree of the offense and the penalties were increased. By the end of the 1950's a large majority of the States banned abortion, however and whenever performed, unless done to save or preserve the life of the mother.[34] The exceptions, Alabama and the District of Columbia, permitted abortion to preserve the mother's health.[35] Three other States permitted abortions that were not "unlawfully" performed or that were not "without lawful justification," leaving interpretation of those standards to the courts.[36] In the past several years, however, a trend toward liberalization of abortion statutes has resulted in adoption, by about one-third of the States, of less stringent laws, most of them patterned after the ALI Model Penal Code ● ● ●

It is thus apparent that at common law, at the time of the adoption of our Constitution, and throughout the major portion of the 19th century, abortion was viewed with less disfavor than under most American statutes currently in effect. Phrasing it another way, a woman enjoyed a substantially broader right to terminate a pregnancy than she does in most States today. At least with respect to the early stage of pregnancy, and very possibly without such a limitation, the opportunity to make this choice was present in this country well into the 19th century. Even later, the law continued for some time to treat less punitively an abortion procured in early pregnancy.

6. *The position of the American Medical Association.* The anti-abortion mood prevalent in this country in the late 19th century was shared by the medical profession. Indeed, the attitude of the profession may have played a significant role in the enactment of stringent criminal abortion legislation during that period. ● ● ●

In 1970, after the introduction of a variety of proposed resolutions, and of a report from its Board of Trustees, a reference committee noted "polarization of the medical profession on this controversial issue" ● ● ●

7. *The position of the American Public Health Association.* In October 1970, the Executive Board of the APHA adopted Standards for Abortion Services. These were five in number:

"a. Rapid and simple abortion referral must be readily available through state and local public health departments, medical societies, or other non-profit organizations. ● ● ●

8. *The position of the American Bar Association.* At its meeting in February 1972 the ABA House of Delegates approved, with 17 opposing votes, the Uniform Abortion Act ● ● ●

Three reasons have been advanced to explain historically the enactment of criminal abortion laws in the 19th century and to justify their continued existence.

It has been argued occasionally that these laws were the product of a Victorian social concern to discourage illicit sexual conduct. Texas, however, does not advance this justification in the present case, and it appears that no court or commentator has taken the argument seriously. ● ● ●

A second reason is concerned with abortion as a medical procedure. When most criminal abortion laws were first enacted, the procedure was a hazardous one for the woman. ● ● ●

Modern medical techniques have altered this situation. ● ● ●

The third reason is the State's interest—some phrase it in terms of duty—in protecting prenatal life. Some of the argument for this justification rests on the theory that a new human life is present from the moment of conception.[45] The State's interest and general obligation to protect life then extends, it is argued, to prenatal life. Only when the life of the pregnant mother herself is at stake, balanced against the life she carries within her, should the interest of the embryo or fetus not prevail. Logically, of course, a legitimate state interest in this area need not stand or fall on acceptance of the belief that life begins at conception or at some other point prior to live birth. In assessing the State's interest, recognition may be given to the less rigid claim that as long as at least *potential* life is involved, the State may assert interests beyond the protection of the pregnant woman alone.

Parties challenging state abortion laws have sharply disputed in some courts the contention that a purpose of these laws, when enacted, was to protect prenatal life.[46] Pointing to the absence of legislative history to support the contention, they claim that most state laws were designed solely to protect the woman. Because medical advances have lessened this concern, at least with respect to abortion in early pregnancy, they argue that with respect to such abortions the laws can no longer be justified by any state interest. There is some scholarly support for this view of original purpose.[47] The few state courts

called upon to interpret their laws in the late 19th and early 20th centuries did focus on the State's interest in protecting the woman's health rather than in preserving the embryo and fetus.[48] Proponents of this view point out that in many States, including Texas,[49] by statute or judicial interpretation, the pregnant woman herself could not be prosecuted for self-abortion or for cooperating in an abortion performed upon her by another.[50] They claim that adoption of the "quickening" distinction through received common law and state statutes tacitly recognizes the greater health hazards inherent in late abortion and impliedly repudiates the theory that life begins at conception.

It is with these interests, and the weight to be attached to them, that this case is concerned.

The Constitution does not explicitly mention any right of privacy. In a line of decisions, however, going back perhaps as far as Union Pacific R. Co. v. Botsford, 141 U.S. 250, 251, 11 S.Ct. 1000, 1001, 35 L.Ed. 734 (1891), the Court has recognized that a right of personal privacy, or a guarantee of certain areas or zones of privacy, does exist under the Constitution. In varying contexts the Court or individual Justices have indeed found at least the roots of that right in the First Amendment, Stanley v. Georgia, 394 U.S. 557, 564, 89 S.Ct. 1243, 1247, 22 L.Ed.2d 542 (1969); in the Fourth and Fifth Amendments ● ● ● in the Ninth Amendment, *id.*, at 486, 85 S.Ct. at 1682 (Goldberg, J., concurring); or in the concept of liberty guaranteed by the first section of the Fourteenth Amendment, see Meyer v. Nebraska, 262 U.S. 390, 399, 43 S.Ct. 625, 626, 67 L.Ed. 1042 (1923). These decisions make it clear that only personal rights that can be deemed "fundamental" or "implicit in the concept of ordered liberty," Palko v. Connecticut, 302 U.S. 319, 325, 58 S.Ct. 149, 152, 82 L.Ed. 288 (1937), are included in this guarantee of personal privacy. They also make it clear that the right has some extension to activities relating to marriage, Loving v. Virginia, 388 U.S.

1, 12, 87 S.Ct. 1817, 1823, 18 L.Ed.2d 1010 (1967), procreation, Skinner v. Oklahoma, 316 U.S. 535, 541–542, 62 S. Ct. 1110, 1113–1114, 86 L.Ed. 1655 (1942), contraception, Eisenstadt v. Baird, 405 U.S. 438, 453–454, 92 S.Ct. 1029, 1038–1039, 31 L.Ed.2d 349 (1972); id., at 460, 463–465, 92 S.Ct. at 1042, 1043–1044 (White, J., concurring), family relationships, Prince v. Massachusetts, 321 U.S. 158, 166, 64 S.Ct. 438, 442, 88 L.Ed. 645 (1944), and child rearing and education ● ● ●

This right of privacy, whether it be founded in the Fourteenth Amendment's concept of personal liberty and restrictions upon state action, as we feel it is, or, as the District Court determined, in the Ninth Amendment's reservation of rights to the people, is broad enough to encompass a woman's decision whether or not to terminate her pregnancy. The detriment that the State would impose upon the pregnant woman by denying this choice altogether is apparent. Specific and direct harm medically diagnosable even in early pregnancy may be involved. Maternity, or additional offspring, may force upon the woman a distressful life and future. Psychological harm may be imminent. Mental and physical health may be taxed by child care. There is also the distress, for all concerned, associated with the unwanted child, and there is the problem of bringing a child into a family already unable, psychologically and otherwise, to care for it. In other cases, as in this one, the additional difficulties and continuing stigma of unwed motherhood may be involved. All these are factors the woman and her responsible physician necessarily will consider in consultation.

On the basis of elements such as these, appellants and some amici argue that the woman's right is absolute and that she is entitled to terminate her pregnancy at whatever time, in whatever way, and for whatever reason she alone chooses. With this we do not agree. Appellants' arguments that Texas either has no valid interest at all in regulating the abortion decision, or no interest strong enough to support any limitation upon the woman's sole determination, is unpersuasive. The Court's decisions recognizing a right of privacy also acknowledge that some state regulation in areas protected by that right is appropriate. As noted above, a state may properly assert important interests in safeguarding health, in maintaining medical standards, and in protecting potential life. At some point in pregnancy, these respective interests become sufficiently compelling to sustain regulation of the factors that govern the abortion decision. The privacy right involved, therefore, cannot be said to be absolute. In fact, it is not clear to us that the claim asserted by some amici that one has an unlimited right to do with one's body as one pleases bears a close relationship to the right of privacy previously articulated in the Court's decisions. The Court has refused to recognize an unlimited right of this kind in the past. Jacobson v. Massachusetts, 197 U.S. 11, 25 S.Ct. 358, 49 L.Ed. 643 (1905) (vaccination); Buck v. Bell, 274 U.S. 200, 47 S.Ct. 584, 71 L.Ed. 1000 (1927) (sterilization).

We therefore conclude that the right of personal privacy includes the abortion decision, but that this right is not unqualified and must be considered against important state interests in regulation.

We note that those federal and state courts that have recently considered abortion law challenges have reached the same conclusion. ● ● ●   most of these courts have agreed that the right of privacy, however based, is broad enough to cover the abortion decision; that the right, nonetheless, is not absolute and is subject to some limitations; and that at some point the state interests as to protection of health, medical standards, and prenatal life, become dominant. We agree with this approach. ● ● ●

The appellee and certain amici argue that the fetus is a "person" within the language and meaning of the Fourteenth Amendment. In support of this they outline at length and in detail the well-known facts of fetal development. If this suggestion of personhood is established, the appellant's case, of course, collapses, for the fetus' right to life is then guaranteed specifically by the Amendment. The appellant conceded as much on reargument.[51] On the other hand, the appellee conceded on reargument [52] that no case could be cited that holds that a fetus is a person within the meaning of the Fourteenth Amendment.

The Constitution does not define "person" in so many words. Section 1 of the Fourteenth Amendment contains three references to "person." The first, in defining "citizens," speaks of "persons born or naturalized in the United States." The word also appears both in the Due Process Clause and in the Equal Protection Clause. "Person" is used in other places in the Constitution ● ● ● But in nearly all these instances, the use of the word is such that it has application only postnatally. None indicates, with any assurance, that it has any possible pre-natal application.[54] All this, together with our observation, *supra*, that throughout the major portion of the 19th century prevailing legal abortion practices were far freer than they are today, persuades us that the word "person," as used in the Fourteenth Amendment, does not include the unborn.[55] This is in accord with the results reached in those few cases where the issue has been squarely presented. McGarvey v. Magee-Womens Hospital, 340 F.Supp. 751 (W.D.Pa.1972); Byrn v. New York City Health & Hospitals Corp., 31 N.Y.2d 194, 335 N.Y.S.2d 390, 286 N.E.2d 887 (1972), appeal pending; Abele v. Markle, —— F.Supp. —— (D.C. Conn.1972), appeal pending. ● ● ●

This conclusion, however, does not of itself fully answer the contentions raised by Texas, and we pass on to other considerations.

The pregnant woman cannot be isolated in her privacy. She carries an embryo and, later, a fetus, if one accepts the medical definitions of the developing young in the human uterus. See Dorland's Illustrated Medical Dictionary, 478–479, 547 (24th. ed. 1965). The situation therefore is inherently different from marital intimacy, or bedroom possession of obscene material, or marriage, or procreation, or education, with which *Eisenstadt, Griswold, Stanley, Loving, Skinner, Pierce*, and *Meyer* were respectively concerned. As we have intimated above, it is reasonable and appropriate for a State to decide that at some point in time another interest, that of health of the mother or that of potential human life, becomes significantly involved. The woman's privacy is no longer sole and any right of privacy she possesses must be measured accordingly.

Texas urges that, apart from the Fourteenth Amendment, life begins at conception and is present throughout pregnancy, and that, therefore, the State has a compelling interest in protecting that life from and after conception. We need not resolve the difficult question of when life begins. When those trained in the respective disciplines of medicine, philosophy, and theology are unable to arrive at any consensus, the judiciary, at this point in the development of man's knowledge, is not in a position to speculate as to the answer. ● ● ● Physicians and their scientific colleagues have regarded that event with less interest and have tended to focus either upon conception or upon live birth or upon the interim point at which the fetus becomes "viable," that is, potentially able to live outside the mother's womb, albeit with artificial aid.[59] Viability is usually placed at about seven months (28 weeks) but may occur earlier, even at 24 weeks. ● ● ● we do not agree that, by adopting one theory of life, Texas may override the rights of the pregnant woman that are at stake. We repeat, however, that the State does have an important and legitimate interest in preserving and protecting the health of the pregnant woman, whether she be a resident of the State or a nonresident who seeks medical consultation and treatment there, and that it has still *another* important and legitimate interest in protecting the potentiality of human life. These interests are separate and distinct. Each grows in substantiality as the woman approaches term and, at a point during pregnancy, each becomes "compelling."

With respect to the State's important and legitimate interest in the health of the mother, the "compelling" point, in the light of present medical knowledge, is at approximately the end of the first trimester. This is so because of the now established medical fact, referred to above at p. 724, that until the end of the first trimester mortality in abortion is less than mortality in normal childbirth. It follows that, from and after this point, a State may regulate the abortion procedure to the extent that the regulation reasonably relates to the preservation and protection of maternal health. Examples of permissible state regulation in this area are requirements as to the qualifications of the person who is to perform the abortion; as to the licensure of that person; as to the facility in which the procedure is to be performed, that is, whether it must be a hospital or may be a clinic or some other place of less-than-hospital status; as to the licensing of the facility; and the like.

This means, on the other hand, that, for the period of pregnancy prior to this "compelling" point, the attending physician, in consultation with his patient, is free to determine, without regulation by the State, that in his medical judgment the patient's pregnancy should be terminated. If that decision is reached, the judgment may be effectuated by an abortion free of interference by the State.

With respect to the State's important and legitimate interest in potential life, the "compelling" point is at viability. This is so because the fetus then presumably has the capability of meaningful life outside the mother's womb. State regulation protective of fetal life after viability thus has both logical and biological justifications. If the State is interested in protecting fetal life after viability, it may go so far as to proscribe abortion during that period except when it is necessary to preserve the life or health of the mother.

Measured against these standards, Art. 1196 of the Texas Penal Code, in restricting legal abortions to those "procured or attempted by medical advice for the purpose of saving the life of the mother," sweeps too broadly. The statute makes no distinction between abortions performed early in pregnancy and those performed later, and it limits to a single reason, "saving" the mother's life, the legal justification for the procedure. The statute, therefore, cannot survive the constitutional attack made upon it here.

This conclusion makes it unnecessary for us to consider the additional challenge to the Texas statute asserted on grounds of vagueness. ● ● ●

To summarize and to repeat:

1. A state criminal abortion statute of the current Texas type, that excepts from criminality only a *life saving* procedure on behalf of the mother, without regard to pregnancy stage and without recognition of the other interests involved, is violative of the Due Process Clause of the Fourteenth Amendment.

(a) For the stage prior to approximately the end of the first trimester, the abortion decision and its effectuation must be left to the medical judgment of the pregnant woman's attending physician.

(b) For the stage subsequent to approximately the end of the first trimester, the State, in promoting its interest in the health of the mother, may, if it chooses, regulate the abortion procedure in ways that are reasonably related to maternal health.

(c) For the stage subsequent to viability the State, in promoting its interest in the potentiality of human life, may, if it chooses, regulate, and even proscribe, abortion except where it is necessary, in appropriate medical judgment, for the preservation of the life or health of the mother.

2. The State may define the term "physician," as it has been employed in the preceding numbered paragraphs of this Part XI of this opinion, to mean only a physician currently licensed by the State, and may proscribe any abortion by a person who is not a physician as so defined. ● ● ●

Our conclusion that Art. 1196 is unconstitutional means, of course, that the Texas abortion statutes, as a unit, must fall. The exception of Art. 1196 cannot be stricken separately, for then the State is left with a statute proscribing all abortion procedures no matter how medically urgent the case.

Although the District Court granted plaintiff Roe declaratory relief, it stopped short of issuing an injunction against enforcement of the Texas statutes. The Court has recognized that different considerations enter into a federal court's decision as to declaratory relief, on the one hand, and injunctive relief, on the other. Zwickler v. Koota, 389 U.S. 241, 252–255, 88 S.Ct. 391, 397–399, 19 L.Ed.2d 444 (1967); Dombrowski v. Pfister, 380 U.S. 479, 85 S. Ct. 1116, 14 L.Ed.2d 22 (1965). We are not dealing with a statute that, on its face, appears to abridge free expression, an area of particular concern under *Dombrowski* and refined in Younger v.

Harris, 401 U.S., at 50, 91 S.Ct., at 753.

We find it unnecessary to decide whether the District Court erred in withholding injunctive relief, for we assume the Texas prosecutorial authorities will give full credence to this decision that the present criminal abortion statutes of that State are unconstitutional.

The judgment of the District Court as to intervenor Hallford is reversed, and Dr. Hallford's complaint in intervention is dismissed. In all other respects the judgment of the District Court is affirmed. Costs are allowed to the appellee.

It is so ordered.

Affirmed in part and reversed in part.

Mr. Justice REHNQUIST, dissenting.

(d). Voluntary Sterilization

SEXUAL STERILIZATION, Va. Code Ann. sec. 32-423(1969).

§ 32-423. Sexual sterilization of person twenty-one years of age or older. — It shall be lawful for any physician or surgeon licensed by this State, when so requested by any person who has attained the age of twenty-one years, to perform, upon such person a vasectomy, or salpingectomy, or other surgical sexual sterilization procedure, as the case may be, provided a request in writing is made by such person and by his or her spouse, if there be one, prior to the performance of such surgical operation and provided further, that prior to or at the time of such request a full and reasonable medical explanation is given by such physician or surgeon to such person as to the meaning and consequences of such operation. No such request shall be necessary for the spouse of the person requesting such surgical operation if the person requesting such operation shall state in writing under oath that his or her spouse has disappeared or that they have been separated continually for a period of more than one year prior thereto. Provided, however, no vasectomy shall be performed pursuant to the provisions of this section prior to thirty days from the date of consent or request therefor; provided further that no salpingectomy or other irrevocable surgical sexual sterilization procedure shall be performed prior to thirty days from the date of consent or request therefor on any female who has not theretofore given birth to a child.

. . . .

STERILIZATION OPERATIONS, N.C. Gen. Stat. sec. 90-271(Supp. 1969).

§ 90-271. Operations lawful; consent required for operation on married person or person over twenty-one. — It shall be lawful for any physician or surgeon licensed by this State and acting in collaboration or consultation with at least one or more physicians or surgeons so licensed, when so requested by any person twenty-one years of age or over, or less than twenty-one years of age if legally married, to perform in a hospital licensed by the Medical Care Commission, upon such person a surgical interruption of vas deferens or Fallopian tubes, as the case may be, provided a request in writing is made by such person at least thirty (30) days prior to the performance of such surgical operation, and provided, further, that prior to or at the time of such request a full and reasonable medical explanation is given by such physician or surgeon to such person as to the meaning and consequences of such operation; and provided, further, that a request in writing is also made at least thirty (30) days prior to the performance of the operation by the spouse of such person, if there be one, unless the spouse has been declared mentally incompetent, or unless a separation agreement has been entered into between the spouse and the person to be operated upon, or unless the spouse and the person to be operated upon have been divorced from bed and board or have been divorced absolutely. (1963, c. 600.)

(e). Promotion of Voluntary Controls

i. OEO emphasis on family planning

THE PUBLIC HEALTH AND WELFARE, 42 U.S.C.A. sec 2808
(a) (5)

§ 2808. General provisions for financial assistance.

(a) Component activities.

The Director may provide financial assistance to community action agencies for the planning, conduct, administration and evaluation of community action programs and components. Those components may involve, without limitation, other activities and supporting facilities designed to assist participants including the elderly poor— ● ● ●

(5) to undertake family planning, consistent with personal and family goals, religious and moral convictions;

. . . .

ii. Social Security Act Assistance

THE PUBLIC HEALTH AND WELFARE, 42 U.S.C.A. sec. 2809
(a) (6)

§ 2809. Special programs and assistance; Project Headstart; Follow Through; Legal Services; Comprehensive Health Services; Upward Bound; Emergency Food and Medical Services; Family Planning; Senior Opportunities and Services; Alcoholic Counseling and Recovery; Drug Rehabilitation.

(a) In order to stimulate actions to meet or deal with particularly critical needs or problems of the poor which are common to a number of communities, the Director may develop and carry on special programs under this section. This authority shall be used only where the Director determines that the objectives sought could not be effectively achieved through the use of authorities under section 2808 of this title, including assistance to components or projects based on models developed and promulgated by him. It shall also be used only with respect to programs which (A) involve activities which can be incorporated into or be closely coordinated with community action programs, (B) involve significant new combinations of resources of new and innovative approaches, or (C) are structured in a way that will, within the limits of the type of assistance or activities contemplated, most fully and effectively promote the purposes of this subchapter. Subject to such conditions as may be appropriate to assure effective and efficient administration, the Director may provide financial assistance to public or private nonprofit agencies to carry on local projects initiated under such special programs; but he shall do so in a manner that will encourage, wherever feasible, the inclusion of the assisted projects in community action programs, with a view to minimizing possible duplication and promoting efficiencies in the use of common facilities and services, better assisting persons or families having a variety of needs, and otherwise securing from the funds committed the greatest possible impact in promoting family and individual self-sufficiency. Programs under this section shall include those described in the following paragraphs: ● ● ●

(6) A "Family Planning" program to provide assistance and services to low-income persons in the field of voluntary family planning, including the provision of information, medical assistance, and supplies. The Director and the Secretary of Health, Education, and Welfare shall coordinate, and assure a full exchange of information concerning, family planning projects within their respective jurisdictions in order to assure the maximum availability of services and in order best to meet the varying needs of different communities. The Secretary of Health, Education, and Welfare shall make the services of Public Health Service officers available to the Director in carrying out this program.

iii. <u>Family Planning Service</u>
and Population Research Act <u>of 1970</u>, P.L. 91-572,
84 STAT. 1504

DECLARATION OF PURPOSE

Sec. 2. It is the purpose of this Act—

(1) to assist in making comprehensive voluntary family planning services readily available to all persons desiring such services;

(2) to coordinate domestic population and family planning research with the present and future needs of family planning programs;

(3) to improve administrative and operational supervision of domestic family planning services and of population research programs related to such services;

(4) to enable public and nonprofit private entities to plan and develop comprehensive programs of family planning services;

(5) to develop and make readily available information (including educational materials) on family planning and population growth to all persons desiring such information;

(6) to evaluate and improve the effectiveness of family planning service programs and of population research;

(7) to assist in providing trained manpower needed to effectively carry out programs of population research and family planning services; and

(8) to establish an Office of Population Affairs in the Department of Health, Education, and Welfare as a primary focus within the Federal Government on matters pertaining to population research and family planning, through which the Secretary of Health, Education, and Welfare (hereafter in this Act referred to as the "Secretary") shall carry out the purposes of this Act.

. . . .

See: Bravenec, "Voluntary Sterilization of Crime: Application of Assault and Battery and of Mayhem," 6 J. Fam. Law 94 (1966).

Sands, "The Therapeutic Abortion Act: An Answer to the Opposition," 13 U.C.L.A. L. Rev. 22 (1966).

Note, "The Abortion Decisions: Roe v. Wade, Doe v. Bolton," 12 J. Fam. L. 459 (1973).

B.   Regulation of Population Distribution

1.   The Right to Travel

EDWARDS v. CALIFORNIA, 314 U.S. 160(1941).

MR. JUSTICE BYRNES delivered the opinion of the Court.

The facts of this case are simple and are not disputed. Appellant is a citizen of the United States and a resident of California. In December, 1939, he left his home in Marysville, California, for Spur, Texas, with the intention of bringing back to Marysville his wife's brother, Frank Duncan, a citizen of the United States and a resident of Texas. When he arrived in Texas, appellant learned that Duncan had last been employed by the Works Progress Administration. Appellant thus became aware of the fact that Duncan was an indigent person and he continued to be aware of it throughout the period involved in this case. The two men agreed that appellant should transport Duncan from Texas to Marysville in appellant's automobile. Accordingly, they left Spur on January 1, 1940, entered California by way of Arizona on January 3, and reached Marysville on January 5. When he left Texas, Duncan had about $20. It had all been spent by the time he reached Marysville. He lived with appellant for about ten days until he obtained financial assistance from the Farm Security Administration. During the ten day interval, he had no employment.

In Justice Court a complaint was filed against appellant under § 2615 of the Welfare and Institutions Code of California, which provides: "Every person, firm or corporation or officer or agent thereof that brings or assists in bringing into the State any indigent person who is not a resident of the State, knowing him to be an indigent person, is guilty of a misdemeanor." On demurrer to the complaint, appellant urged that the Section violated several provisions of the Federal Constitution. The demurrer was overruled, the cause was tried, appellant was convicted and sentenced to six months imprisonment in the county jail, and sentence was suspended.

On appeal to the Superior Court of Yuba County, the facts as stated above were stipulated. The Superior Court, although regarding as "close" the question of the validity of the Section, felt "constrained to uphold the statute as a valid exercise of the police power of the State of California." Consequently, the conviction was affirmed. No appeal to a higher state court was open to appellant. We noted probable jurisdiction early last term, and later ordered reargument (313·U. S. 545) which has been held.

At the threshold of our inquiry a question arises with respect to the interpretation of § 2615. ● ● ●

Neither under these forerunners nor under § 2615 itself does the term "indigent person" seem to have been accorded an authoritative interpretation by the California courts. The appellee claims for the Section a very limited scope. It urges that the term "indigent person" must be taken to include only persons who are presently destitute of property and without resources to obtain the necessities of life, and who have no relatives or friends able and willing to support them. It is conceded, however, that the term is not confined to those who are physically or mentally incapacitated. While the generality of the language of the Section contains no hint of these limitations, we are content to assign to the term this narrow meaning.

Article I, § 8 of the Constitution delegates to the Congress the authority to regulate interstate commerce. And it is settled beyond question that the transportation of persons is "commerce," within the meaning of that provision.[1] It is nevertheless true, that the States are not wholly precluded from exercising their police power in matters of local concern even though they may thereby affect interstate commerce. *California* v. *Thompson,* 313 U. S. 109, 113. The issue presented in this case, therefore, is whether the prohibition embodied in § 2615 against the "bringing" or transportation of indigent persons into California is within the police power of that State. We think that it is not, and hold that it is an unconstitutional barrier to interstate commerce.

The grave and perplexing social and economic dislocation which this statute reflects is a matter of common knowledge and concern. We are not unmindful of it. We appreciate that the spectacle of large segments of our population constantly on the move has given rise to urgent demands upon the ingenuity of government. ● ● ●
The State asserts that the huge influx of migrants into California in recent years has resulted in problems of health, morals, and especially finance, the proportions of which are staggering. It is not for us to say that this is not true. We have repeatedly and recently affirmed, and we now reaffirm, that we do

not conceive it our function to pass upon "the wisdom, need, or appropriateness" of the legislative efforts of the States to solve such difficulties. See *Olsen* v. *Nebraska*, 313 U. S. 236, 246.

But this does not mean that there are no boundaries to the permissible area of State legislative activity. There are. And none is more certain than the prohibition against attempts on the part of any single State to isolate itself from difficulties common to all of them by restraining the transportation of persons and property across its borders. It is frequently the case that a State might gain a momentary respite from the pressure of events by the simple·expedient of shutting its gates to the outside world. But, in the words of Mr. Justice Cardozo: "The Constitution was framed under the dominion of a political philosophy less parochial in range. It was framed upon the theory that the peoples of the several States must sink or swim together, and that in the long run prosperity and salvation are in union and not division." *Baldwin* v. *Seelig*, 294 U. S. 511, 523.

It is difficult to conceive of a statute more squarely in conflict with this theory than the Section challenged here. Its express purpose and inevitable effect is to prohibit the transportation of indigent persons across the California border. The burden upon interstate commerce is intended and immediate; it is the plain and sole function of the statute. Moreover, the indigent non-residents who are the real victims of the statute are deprived of the opportunity to exert political pressure upon the California legislature in order to obtain a change in policy. *South Carolina Highway Dept.* v. *Barnwell Bros.*, 303 U. S. 177, 185, n. 2. We think this statute must fail under any known test of the validity of State interference with interstate commerce.

It is urged, however, that the concept which underlies § 2615 enjoys a firm basis in English and American history.[2] This is the notion that each community should care for its own indigent, that relief is solely the responsibility of local government. Of this it must first be said that we are not now called upon to determine anything other than the propriety of an attempt by a State to prohibit the transportation of indigent non-residents into its territory. The nature and extent of its obligation to afford relief to newcomers is not here involved. We do, however, suggest that the theory of the Elizabethan poor laws no longer fits the facts. Recent years, and particularly the past decade, have been marked by a growing recognition that in an industrial society the task of providing assistance to the needy has ceased to be local in character. The duty to share the burden, if not wholly to assume it, has been recognized not only by State governments, but by the Federal government as well. The changed attitude is reflected in the Social Security laws under which the Federal and State governments coöperate for the care of the aged, the blind and dependent children. ● ● ●

What has been said with respect to financing relief is not without its bearing upon the regulation of the transportation of indigent persons. For the social phenomenon of large-scale interstate migration is as certainly a matter of national concern as the provision of assistance to those who have found a permanent or temporary abode. Moreover, and unlike the relief problem, this phenomenon does not admit of diverse treatment by the several States. The prohibition against transporting indigent non-residents into one State is an open invitation to retaliatory measures, and the burdens upon the transportation of such persons become cumulative. Moreover, it would be a virtual impossibility for migrants and those who transport them to acquaint themselves with the peculiar rules of admission of many States. ● ● ●

There remains to be noticed only the contention that the limitation upon State power to interfere with the interstate transportation of persons is subject to an exception in the case of "paupers." It is true that support for this contention may be found in early decisions of this Court. In *City of New York* v. *Miln*, 11 Pet. 102, at 143, it was said that it is "as competent and as necessary for a State to provide precautionary measures against the moral pestilence of paupers, vagabonds, and possibly convicts, as it is to guard against the physical pestilence, which may arise from unsound and infectious articles imported, . . ." This language has been casually repeated in numerous later cases up to the turn of the century. ● ● ●
In none of these cases, however, was the power of a State to exclude "paupers" actually involved.

Whether an able-bodied but unemployed person like Duncan is a "pauper" within the historical meaning of the term is open to considerable doubt. See 53 Harvard L. Rev. 1031, 1032. But assuming that the term is applicable to him and to persons similarly situated, we do not consider ourselves bound by the language referred to. *City of New York* v. *Miln* was decided in 1837. Whatever may have been the notion then prevailing, we do not think that it will now be seriously contended that because a person is without employment and without funds he constitutes a "moral pestilence." Poverty and immorality are not synonymous.

We are of the opinion that § 2615 is not a valid exercise of the police power of California; that it imposes an unconstitutional burden upon interstate commerce, and that the conviction under it cannot be sustained. In the view we have taken it is unnecessary to decide whether the Section is repugnant to other provisions of the Constitution.

Reversed.

. . . .

2. Discrimination Against Non-Residents

(a). Welfare Payments

SHAPIRO v. THOMPSON, 394 U.S. 618 (1968).

MR. JUSTICE BRENNAN delivered the opinion of the Court.

These three appeals were restored to the calendar for reargument. 392 U. S. 920 (1968). Each is an appeal from a decision of a three-judge District Court holding unconstitutional a State or District of Columbia statutory provision which denies welfare assistance to residents of the State or District who have not resided within their jurisdictions for at least one year immediately preceding their applications for such assistance.[1] We affirm the judgments of the District Courts in the three cases.

In No. 9, the Connecticut Welfare Department invoked § 17-2d of the Connecticut General Statutes[2] to deny the application of appellee Vivian Marie Thompson for assistance under the program for Aid to Families with Dependent Children (AFDC). She was a 19-year-old unwed mother of one child and pregnant with her second child when she changed her residence in June 1966 from Dorchester, Massachusetts, to Hartford, Connecticut, to live with her mother, a Hartford resident. She moved to her own apartment in Hartford in August 1966, when her mother was no longer able to support her and her infant son. Because of her pregnancy, she was unable to work or enter a work training program. Her application for AFDC assistance, filed in August, was denied in November solely on the ground that, as required by § 17-2d, she had not lived in the State for a year before her application was filed. She brought this action in

the District Court for the District of Connecticut where
a three-judge court, one judge dissenting, declared § 17–
2d unconstitutional. 270 F. Supp. 331 (1967). The
majority held that the waiting-period requirement is
unconstitutional because it "has a chilling effect on the
right to travel." *Id.*, at 336. The majority also held
that the provision was a violation of the Equal Protection
Clause of the Fourteenth Amendment because the denial
of relief to those resident in the State for less than a year
is not based on any permissible purpose but is solely designed, as "Connecticut states quite frankly," "to protect
its fisc by discouraging entry of those who come needing
relief." *Id.*, at 336–337. We noted probable jurisdiction.
389 U. S. 1032 (1968).

In No. 33, there are four appellees. Three of them—
appellees Harrell, Brown, and Legrant—applied for and
were denied AFDC aid. The fourth, appellee Barley,
applied for and was denied benefits under the program
for Aid to the Permanently and Totally Disabled. The
denial in each case was on the ground that the applicant
had not resided in the District of Columbia for one year
immediately preceding the filing of her application, as
required by § 3–203 of the District of Columbia Code.[3]

• • •

The several cases were consolidated for trial, and a
three-judge District Court was convened.[4] The court,
one judge dissenting, held § 3–203 unconstitutional. 279
F. Supp. 22 (1967). The majority rested its decision on
the ground that the one-year requirement was unconstitutional as a denial of the right to equal protection
secured by the Due Process Clause of the Fifth Amendment. We noted probable jurisdiction. 390 U. S. 940
(1968).

In No. 34, there are two appellees, Smith and Foster,
who were denied AFDC aid on the sole ground that they
had not been residents of Pennsylvania for a year prior
to their applications as required by § 432 (6) of the
Pennsylvania Welfare Code. • • •

A three-judge District Court for
the Eastern District of Pennsylvania, one judge dissenting, declared § 432 (6) unconstitutional. 277 F. Supp. 65
(1967). The majority held that the classification established by the waiting-period requirement is "without
rational basis and without legitimate purpose or function"
and therefore a violation of the Equal Protection Clause.
Id., at 67. The majority noted further that if the
purpose of the statute was "to erect a barrier against
the movement of indigent persons into the State or to

effect their prompt departure after they have gotten there," it would be "patently improper and its implementation plainly impermissible." *Id.,* at 67–68. We noted probable jurisdiction. 390 U. S. 940 (1968).

There is no dispute that the effect of the waiting-period requirement in each case is to create two classes of needy resident families indistinguishable from each other except that one is composed of residents who have resided a year or more, and the second of residents who have resided less than a year, in the jurisdiction. On the basis of this sole difference the first class is granted and the second class is denied welfare aid upon which may depend the ability of the families to obtain the very means to subsist—food, shelter, and other necessities of life. In each case, the District Court found that appellees met the test for residence in their jurisdictions, as well as all other eligibility requirements except the requirement of residence for a full year prior to their applications. On reargument, appellees' central contention is that the statutory prohibition of benefits to residents of less than a year creates a classification which constitutes an invidious discrimination denying them equal protection of the laws.[6] We agree. The interests which appellants assert are promoted by the classification either may not constitutionally be promoted by government or are not compelling governmental interests.

Primarily, appellants justify the waiting-period requirement as a protective device to preserve the fiscal integrity of state public assistance programs. It is asserted that people who require welfare assistance during their first year of residence in a State are likely to become continuing burdens on state welfare programs. Therefore, the argument runs, if such people can be deterred from entering the jurisdiction by denying them welfare benefits during the first year, state programs to assist long-time residents will not be impaired by a substantial influx of indigent newcomers.[7]

There is weighty evidence that exclusion from the jurisdiction of the poor who need or may need relief was the specific objective of these provisions. In the Congress, sponsors of federal legislation to eliminate all residence requirements have been consistently opposed by representatives of state and local welfare agencies who have stressed the fears of the States that elimination of the requirements would result in a heavy influx of individuals into States providing the most generous benefits. ● ● ●

We do not doubt that the one-year waiting-period device is well suited to discourage the influx of poor families in need of assistance. An indigent who desires to migrate, resettle, find a new job, and start a new life will doubtless hesitate if he knows that he must risk making the move without the possibility of falling back on state welfare assistance during his first year of residence, when his need may be most acute. But the purpose of inhibiting migration by needy persons into the State is constitutionally impermissible.

This Court long ago recognized that the nature of our Federal Union and our constitutional concepts of personal liberty unite to require that all citizens be free to travel throughout the length and breadth of our land uninhibited by statutes, rules, or regulations which unreasonably burden or restrict this movement. ● ● ●

Thus, the purpose of deterring the in-migration of indigents cannot serve as justification for the classification created by the one-year waiting period, since that purpose is constitutionally impermissible. If a law has "no other purpose . . . than to chill the assertion of constitutional rights by penalizing those who choose to exercise them, then it [is] patently unconstitutional." *United States* v. *Jackson*, 390 U. S. 570, 581 (1968).

Alternatively, appellants argue that even if it is impermissible for a State to attempt to deter the entry of all indigents, the challenged classification may be justified as a permissible state attempt to discourage those indigents who would enter the State solely to obtain larger benefits. ● ● ●

More fundamentally, a State may no more try to fence out those indigents who seek higher welfare benefits than it may try to fence out indigents generally. Implicit in any such distinction is the notion that indigents who enter a State with the hope of securing higher welfare benefits are somehow less deserving than indigents who do not take this consideration into account. But we do not perceive why a mother who is seeking to make a new life for herself and her children should be regarded as less deserving because she considers, among others factors, the level of a State's public assistance. Surely such a mother is no less deserving than a mother who moves into a particular State in order to take advantage of its better educational facilities.

Appellants argue further that the challenged classification may be sustained as an attempt to distinguish between new and old residents on the basis of the contribution they have made to the community through the payment of taxes. We have difficulty seeing how long-term residents who qualify for welfare are making a greater present contribution to the State in taxes than indigent residents who have recently arrived. ● ● ●

In sum, neither deterrence of indigents from migrating to the State nor limitation of welfare benefits to those regarded as contributing to the State is a constitutionally permissible state objective.

Appellants next advance as justification certain administrative and related governmental objectives allegedly served by the waiting-period requirement.[12] They argue that the requirement (1) facilitates the planning of the welfare budget; (2) provides an objective test of residency; (3) minimizes the opportunity for recipients fraudulently to receive payments from more than one jurisdiction; and (4) encourages early entry of new residents into the labor force.

At the outset, we reject appellants' argument that a mere showing of a rational relationship between the waiting period and these four admittedly permissible state objectives will suffice to justify the classification. See *Lindsley* v. *Natural Carbonic Gas Co.,* 220 U. S. 61, 78 (1911); *Flemming* v. *Nestor,* 363 U. S. 603, 611 (1960); *McGowan* v. *Maryland,* 366 U. S. 420, 426 (1961). The waiting-period provision denies welfare benefits to otherwise eligible applicants solely because they have recently moved into the jurisdiction. But in moving from State to State or to the District of Columbia appellees were exercising a constitutional right, and any classification which serves to penalize the exercise of that right, unless shown to be necessary to promote a *compelling* governmental interest, is unconstitutional. Cf. *Skinner* v. *Oklahoma,* 316 U. S. 535, 541 (1942); *Korematsu* v. *United States,* 323 U. S. 214, 216 (1944); *Bates* v. *Little Rock,* 361 U. S. 516, 524 (1960); *Sherbert* v. *Verner,* 374 U. S. 398, 406 (1963).

The argument that the waiting-period requirement facilitates budget predictability is wholly unfounded. ● ● ●

The argument that the waiting period serves as an administratively efficient rule of thumb for determining residency similarly will not withstand scrutiny. ● ● ●

Similarly, there is no need for a State to use the one-year waiting period as a safeguard against fraudulent receipt of benefits;[18] for less drastic means are available, and are employed, to minimize that hazard. ●●●

Pennsylvania suggests that the one-year waiting period is justified as a means of encouraging new residents to join the labor force promptly. But this logic would also require a similar waiting period for long-term residents of the State. A state purpose to encourage employment provides no rational basis for imposing a one-year waiting-period restriction on new residents only.

We conclude therefore that appellants in these cases do not use and have no need to use the one-year requirement for the governmental purposes suggested. Thus, even under traditional equal protection tests a classification of welfare applicants according to whether they have lived in the State for one year would seem irrational and unconstitutional.[20] But, of course, the traditional criteria do not apply in these cases. Since the classification here touches on the fundamental right of interstate movement, its constitutionality must be judged by the stricter standard of whether it promotes a *compelling* state interest. Under this standard, the waiting-period requirement clearly violates the Equal Protection Clause.[21] ●●●

The waiting-period requirement in the District of Columbia Code involved in No. 33 is also unconstitutional even though it was adopted by Congress as an exercise of federal power. In terms of federal power, the discrimination created by the one-year requirement violates the Due Process Clause of the Fifth Amendment. "[W]hile the Fifth Amendment contains no equal protection clause, it does forbid discrimination that is 'so unjustifiable as to be violative of due process.'" *Schneider* v. *Rusk*, 377 U. S. 163, 168 (1964); *Bolling* v. *Sharpe*, 347 U. S. 497 (1954). For the reasons we have stated in invalidating the Pennsylvania and Connecticut provisions, the District of Columbia provision is also invalid—the Due Process Clause of the Fifth Amendment prohibits Congress from denying public assistance to poor persons otherwise eligible solely on the ground that they have not been residents of the District of Columbia for one year at the time their applications are filed.

Accordingly, the judgments in Nos. 9, 33, and 34 are

Affirmed.

(b). <u>Right to Vote</u>

<u>DUNN v. BLUMSTEIN,</u> 405 U.S. 330, 92 S. Ct. 995(1972).

MR. JUSTICE MARSHALL delivered the opinion of the Court.

Various Tennessee public officials (hereinafter Tennessee) appeal from a decision by a three-judge federal court holding that Tennessee's durational residence requirements for voting violate the Equal Protection Clause of the United States Constitution. The issue arises in a class action for declaratory and injunctive relief brought by appellee James Blumstein. Blumstein moved to Tennessee on June 12, 1970, to begin employment as an assistant professor of law at Vanderbilt University in Nashville. With an eye toward voting in the upcoming August and November elections, he attempted to register to vote on July 1, 1970. The county registrar refused to register him, on the ground that Tennessee law authorizes the registration of only those persons who, at the time of the next election, will have been residents of the State for a year and residents of the county for three months.

After exhausting state administrative remedies, Blumstein brought this action challenging these residence requirements on federal constitutional grounds.[1] A three-judge court, convened pursuant to 28 U. S. C. §§ 2281, 2284, concluded that Tennessee's durational residence requirements were unconstitutional (1) because they impermissibly interfered with the right to vote and (2) because they created a "suspect" classification penalizing some Tennessee residents because of recent interstate movement.[2] 337 F. Supp. 323 (MD Tenn. 1970). We noted probable jurisdiction, 401 U. S. 934 (1971). For the reasons that follow, we affirm the decision below.[3]

The subject of this lawsuit is the durational residence requirement. Appellee does not challenge Tennessee's power to restrict the vote to bona fide Tennessee residents. Nor has Tennessee ever disputed that appellee was a bona fide resident of the State and county when he attempted to register.[4] But Tennessee insists that, in addition to *being* a resident, a would-be voter must *have been* a resident for a year in the State and three months in the county. It is this additional *durational* residence requirement that appellee challenges.

Durational residence laws penalize those persons who have traveled from one place to another to establish a new residence during the qualifying period. Such laws divide residents into two classes, old residents and new residents, and discriminate against the latter to the extent of totally denying them the opportunity to vote.[5] The constitutional question presented is whether the Equal Protection Clause of the Fourteenth Amendment permits a State to discriminate in this way among its citizens.

To decide whether a law violates the Equal Protection Clause, we look, in essence, to three things: the character of the classification in question; the individual interests affected by the classification; and the governmental interests asserted in support of the classification. ● ● ●

In the present case, whether we look to the benefit withheld by the classification (the opportunity to vote) or the basis for the classification (recent interstate travel) we conclude that the State must show a substantial and compelling reason for imposing durational residence requirements.

Durational residence requirements completely bar from voting all residents not meeting the fixed durational standards. By denying some citizens the right to vote, such laws deprive them of " 'a fundamental political right, . . . preservative of all rights.' " *Reynolds* v. *Sims,* 377 U. S. 533, 562 (1964). ● ● ●

This "equal right to vote,"   ● ● ●   is not absolute; the States have the power to impose voter qualifications, and to regulate access to the franchise in other ways. See, *e. g., Carrington* v. *Rash, supra,* at 91; *Oregon* v. *Mitchell,* 400 U. S. 112, 144 (opinion of DOUGLAS, J.), 241 (separate opinion of BRENNAN, WHITE, and MARSHALL, JJ.), 294 (opinion of STEWART, J., concurring and dissenting, with whom BURGER, C. J., and BLACKMUN, J., joined). But, as a general matter, "before that right [to vote] can be restricted, the purpose of the restriction and the assertedly overriding interests served by it must meet close constitutional scrutiny." ● ● ●

if a chal-
lenged statute grants the right to vote to some citizens
and denies the franchise to others, "the Court must determine whether the exclusions are *necessary* to promote
a *compelling* state interest." *Id.*, at 627 (emphasis
added); *Cipriano* v. *City of Houma, supra*, at 704;
City of Phoenix v. *Kolodziejski*, 399 U. S. 204, 205, 209
(1970). Cf. *Harper* v. *Virginia Board of Elections,
supra*, at 670. This is the test we apply here.[7]

⬩ ⬩ ⬩ Tennessee's dura-
tional residence laws classify bona fide residents on the
basis of recent travel, penalizing those persons, and only
those persons, who have gone from one jurisdiction to
another during the qualifying period. Thus, the durational residence requirement directly impinges on the
exercise of a second fundamental personal right, the right
to travel. ⬩ ⬩ ⬩

Obviously,
durational residence laws single out the class of
bona fide state and county residents who have recently exercised this constitutionally protected right, and
penalize such travelers directly. We considered such a
durational residence requirement in *Shapiro* v. *Thompson,
supra*, where the pertinent statutes imposed a one-year
waiting period for interstate migrants as a condition to
receiving welfare benefits. Although in *Shapiro* we
specifically did not decide whether durational residence
requirements could be used to determine voting eligibility,
id., at 638 n. 21, we concluded that since the right to
travel was a constitutionally protected right, "any classification which serves to penalize the exercise of that right,
unless shown to be necessary to promote a *compelling*
governmental interest, is unconstitutional." ⬩ ⬩ ⬩

Tennessee attempts to distinguish *Shapiro* by urging
that "the vice of the welfare statute in *Shapiro* . . . was
its objective to deter interstate travel." Brief for Appellants 13. In Tennessee's view, the compelling-state-interest test is appropriate only where there is "some
evidence to indicate a deterrence of or infringement on
the right to travel . . . ." *Ibid.* Thus, Tennessee seeks
to avoid the clear command of *Shapiro* by arguing that
durational residence requirements for voting neither
seek to nor actually do deter such travel. In essence,
Tennessee argues that the right to travel is not abridged
here in any constitutionally relevant sense.

This view represents a fundamental misunderstanding of the law.[8] It is irrelevant whether disenfranchisement or denial of welfare is the more potent deterrent to travel. *Shapiro* did not rest upon a finding that denial of welfare actually deterred travel. Nor have other "right to travel" cases in this Court always relied on the presence of actual deterrence.[9] In *Shapiro* we explicitly stated that the compelling-state-interest test would be triggered by "any classification which serves to *penalize* the exercise of that right [to travel] . . . ." ● ●●

It is not sufficient for the State to show that durational residence requirements further a very substantial state interest. In pursuing that important interest, the State cannot choose means that unnecessarily burden or restrict constitutionally protected activity. Statutes affecting constitutional rights must be drawn with "precision," *NAACP* v. *Button,* 371 U. S. 415, 438 (1963); *United States* v. *Robel,* 389 U. S. 258, 265 (1967), and must be "tailored" to serve their legitimate objectives. *Shapiro* v. *Thompson, supra,* at 631. And if there are other, reasonable ways to achieve those goals with a lesser burden on constitutionally protected activity, a State may not choose the way of greater interference. If it acts at. all, it must choose "less drastic means." *Shelton* v. *Tucker,* 364 U. S. 479, 488 (1960).

We turn, then, to the question of whether the State has shown that durational residence requirements are needed to further a sufficiently substantial state interest.

● ● ●

Tennessee tenders "two basic purposes" served by its durational residence requirements:

> "(1) INSURE PURITY OF BALLOT BOX— Protection against fraud through colonization and inability to identify persons offering to vote, and
>
> "(2) KNOWLEDGEABLE V O T E R — Afford some surety that the voter has, in fact, become a member of the community and that as such, he has a common interest in all matters pertaining to its government and is, therefore, more likely to exercise his right more intelligently." Brief for Appellants 15, citing 18 Am. Jur., Elections, § 56, p. 217.

We·consider each in turn.

Preservation of the "purity of the ballot box" is a formidable-sounding state interest. The impurities feared, variously called "dual voting" and "colonization," all involve voting by nonresidents, either singly or in groups. The main concern is that nonresidents will temporarily invade the State or county, falsely swear that they are residents to become eligible to vote, and, by voting, allow a candidate to win by fraud. Surely the prevention of such fraud is a legitimate and compelling government goal. But it is impossible to view durational residence requirements as necessary to achieve that state interest.

Preventing fraud, the asserted evil that justifies state lawmaking, means keeping nonresidents from voting. But, by definition, a durational residence law bars *newly arrived* residents from the franchise along with non-residents. The State argues that such sweeping laws are necessary to prevent fraud because they are needed to identify bona fide residents. This contention is particularly unconvincing ● ● ●

Our conclusion that the waiting period is not the least restrictive means necessary for preventing fraud is bolstered by the recognition that Tennessee has at its disposal a variety of criminal laws that are more than adequate to detect and deter whatever fraud may be feared.[24] At least six separate sections of the Tennessee Code define offenses to deal with voter fraud. ● ● ●

The argument that durational residence requirements further the goal of having "knowledgeable voters" appears to involve three separate claims. The first is that such requirements "afford some surety that the voter has, in fact, become a member of the community." But here the State appears to confuse a bona fide residence requirement with a durational residence requirement. As already noted, a State does have an interest in limiting the franchise to bona fide members of the community. But this does not justify or explain the exclusion from the franchise of persons, not because their bona fide residence is questioned, but because they are recent rather than longtime residents.

The second branch of the "knowledgeable voters" justification is that durational residence requirements assure that the voter "has a common interest in all matters pertaining to [the community's] government . . . ." By this, presumably, the State means that it may require a period of residence sufficiently lengthy to impress upon

its voters the local viewpoint. This is precisely the sort
of argument this Court has repeatedly rejected. In
Carrington v. *Rash*, for example, the State argued that
military men newly moved into Texas might not have
local interests sufficiently in mind, and therefore could
be excluded from voting in state elections. This Court
replied:

> "But if they are in fact residents, . . . they, as all
> other qualified residents, have a right to an equal
> opportunity for political representation. . . . 'Fenc-
> ing out' from the franchise a sector of the popu-
> lation because of the way they may vote is consti-
> tutionally impermissible." 380 U. S., at 94.

See 42 U. S. C. § 1973aa–1 (a)(4).

Similarly here, Tennessee's hopes for voters with a
"common interest in all matters pertaining to [the community's] government" is impermissible.[27] To para-
phrase what we said elsewhere, "All too often, lack of a
['common interest'] might mean no more than a different interest." *Evans* v. *Cornman*, 398 U. S., at 423.

● ● ●

Finally, the State urges that a longtime resident is
"more likely to exercise his right [to vote] more intelli-
gently." To the extent that this is different from the
previous argument, the State is apparently asserting an
interest in limiting the franchise to voters who are
knowledgeable about the issues. In this case, Tennessee argues that people who have been in the State
less than a year and the county less than three months
are likely to be unaware of the issues involved in the
congressional, state, and local elections, and therefore
can be barred from the franchise. We note that the
criterion of "intelligent" voting is an elusive one, and
susceptible of abuse. But without deciding as a general
matter the extent to which a State can bar less knowledgeable or intelligent citizens from the franchise, cf.
Evans v. *Cornman*, 398 U. S., at 422; *Kramer* v. *Union
Free School District*, 395 U. S., at 632; *Cipriano* v. *City
of Houma*, 395 U. S., at 705,[29] we conclude that durational residence requirements cannot be justified on this
basis. ● ● ●
          the durational residence requirements in this
case founder because of their crudeness as a device for

achieving the articulated state goal of assuring the knowledgeable exercise of the franchise. The classifications created by durational residence requirements obviously permit any longtime resident to vote regardless of his knowledge of the issues—and obviously many longtime residents do not have any. On the other hand, the classifications bar from the franchise many other, admittedly new, residents who have become at least minimally, and often fully, informed about the issues. Indeed, recent migrants who take the time to register and vote shortly after moving are likely to be those citizens, such as appellee, who make it a point to be informed and knowledgeable about the issues.   ● ● ●

Concluding that Tennessee has not offered an adequate justification for its durational residence laws, we affirm the judgment of the court below.

Affirmed.

3.   Emergency Justification for Large-Scale Relocation

KOREMATSU v. UNITED STATES, 323 U.S. 214(1944).

MR. JUSTICE BLACK delivered the opinion of the Court.

The petitioner, an American citizen of Japanese descent, was convicted in a federal district court for remaining in San Leandro, California, a "Military Area," contrary to Civilian Exclusion Order No. 34 of the Commanding General of the Western Command, U. S. Army, which directed that after May 9, 1942, all persons of Japanese ancestry should be excluded from that area. No question was raised as to petitioner's loyalty to the United States. The Circuit Court of Appeals affirmed,[1] and the importance of the constitutional question involved caused us to grant certiorari.

It should be noted, to begin with, that all legal restrictions which curtail the civil rights of a single racial group are immediately suspect. That is not to say that all such restrictions are unconstitutional. It is to say that courts must subject them to the most rigid scrutiny. Pressing public necessity may sometimes justify the existence of such restrictions; racial antagonism never can.

In the instant case prosecution of the petitioner was begun by information charging violation of an Act of Congress, of March 21, 1942, 56 Stat. 173, which provides that

". . . whoever shall enter, remain in, leave, or commit any act in any military area or military zone prescribed, under the authority of an Executive order of the President, by the Secretary of War, or by any military commander designated by the Secretary of War, contrary to the restrictions applicable to any such area or zone or contrary to the order of the Secretary of War or any such military commander, shall, if it appears that he knew or should have known of the existence and extent of the restrictions or order and that his act was in violation thereof, be guilty of a misdemeanor and upon conviction shall be liable to a fine of not to exceed $5,000 or to imprisonment for not more than one year, or both, for each offense."

Exclusion Order No. 34, which the petitioner knowingly and admittedly violated, was one of a number of military orders and proclamations, all of which were substantially based upon Executive Order No. 9066, 7 Fed. Reg. 1407. That order, issued after we were at war with Japan, declared that "the successful prosecution of the war requires every possible protection against espionage and against sabotage to national-defense material, national-defense premises, and national-defense utilities. . . ."

One of the series of orders and proclamations, a curfew order, which like the exclusion order here was promulgated pursuant to Executive Order 9066, subjected all persons of Japanese ancestry in prescribed West Coast military areas to remain in their residences from 8 p. m. to 6 a. m. As is the case with the exclusion order here, that prior curfew order was designed as a "protection against espionage and against sabotage." In *Hirabayashi* v. *United States*, 320 U. S. 81, we sustained a conviction obtained for violation of the curfew order. The Hirabayashi conviction and this one thus rest on the same 1942 Congressional Act and the same basic executive and military orders, all of which orders were aimed at the twin dangers of espionage and sabotage. ● ● ●

In the light of the principles we announced in the *Hirabayashi* case, we are unable to conclude that it was beyond the war power of Congress and the Executive to exclude those of Japanese ancestry from the West Coast war area at the time they did. True, exclusion from the area in which one's home is located is a far greater deprivation than constant confinement to the home from 8 p. m. to 6 a. m. Nothing short of apprehension by the proper military authorities of the gravest imminent danger to the public safety can constitutionally justify either. But exclusion from a threatened area, no less than curfew, has a definite and close relationship to the prevention of espionage and sabotage. The military authorities, charged with the primary responsibility of defending our shores, concluded that curfew provided inadequate protection and ordered exclusion. They did so, as pointed out in our *Hirabayashi* opinion, in accordance with Congressional authority to the military to say who should, and who should not, remain in the threatened areas.

In this case the petitioner challenges the assumptions upon which we rested our conclusions in the *Hirabayashi* case. He also urges that by May 1942, when Order No. 34 was promulgated, all danger of Japanese invasion of the West Coast had disappeared. After careful consideration of these contentions we are compelled to reject them.

● ● ●

Like curfew, exclusion of those of Japanese origin was deemed necessary because of the presence of an unascertained number of disloyal members of the group, most of whom we have no doubt were loyal to this country. It was because we could not reject the finding of the military authorities that it was impossible to bring about an immediate segregation of the disloyal from the loyal that we sustained the validity of the curfew order as applying to the whole group. In the instant case, temporary exclusion of the entire group was rested by the military on the same ground. The judgment that exclusion of the whole group was for the same reason a military imperative answers the contention that the exclusion was in the nature of group punishment based on antagonism to those of Japanese origin. ● ● ●

We uphold the exclusion order as of the time it was made and when the petitioner violated it. Cf. *Chastleton Corporation* v. *Sinclair*, 264 U. S. 543, 547; *Block* v. *Hirsh*, 256 U. S. 135, 154–5. In doing so, we are not unmindful of the hardships imposed by it upon a large group of American citizens. Cf. *Ex parte Kawato*, 317 U. S. 69, 73. But hardships are part of war, and war is an aggregation of hardships. All citizens alike, both in and out of uniform, feel the impact of war in greater or lesser measure. Citizenship has its responsibilities as well as its privileges, and in time of war the burden is always heavier. Compulsory exclusion of large groups of citizens from their homes, except under circumstances of direst emergency and peril, is inconsistent with our basic governmental institutions. But when under conditions of modern warfare our shores are threatened by hostile forces, the power to protect must be commensurate with the threatened danger. ● ● ●

It is said that we are dealing here with the case of imprisonment of a citizen in a concentration camp solely because of his ancestry, without evidence or inquiry concerning his loyalty and good disposition towards the United States. Our task would be simple, our duty clear, were this a case involving the imprisonment of a loyal citizen in a concentration camp because of racial prejudice. Regardless of the true nature of the assembly and relocation centers—and we deem it unjustifiable to call them concentration camps with all the ugly connotations that term implies—we are dealing specifically with nothing but an exclusion order. To cast this case into outlines of racial prejudice, without reference to the real military dangers which were presented, merely confuses the issue. Korematsu was not excluded from the Military Area because of hostility to him or his race. He *was* excluded because we are at war with the Japanese Empire, because the properly constituted military authorities feared an invasion of our West Coast and felt constrained to take proper security measures, because they decided that the military urgency of the situation demanded that all citizens of Japanese ancestry be segregated from the West Coast temporarily, and finally, because Congress, reposing its confidence in this time of war in our military leaders—as inevitably it must—determined that they should have the power to do just this. There was evidence of disloyalty on the part of some, the military authorities considered that the need for action was great, and time was short. We cannot—by availing ourselves of the calm perspective of hindsight— now say that at that time these actions were unjustified.

Affirmed.

● ● ●

Mr. Justice Roberts.

I dissent, because I think the indisputable facts exhibit a clear violation of Constitutional rights.

GARRETT v. CITY OF HAMTRAMCK, 357 F. Supp. 925 (E.D. Mich. 1973).

KEITH, District Judge.

After an extensive trial, this Court found in its opinion of November 22, 1971, 335 F.Supp. 16 (D.C.1971), that the defendants have intentionally planned and implemented a series of urban renewal projects and other government programs designed to remove a substantial portion of Black citizens from the city, in violation of plaintiffs' federal statutory and constitutional rights. Pursuant to that opinion, the Court ordered the parties to submit a proposed program designed to remedy the wrongs suffered and continuing to be suffered by virtue of defendants' conduct.

Having studied the submissions of the parties, and held hearings with respect thereto, the Court makes the following Findings of Fact in addition to those in its opinion of November 22, 1971:

1. Defendants' past actions have intentionally and unlawfully displaced at least 467 to 556 housing units occupied by Black familes and individuals.

● ● ●

2. Defendants' ongoing urban renewal activities (and other official activities related thereto) will soon be responsible for displacing at least 497 to 508 additional housing units, for which adequate replacement housing must be found. ● ● ●

3. Approximately 600 of these units (described in paragraphs 1 and 2) have been or now are occupied by low and moderate income families eligible for housing subsidies under 12 U.S.C. § 1701 et seq. and 42 U.S.C. § 1401 et seq.

4. No more than 25% of these units (described in paragraphs 1 and 2) have been or are being occupied by the elderly.

5. The 964 to 1,064 housing units needed to accommodate this displaced population should consist of approximately 50% one-bedroom, 25% two-bedroom, 15% three-bedroom, 7% four-bedroom, and 3% five-bedroom units.

6. Because of the extremely low vacancy rate and the racially discriminatory and closed nature of the Hamtramck real estate market, these 964 to 1,064 replacement housing units cannot be obtained from the present private housing market in the City of Hamtramck.

7. Consistent with good planning, at least 430–440 housing units can be built in the Wyandotte (R–31) area, and at least 100–120 housing units can be built on a site located along the extreme northeastern corner of the city between Alpena Avenue and the corporate boundary line. Very few additional housing units can be newly built in Hamtramck without clearance of existing structures.

8. For the reasons set forth in paragraph 6, the 404–534 replacement units which will be needed in addition to those constructed in the Wyandotte (R–31) and Alpena Avenue areas cannot be obtained from the present private housing market in the City of Hamtramck unless the following specific measures are taken: (a) implementation of a system to give public notice of all the residences offered for rent or sale in Hamtramck; (b) clarification of the acts which constitute discrimination under the Hamtramck Fair Housing Ordinance; (c) elimination of various exemptions from said Ordinance which presently make it ineffective; (d) implementation of a system whereby all homeowners in Hamtramck who move into new units in the Wyandotte or Alpena areas give a first option on their present homes, at a fair price, either to displacees or to the City for rehabilitation and/or resale to displacees; (e) implementation of a system which assures that when displacees who are eligible for government housing subsidies request assistance in finding a home, City officials will accompany them to inspect homes for sale or rent, and will acquaint the owners or landlords with the various applicable government subsidy programs which guaranty certain

purchase or rental payments.

9. Unless there are certain rezonings, elimination of variances, and prohibitions against demolition, industrial expansion will continue to eliminate residential units in Hamtramck which are vital to maintaining the housing supply available to the plaintiff displacees.

10. Many eligible displacees will not be able to learn about and respond to their opportunity for housing in Hamtramck, pursuant to this Court's Order, unless there is an affirmative marketing strategy by which every reasonable effort is made to notify displacees personally and afford them all an equal opportunity to apply for the available housing units.

11. Many displacees will not be able to afford to move back to take advantage of their housing opportunity in Hamtramck unless they receive adequate moving expenses and other relocation payments.

In view of all the above, the Court finds that the following provisions of this Order are individually and collectively necessary to remedy the unlawful actions of defendants. Therefore,

It is hereby ordered:

I. Defendants City of Hamtramck and its officials ("city") and U.S. Department of Housing and Urban Development and its officials ("HUD") shall, after consultation with plaintiffs, design and implement an amended renewal plan for the Wyandotte Area of Hamtramck. Under such plan, the Wyandotte Area shall be devoted to maximum residential use, consistent with sound urban planning, so as to provide a source of adequate relocation housing for those individuals ("displacees") who have been and are to be displaced from their homes by urban renewal projects, and by other actions of defendants found unlawful by this Court's opinion of November 22, 1971.[1] ● ● ●

C. If, in administering the plan, any quotas or administrative guidelines with regard to demographic makeup of tenants eligible for publicly subsidized housing programs shall conflict with maximum use of Wyandotte for displacees, defendants shall adjust or waive such quotas or guidelines. ● ● ●

E. To the extent that the Wyandotte renewal plan may conflict with any zoning ordinances, these ordinances shall be deemed inapplicable to the extent of any such inconsistency. ● ● ●

II. Since the new units to be constructed in Wyandotte will fall far short of the number needed to accommodate the displacees, defendants shall, in consultation with plaintiffs, design and implement a plan for the seven-acre tract of land located along the extreme northeastern corner of Hamtramck between Alpena Avenue and the corporate boundary line (hereafter, the "Alpena area"). Defendants shall begin land acquisition in this area immediately, through condemnation if necessary. The plan to be developed shall utilize at least four acres of the Alpena area for residential purposes and shall provide for construction of at least 100 units. ● ● ●

III. All individuals or families who wish to rent or purchase units in the Wyandotte or Alpena areas, and who own a home in Hamtramck, shall be required, as a condition of applying for entry into the subsidized Wyandotte or Alpena developments, to sign an agreement to offer their home for sale to any willing purchaser (including the Hamtramck Housing Commission) referred by the city's relocation officials; provided, however, that (1) in no event shall the owner be obliged to accept a lesser price for his home from a purchaser referred by city relocation officials than he is offered in good faith by another bidder who does not come through relocation channels; and provided, further, that (2) the owner's obligation to give the city or displacees this "first option" shall terminate if no willing purchaser has come forward through this channel, and is prepared to close the transaction, by the date on which the owner is permitted (by his rental or purchase agreement) to move into the Wyandotte or Alpena housing unit.

● ● ●

IV. In order to make known to displacees the housing and benefits available pursuant to this Court's Order, defendants shall retain the services of an established private research and interviewing firm to design the details and carry out the mechanics of a notification process. This process shall comply with all the minimum requirements of a relocation assistance advisory program, as contained in 24 C.F.R. §§ 42.100–42.115 (1972) and Act No. 227, Mich.Public Acts of 1972, § 3; and, in addition, shall contain the following essential elements:

A. Periodic notices, over sustained periods of time, in the newspapers and radio stations directed especially at the Black community in the Metropolitan Detroit Area, as well as in the other, more widely received newspapers, radio, and television stations;

B. A sustained effort to trace all displacees and make personal visits to their present homes, at a time convenient to each displacee, in order to explain thoroughly the relocation opportunities, answer all questions, and fill out application forms; ● ● ●

V. In order to choose from among eligible applicants for housing units made available pursuant to this Court's Order in Wyandotte, Alpena, or in units acquired by defendants from the existing housing stock, under Part III of this Order or otherwise, defendants shall establish objective rules of priority which shall provide that:

A. All eligible displacees shall share a first and equal priority as to units made available at each stage or section of development of Wyandotte or Alpena. Units from the existing housing stock, obtained by defendants pursuant to Part III of this Order or otherwise, shall be deemed part of whatever section of Wyandotte or Alpena is then available for applications. If no such section is

then available, these units will be deemed a separate "section" for purposes of application priorities.

B. To the greatest extent possible, personal notice shall be given to all displacees, wherever located, as each section is opened for applications. ● ● ●

F. Administration - of this priority system shall be on a nondiscriminatory basis—to be judged, in part, by the extent of the defendants' affirmative efforts to locate Black displacees and facilitate their participation in the system for providing relocation housing units.

G. If any of the new units in a particular development section have not been taken by eligible displacees within 30 days of the date such units are ready for occupancy (see "B" above), they shall be offered to the general public— consistent with the guidelines governing the particular HUD subsidy program under which the units have been financed. ● ● ●

VI. The defendants shall initiate a thorough study and review of the residential potential of the Grand Haven area[3] to determine whether it may appropriately be used to provide relocation housing for displacees, and otherwise be developed for improved residential use. In order to preserve the status quo during this study: ● ● ●

VII. In order to preserve the desirable residential character of areas where industrial expansion threatens to destroy further housing units needed to effectuate this Court's Order, defendants shall rezone to category R–2, permitting two-family dwellings, the following areas: ● ● ●

VIII. Until the relocation housing requirements of all eligible displacees have been met, defendants are hereby enjoined from taking any action (e. g., through condemnation, acquisition, or issuance of demolition permits), which will facilitate the elimination of housing units in the city, unless a corresponding number of new units (in addition to those built pursuant to Parts I and II of this Order) are provided within the city.

IX. In order to break down the pervasive pattern of private discrimination within the tightly closed Hamtramck housing market, defendant city shall amend its open housing ordinance, Hamtramck, Mich.Ord.No. 347 (1972), in a manner which will permit the application of the ordinance to a significant percentage of real estate transactions in Hamtramck and assure that all who seek housing in Hamtramck will have an equal opportunity to learn about and gain access to any available housing. The current Hamtramck open housing ordinance is hereby declared insufficient to accomplish those ends or to comply with this Court's prior order of November 22, 1971. ● ● ●

X. In order to assure that displacees obtain access on a nondiscriminatory basis to the existing private housing market in Hamtramck, defendants shall establish a procedure whereby relocation and/or public housing officials, as appropriate, (a) will accompany displacees who wish to inspect Hamtramck housing units offered for rent or sale on the open market, (b) will attempt to persuade the owner to rent or sell the unit to the displacee (on a nondiscriminatory basis); and (c) if the displacee is eligible for public housing, attempt to persuade the owner to rent or sell the unit under the applicable federal or state leased housing or acquisition program, for the benefit of low-income families.

XI. As a matter of providing complete equitable relief, in order to assure that displacees can take advantage of the relocation housing made available by this Order, defendants shall jointly adopt procedures and provide funds for adequate moving expenses and other relocation payments to displacees. ● ● ●

XII. The defendants shall assume responsibility for assuring that all displacees who are living in substandard units and express a desire to relocate, but who cannot find suitable relocation housing in Hamtramck, under the provisions of this Order or otherwise, will be provided with decent, safe, and sanitary housing in Detroit or elsewhere in the Metropolitan Area, in accordance with the criteria and provisions of 42 U.S.C.A. §§ 4625(c)(3) and 4626(a) (Supp.1972); 24 C.F.R. § 42.120 (1972) and 37 Fed. Reg. 14768 (1972); and will be provided with the relocation payments proposed for all displacees in Part XI, *supra*.

XIII. This Court shall retain jurisdiction over this matter for the entry of such further orders as may be appropriate to effectuate the provisions of this Order.

5.   New Town Development

HOUSING AND URBAN DEVELOPMENT ACT OF 1970, 1 U.S. Congr. & Adm. News '70 2098, P.L. 91-609, 84 STAT. 1770.

FINDINGS AND PURPOSE

SEC. 710. (a) The Congress finds that this Nation is likely to experience during the remaining years of this century a population increase of about seventy-five million persons.

(b) The Congress further finds that continuation of established patterns of urban development, together with the anticipated increase in population, will result in (1) inefficient and wasteful use of land resources which are of national economic and environmental importance; (2) destruction of irreplaceable natural and recreational resources and increasing pollution of air and water; (3) diminished opportunity for the private homebuilding industry to operate at its highest potential capacity in providing good housing needed to serve the expanding population and to replace substandard housing; (4) costly and inefficient public facilities and services at all levels of government; (5) unduly limited options for many of our people as to where they may live, and the types of housing and environment in which they may live; (6) failure to make the most economic use of present and potential resources of many of the Nation's smaller cities and towns, including those in rural and economically depressed areas, and decreasing employment and business opportunities for their residents; (7) further lessening of employment and business opportunities for the residents of central cities and of the ability of such cities to retain a tax base adequate to support vital services for all their citizens, particularly the poor and disadvantaged; (8) further separation of people within metropolitan areas by income and by race; (9) further increases in the distances between the places where people live and where they work and find recreation; and (10) increased cost and decreased effectiveness of public and private facilities for urban transportation.

(c) The Congress further finds that better patterns of urban development and revitalization are essential to accommodate future population growth; to prevent further deterioration of the Nation's physical and social environment; and to make positive contributions to improving the overall quality of life within the Nation.

(d) The Congress further finds that the national welfare requires the encouragement of well-planned, diversified, and economically sound new communities, including major additions to existing communities, as one of several essential elements of a consistent national program for bettering patterns of development and renewal.

(e) The Congress further finds that desirable new community development on a significant national scale has been prevented by difficulties in (1) obtaining adequate financing at moderate cost for enterprises which involve large initial capital investment, extensive periods before investment can be returned, and irregular patterns of return; (2) the timely assembly of sufficiently large sites in economically favorable locations at reasonable cost: and (3) making necessary arrangements, among all private and public organizations involved, for providing site and related improvements (including streets, sewer and water facilities, and other public and community facilities) in a timely and coordinated manner.

(f) It is, therefore, the purpose of this part to provide private developers and State and local public bodies and agencies (including regional or metropolitan public bodies and agencies) with financial and other assistance necessary for encouraging the orderly development of well-planned, diversified, and economically sound new communities, including major additions to existing communities, and to do so in a manner which will rely to the maximum extent on private enterprise; strengthen the capacity of State and local governments to deal with local problems; preserve and enhance both the natural and urban environment; increase for all persons, particularly members of minority groups, the available choices of locations for living and working, thereby providing a more just economic and social environment; encourage the fullest utilization of the economic potential of older central cities, smaller towns, and rural communities; assist in the efficient production of a steady supply of residential, commercial, and industrial building sites at reasonable cost; increase the capability of all segments of the home-building industry, including both small and large producers, to utilize improved technology in producing the large volume of well-designed, inexpensive housing needed to accommodate population growth; help create neighborhoods designed for easier access between the places where people live and the places where they work and find recreation; and encourage desirable innovation in meeting domestic problems whether physical, economic, or social. It is also the purpose of this part to improve the organizational capacity of the Federal Government to carry out programs of assistance for the development of new communities and the revitalization of the Nation's urban areas.

See: Sections 711-729, 1 U.S. Congr. & Adm. News '70 2098

. . . .

See: Comment, "The Right to Travel: Another Constitutional Standard for Local Land Use Regulations," 39 U. Chi. L. Rev. 612(1972).

Miller & Davidson, "Observations on Population Policy-Making and the Constitution," 40 Geo. Wash. L. Rev. 618(1972).

Driver, "Population Policies of State Government in the United States: Some Preliminary Observations," 15 Vill. L. Rev. 818(1970).

Montgomery, "The Population Explosion and the United States Law," 22 Hastings L.J. 629(1971).

Rose, "New Directions in Planning Law: A Review of the 1972-1973 Judicial Decisions," J. American Inst. Planners (July, 1974).

A. Pesticides

1. Procedure to Determine Safe Tolerance

ENVIRONMENTAL DEFENSE FUND, INC. v. FINCH, 428
F.2d 1083 (C.A.D.C. 1970).

J. SKELLY WRIGHT, Circuit Judge:

The pesticide DDT has been one of the most widely used chemicals to control various insect populations and to protect agricultural crops from destruction by insects. Recent scientifc studies have, however, raised serious questions about the effect on the environment and on human health of the continued use of DDT. ● ● ●

On the basis of these recent studies, petitioners [2] here filed a petition with the Secretary of Health, Education and Welfare, under applicable statutory provisions,[3] proposing that the Secretary establish a "zero tolerance" for DDT residues in or on raw agricultural commodities. The Secretary rejected the petition as legally insufficient since petitioners had not shown any "practicable method" of removing the residues of the persistent pesticide DDT from raw agricultural commodities. Consequently, he refused to publish petitioners' proposal in the Federal Register, an action which would have triggered a series of informal and formal administrative procedures, including study of the proposal by a specially appointed committee of scientists and formal administrative hearings open to all interested parties.[4]

In this court, petitioners urge that the Secretary's order refusing to publish their proposal should be reversed on two grounds. First, they argue that their petition, properly interpreted, met all the statutory requirements, including that of "practicability." Second, they urge that the 1958 amendment to the Food, Drug and Cosmetic Act, which requires the Secretary to ban any food additive which is found to induce cancer in experimental animals (the Delaney amendment),[5] must

be read to require the Secretary not merely to publish their proposal but to establish the "zero tolerance" forthwith.

At the outset, we reject respondents' position that any action by HEW on petitioners' proposal must await action, in the first instance, by the Department of Agriculture. The federal government regulates the use of pesticides through two statutes, the Food, Drug and Cosmetic Act [6] (FDCA), administered by the Secretary of HEW, and the Federal Insecticide, Fungicide and Rodenticide Act [7] (FIFRA), administered by the Secretary of Agriculture.

FIFRA regulates the shipment of pesticides, called "economic poisons," in interstate commerce. Under the provisions of that Act, every economic poison marketed in interstate commerce must be registered. To be registered, an economic poison must meet certain requirements relating to labeling, agricultural usefulness, and safety. These requirements apply to all pesticides, whether or not used on food crops. FDCA regulates pesticides only to the extent of controlling the residue of a pesticide which can safely remain in or on raw agricultural commodities. ● ● ● the Secretary of HEW is authorized to establish maximum permissible amounts, called tolerances, for pesticide residues; if the pesticide residue is below the tolerance, the commodity is not considered "adulterated." 21 U.S.C. § 346a.

The heart of the regulatory scheme lies in the establishment of these tolerances. Without detailing the elaborate procedures involved, we note that the Act provides two general commands to the Secretary of HEW in establishing tolerances. First, the Act directs the Secretary of HEW to establish tolerances "to the extent necessary to protect the public health." 21 U.S.C. § 346a(b). In making this judgment, the Secretary is required by the Act to consider the necessity for an adequate food supply, other ways in which the consumer might be affected by the same pesticide, and the opinion of the Secretary of Agriculture as to the agricultural usefulness of the pesticide involved. *Ibid.* Second, the general instruction to establish tolerances is modified by the authorization to establish a zero tolerance—a ban on any residue at all—"if the scientific data before the Secretary does not justify the establishment of a greater tolerance." *Ibid.* In the words of both Senate and House Reports on this legislation:

"Before any pesticide-chemical residue may remain in or on a raw agricultural commodity, scientific data must be presented to show that the pesticide-chemical residue is safe from the standpoint of the food consumer. The burden is on the person proposing the tolerance or exemption to establish the safety of such pesticide-chemical residue." [8]

While it is obvious that the responsibilities of the two Secretaries are interrelated and ought to be coordinated, we think their individual responsibilities are quite clear and quite separate. The Secretary of HEW is given the primary responsibility for determining the amount of residue of a pesticide which can safely—from the viewpoint of the food consumer—be left on raw agricultural commodities. It is true that in establishing a tolerance the Secretary of HEW must take into account the Agriculture Secretary's opinion regarding the agricultural usefulness of the pesticide, but that is only one of many factors which HEW must consider. In our judgment, the Act's language requires that HEW make its own independent judgment, based on public health considerations, as to the tolerance which should be set for pesticide residues on raw agricultural commodities and not abdicate its responsibility to the Department of Agriculture. [9]

Respondents suggest, however, that the problem posed by DDT's "persistence" somehow alters these basic responsibilities. They argue that, as a result of DDT's persistence, DDT remains in the air, water and soil for a sufficient length of time to be carried over from season to season and from one crop to another. As a result, according to this argument, DDT must first be deregistered by Agriculture, and the chemical allowed to gradually disappear, before HEW can reasonably enact zero tolerances. We note in passing that this argument would apparently mean that HEW would *never* have to act since, according to the argument's premise, DDT would have disappeared.

But, in any event, we do not see how the fact that there is a new, and quite difficult, dimension present in any decision to revise present DDT tolerances operates to relieve HEW of its statutory responsibility. DDT's persistence will obviously affect any action taken by HEW; in all probability it will require that agency to bring creativity and imagination to bear in the search for a workable solution to the problem. ● ● ●

One of the strengths of administrative agencies has always been thought to be the expertise which reposes in specialized administrators. [12] Presumably that was one of the reasons Congress thought it wise to divide responsibilities for different aspects of pesticide regulation between the Departments of Agriculture and HEW: each has a particular specialty and focus. For either department to relinquish its responsibility would destroy the regulatory scheme enacted by Congress. Consequently, we believe that HEW had and continues to have a responsibility to appraise the continuing safety of pesticide tolerance levels; it should, of course, continue to coordinate its operations with the Department of Agriculture, as it presently does. But it may not relinquish or evade its own responsibilities.

The Commissioner of Food and Drugs, acting as the delegate of the Secretary of HEW, rejected petitioners' petition on the ground that it did not satisfy Section 408(d) (1) (E) of the FDCA, 21 U.S.C. § 346a(d) (1) (E), which requires data showing "practicable methods for removing residue which exceeds any proposed tolerance." [13] This alleged deficiency also derives from·the fact that DDT is a "persistent" pesticide, i. e., it does not decay quickly, but remains in its toxic form in the environment (and increasingly in human bodies) for a period of years. Thus even if all applications of DDT were to cease tomorrow, substantial and detectable residues of DDT would apparently continue to exist in many raw agricultural commodities. Under these circumstances, establishing a zero tolerance for DDT on all commodities, effective immediately, would mean that a substantial proportion of food in the United States would still be "adulterated" within the meaning of the FDCA.

In their supplement to their petition, however, petitioners made clear that they were not seeking this infeasible, major disruption of the country's food supply. Specifically, they suggested:

"* * * At a minimum, the Secretary should establish a zero tolerance for DDT and its residues on all raw agricultural commodities with the possible exemption from seizure of any commodities in which it can be established that any residues are the consequence of applications of DDT that were made prior to the announcement by the Secretary of the zero tolerance."

This is certainly one possible solution leading to the gradual elimination of a persistent pesticide from the environment.

In any event, we think HEW's emphasis on the "practicability" requirement is seriously misplaced, as disclosed by the most cursory examination of the legislative history of the provision.

• • •

In our judgment, the Commissioner of Food and Drugs failed to apply a "rule of reason" in assessing·the present petition. Instead of publishing petitioners' proposal, which would begin an administrative process designed to bring forth constructive alternatives for dealing with an admittedly difficult but vitally important problem, the Commissioner chose to stop petitioners at the door. Moreover, he chose to rely on a requirement which cannot be applied literally to the present case. Everyone agrees that there is no way to remove DDT from the environment *immediately*. The questions to be answered are how great is the present danger and what steps ought to be taken immediately in response to that danger.

These are basically matters for exploration and judgment which in the last analysis will rest with HEW. • • •

The administrative process, the process which Congress intended to focus on and illuminate these problems, has not been permitted to begin. In our view, the petition does comply with all statutory prerequisites, and this case must, therefore, be remanded to the Secretary of HEW with directions to file petitioners' proposal and to publish it in the Federal Register, as provided in 21 U.S.C. § 346a(d) (1).

Petitioners here argue that any remand order should not permit the Secretary to consider "whether it is appropriate to continue, for any period of time, using DDT; rather, the Secretary should consider only the solution that should be implemented to afford the consuming public the greatest possible protection from continued exposure to that cancer-producing poison." Petitioners contend that this result is compelled by 21 U.S.C. § 348(c) (3) (A), the so-called Delaney amendment, which requires the Secretary to ban any *food additive* which has been found to cause cancer in experimental animals.[17] Since we have decided that a remand is necessary, we think it appropriate to indicate our views on this question.

Several related events which occurred in the late 1950's form the basis for petitioners' argument that the Delaney amendment, or at least the principle it embodies, applies to pesticide chemicals. • • •

While we agree that these events are not without legal significance, we do not think the Delaney anticancer·amendment can be held to apply full force to pesticide chemicals. • • •

On remand, therefore, the Secretary must consider the scientific evidence presented and determine whether continued tolerances for DDT are consistent with the intent of Congress.[27] If the evidence demonstrates that DDT is a carcinogen and the Secretary proposes to continue in effect any DDT tolerances on raw agricultural commodities, he would, of course, be required to explain the basis on which he determined such tolerances to be "safe."

The petition for review is granted, the order of the Secretary of HEW is reversed, and the case is remanded with instructions to publish petitioners' proposal in the Federal Register and commence the administrative process contemplated by the provisions of the Food, Drug and Cosmetic Act.

So ordered.

. . . .

For a discussion of environmental toxicants in general, including pesticides and radio-active materials see Yannacone & Cohen, Environmental Rights and Remedies Sec. 8:4.

For additional information see:

1. Merta, The Complete Handbook of Pesticides (1972).

2. Watt, (ed.) Systems Analysis in Ecology (1966).

3. Patten, (ed.) Systems Analysis and Simulation in Ecology (1971).

4. Toxic Substances, (Council on Environmental Quality, 1971).

2. Federal Insecticide, Fungicide, and Rodenticide Act, 7 U.S.C. sec. 135 et seq. (1964)

(a). Definition of "economic poison"

§ 135. Definitions.

For the purposes of sections 135 to 135k of this title—

(a) The term "economic poison" means (1) any substance or mixture of substances intended for preventing, destroying, repelling, or mitigating any insects, rodents, nematodes, fungi, weeds, and other forms of plant or animal life or viruses, except viruses on or in living man or other animals, which the Secretary shall declare to be a pest, and (2) any substance or mixture of substances intended for use as a plant regulator, defoliant or desiccant.

. . . .

(b). Prohibition of Misbranding of Economic Poisons

§ 135a. Prohibited acts.

(a) It shall be unlawful for any person to distribute, sell, or offer for sale in any Territory or in the District of Columbia, or to ship or deliver for shipment from any State, Territory, or the District of Columbia. to any other State, Territory, or the District of Columbia, or to any foreign country, or to receive in any State, Territory, or the District of Columbia from any other State, Territory or the District of Columbia, or foreign country, and having so received, deliver or offer to deliver in the original unbroken package to any other person, any of the following:

(1) Any economic poison which is not registered pursuant to the provisions of section 135b of this title, or any economic poison if any of the claims made for it or any of the directions for its use differ in substance from the representations made in connection with its registration, or if the composition of an economic poison differs from its composition as represented in connection with its registration: *Provided,* That in the discretion of the Administrator, a change in the labeling or formula of an economic poison may be made within a registration period without requiring re-registration of the product.

. . . .

(c). Registration of Economic Poisons

§ 135b. Registration of economic poisons.

(a) General requirement; single economic poisons; supplement statements; filing and contents of statements.

Every economic poison which is distributed, sold, or offered for sale in any Territory or the District of Columbia, or which is shipped or delivered for shipment from any State, Territory, or the District of Columbia to any other State, Territory, or the District of Columbia, or which is received from any foreign country shall be registered with the Administrator: *Provided,* That products which have the same formula, are manufactured by the same person, the labeling of which contains the same claims, and the labels of which bear a designation identifying the product as the same economic poison may be registered as a single economic poison; and additional names and labels shall be added by supplement statements; the applicant for registration shall file with the Administrator a statement including—

(1) the name and address of the applicant for registration and the name and address of the person whose name will appear on the label, if other than the applicant for registration;

(2) the name of the economic poison;

(3) a complete copy of the labeling accompanying the economic poison and a statement of all claims to be made for it, including the directions for use; and

(4) if requested by the Administrator, a full description of the tests made and the results thereof upon which the claims are based.

(d). Unlawful Acts

See: section 135a(a) at VI., A.2b., supra

(3) Any economic poison which contains any substance or substances in quantities highly toxic to man, determined as provided in section 135d of this title, unless the label shall bear, in addition to any other matter required by sections 135 to 135k of this title—

(a) the skull and crossbones;

(b) the word "poison" prominently (IN RED) on a background of distinctly contrasting color; and

(c) a statement of an antidote for the economic poison.

. . . .

(e). Penalties

i. Civil Penalties

§ 135g. Seizures; disposition; costs against claimant.

(a) Any economic poison or device that is being transported from one State, Territory, or District to another, or, having been transported, remains unsold or in original unbroken packages, or that is sold or offered for sale in the District of Columbia or any Territory, or that is imported from a foreign country, shall be liable to be proceeded against in any district court of the United States in the district where it is found and seized for confiscation by a process of libel for condemnation—

(1) in the case of an economic poison—

(a) if it is adulterated or misbranded;

(b) if it is not registered pursuant to the provisions of section 135b of this title;

(c) if it fails to bear on its label the information required by sections 135 to 135k of this title; or

(d) if it is a white powder economic poison and is not colored as required under said sections; or

(2) in the case of a device if it is misbranded.

(b) If the article is condemned it shall, after entry of the decree, be disposed of by destruction or sale as the court may direct and the proceeds, if sold, less the legal costs, shall be paid into the Treasury of the United States, but the article shall not be sold contrary to the provisions of sections 135 to 135k of this title or of the laws of the jurisdiction in which it is sold: *Provided,* That upon the payment of the costs of the libel proceedings and the execution and delivery of a good and sufficient bond conditioned that the article shall not be sold or otherwise disposed of contrary to the provisions of said sections or the laws of any State, Territory, or District in which sold, the court may direct that such articles be delivered to the owner thereof. The proceedings of such libel cases shall conform, as near as may be, to the proceedings in admiralty, except that either party may demand trial by jury of any issue of fact joined in any case, and all such proceedings shall be at the suit of and in the name of the United States.

(c) When a decree of condemnation is entered against the article, court costs and fees, storage, and other proper expenses shall be awarded against the person, if any, intervening as claimant of the article. • • •

§ 135h. Imports; prohibition against delivery; penal bonds; imposition of costs; liens.

The Secretary of the Treasury shall notify the Administrator of the arrival of economic poisons and devices offered for importation and shall deliver to the Administrator, upon his request, samples of economic poisons or devices which are being imported or offered for import into the United States, giving notice to the owner or consignee, who may appear before the Administrator and have the right to introduce testimony. If it appears from the examination of a sample that it is adulterated, or misbranded or otherwise violates the prohibitions set forth in sections 135 to 135k of this title, or is otherwise dangerous to the health of the people of the United States, or is of a kind forbidden entry into or forbidden to be sold or restricted in sale in the country in which it is made or from which it is exported, the said article may be refused admission, and the Secretary of the Treasury shall refuse delivery to the consignee and shall cause the destruction of any goods refused delivery which shall not be exported by the consignee within three months from the date of notice of such refusal under such regulations as the Secretary of the Treasury may prescribe: *Provided,* That the Secretary of the Treasury may deliver to the consignee such goods pending examination and decision in the matter on execution of a penal bond for the amount of the full invoice value of such goods, together with the duty thereon, and on refusal to return such goods for any cause to the custody of the Secretary of the Treasury, when demanded, for the purpose of excluding them from the country, or for any other purpose, said consignee shall forfeit the full amount of the bond: *And provided further,* That all charges for storage, cartage, and labor on goods which are refused admission or delivery shall be paid by the owner or consignee, and in default of such payment shall constitute a lien against any future importation made by such owner or consignee. • • •

ii. Criminal Penalties

§ 135f. Penalties.

(a) Any person violating section 135a (a) (1) of this title shall be guilty of a misdemeanor and shall on conviction be fined not more than $1,000.

(b) Any person violating any provision other than section 135a (a) (1) of this title shall be guilty of a misdemeanor and shall upon conviction be fined not more than $500 for the first offense, and on conviction for each subsequent offense be fined not more than $1,000 or imprisoned for not more than one year, or both such fine and imprisonment: *Provided,* That an offense committed more than five years after the last previous conviction shall be considered a first offense. An article the registration of which has been terminated may not again be registered unless the article, its labeling, and other material required to be submitted appear to the Administrator to comply with all the requirements of sections 135 to 135k of this title.

(c) Notwithstanding any other provision of this section, in case any person, with intent to defraud, uses or reveals information relative to formulas of products acquired under the authority of section 135b of this title, he shall be fined not more than $10,000 or imprisoned for not more than three years, or both such fine and imprisonment.

. . . .

3. Federal Food, Drug and Costmetic Act, 21 U.S.C.A. sec. 342 et seq. (1964).

(a). Definition of "adulterated"

§ 342. Adulterated food

A food shall be deemed to be adulterated—

Poisonous, insanitary, etc., ingredients

(a) (1) If it bears or contains any poisonous or deleterious substance which may render it injurious to health; but in case the substance is not an added substance such food shall not be considered adulterated under this clause if the quantity of such substance in such food does not ordinarily render it injurious to health; or (2) (A) if it bears or contains any added poisonous or added deleterious substance (other than one which is (i) a pesticide chemical in or on a raw agricultural commodity; (ii) a food additive; (iii) a color additive; or (iv) a new animal drug) which is unsafe within the meaning of section 346 of this title, or (B) if it is a raw agricultural commodity and it bears or contains a pesticide chemical which is unsafe within the meaning of section 346a(a) of this title, or (C) if it is, or it bears or contains, any food additive which is unsafe within the meaning of section 348 of this title ‹ • •   or (D) if it is, or it bears or contains, a new animal drug (or conversion product thereof) which is unsafe within the meaning of section 360b of this title; or (3) if it consists in whole or in part of any filthy, putrid, or decomposed substance, or if it is otherwise unfit for food; or (4) if it has been prepared, packed, or held under insanitary conditions whereby it may have become contaminated with filth, or whereby it may have been rendered injurious to health; or (5) if it is, in whole or in part, the product of a diseased animal or of an animal which has died otherwise than by slaughter; or (6) if its container is composed, in whole or in part, of any poisonous or deleterious substance which may render the contents injurious to health; or (7) if it has been intentionally subjected to radiation, unless the use of the radiation was in conformity with a regulation or exemption in effect pursuant to section 348 of this title.

(b). <u>Foods Containing Pesticide</u>
<u>Chemicals</u>

§ 346a. Tolerances for pesticide chemicals in or on raw agricultural commodities

Conditions of safety

(a) Any poisonous or deleterious pesticide chemical ● ● ●
added to a raw agricultural commodity, shall be deemed unsafe ● ● ●
unless—

(1) a tolerance for such pesticide chemical in or on the raw agricultural commodity has been prescribed by the Administrator of the Environmental Protection Agency under this section and the quantity of such pesticide chemical in or on the raw agricultural commodity is within the limits of the tolerance so prescribed; or

(2) with respect to use in or on such raw agricultural commodity, the pesticide chemical has been exempted from the requirement of a tolerance by the Administrator under this section.

● ●

(c). <u>Regulations Establishing</u>
<u>Tolerances</u>, sec. 346a(b)

Establishment of tolerances

(b) The Administrator shall promulgate regulations establishing tolerances with respect to the use in or on raw agricultural commodities of poisonous or deleterious pesticide chemicals and of pesticide chemicals which are not generally recognized, among experts qualified by scientific training and experience to evaluate the safety of pesticide chemicals, as safe for use, to the extent necessary to protect the public health. In establishing any such regulation, the Administrator shall give appropriate consideration, among other relevant factors, (1) to the necessity for the production of an adequate, wholesome, and economical food supply; (2) to the other ways in which the consumer may be affected by the same pesticide chemical or by other related substances that are poisonous or deleterious; and (3) to the opinion submitted with a certification of usefulness under subsection (*l*) of this section. Such regulations shall be promulgated in the manner prescribed in subsection (d) or (e) of this section. In carrying out the provisions of this section relating to the establishment of tolerances, the Administrator may establish the tolerance applicable with respect to the use of any pesticide chemical in or on any raw agricultural commodity at zero level if the scientific data before the Administrator does not justify the establishment of a greater tolerance.

B. Radioactive Materials

1. Atomic Energy Act, 42 U.S.C.A. 2012(1964)

(a). Powers of the Atomic Energy Commission

§ 2073. Domestic distribution of special nuclear material— Licenses

(a) The Commission is authorized (i) to issue licenses to transfer or receive in interstate commerce, transfer, deliver, acquire, possess, own, receive possession of or title to, import, or export under the terms of an agreement for cooperation arranged pursuant to section 2153 of this title, special nuclear material. make special nuclear material available for the period of the , and, (iii) to distribute special nuclear material within the United States to qualified applicants requesting such material—

(1) for the conduct of research and development activities of the types specified in section 2051 of this title;

(2) for use in the conduct of research and development activities or in medical therapy under a license issued pursuant to section 2134 of this title;

(3) for use under a license issued pursuant to section 2133 of this title;

(4) for such other uses as the Commission determines to be appropriate to carry out the purposes of this chapter.

. . . .

(b). Definition of "Special Nuclear Material"

§ 2014

(aa) The term "special nuclear material" means (1) plutonium, uranium enriched in the isotope 233 or in the isotope 235, and any other material which the Commission, pursuant to the provisions of section 2071 of this title, determines to be special nuclear material but does not include source material; or (2) any material artificially enriched by any of the foregoing, but does not include source material.

. . . .

(c). Prohibited Acts

§ 2077. Unauthorized dealings in special nuclear material— Handling by persons

(a) Unless authorized by a general or specific license issued by the Commission, which the Commission is authorized to issue pursuant to section 2073 of this title, no person may transfer or receive in interstate commerce, transfer, deliver, acquire, own, possess, receive possession of or title to, or import into or export from the United States any special nuclear material.

(b). It shall be unlawful for any person to directly or indirectly engage in the production of any special nuclear material outside of the United States except (1) under an agreement for cooperation made pursuant to section 2153 of this title, or (2) upon authorization by the Commission after a determination that such activity will not be inimical to the interest of the United States.

. . . .

(d). Licensing Requirements

§ 2014. Definitions

The intent of Congress in the definitions as given in this section should be construed from the words or phrases used in the definitions. As used in this chapter: ● ● ●

(e) The term "byproduct material" means any radioactive material (except special nuclear material) yielded in or made radioactive by exposure to the radiation incident to the process of producing or utilizing special nuclear material.

● ● ●

§ 2133. Commercial licenses—Conditions

(a) Subsequent to a finding by the Commission as required in section 2132 of this title, the Commission may issue licenses to transfer or receive in interstate commerce, manufacture, produce, transfer, acquire, possess, use, import, or export under the terms of an agreement for cooperation arranged pursuant to section 2153 of this title, such type of utilization or production facility. ● ● ●

Nonexclusive basis

(b) The Commission shall issue such licenses on a nonexclusive basis to persons applying therefor (1) whose proposed activities will serve a useful purpose proportionate to the quantities of special nuclear material or source material to be utilized; (2) who are equipped to observe and who agree to observe such safety standards to protect health and to minimize danger to life or property as the Commission may by rule establish; and (3) who agree to make available to the Commission such technical information and data concerning activities under such licenses as the Commission may determine necessary to promote the common defense and security and to protect the health and safety of the public. All such information may be used by the Commission only for the purposes of the common defense and security and to protect the health and safety of the public.

License period

(c) Each such license shall be issued for a specified period, as determined by the Commission, depending on the type of activity to be licensed, but not exceeding forty years, and may be renewed upon the expiration of such period.

Limitations

(d) No license under this section may be given to any person for activities which are not under or within the jurisdiction of the United States ● ● ●

No license may be issued to an alien or any any [1] corporation or other entity if the Commission knows or has reason to believe it is owned, controlled, or dominated by an alien, a foreign corporation, or a foreign government. In any event, no license may be issued to any person within the United States if, in the opinion of the Commission, the issuance of a license to such person would be inimical to the common defense and security or to the health and safety of the public.

* * *

§ 2134. Medical therapy, research, and development licenses; limitations

(a) The Commission is authorized to issue licenses to persons applying therefor for utilization facilities for use in medical therapy. * * *

(b) The Commission is authorized to issue licenses to persons applying therefor for utilization and production facilities involved in the conduct of research and development activities leading to the demonstration of the practical value of such facilities for industrial or commercial purposes. * * *

(d) No license under this section may be given to any person for activities which are not under or within the jurisdiction of the United States * * * No license may be issued to any corporation or other entity if the Commission knows or has reason to believe it is owned, controlled, or dominated by an alien, a foreign corporation, or a foreign government. In any event, no license may be issued to any person within the United States if, in the opinion of the Commission, the issuance of a license to such person would be inimical to the common defense and security or to the health and safety of the public.

. . . .

(e). Penalties

§ 2282. Civil penalties for violations of licensing requirements; notice; collection of penalties

(a) Any person who (1) violates any licensing provision of section 2073, 2077, 2092, 2093, 2111, 2112, 2131, 2133, 2134, 2137, or 2139 of this title or any rule, regulation, or order issued thereunder, or any term, condition, or limitation of any license issued thereunder, or (2) commits any violation for which a license may be revoked under section 2236 of this title, shall be subject to a civil penalty, to be imposed by the Commission, of not to exceed $5,000 for each such violation: *Provided,* That in no event shall the total penalty payable by any person exceed $25,000 for all violations by such person occurring within any period of thirty consecutive days. If any violation is a continuing one, each day of such violation shall constitute a separate violation for the purpose of computing the applicable civil penalty. The Commission shall have the power to compromise, mitigate, or remit such penalties.

. . . .

(f). Standards of Possession and Use of Materials

§ 2201. General duties of Commission

In the performance of its functions the Commission is authorized to—

Standards governing use and possession of material

(b) establish by rule, regulation, or order, such standards and instructions to govern the possession and use of special nuclear material, source material, and byproduct material as the Commission may deem necessary or desirable to promote the common defense and security or to protect health or to minimize danger to life or property;

. . . .

2. Suits to Enjoin Detonation of Nuclear Devices

CROWTHER v. SEABORG, 312 F. Supp. 1205(D.C. Colo. 1970).

ARRAJ, Chief Judge.

INTRODUCTION

Project Rulison

Project Rulison is a joint experiment sponsored by the Atomic Energy Commission (AEC), the Department of Interior and Austral Oil Company, Inc., (Austral). The program manager is CER Geonuclear Corporation (CER). Rulison is a part of the Plowshare Program of the AEC, which is designed to develop peaceful use of nuclear explosive technology. The specific purpose of the project is to study the economic and technical feasibility of nuclear stimulation of the low permeability gas bearing Mesaverde sandstone formation in the Rulison Field of Colorado. "Nuclear stimulation" is the detonation of a nuclear device in the formation which will create a cavity and attendant fracture system that will stimulate the production of natural gas from the formation. The Mesaverde formation, because of its low permeability, does not produce natural gas in commercial quantities, although it does contain a significant gas reserve.

The nuclear device was detonated at a depth of 8,431 feet at the Rulison site near Rulison, Colorado, on September 10, 1969. Prior to this detonation all three of the lawsuits dealing with the project had been filed and hearings held at which the various plaintiffs sought a preliminary injunction to halt the detonation. This Court denied the preliminary injunctions and the denials were sustained by the Tenth Circuit Court of

Appeals, 415 F.2d 437 (10th Cir. 1969) and No. 453–69. All three cases, Civil Actions C–1702, C–1712 and C–1722, are against essentially the same defendants, and this coupled with the identity of the subject matter rendered consolidation of the cases feasible. At the trial of the consolidated cases the plaintiffs sought a permanent injunction against the defendants to prohibit the planned flaring of the gas contained within the cavity created by the nuclear detonation. These plans will be discussed in detail below, but the general purpose of the proposed flaring is to determine the extent of stimulation of production, the dimensions and configuration of the cavity and fracture system, and the technical and economic feasibility of the entire project.

Identity of Parties

The plaintiffs in Civil Action C–1702 are: (1) Charles Morgan Smith, a resident of Colorado who owns property approximately seven miles from the Project Rulison site; (2) James Hopkins Smith, III, the son of the plaintiff Charles Morgan Smith, who occasionally accompanies his father to the property referred to above; (3) Richard L. Crowther, a resident of Colorado who owns real estate approximately thirty miles from Project Rulison; and (4) Willard Eames, a resident of Colorado who owns property approximately three and one-half miles from the Project Rulison site.

The defendants in Civil Action C–1702 are: (1) Dr. Glenn T. Seaborg, Chairman of the AEC; (2) Austral Oil Company, Inc., a Delaware corporation licensed to do business in Colorado; and (3) CER Geonuclear Corporation, a Delaware corporation licensed to do business in Colorado.

The plaintiff in Civil Action C–1712 is the Colorado Open Space Coordinating Council, Inc., (COSCC). COSCC is a nonprofit, public benefit corporation organized and existing under the laws of Colorado. COSCC purports to bring suit as a class action on behalf of all those persons entitled to the protection of their health, and on behalf of all those entitled to the full benefit, use and enjoyment of the natural resources of the State of Colorado.

The defendants in Civil Action C–1712 are: (1) Dr. Seaborg; (2) Austral; and (3) CER.

The plaintiff in Civil Action C–1722 is Martin G. Dumont, District Attorney for the Ninth Judicial District of the State of Colorado, on behalf of the people of the State.

The defendants in Civil Action C–1722 are: (1) Dr. Seaborg, substituted for defendant Atomic Energy Commission by stipulation of October 8, 1969; (2) Austral; (3) CER; and (4) Claude Hayward, the owner of the property on which the Rulison detonation occurred.

ISSUES PRESENTED

The parties were unable to agree upon the wording of the factual issues in the submitted pretrial order. Our review of the evidence presented at trial, the numerous pleadings, and the briefs of the parties filed leads to the conclusion that the following outlined issues of fact and law satisfactorily delineate the areas of contention among the parties. These issues as set out will govern the order of disposition of the three suits in this opinion.

Issues of Law

Because the defendants reserved certain issues relating to the jurisdiction of the Court, these will be disposed of first. The first four issues of law may be considered the jurisdictional issues presented.

1. Do the plaintiffs have standing to sue?

2. Is there a justiciable controversy entitling plaintiffs to declaratory relief?

3. Are the plaintiffs' actions unconsented suits against the United States?

4. Are the plaintiffs seeking review of and an injunction against discretionary acts of the AEC which are not subject to judicial review?

5. Is the AEC following its Congressional mandate and its own rules and regulations in that the actions and plans for protecting health and minimizing danger to life and property are a reasonable exercise of its statutory authority?

6. Are the plaintiffs entitled to an order directing the AEC to answer all questions and to turn over to the plaintiffs all information regarding Project Rulison?

Issues of Fact

The ultimate issue of fact presented by these cases is whether the proposed flaring of gas from the Rulison cavity will endanger life, health and property of the plaintiffs or any other similarly situated, in contravention of the mandate of the Atomic Energy Act. In determining this issue, five subsidiary issues have been raised by the parties and must be disposed of. These are:

1. Do the Rulison plans make reasonably adequate provision for the protection of the health and safety of human, plant and animal life?

2. Are these plans for flaring within the radiation protection standards of the AEC and the Federal Radiation Council (FRC)?

3. Are the defendants prepared and equipped to actually implement the plans for flaring, thus insuring the protection of health and safety?

4. Are there safe economical alternatives to the proposed flaring as a means of determining the effectiveness of the Rulison detonation?

5. Are the FRC and AEC radiation protection standards themselves reasonably adequate to protect life, health and property?

● ● ●

Having determined the five subsidiary issues of fact presented by this case, we find that the ultimate issue of fact must be resolved in favor of the defendants. The proposed flaring of gas from the Rulison cavity has not been shown to present a danger to life, health or property of the plaintiffs, or any others similarly situated.

Fifth Legal Issue

Our findings and conclusions on the factual issues show that this phase of the Rulison project and its flaring phase do not present a threat to health and safety. They show that the AEC has planned its activities and is carrying them out with all due regard to the health and safety of the public. They show that the radiation dose from the flaring will be within the radiation standards of the AEC and other radiation protection institutions. They show that in the event of an accident which creates a danger of an excessive exposure, plans will be implemented to limit exposure to the established guidelines. Thus, plaintiffs have failed to show the probability of irreparable damage if the flaring is not enjoined, and have failed to establish a right to the specific injunctive relief sought. Crowther v. Seaborg, 415 F.2d 437, 439 (10th Cir. 1969).

We conclude that the evidence shows that the AEC is following the Congressional mandate and its own rules and regulations, and that the actions and plans of the AEC in the prosecution of the conclusory phase of Project Rulison constitute a reasonable exercise of its statutory authority to conduct research in the utilization of atomic energy while providing for the protection of the health and safety of the public. 42 U.S.C.A. § 2051(a), (d).

Lest our ruling today be misunderstood, some additional words are required. This opinion, our findings, conclusions and ruling apply only to the specific factual situation presented by this litigation. We approve only of the flaring of the gas from the one well in the Rulison unit in which a nuclear device was detonated on September 10, 1969. We are not here and now approving continued detonations and flaring operations in the Rulison field. Such determination must be made in the context of a specific factual situation, in light of contemporary knowledge of science and medicine of the dangers of radioactivity, at the time such projects are conceived and executed.

Further, although we have found that the plans for the flaring do provide reasonably for the health and safety of the public and that the specific plans for surveillance are reasonable, we determine that the Court should retain jurisdiction in order to insure that the plans we today approve as reasonable are in fact reasonably and safely executed. To aid this retention of jurisdiction we further determine that the defendants should file with this Court data and reports of the information collected by the surveillance system outlined in Appendix A.

This memorandum opinion and order shall serve as the findings of fact and conclusions of law of the Court as required by Rule 52 of the Federal Rules of Civil Procedure.

It is therefore

Ordered that the complaint in Civil Action C–1722, Dumont v. Glenn Seaborg, et al., shall be and is hereby dismissed. It is further

Ordered that the requests of the plaintiffs in Civil Actions C–1702 and C–1712 for a permanent injunction enjoining the defendants from the flaring of the gases contained in the Rulison cavity shall be and is hereby denied. It is further

Ordered that defendant Glenn Seaborg or his responsible agent comply fully with the information and data dissemination plan outlined in Appendix A to this opinion, insuring the distribution of such data to the Rulison Open File as indicated, the Colorado State Public Health Department, and also to this Court, when they first become available. It is further

Ordered that the Court shall and it hereby does retain jurisdiction of the parties and subject matter of this proceeding for purposes of assuring that further activities in connection with this phase of the Rulison Project will be carried out in accordance with the plans as approved by the Court, and for such other and further action as may be deemed appropriate in the premises.

3.   AEC Must Comply with NEPA

CALVERT CLIFFS' COORDINATING COMM., INC. v. UNITED STATES ATOMIC ENERGY COMMISSION, 449 F. 2d 1109 (Ct. App. D.C., 1971).

J. SKELLY WRIGHT, Circuit Judge:

These cases are only the beginning of what promises to become a flood of new litigation—litigation seeking judicial assistance in protecting our natural environment. Several recently enacted statutes attest to the commitment of the Government to control, at long last, the destructive engine of material "progress." [1] But it remains to be seen whether the promise of this legislation will become a reality. Therein lies the judicial role. In these cases, we must for the first time interpret the broadest and perhaps most important of the recent statutes: the National Environmental Policy Act of 1969 (NEPA). [2] We must assess claims that one of the agencies charged with its administration has failed to live up to the congressional mandate. ● ● ●

NEPA, like so much other reform legislation of the last 40 years, is cast in terms of a general mandate and broad delegation of authority to new and old administrative agencies. It takes the major step of requiring all federal agencies to consider values of environmental preservation in their spheres of activity, and it prescribes certain procedural measures to ensure that those values are in fact fully respected. Petitioners argue that rules recently adopted by the Atomic Energy Commission to govern consideration of environmental matters fail to satisfy the rigor demanded by NEPA. The Commission, on the other hand, contends that the vagueness of the NEPA mandate and delegation leaves much room for discretion and that the rules challenged by petitioners fall well within the broad scope of the Act. We find the policies embodied in NEPA to be a good deal clearer and more demanding than does the Commission. We conclude that the Commission's procedural rules do not comply with the congressional policy. Hence we remand these cases for further rule making.

We begin our analysis with an examination of NEPA's structure and approach and of the Atomic Energy Commission rules which are said to conflict with the requirements of the Act. The relevant portion of NEPA is Title I, consisting of five sections. [3] Section 101 sets forth the Act's basic substantive policy: that the federal government "use all practicable means and measures" to protect environmental values. Congress did not establish environmental protection as an exclusive goal; rather, it desired a reordering of priorities, so that environmental costs and benefits will assume their proper place along with other considerations. ● ● ●

Thus the general substantive policy of the Act is a flexible one. It leaves room for a responsible exercise of discretion and may not require particular substantive results in particular problematic instances. However, the Act also contains very important "procedural" provisions—provisions which are designed to see that all federal agencies do in fact exercise the substantive discretion given them. These provisions are not highly flexible. Indeed, they establish a strict standard of compliance.

NEPA, first of all, makes environmental protection a part of the mandate of every federal agency and department. The Atomic Energy Commission, for example, had continually asserted, prior to NEPA, that it had no statutory authority to concern itself with the adverse environmental effects of its actions. [4] Now, however, its hands are no longer tied. It is not only permitted, but compelled, to take environmental values into account. Perhaps the greatest importance of NEPA is to require the Atomic Energy Commission and other agencies to *consider* environmental issues just as they consider other matters within their mandates. This compulsion is most plainly stated in Section 102. ● ● ●

Senator Jackson NEPA's principal sponsor, stated that "[n]o agency will [now] be able to maintain that it has no mandate or no requirement to consider the environmental consequences of its actions." [6] He characterized the requirements of Section 102 as "action-forcing" and stated that "[o]therwise, these lofty declarations [in Section 101] are nothing more than that." [7]

The sort of consideration of environmental values which NEPA compels is clarified in Section 102(2) (A) and (B). In general, all agencies must use a "systematic, interdisciplinary approach" to environmental planning and evaluation "in decisionmaking which may have an impact on man's environment." In order to include all possible environmental factors in the decisional equation, agencies must "identify and develop methods and procedures * * * which will insure that presently unquantified environmental amenities and values may be given appropriate consideration in decisionmaking along with economic and technical considerations." [8] "Environmental amenities" will often be in conflict with "economic and technical considerations." To "consider" the former "along with" the latter must involve a balancing process. In some instances environmental costs may outweigh economic and technical benefits and in other instances they may not. But NEPA mandates a rather finely tuned and "systematic" balancing analysis in each instance.[9]

To ensure that the balancing analysis is carried out and given full effect, Section 102(2) (C) requires that responsible officials of all agencies prepare a "detailed statement" covering the impact of particular actions on the environment, the environmental costs which might be avoided, and alternative measures which might alter the cost-benefit equation. The apparent purpose of the "detailed statement" is to aid in the agencies' own decision making process and to advise other interested agencies and the public of the environmental consequences of planned federal action. Beyond the "detailed statement," Section 102(2) (D) requires all agencies specifi-

cally to "study, develop, and describe appropriate alternatives to recommended courses of action in any proposal which involves unresolved conflicts concerning alternative uses of available resources." This requirement, like the "detailed statement" requirement, seeks to ensure that each agency decision maker has before him and takes into proper account all possible approaches to a particular project (including total abandonment of the project) which would alter the environmental impact and the cost-benefit balance. Only in that fashion is it likely that the most intelligent, optimally beneficial decision will ultimately be made. Moreover, by compelling a formal "detailed statement" and a description of alternatives, NEPA provides evidence that the mandated decision making process has in fact taken place and, most importantly, allows those removed from the initial process to evaluate and balance the factors on their own.

Of course, all of these Section 102 duties are qualified by the phrase "to the fullest extent possible." We must stress as forcefully as possible that this language does not provide an escape hatch for footdragging agencies; it does not make NEPA's procedural requirements somehow "discretionary." Congress did not intend the Act to be such a paper tiger. Indeed, the requirement of environmental consideration "to the fullest extent possible" sets a high standard for the agencies, a standard which must be rigorously enforced by the reviewing courts. ● ● ●
Thus the Section 102 duties are not inherently flexible. They must be complied with to the fullest extent, unless there is a clear conflict of *statutory* authority.[12] Considerations of administrative difficulty, delay or economic cost will not suffice to strip the section of its fundamental importance.

We conclude, then, that Section 102 of NEPA mandates a particular sort of careful and informed decisionmaking process and creates judicially enforceable duties. The reviewing courts probably cannot reverse a substantive decision on its merits, under Section 101, unless it be shown that the actual balance of costs and benefits that was struck was arbitrary or clearly gave insufficient weight to environmental values. But if the decision was reached procedurally without individualized consideration and balancing of environmental factors—conducted fully and in good faith—it is the responsibility of the courts to reverse. As one District Court has said of Section 102 requirements: "It is hard to imagine a clearer or stronger mandate to the Courts." [13]

In the cases before us now, we do not have to review a particular decision by the Atomic Energy Commission granting a construction permit or an operating license. Rather, we must review the Commission's recently promulgated rules which govern consideration of environmental values in all such individual decisions.[14] The rules were devised strictly in order to comply with the NEPA procedural requirements—but petitioners argue that they fall far short of the congressional mandate. ● ● ●
The procedure for environmental study and consideration ● ● ●
is as follows: Each applicant for an initial construction permit must submit to the Commission his own "environmental report," presenting his assessment of the environmental impact of the planned facility and possible alternatives which would alter the impact. When construction is completed and the applicant applies for a license to operate the new facility, he must again submit an "environmental report" noting any factors which have changed since the original report. At each stage, the Commission's regulatory staff must take the applicant's report and prepare its own "detailed statement" of environmental costs, benefits and alternatives. The statement will then be circulated to other interested and responsible agencies and made available to the public. After comments are received from those sources, the staff must prepare a final "detailed statement" and make a final recommendation on the application for a construction permit or operating license.

Up to this point ● ● ●
petitioners have raised no challenge. However, they do attack four other, specific parts of the rules which, they say, violate the requirements of Section 102 of NEPA. Each of these parts in some way limits full consideration and individualized balancing of environmental values in the Commission's decision making process. (1) Although environmental factors must be considered by the agency's regulatory staff under the rules, such factors need not be considered by the hearing board conducting an independent review of staff recommendations, unless affirmatively raised by outside parties or staff members. (2) Another part of the procedural rules prohibits any such party from raising non-radiological environmental issues at any hearing if the notice for that hearing appeared in the Federal Register before March 4, 1971. (3) Moreover, the hearing board is prohibited from conducting an independent evaluation and balancing of certain environmental factors if other responsible agencies have already certified that their own environmental standards are satisfied by the proposed federal action. (4) Finally, the Commission's rules provide that when a construction permit for a facility has been issued before NEPA compliance was required and when an operating license has yet to be issued, the agency will not formally consider environmental factors or require modifications in the proposed facility until the time of the issuance of the operating license. ● ● ●
We believe that the Commission's crabbed interpretation of NEPA makes a mockery of the Act. ● ● ●
Congress passed the final version of NEPA in late 1969, and the Act went into full effect on January 1, 1970. Yet the Atomic Energy Commission's rules prohibit any consideration of environmental issues by its hearing boards at proceedings officially noticed before March 4, 1971.[22] This is 14 months after the effective date of NEPA. And the hearings affected may go on for as much as a year longer until final action is taken. The result is that major federal actions having a significant environmental impact may be taken by the Commission, without full NEPA compliance, more than two years after the Act's effective date. In view of the importance of environmental consideration during the agency review process ● ● ●
such a time lag is shocking.

The Commission explained that its very long time lag was intended "to provide an orderly period of transition in the conduct of the Commission's regulatory proceedings and to avoid unreasonable delays in the construction and operation of nuclear power plants urgently needed to meet the national requirements for electric power." [23] Before this court, it has claimed authority for its action, arguing that "the statute did not lay down detailed guidelines and inflexible timetables for its implementation; and we find in it no bar to agency provisions which are designed to accommodate transitional implementation problems." [24]

Again, the Commission's approach to statutory interpretation is strange indeed—so strange that it seems to reveal a rather thoroughgoing reluctance to meet the NEPA procedural obligations in the agency review process, the stage at which deliberation is most open to public examination and subject to the participation of public intervenors. The Act, it is true, lacks an "inflexible timetable" for its implementation. But it does have a clear effective date, consistently enforced by reviewing courts up to now. Every federal court having faced the issues has held that the procedural requirements of NEPA must be met in order to uphold federal action taken after January 1, 1970.[25] The absence of a "timetable" for compliance has never been held sufficient, in itself, to put off the date on which a congressional mandate takes effect. The absence of a "timetable," rather, indicates that compliance is required forthwith. ● ● ●

No doubt the process formulating procedural rules to implement NEPA takes some time. Congress cannot have expected that federal agencies would immediately begin considering environmental issues on January 1, 1970. But the effective date of the Act does set a time for agencies to begin adopting rules and it demands that they strive, "to the fullest extent possible," to be prompt in the process. The Atomic Energy Commission has failed in this regard. ● ● ●

In the end, the Commission's long delay seems based upon what it believes to be a pressing national power crisis. Inclusion of environmental issues in pre-March 4, 1971 hearings might have held up the licensing of some power plants for a time. But the very purpose of NEPA was to tell federal agencies that environmental protection is as much a part of their responsibility as is protection and promotion of the industries they regulate. Whether or not the spectre of a national power crisis is as real as the Commission apparently believes, it must not be used to create a blackout of environmental consideration in the agency review process. NEPA compels a case-by-case examination and balancing of discrete factors. Perhaps there may be cases in which the need for rapid licensing of a particular facility would justify a strict time limit on a hearing board's review of environmental issues; but a blanket banning of such issues until March 4, 1971 is impermissible under NEPA. ● ● ●

The sweep of NEPA is extraordinarily broad, compelling consideration of any and all types of environmental impact of federal action. However, the Atomic Energy Commission's rules specifically exclude from full consideration a wide variety of environmental issues. First, they provide that no party may raise and the Commission may not independently examine any problem of water quality—perhaps the most significant impact of nuclear power plants. Rather, the Commission indicates that it will defer totally to water quality standards devised and administered by state agencies and approved by the federal government under the Federal Water Pollution Control Act.[30] Secondly, the rules provide for similar abdication of NEPA authority to the standards of other agencies:

"With respect to those aspects of environmental quality for which environmental quality standards and requirements have been established by authorized Federal, State, and regional agencies, proof that the applicant is equipped to observe and agrees to observe such standards and requirements will be considered a satisfactory showing that there will not be a significant, adverse effect on the environment. Certification by the appropriate agency that there is reasonable assurance that the applicant for the permit or license will observe such standards and requirements will be considered dispositive for this purpose." [31] The most the Commission will do is include a condition in all construction permits and operating licenses requiring compliance with the water quality or other standards set by such agencies.[32] The upshot is that the NEPA procedures, viewed by the Commission as superfluous, will wither away in disuse, applied only to those environmental issues wholly unregulated by any other federal, state or regional body.

We believe the Commission's rule is in fundamental conflict with the basic purpose of the Act. NEPA mandates a case-by-case balancing judgment on the part of federal agencies. In each individual case, the particular economic and technical benefits of planned action must be assessed and then weighed against the environmental costs; alternatives must be considered which would affect the balance of values. ● ● ●

Certification by another agency that its own environmental standards are satisfied involves an entirely different kind of judgment. Such agencies, without overall responsibility for the particular federal action in question, attend only to one aspect of the problem: the magnitude of certain environmental costs. They simply determine whether those costs exceed an allowable amount. Their certification does not mean that they found no environmental damage whatever. In fact, there may be significant environmental damage (e. g., water pollution), but not quite enough to violate applicable (e. g., water quality) standards. Certifying agencies do not attempt to weigh that damage against the opposing benefits. Thus the balancing analysis remains to be done. It may be that the environmental costs, though passing prescribed standards, are nonetheless great enough to outweigh the particular economic and technical benefits involved in the planned action. The only agency in a position to make such a judgment is the agency with overall responsibility for the proposed federal action— the agency to which NEPA is specifically directed.

The Atomic Energy Commission, abdicating entirely to other agencies' certifications, neglects the mandated balancing analysis. Concerned members of the public are thereby precluded from raising a wide range of environmental issues in order to affect particular Commission decisions. And the special purpose of NEPA is subverted.

Arguing before this court, the Commission has made much of the special environmental expertise of the agencies which set environmental standards. NEPA did not overlook this consideration. ● ● ● the Congress was surely cognizant of federal, state and local agencies "authorized to develop and enforce environmental standards." But it provided, in Section 102(2) (C), only for full consultation. It most certainly did not authorize a total abdication to those agencies. Nor did it grant a license to disregard the main body of NEPA obligations. ● ● ●

Petitioners' final attack is on the Commission's rules governing a particular set of nuclear facilities: those for which construction permits were granted without consideration of environmental issues, but for which operating licenses have yet to be issued. These facilities, still in varying stages of construction, include the one of most immediate concern to one of the petitioners: the Calvert Cliffs nuclear power plant on Chesapeake Bay in Maryland.

The Commission's rules recognize that the granting of a construction permit before NEPA's effective date does not justify bland inattention to environmental consequences until the operating license proceedings, perhaps far in the future. The rules require that measures be taken *now* for environmental protection. Specifically, the Commission has provided for three such measures during the pre-operating license stage. First, it has required that a condition be added to all construction permits, "whenever issued," which would oblige the holders of the permits to observe all applicable environmental standards imposed by federal or state law. Second, it has required permit holders to submit their own environmental report on the facility under construction. And third, it has initiated procedures for the drafting of its staff's "detailed environmental statement" in advance of operating license proceedings.

The one thing the Commission has refused to do is take any independent action based upon the material in the environmental reports and "detailed statements." Whatever environmental damage the reports and statements may reveal, the Commission will allow construction to proceed on the original plans. It will not even consider requiring alterations in those plans (beyond compliance with external standards which would be binding in any event), though the "detailed statements" must contain an analysis of possible alternatives and may suggest relatively inexpensive but highly beneficial changes. Moreover, the Commission has, as a blanket policy, refused to consider the possibility of temporarily halting construction in particular cases pending a full study of a facility's environmental impact. It has also refused to weigh the pros and cons of "backfitting" for particular facilities (alteration of already constructed portions of the facilities in order to incorporate new technological developments designed to protect the environment). Thus reports and statements will be produced, but nothing will be done with them. Once again, the Commission seems to believe that the mere drafting and filing of papers is enough to satisfy NEPA.

The Commission appears to recognize the severe limitation which its rules impose on environmental protection. Yet it argues that full NEPA consideration of alternatives and independent action would cause too much delay at the pre-operating license stage. It justifies its rules as the most that is "practicable, in the light of environmental needs and 'other essential considerations of national policy'." [42] It cites, in particular, the "national power crisis" as a consideration of national policy militating against delay in construction of nuclear power facilities.

The Commission relies upon the flexible NEPA mandate to "use all practicable means consistent with other essential considerations of national policy." As we have previously pointed out, however, that mandate applies only to the substantive guidelines set forth in Section 101 of the Act. ● ● ●

The procedural duties, the duties to give full *consideration* to environmental protection, are subject to a much more strict standard of compliance. By now, the applicable principle should be absolutely clear. NEPA requires that an agency must—to the *fullest* extent possible under its other statutory obligations—consider alternatives to its actions which would reduce environmental damage. That principle establishes that consideration of environmental matters must be more than a *pro forma* ritual. Clearly, it is pointless to "consider" environmental costs without also seriously considering action to avoid them. Such a full exercise of substantive discretion is required at every important, appropriate and nonduplicative stage of an agency's proceedings. *See* text at page 1114 *supra.*

The special importance of the pre-operating license stage is not difficult to fathom. In cases where environmental costs were not considered in granting a construction permit, it is very likely that the planned facility will include some features which do significant damage to the environment and which could not have survived a rigorous balancing of costs and benefits. At the later operating license proceedings, this environmental damage will have to be fully considered. But by that time the situation will have changed radically. Once a facility has been completely constructed, the economic cost of any alteration may be very great. In the language of NEPA, there is likely to be an "irreversible and irretrievable commitment of resources," which will inevitably restrict the Commission's options. Either the licensee will have to undergo a major expense in making alterations in a completed facility or the environmental harm will have to be tolerated. It is all too probable that the latter result would come to pass.

By refusing to consider requirement of alterations until construction is completed, the Commission may effectively foreclose the environmental protection desired by Congress. It may also foreclose rigorous consideration of environmental factors at the eventual operating license proceedings. If "irreversible and irretrievable commitment[s] of resources" have already been made, the license hearing (and any public intervention therein) may become a hollow exercise. This hardly amounts to consideration of environmental values "to the fullest extent possible."

A full NEPA consideration of alterations in the original plans of a facility, then, is both important and appropriate well before the operating license proceedings. It is not duplicative if environmental issues were not considered in granting the construction permit. And it need not be duplicated, absent new information or new developments, at the operating license stage. In order that the pre-operating license review be as effective as possible, the Commission should consider very seriously the requirement of a temporary halt in construction pending its review and the "backfitting" of technological innovations. For no action which might minimize environmental damage may be dismissed out of hand. Of course, final operation of the facility may be delayed thereby. But some delay is inherent whenever the NEPA consideration is conducted—whether before or at the license proceedings. It is far more consistent with the purposes of the Act to

delay operation at a stage where real environmental protection may come about than at a stage where corrective action may be so costly as to be impossible.

Thus we conclude that the Commission must go farther than it has in its present rules. It must consider action, as well as file reports and papers, at the pre-operating license stage. As the Commission candidly admits, such consideration does not amount to a retroactive application of NEPA. Although the projects in question may have been commenced and initially approved before January 1, 1970, the Act clearly applies to them since they must still pass muster before going into full operation.[43] All we demand is that the environmental review be as full and fruitful as possible. We hold that ● ● ● the Commission must revise its rules governing consideration of environmental issues. We do not impose a harsh burden on the Commission. For we require only an exercise of substantive discretion which will protect the environment "to the fullest extent possible." No less is required if the grand congressional purposes underlying NEPA are to become a reality.

Remanded for proceedings consistent with this opinion.

4. Tort Liability

See: High Voltage Engineering Corp. v. Pierce, 359 F. 2d 33 (Ct. App. 10th N.M., 1966), supra, I,D,5 and Mahoney v. U.S., 220 F. Supp. 823 (D.C. Tenn., 1963), aff'd. 339 F. 2d 605.

. . . .

C. Solid Waste Disposal

1. Disposal Site as Nuisance

TOWN OF CLAYTON v. MAYFIELD, 82 N.M. 596, 485 P.2d 352(1971).

COMPTON, Chief Justice.

From an order enjoining appellants from operating a junk yard upon premises located within the Town of Clayton, New Mexico, and directing appellants to abate the nuisance by removing the accumulated junk therefrom, the appellant, S. D. Mayfield, has appealed.

Appellant has raised several points of alleged error. The controlling issue, however, is whether the actions of the appellant constitute an abatable common law nuisance. The trial court specifically found that appellant's operation of the junk yard constituted a common law public nuisance as being contrary to the public health, safety and welfare.

Appellant asserts that the finding has no substantial support in the evidence. The junk yard was unfenced. There is evidence substantial in character that the junk yard constituted a fire and health hazard due to the accumulation of combustible materials in and around the cars; that the accumulation of water in and under the cars created a breeding ground for mosquitoes; that the accumulation of old cars were readily accessible, and attractive to young children, thus posing a safety hazard. Appellant himself testified that he intended to burn the old cars on the premises while processing them and that due to the nature of the combustible material in the cars, a great deal of smoke would be created. And there is evidence that the value of residential property in the area had decreased due to the presence of appellant's operation.

It is firmly established in this jurisdiction that nuisances that adversely affect the public health, welfare or safety may be enjoined. Mahone v. Autry, 55 N.M. 111, 227 P.2d 623, and cases cited therein.

Appellant asserts that appellee had an adequate remedy at law through the enforcement of one of various town ordinances. It is noted that all the ordinances referred to by him contain penal provisions for violations. The fact that acts constituting a public nuisance are punishable criminally does not deprive equity of its power to enjoin a public nuisance where there is ample proof of irreparable injury to the public health, welfare or safety. State ex rel. Marron v. Compere, 44 N.M. 414, 103 P.2d 273. We think this is a proper case for injunctive relief.

A discussion of other points urged by appellant would serve no beneficial purpose. The judgment should be affirmed.

It is so ordered.

2. Zoning Problems

VOGELAAR v. POLK COUNTY ZONING BOARD, 188 N.W. 2d 860 (Iowa, 1971).

REYNOLDSON, Justice.

The trial court sustained the action of defendant Polk County Zoning Board of Adjustment in issuing a permit for construction of a sanitary landfill to defendant Des Moines Metropolitan Area Solid Waste Agency. Plaintiffs are landowners and residents in the area of the landfill site. They appeal and we affirm.

The landfill property is a 400 aere tract known as the Pomerantz farm. It is located approximately seven miles East of the Des Moines City limits in Polk County, Iowa. The real estate is in an unincorporated area zoned A-1, Agricultural District, under the county zoning ordinance. This ordinance provides for establishment of garbage disposal and dumps, including landfills, on property zoned A-1, but only by special permit following a public hearing.

The viability of the Waste Agency, created by a number of municipalities pursuant to chapter 28E, Code, 1971, was recognized by this court in Goreham v. Des Moines Met. Area Solid Waste Agency, 179 N.W.2d 449 (Iowa 1970). Responding to acute needs and to chapter 406, Code, 1971 (requiring the establishment of a sanitary solid waste disposal facility by every town, city and county), the Waste Agency purchased the Pomerantz farm and applied to defendant Board of Adjustment for a special use permit to construct a sanitary landfill. Following a public hearing on May 21, 1970, the board issued the requested permit subject to certain conditions and restrictions.

On June 15, 1970, plaintiffs filed a petition for writ of certiorari under provisions of § 358A.18, Code, 1971, alleging the defendant board had acted illegally in granting the special use permit. • • •

Exercising its discretion to hear evidence pursuant to § 358A.21, Code, 1971, the court received testimony of Waste Agency's investigations and studies relating to the construction and operation of the landfill. Testimony was adduced from which the court found the geophysical composition of the Pomerantz farm will not allow surface water to penetrate through to the permanent water table. Evidence indicated the planned operation will prevent percolating waters from flowing through deposited waste and contaminating the local water supply. Burning on this site will be prohibited. The erection of barrier fences will prevent blowing matter from being carried away from the area. Each day's waste, projected to be 300 truck loads, will be sealed in cells in a manner eliminating leakage from one to another. In addition, defendant agency plans to limit esthetic impairment by screening the landfill site with stockpiled fill dirt and trees.

Following the testimony the trial court held there was substantial evidence to support defendant board's decision to issue the permit. Plaintiffs' petition was dismissed and the writ annulled by ruling entered November 3, 1970.

Plaintiffs' 13 page brief, citing no case authority, presents three issues relied upon for reversal. These are (1) the decree of the trial court is contrary to the provisions of subsection 3 of § 358A.15, Code, 1971, (2) the decree of the trial court is contrary to the public interest, (3) the decree of the trial court allows the creation of a public nuisance contrary to the provisions of chapter 657, Code, 1971.

I. Plaintiffs assert the decree of the trial court is contrary to the provisions of subsection 3 of § 358A.15. This contention exposes plaintiffs' confusion concerning the powers of defendant board itemized under § 358A.15. The section cited relates solely to powers of the county zoning board of adjustment, not to powers of a reviewing trial court.

Further, analysis of the application made by the Waste Agency to defendant board subsumes the action under the *original jurisdiction* granted in subsection 2, § 358A.15. Under subsection 2 the board of adjustment is authorized to hear and decide *special exceptions* to the terms of the ordinance.

In contrast, under subsection 3 of § 358A.-15, the board is given power to authorize *upon appeal*, in specific cases, such *variance* from the terms of the ordinance as will not be contrary to the public interest. Under § 358A.13 *appeals* to a board of adjustment may be taken by any person aggrieved or by any county officer, department, board or bureau affected *by a decision of the administrative officer*.

As used in the context of zoning ordinances, a "variance" is authority extended to the owner to use property in a manner forbidden by the zoning enactment, where literal enforcement would cause him undue hardship; while an "exception" allows him to put his property to a use which the enactment expressly permits. Moody v. City of University Park, 278 S.W.2d 912, 919–920 (Tex.Civ.App.1955). See also Rosenfeld v. Zoning Board of Appeals, 19 Ill.App.2d 447, 450, 154 N.E.2d 323, 325 (1958).

The two concepts are well clarified in Depue v. City of Clinton, 160 N.W.2d 860, 864 (Iowa 1968). In that decision we quoted with approval the following from Cunningham, Land-Use Control—The State and Local Programs, 50 Iowa L.Rev. 367, 399–400:

"Since World War II, however, most courts have come to recognize that a 'special exception' permits in a particular district a use not otherwise permitted when certain conditions specifically set out in the ordinance are satisfied * * *. A 'variance', on the other hand, relaxes the zoning regulations when literal enforcement would result in 'unnecessary hardship'."

The "special use permit" granted defendant waste agency falls within the modification authorized by § 358A.15(2) and is a "special exception", rather than a "variance" authorized by § 358A.15(3). Plaintiffs' argument that trial court's ruling was contrary to § 358A.15(3) misses its mark completely. The proceeding was under § 358A.15(2) throughout.

II. Plaintiffs next contend trial court's holding is contrary to the public interest. This issue was not raised below unless it can be read into the allegations of subparagraph 2(a) (4) of the petition that the landfill operation will cause pollution of atmosphere and water. The trial court concluded the issuance of the special permit was proper, essential, and advantageous to the public good. The scope of our review thus becomes important.

•   •   •

we have held repeatedly in similar appeals our review is on assigned errors only. Zilm v. Zoning Board of Adjustment, Polk County, 260 Iowa 787, 150 N.W.2d 606 (1967); Jersild v. Sarcone, 260 Iowa 288, 149 N.W.2d 179 (1967); Schultz v. Board of Adjust. of Pottawattamie Co., 258 Iowa 804, 139 N.W.2d 448 (1966). The findings of fact by the trial court, set out above, are supported by substantial evidence and are binding on this court. Rule 344(f) (1), R.C.P.

This court also notes defendants' affirmative contention that a sanitary landfill is commensurate with the public policy of the State of Iowa. Section 406.3, Code, 1971, makes mandatory upon every city, town and county the establishment of a sanitary solid waste disposal project. Sanitary landfills have been held by this court to qualify as a bona fide waste disposal method in Schultz v. Board of Adjust. of Pottawattamie Co., 258 Iowa 804, 139 N.W.2d 448 (1966). Plaintiffs do not demonstrate the proposed landfill conflicts with the requirements of § 406.3. This coupled with trial court's substantiated findings of fact referred to above compel this court to hold the proposed landfill not contrary to the public interest.

III. The remaining issue advanced by plaintiffs, that the landfill would create a public nuisance contrary to chapter 657, Code, 1971, was stipulated out of the case by the parties at trial. Plaintiffs' counsel readily so conceded in argument before us, observing that this ground was reserved "for another lawsuit". An issue not presented to or passed upon by the trial court cannot be raised or reviewed on appeal. Rouse v. Rouse, 174 N.W.2d 660 (Iowa 1970); Volkswagen Iowa City, Inc. v. Scott's Incorporated, 165 N.W.2d 789 (Iowa 1969).

The judgment of the trial court must be affirmed. In view of this holding we do not find it necessary to decide the questions raised in the cross-appeal filed by the Waste Agency.

Affirmed.

. . . .

COX v. TOWNSHIP OF NEW SEWICKLEY, 284 A. 2d 829 (Pa. 1971).

WILKINSON, Judge.

The appellants in these two cases challenge the constitutionality of the provisions of the New Sewickley Township Junk Dealer and Junk Yard Ordinance of 1968.
. . .
Immediately following its enactment on June 13, 1968, effective June 18, 1968, these actions were instituted to enjoin its enforcement. After a hearing, a preliminary injunction issued. A full hearing was held on August 21, 1968, continued to and concluded on August 26, 1968. . . .
The court, on June 4, 1970, filed its Opinion and Decree Nisi, modifying the Preliminary Injunction so as to continue it only as to those parts of the ordinance which the court had found unconstitutional, thereby vacating it with regard to the constitutional provisions of the ordinance that remained. The decision of the lower court is affirmed. . . .

It the lower court's opinion did not deal in detail with many points that are no longer in issue, we would affirm on that scholarly opinion. Instead, we will take each provision of the ordinance which appellants contest and quote, with approval, from portions of the treatment it received by President Judge Sawyer. The references will be to the sections of Ordinance 31 which have been declared to be constitutional by the court below and have been put in issue by appellants in this appeal:

"Section 6. License fee.

The annual license fee established by Section 6 of this ordinance is $200. Plaintiffs allege that the license fee was set at the maximum allowed by law without regard to the actual costs involved.

In Commonwealth ex rel. Hines v. Winfree, 408 Pa. 128, 136–137, 182 A.2d 698 (1962), the court states:

'In determining the reasonableness of the amount of a license fee two principles must be borne in mind: (a) the party who claims that the amount of a license fee is unreasonable has the burden of so proving and (b) in matters of this character municipalities must be given reasonable latitude in fixing charges to cover anticipated expenses to be incurred in the enforcement of the ordinance and all doubt should be resolved in favor of the reasonableness of the fee. Wm. Laubach & Sons v. Easton, 347 Pa. 542, 550, 32 A.2d 881.' . . .
There are several Pennsylvania cases where junkyard license fees of varying amounts have been upheld where there has not been sufficient evidence to overcome the presumption of reasonableness of the fee and where the fee is commensurate with the cost of regulation and inspection.

. . .

Under Section 14 of the ordinance, the township chief of police is required to regularly inspect the premises of every licensee for the purpose of determining that the licensee has established and maintained his premises in full compliance with the provisions of the Ordinance. • • • There are various costs to be considered in connection with these inspections, including the officer's salary, travel time, mileage, and the cost of his written reports. The $200 fee required by Section 6 is not so disproportionate to the costs reasonably expected to be incurred by the Township in issuing and regulating licenses under this ordinance as to render said fee invalid."

"Section 13.

.   .   .   .   .

Sub-section 13(d) specifies certain setback provisions regulating the location of junkyards. Sub-section 13(f) relating to fencing and stacking, and Sub-section 13(g) providing for the planting of shrubbery are intended to apply in conjunction with Sub-section 13(d).

Contrary to plaintiffs' contention, Sub-section 13(d) and 13(f) relating to setbacks and fencing are not so vague and indefinite as to be incapable of reasonable application.

.   .   .   .   .   .

Regulations governing the fencing and screening of junkyards have been held invalid in other jurisdictions when based solely on aesthetic considerations. • •• On the other hand, regulations governing the fencing and screening of junkyards, even though aesthetic factors were involved in their adoption, have been upheld in other jurisdictions on considerations of public safety. • • • Subsection 13(d) of the New Sewickley Township ordinance contains the following set-back provisions:

'No junk shall be stored or accumulated nor shall any structure be erected within twenty-five (25) feet of the side and rear lines of the licensed premises nor within seventy-five (75) feet of any existing dwelling house erected upon premises adjacent to the licensed prem-

ises. Nor shall any junk be stored or accumulated or any structure be erected that is used in connection with said junk yard within forty (40) feet of that line of the licensed premises abutting a public street or highway within the Township of New Sewickley. PROVIDED: That in cases where two or more lines of the licensed premises abut public streets or highways within the Township one line only of such premises shall be governed by the above-provided set-back of forty (40) feet. PROVIDED: That nothing contained in this sub-section shall apply to existing structures pertaining to and being used in connection with junkyards presently established and operating.'

There are specific safety factors behind the set-back requirements of Subsection 13(d). With respect to traffic safety, the Township Supervisors were concerned about the possible obstruction of view created by the storing of 'junk' cars along the side of the highway (T–138) and the danger of drivers traveling to the center of the road to avoid 'junk' cars parked along the side of the road (T–139, 140). The set-back requirement would also lessen the dangers from fire and explosion which might result from junkyard operations. For these reasons, the set-back requirements of Subsection 13(d) are substantially related to the safety of the community and are, therefore, valid and constitutional, and constitute a proper exercise of the police power of the Township.

Subsection 13(f) provides that junkyards must be enclosed by a fence or wall not less than six feet in height. There is evidence to indicate that this is a reasonable requirement, substantially related to the safety of the community. • •• We, therefore, conclude that the fencing requirement is valid and constitutional and a legitimate exercise of the police power.

Subsection 13(f) also provides that no two or more vehicles or major parts thereof may be stacked on top of one another or otherwise as to protrude above the fence. It is apparent that one of the principal purposes behind this requirement is aesthetics. However, the stacking requirement is related to the public safety to the extent that it helps to control the spread of fires and to reduce the danger of injury to persons in the junkyards and is, therefore, valid and constitutional and a legitimate exercise of the police power of the township.

The planting requirement of Subsection 13(g) is based on aesthetic considerations. The township argues that a regulation, even though based on aesthetic considerations, which serves to promote the general welfare is a legitimate exercise of the police power.

The decision of the Pennsylvania Supreme Court in Bilbar Const. Co. v. Easttown Twp. Board of Adjustment, 393 Pa. 62, 73, 141 A.2d 851 (1958), and Best v. Zoning Board of Adjustment, 393 Pa. 106, 116, 141 A.2d 606 (1958), indicates that the concept of the general welfare admits of aesthetic considerations and may be a sufficient basis to justify a police power regulation. In *Bilbar* and *Best,* the Pennsylvania Supreme Court held that general welfare alone, unconnected with health, safety or morals was a justifiable basis for zoning.

Without imposing undue hardship on junkyard operators, the planting requirement serves to screen unsightly junkyards from public view. Keeping in mind that the community has a definite interest in preserving the value of property in the community, in providing a pleasant environment for its citizens, and in protecting the scenic value of the community for its residents and visitors, the planting requirement serves to promote the general welfare of the Township of New Sewickley and is, therefore, valid and constitutional and a legitimate exercise of the police power.

.   .   .   .   .   .

Even though it might be difficult or expensive for plaintiffs to comply with Section 13 of New Sewickley Township Ordinance No. 31, the interests of the community outweigh this consideration. It is apparent that aesthetic considerations were involved to one degree or another in the adoption of the set-back, fencing, stacking and planting regulations found in Section 13. However, these regulations do bear a substantial relationship to proper objects of the police power, namely, public health and safety, and the general welfare, and are therefore a legitimate exercise of that power."

"Section 15.

The 20-foot space required by Section 15 between rows of junk might be unreasonable if its only purpose was to facilitate inspection of junkyards. Obviously the junkyards could be adequately inspected with far less space between the rows. However, the spacing requirement is necessary in order to allow fire and emergency equipment to maneuver within the junkyards. It might also be noted that this 20-foot space helps to prevent the spread of fires. To the extent that it serves to lessen the dangers from fires in junkyards in New Sewickley Township, the 20-foot spacing provision is a reasonable requirement serving to protect the safety of the community and is therefore valid, constitutional and a legitimate exercise of the police power. ● ● ●

Section 17 which requires a 20-foot set-back from any river or stream or any other natural water course is substantially related to the public safety in that it helps to prevent pollution of these waterways and is therefore valid, constitutional and a legitimate exercise of the police power. ● ● ●   While this set-back applies to a significant portion of plaintiffs' land, 20 feet on either side of any natural water course, its benefit to the community outweighs any inconvenience caused to the plaintiffs.

●   ●   ●

The record in this case more than amply supports the lower court's findings that the provisions here in issue are reasonable.

Affirmed.

314

3. State Solid Waste Disposal Legislation

RINGLIEB v. TOWNSHIP OF PARSIPPANY-TROY HILLS,
59 N.J. 348, 283 A.2d 97(1971).

PER CURIAM.

The judgment is affirmed for the reasons expressed by Judge Joseph H. Stamler in his oral opinion which reads as follows:

● ● ● On May 6, 1970 the Legislature approved two pieces of legislation concerning solid waste. Chapter 39 of the Laws of 1970 concerned itself with solid waste management and the title of that statute read that it was "An Act Concerning Solid Waste Management creating an Advisory Council on Solid Waste Management in the State Department of Environmental Protection and Relating to the Department's Functions, Powers and Duties".

This statute, Chapter 39, was incorporated into our laws as N.J.S. 13:1E–1 et seq. and in Section 2 the Legislature expressed its concern when it made the following findings and declarations: "The collection, disposal and utilization of solid waste is a matter of grave concern to all citizens and is an activity thoroughly affected with the public interest; that the health, safety and welfare of the people of this State require efficient and reasonable solid waste collection and disposal service or efficient utilization of such waste, and that the current solid waste crisis should be resolved not only by the enforcement of more stringent and realistic regulations upon the solid waste industry but also through the development and formulation of statewide, regional, county and intercounty plans for solid waste management and guidelines to implement the plans."

Throughout that statute there is no mention of the concern of the Legislature below the inter-county level but by that statute, 13:1E–9, the Legislature provided that the codes, rules and regulations shall be observed throughout the State and shall be enforced by the Department and every local Board of Health. Thereafter the procedure for penalty provisions is set forth in actions commenced by the Commissioner of Environmental Control or by a local Board of Health. The rules and regulations have already been promulgated and adopted and these appear as Chapter 8, "Refuse Disposal." ● ● ●

On the same day the Legislature passed the Solid Waste Utility Control Act of 1970, and there are legislative findings made there in N.J.S. 48:13A–2 which restate the grave concern of all citizens and of the Legislature in the industry affected and makes a public utility out of those people who are engaged in solid waste collection and disposal and it gives to the Public Utility Commission the duty of establishing and enforcing standards and rates for the regulating of the economic aspects of the solid waste collection, disposal and utilization service. Under the two statutes anyone seeking to engage in this operation would be required to comply with stringent requirements and would first, before qualified as a public utility, be required to be found by the Board of Public Utilities Commissioners as qualified by experience, training or education to engage in the business, to furnish proof of financial responsibility and, most importantly, hold a certificate of public convenience and necessity issued by the Board of Public Utility Commissioners.

● ● ●

In Section 8 of the same statute the Public Utility Commission (the Board) can order any person in this State engaged in the solid waste collection business or the solid waste disposal business to extend his collection or disposal service into any area of the State where service has been discontinued in accordance with sections of the Public Utility Act heretofore enacted. R.S. 48:2–27.

A reading of both acts together with the regulation adopted seems to be a comprehensive plan on the part of the State to control all facets of this industry.

All counsel have acknowledged on this motion that the need was great for the

State to step in and do something, that the concern was partially economic and rising costs, but there was also concern in the Department of Environmental Protection about where our land was going when it would be overwhelmed with sewage and disposal problems.

So that this act was in existence when on October 13th, 1970 Parsippany-Troy Hills passed an ordinance. The ordinance was entitled "An Ordinance Providing for Establishing, Licensing, Operating, Regulating, Maintaining, and Controlling Sanitary Landfills in the Township of Parsippany-Troy Hills." There is no question but that the industry there sought to be regulated, the type of industry, was well within the limitations and requirements as imposed by Chapter 39 and Chapter 40.

After the passage of the ordinance heretofore referred to plaintiffs, Conrad J. Ringlieb, Helen Elaine Ringlieb and Frieda Ringlieb—and as the complaint was amended by order of this Court, Sharkey Farms, Inc.—brought an action against the Township of Parsippany-Troy Hills, George F. Kugler, Jr., Attorney General of the State of New Jersey, the Department of Environmental Protection and the Board of Public Utility Commissioners.

In relevant part, so far as this motion is concerned, plaintiffs, who were owners and operators of the sanitary land site in Parsippany-Troy Hills, asked this Court to determine that the Legislature by Chapter 39 and Chapter 40 preempted the entire industry and the regulation of that industry of sanitary landfills by the enactment of the two statutes heretofore referred to. ● ● ●

The defendant municipality cross moves for summary judgment and takes the position that the statutes do not preclude the municipality from passing an ordinance regulating the same industry.

The Court has examined the ordinance and feels that absent state statutes such ordinance would serve a very useful purpose in protecting the health of individuals in the municipality but the state statute, admittedly by defendant, in one or another respect, conflicts with or duplicates that which is required by the ordinance.

I have compared the ordinance with the statutes in question and with the regulations under the statute in question, Chapter 8, "Refuse Disposal" and there is much duplication and overlapping, requiring double effort and serving no useful purpose.

It is well-established that municipalities in our State have no power other than those delegated to them by the Legislature and by our State Constitution. The State may withhold from or grant a given power to a municipality. The question of preemption must be determined absent an express exclusion from the field by the State by the Courts ascertaining the legislative intent.

In our Constitution, Article 4, Section 7, Paragraph 11, our Courts are enjoined by this constitutional provision, to liberally construe all laws in favor of municipal corporations. Local government should be given every advantage to manage and operate its affairs but the Constitution expressly states that the municipalities have not only the powers granted in express terms but also those of necessary or fair implication or incident to powers expressly conferred or essential thereto, but it concludes with the following limitation: that none of these powers, whether they are express or by implication inconsistent with or prohibited by the Constitution or state statute, shall be inferred as going from the State. Attached to every ordinance there is an implied condition that it must yield to the predominant power of the State. ● ● ●

Here the fair reading of Chapter 39 and of Chapter 40, and especially with a view of close scrutiny on the legislative findings, there is an intention disclosed certainly by the Legislature to make uniform this industry throughout the State. ● ● ●

I have searched to find whether or not there is some statute which specifically regulated or delegated the power to a municipality to regulate sanitary landfills. I could find none. ●● ●

I find here that the plaintiff, when approved and certificated by the board under the two statutes, operates under the regulations. I find him to be a public utility according to constitutional state legislation, serving a function which is plainly essential to public health. For this the certificate of necessity so provides and requires; and that he is an instrumentality, the plaintiff is an instrumentality, who operates not only with the express approval but under a charged duty with stringent penalties under the eye of the Department of Environmental Protection and the Public Utilities Board. ● ● ●

This Court concludes that the Legislature by Chapter 39 of the Laws of 1970 and Chapter 40 of the Laws of 1970 has preempted the field of solid waste collection and disposal and management under both statutes and that municipalities who are protected in part under the statute generally for every operation requires a certification that it does not violate the land use provisions of the municipality before approval. It is protected to that extent and can take such steps as it deems necessary when the occasion arises to impose upon the Department of Environmental Control or the Public Utilities Commission the additional protection that it feels it needs but it cannot do so by an ordinance which involves penalties or requires a person to go through the same procedures, the same requirements, almost word for word the same, as is required by the State.

An order for summary judgment in favor of plaintiffs ● ● ● will be entered. The motion of defendant Parsippany-Troy Hills for summary judgment in its favor is denied.

. . . .

For a description of solid waste control laws, broken down by states, see Grad, Treatise On Environmental Law Sec. 4.02.

See also:

1. Tofner & Clark, Intergovernmental Approaches to Solid Waste Management (1971).

2. Regionalized Solid Waste Management, (Technical Guidance Center for Environmental Quality, 1972).

4. Federal Solid Waste Disposal Act of 1965, 42 U.S.C.A. 3251

(a). Congressional Findings

FINDINGS AND PURPOSES

Sec. 202. (a) The Congress finds—

(1) that the continuing technological progress and improvement in methods of manufacture, packaging, and marketing of consumer products has resulted in an ever-mounting increase, and in a change in the characteristics, of the mass of material discarded by the purchaser of such products;

(2) that the economic and population growth of our Nation, and the improvements in the standard of living enjoyed by our population, have required increased industrial production to meet our needs, and have made necessary the demolition of old buildings, the construction of new buildings, and the provision of highways and other avenues of transportation, which, together with related industrial, commercial, and agricultural operations, have resulted in a rising tide of scrap, discarded, and waste materials;

(3) that the continuing concentration of our population in expanding metropolitan and other urban areas has presented these communities with serious financial, management, intergovernmental, and technical problems in the disposal of solid wastes resulting from the industrial, commercial, domestic, and other activities carried on in such areas;

(4) that inefficient and improper methods of disposal of solid wastes result in scenic blights, create serious hazards to the public health, including pollution of air and water resources, accident hazards, and increase in rodent and insect vectors of disease, have an adverse effect on land values, create public nuisances, otherwise interfere with community life and development;

(5) that the failure or inability to salvage and reuse such materials economically results in the unnecessary waste and depletion of our natural resources; and

(6) that while the collection and disposal of solid wastes should continue to be pimarily the function of State, regional, and local agencies, the problems of waste disposal as set forth above have become a matter national in scope and in concern and necessitate Federal action through financial and technical assistance and leadership in the development, demonstration, and application of new and improved methods and processes to reduce the amount of waste and unsalvageable materials and to provide for proper and economical solid-waste disposal practices.

(b). Purposes of the Act

Section 202(b)

(b) The purposes of this Act therefore are—

(1) to initiate and accelerate a national research and development program for new and improved methods of proper and economic solid-waste disposal, including studies directed toward the conservation of natural resources by reducing the amount of waste and unsalvageable materials and by recovery and utilization of potential resources in solid wastes; and

(2) to provide technical and financial assistance to State and local governments and interstate agencies in the planning, development, and conduct of solid-waste disposal programs.

• •

For a general discussion of legal problems that arise in solid waste disposal see: "Problems of Solid Waste Disposal," 35 Albany L. Rev. 91 (1970).

See also:

1. "Legal Framework of Solid Waste Disposal," 3 Indiana Legal Forum 415 (1970).

2. Policies for Solid Waste Management, (Public Health Service, Bureau of Solid Waste Management, 1970).

3. Solid Waste Management: Abstracts and Excerpts from the Literature, (Public Health Service, 1970).